THE FRAGILE BOND

THE FRAGILE BOND

In Search of an Equal, Intimate and
Enduring Marriage

Augustus Y. Napier, Ph.D.

PERENNIAL LIBRARY

HARPER & ROW, PUBLISHERS, New York
Grand Rapids, Philadelphia, St. Louis, San Francisco
London, Singapore, Sydney, Tokyo, Toronto

First PERENNIAL LIBRARY edition published 1990

Designed by Joan Greenfield

Library of Congress has catalogued the hardcover edition of this title as follows:

Napier, Augustus.
  The fragile bond.

  1. Marriage—United States.   2. Marriage—Psychological aspects.   I. Title.
HQ728.N27   1988   306.8'1   88-45047
ISBN 0-06-015984-7

ISBN 0-06-091598-6 (pbk.)

  91 92 93 94 AC / FG 10 9 8 7 6 5 4 3

To Margaret, without whom I cannot imagine myself

And to my children, Sarah, Mark, and Julia,
who have helped me be myself

Contents

Acknowledgments

IN THE FIRST DAYS of my apprenticeship as a family therapist, I was intrigued to discover how fiercely entangled with each other family members are. In spite of my efforts, a teenager seemed determined to get arrested in order to distract his parents from fighting; a man who hated his father's abuse ended up abusing his own kids; a woman who married in defiance of her mother seemed to be doing everything in her power to fulfill her mother's prediction that the marriage would fail. Frustrated, I began to talk to my mentor, Dr. Carl Whitaker, about how loyal families were to each other, and how loyal they were, sometimes, to their own suffering. With a knowing smile, Whitaker handed me a copy of a recently published book, *Invisible Loyalties*, by Ivan Boszormenyi-Nagy and Geraldine Spark. As I began to decipher the difficult first section of the book, written by Dr. Boszormenyi-Nagy, I felt exhilarated. Not only did his ideas make sense, but they made human behavior seem less perversely self-destructive.

As with many other family therapists of my generation, my thinking was reshaped by this book—not only about families, but about human causality. The idea that we are all powerfully driven by our loyalty to those we love is simple enough, but through Boszormenyi-Nagy's work, we come to understand that we are also in pursuit of an intricate "relational justice." In example after example, we see that the excesses of this generation are often unconscious attempts to "balance the books" on the prior generation's injustices. As we try to work out the pain and the frustration of the past, we complicate the present.

Boszormenyi-Nagy writes about our indebtedness to our forebears. While I have acknowledged certain of his ideas in the text of this book, I owe him more than these citations can convey. His interest in justice in relationships transcends clinical considerations; and I am grateful for the complex, humane view of the human struggle which informs all his writings.

My work with families has also been enriched through my association with Al Pesso. His therapeutic approach to historical issues has been deeply exciting to me, and it formed a useful metaphor for viewing a number of relationship issues outside the therapy context.

My wife, Margaret, and I owe deep appreciation to Dr. Jackie Damgaard, who was our therapist at a critical moment in the life of our family. Her insightfulness, her caring, and her willingness to confront us were extremely helpful; and she gave us much more than her role demanded.

My deepest indebtedness in the writing of this book, however, is to Margaret. Not only did she consent to my writing about our marriage, but she helped in many ways with the writing itself. She worked on the entire text through its several drafts; and every time I lost confidence in the book, she offered me absolutely vital encouragement. Margaret's presence pervades this book; and while I am its author, she is as integral to its contents as she is to my life.

Though I didn't always feel it at the time, I am appreciative now that Margaret sometimes struggled to get me to put this book down: to be psychologically as well as physically present in our family. As the reader will see, our battles over my workaholism have been pivotal in our relationship, and I am immensely grateful to Margaret that she fought with me to value the experience of today, and to decide my sometimes divided loyalties in favor of my present-day— as opposed to my childhood—family.

As the only surviving member of my father's family, my beloved aunt Alice not only helped me understand some important aspects of my father's family history, but she encouraged me to write about them. For this help and permission, and for her long and caring interest in my life, I am especially grateful.

I am also indebted to my editor, Carol Cohen, for her patience, support, and tact in seeing me through the completion of this manuscript. Her reassuring voice on the telephone helped me steer a surer course.

Several colleagues read the manuscript, and I am especially appreciative of Carl Johnson's detailed and very helpful suggestions. My daughter Sarah took time from the editorship of her college newspaper to help me edit several chapters, and she offered a number of perceptive recommendations.

Our office manager, Paula Bokros, handled not only the technical aspects of word-processing, but she made Margaret's and my life so much easier and more pleasant through her efficiency, her protectiveness of our time, and her good humor. She was one of this book's first readers, and her reactions were especially important.

Finally, I owe a great debt to our clients, whose stories are found throughout these pages. While certain details have been changed to protect the identities of our clients, and while in some instances two similar situations have been combined, I have tried to remain true to the dynamics and the speech of actual families. I hope that I have been respectful and caring in telling these stories, for these are people who have taught Margaret and me, and whom we have come to love.

Atlanta, Georgia
June 1988

Introduction

IT IS AN ATTRACTIVE, brown-shingled house with green shutters, lovingly landscaped by the couple who raised their three children there. As with many homes, its exterior is deceptive, for what happens inside is often difficult and painful. The struggles that take place within this house, however, are of a special kind. Here not one but many families work, usually with great intensity, to transform their lives. Within these walls there is a deliberate and structured hopefulness about the future of marriages and families, and a strong commitment to change. If I were to name the four corners of this rather plain building, I would call them hope, honesty, caring, and work.

This renovated structure, which we call The Family Workshop, is the professional home of six Atlanta marriage and family therapists: Carl Johnson and Jeanne Montgomery, who have been friends and co-workers for many years, are both veterans of an inner-city family-therapy agency, and are wise in the ways of the families of errant adolescents. Gail Hagler, the mother of four grown children, is interested in families where there is addiction. Jerry Pickens, who dances in and out as he juggles his practice with a college teaching job, often works with the families of young adults. Though Margaret and I share a bedroom at home, we have offices across the hall from each other here; one of them is often vacant, however, because we are also each other's favorite co-therapist. Paula Bokros, our warmly outgoing and take-charge office manager, supports and nurtures us all.

Margaret and I have been professional partners for fourteen years. Our habit of working together began as an experiment, a kind of marital hobby. Though we didn't think of it that way in the beginning, it was probably also a way of reaching out to each other, of bridging the traditional roles which we initially adopted and which were taking us farther and farther apart.

We are all, of course, the products of our own generation. Born in the shadow of World War II, Margaret and I grew up in its optimistic and expansive aftermath, "coming of age" in the placid fifties. When we married in 1963, our expectations, like those of most of our friends, were traditional. Margaret might have a career, but I was *going* to have a career; and our children would be primarily her responsibility. So we were—and are still—members of that generation on whom the rules, and for whom the possibilities, changed. Part of this book concerns our struggle to adapt to those new rules and possibilities. But our story is only one theme in a larger examination of the institution of marriage itself.

Margaret and I knew each other for four years before we married; and while our relationship went through a period of great strain during that time, there was never any doubt in either of our minds that Margaret was my equal. If anything, I was threatened by her intelligence, her social poise, her competence. But the moment we married, changes began to take place in our lives that were so unconscious that I can only liken them to a kind of socially induced hypnosis.

We were both teaching at a small college in Georgia when we married, and our jobs and salaries were identical. As soon as we set up housekeeping in an apartment near the campus, however, our daily routines became far from alike. The day would begin with Margaret's fixing breakfast for both of us, then straightening up the apartment before we left for our first classes. In the evening I would read or grade papers while she cooked dinner. After dinner I would clear the table, but Margaret did the dishes. At about nine in the evening she would finally get to her other work, which included finishing her master's thesis as well as grading papers and preparing lectures. Then, since I had had ample opportunity to rest, I would often want to make love.

In retrospect, it seems somewhat amazing that for several months neither of us questioned this arrangement—until the incident of the card tables. We didn't have desks to work on at that time, but we did have two card tables, one of which functioned as our dining table. It fell to Margaret to clear her work space every night to make a place for our dinner, while I got to have a "permanent" desk. And around this particular injustice Margaret's anger finally surfaced.

Margaret had been working at her "desk" during the afternoon, and when she started to clear it to set the table, she sighed loudly. Hearing her sigh, I asked what was wrong.

"I'm tired of having to clear off my desk," she said tersely.

"I'm sorry," I said sympathetically. "I guess one of us has to do it."

"So why should it be *me*?" she said in an unmistakably angry voice. I looked up. She was standing at that wobbly little table, tears streaming down her face.

"What's wrong, darling?" I asked again.

"You don't *know*? You don't even notice, do you?" I had no idea what she was talking about. "You don't even notice how much I'm doing, and how little you're doing." She began to enumerate some of her daily chores. "You also don't notice that the minute I sit down to work on my thesis, you become amorous. You don't notice much."

Surprised, and feeling unjustly attacked, I defended myself: "Look, I pay the bills every month; I service the car; I deal with the landlord."

"How much time do those things take? My jobs take hours, every day!"

"Well, if you want to be picky about it!" I countered.

"Picky!" She was absolutely furious. "How about *fair*?!

It was our first fight, and it lasted for a couple of hours. At the end, I agreed to "help" more, and I later did so. Neither of us realized then that the ultimate responsibility for our household still remained with Margaret; nor did we know what a stubbornly entrenched issue we had touched. In the years that followed, we remained in the spell of these deeply learned injunctions about who we were and how we were to behave.

At the time of our marriage, Margaret taught French and I taught English. When I decided to become a therapist, Margaret hurried to finish her thesis so that she could support us while I took the courses that would qualify me for graduate school. I was later offered a fellowship in the University of North Carolina's doctoral program in clinical psychology, and Margaret applied to nearby Duke University; she had become interested in working with emotionally disturbed children. For two years, supported by fellowships and loans, we worked shoulder to shoulder in a fairly equal arrangement. Margaret got another master's degree—in special education with emotionally disturbed children; I plunged on toward the doctoral degree.

The decision to have a child is more binding than the decision to marry. Within the space of a year, our cozy "social" arrangement, which we reassure ourselves that we could escape if we decided to, is transformed. One day we are Gus and Margaret, joined by a fragile if loving conjunction; the next we are joined by a human life. This frighteningly valuable and needy creature is both of us, and something more: itself. We realize that there is no escaping this commingling of ourselves in a child's being.

If setting up housekeeping induces us to begin to play predictable, time-worn roles, childbearing plunges most of us into a deep, sleepwalking trance. We become Mother and Father, with the weight of centuries on our shoulders. Suddenly I am terrified that I will not be able to pay the rent, and Margaret is frightened that Sarah, born soon after Margaret's graduation from Duke, will stop breathing in the night. We have become a family, that solitary and mysteriously intense little band through which we have all migrated across the centuries.

Our decision to conceive Sarah when we did was dictated partly by the pressures of time: Margaret was twenty-seven when Sarah was born, and in the days before amniocentesis that seemed late enough. For both of us this was an unambivalent, enthusiastic decision; but especially for Margaret. She wanted to have a career, but she had an intense desire to have and to raise children. I too badly wanted to be a father.

What followed the conscious decision to have a child seemed much less freely willed than the original decision. One look at tiny Sarah and all thoughts of substitute care vanished. She needed us; and in those days, that meant she needed Margaret. The choices we were making now seemed "automatic," preordained, easy. It was their consequences that were difficult: Margaret's anxiety about her mothering, and her chronic fatigue; my panic about being a good provider; and our increasing difficulty in understanding each other's experience.

During my work on the doctorate, I became interested in psychotherapy with families; and as I completed my course work and began to look for an internship in a medical setting, I realized that I might be able to study with Dr. Carl Whitaker, professor of psychiatry at the University of Wisconsin and one of the pioneers in the emerging field of family therapy. For reasons that will become clear to the reader, I knew that an apprenticeship to Carl would offer me a number of advantages.

When Wisconsin accepted me for the internship, there was no question about our moving. Hearing the resolve in my voice, Margaret agreed readily. By the time our little band arrived in Madison in the summer of 1968, Margaret was pregnant again.

I can now understand a little of what it must have been like for her: no job, no friends, in a small apartment in a new city, with a toddler and very soon a second baby. And with a husband who was literally captivated by his work. Not only did the training experience turn out to be fascinating—seeing family after family as the apprentice co-therapist of a brilliant and powerful man—but the personal interest Carl began to develop in my professional growth met a deeper need in me for a supportive father-figure.

During that first year, I completed the extensive requirements for an internship, spent a lot of extra time with Carl, and wrote my dissertation. I was hardly ever home. Margaret and I had a routine Saturday-morning fight, because she wanted one hour of my time so that we could take a long walk. I did it, but I was often preoccupied. My obsession with being competent and successful took most of my energy.

Even when the dissertation and the internship were finally finished, it was clear that my training wasn't. Becoming an accomplished family therapist is, in Whitaker's words, "a ten-year project." When I was offered a postdoctoral fellowship for the following year, I leapt at it. My hours were a little better the second year, but I still lived at work.

In Wisconsin, winter begins in late October, and it doesn't really end until mid-May. "When I think of those first two years," Margaret says today, "I still get very angry. I felt virtually alone with two babies. If it hadn't been for Lola and Sally and some of the other women in the neighborhood who also had children, I don't know how I would have managed." And I reply: "I wish that I had done it differently; I wish I had given you, and the kids, more. I'm sorry." Indeed.

After the postdoctoral year, I wanted to stay in Madison to continue my work with Carl "a little longer," and I had been offered a job teaching family therapy to the staff of a nearby clinic. I was also invited to join the clinical faculty of the department of psychiatry. "I'm tired of being a student's wife," Margaret argued. "If we are staying here, I want a house, a decent car, a regular life. I want to really *be* somewhere."

We stumbled on it in an ad: "Older house on Lake Wingra, needs repair." The state capital, and the site of a great university, Madison is a marvelous city, spread among four adjoining lakes. The smallest, Wingra, is surrounded by the university Arboretum and by city parks. "There aren't any houses on Lake Wingra," we said to each other. There were, as it turned out, three; and one of them, a run-down stucco structure built in 1914, was for sale. We found it at dusk on a snowy evening in January; from the front door one saw a quiet city neighborhood, from the back door only lake and woods. We stood there holding hands in the half-light, falling in love with a house and a place. Later that night we got on the phone to borrow money from our families for the down payment, and we decided that if I added some private practice to my salary, we could do it.

Years later, after we moved to Atlanta, we knew a younger couple with an infant who bought an enormous, run-down house. "I know how she feels," Margaret confided. "That house looks like it will provide her safety, a kind of protection from the world. What she doesn't know yet is that it can become a prison."

And so we acquired traditional lives: one paying job, two kids, a house, a neighborhood, friends. I had more time now and relaxed a little, and we started to explore this place that was home. Around us, the world was in flames: the Vietnam war protests rocked the city daily, but they hardly touched our lives. Watching this turmoil from the distance of another generation, we drove through the barricades to go picnicking in the country with our kids.

Nor were we strongly affected by the early influences of the women's movement, which also surfaced in Madison. I remember seeing the struggle of two psychiatry residents who were husband and wife trying to get permission from the department to each work half-time so that they could share the care of their infant. They had to threaten to quit the residency, but they won. I felt admiring, and vaguely uneasy about the model of marriage and parenting which they were attempting. It was certainly not ours.

The decision to stay in Madison "a little longer" became, in fact, ten years. I quit the salaried job and expanded my private practice; I later taught in another department at the university as well. As I worked with Carl, I began to do workshops around the country, and to write papers with him.

Full of energy, Margaret was determined not to become imprisoned by this wonderful old house into which we poured years of weekend work. As Sarah approached school age and had a difficult experience in kindergarten, Margaret began to look seriously at the local schools. They seemed rigid, traditional, unimaginative. With a group of five other women, she began to put pressure on the neighborhood school to develop some experimental classrooms.

This group of women had become interested in the British open classroom, an approach to education that was developed during World War II when British children were taught in ungraded classrooms outside cities. In this approach, sometimes called the "integrated day," academic subjects are learned and "integrated" through individualized structured projects. When the public schools refused to incorporate these methods into a few model classes, Margaret and her friends rented space in a vacant school building, hired a couple of excellent teachers, and founded Wingra School. The other fathers and I built bookcases and tables, and Sarah began first grade at her mother's school.

A year later, at about the time Julia was born, Margaret assumed the directorship of Wingra. Suddenly she was a working mother, running meetings with a nursing baby in her lap. Two years later, the school had classrooms from kindergarten through sixth grade, and a waiting list.

In many ways, our lives seemed secure and satisfying. I was a more involved father, and Margaret had developed an exciting career—one that allowed her to be at home at least half the time. When she was at school, Julia was often with her. We also hired a wonderful college student, Mary, who cared for Julia three mornings a week.

But for both of us, something was missing. While our lives seemed to be progressing satisfactorily, they felt all too separate. Margaret had her world, I mine; and we still had difficulty understanding each other's experiences. Margaret resented my five o'clock appointments and trips out of town for workshops; I was envious of her many friendships and her intimate relationships with our children. As we complained to each other, the subtle implication was that each found the other to be guilty of a kind of infidelity. Each complained to the other: "You have a higher priority than our relationship."

Margaret and I had once talked hesitantly about the possibility of working together; we had even tried it—one anxious interview with a couple, soon after I got my doctorate. The couple didn't come back, and, feeling devastated, we dismissed the idea.

One day, more than five years later, I was working with a couple in which the pregnant wife was frightened about the impending delivery. As she talked about her fear, I tried to reassure her that most births are normal and ordinary, and I tried to teach her some relaxation techniques. Nothing worked. Suddenly, with a reassuring certainty, I saw Margaret's smiling face. It was her smile at Julia's recent birth that I saw then, and Margaret's words that I heard: "It was the peak experience of my life."

"I know someone who can help you," I said to the wife. Margaret breezed into the therapy, and the young woman was immediately reassured. She had an uneventful delivery, and Margaret stayed on. After five separate years of confidence-building experience, working together now seemed easier. Soon we saw another couple, then a family. I admired the way Margaret said exactly what she thought. She seemed to be able to cut through the surface talk much more successfully than I could; and she was more outgoing. At home, we talked about our cases, trying to stay out of earshot of the kids, and Margaret began to read the family-therapy literature. There was, in the chemistry of this new experiment, something very exciting for both of us.

But even as we first began to work together, I doubted some part of my motives. Was I jealous of Margaret's success at Wingra? Did I want to take her away from it? Did I want to tie her to me? While I didn't articulate these questions to myself clearly, I sensed a mischievous undertone in my intentions. Unfortunately, the future was to expose not only my questionable unconscious motives, but Margaret's problems as well.

Many therapists are drawn to their work through an interest in solving their own difficulties. We begin by being intellectually curious about certain issues; but on some level we know that if we are to be capable practitioners, we must eventually get help ourselves. The stimulus of working closely with patients is so charged, so intimate, that there is simply no hiding one's own neuroses. Sooner or later, our patients confront us with the problems we have not solved, and we must ask for help, or risk using our patients for our own "therapy," or leave the field. In my opinion, all really competent therapists have been successful patients.

This confrontation with the self is especially likely if the "patient" is a couple or family. In this setting, we are literally surrounded by a relationship struggle. While an individual therapist may be able to keep his or her client at a distance, the power of a family's struggle is highly engaging—especially since the couple or family may actively attempt to draw us into their battles. And if the therapist is a married couple, there is yet another vulnerability: the ragged edge of our own battle with each other is likely to be exposed.

In attempting to become partners in both our professional and personal lives, Margaret and I began to realize what a difficult job we had undertaken. How could we develop a relationship that was both deeply intimate and thoroughly equal? Could we manage to be autonomous, to maintain our separate identities, and yet work closely together? Could we achieve real parity, real equality between ourselves, something we increasingly saw at least our women clients wanting in their marriages? Could we combine two careers and yet manage to raise our children successfully? Could we offer our clients an example of a growing, changing relationship; or would we be living a kind of professional lie?

For a number of years we did not see the underlying problems in our marriage. Initially these problems seemed to be mostly mine. Like many women today, Margaret badly wanted to be an attentive and responsible parent, and to have a stimulating career. When she attempted this difficult feat of balance, she found that my behavior proved a formidable obstacle. As she began to confront me about my often subtle opposition, I was plunged into an acute awareness of my problems in dealing with the changes in her expectations.

Looking around me, particularly at our male clients, I realized how many men were having difficulty understanding and supporting their wives in the new roles that were increasingly available to women. While women were changing, we were not. We were not doing our share of the housework; we were not changing appreciably the amount of time we were spending with our children, or the responsibility we felt for them. In a thousand ways we not only failed to support our wives, but we were downright opposed to the changes in their lives.

Some women responded to this resistance in their husbands (and of course they faced even tougher challenges in the workplace) by compromising their careers; some became "superwomen," and laboriously carried the new demands of career as well as their old responsibilities for home and children; some women left their marriages. But in almost every couple we saw, the women were angry and resentful, the men were deeply—if often silently—threatened. "Why," I asked myself, "are we men having so much difficulty dealing with the changes in our wives?" This question, with which I struggled for a number of years, forms a major theme in this book. I attempt to outline some of the origins of these problems in men, and I make a number of suggestions to men who are attempting to adapt to the new world of men's and women's roles.

As Margaret and I struggled to deal with our own marriage, and to help our clients, it became increasingly evident to us that there are also, as one would expect, a number of unsolved problems on the woman's side of this difficult equation. For example, Margaret sometimes asked me to take responsibility for a certain activity of one of our kids, and she would then interfere with my efforts to do what she asked. She would ask me for support or encouragement in dealing with a career decision, and would then resent my suggestions and blame me for her difficulties. Like many other women, she was attempting to do something that her mother had not done, and at times she lacked both a model for what she was trying to accomplish, and internal "permission" to make certain changes in her life.

Like most other couples, we learned that our intention to behave in a certain way was often undermined by powerful and largely unconscious forces. I wanted to support Margaret in having a separate, equal career; but this rational wish was repeatedly undercut by less charitable impulses. Margaret too seemed unable to act in ways that she consciously wanted to.

As we struggled, we both began to ask ourselves: "What are the fundamental obstacles to a marriage that is both deeply intimate and profoundly equal?" This larger question forms the basic theme in this book.

While any question about the structure of the family ultimately involves examining the larger society within which we all live, our expertise and experience lie in a different direction. Whatever the struggles of adults, we have learned to look inward, and backward in time, into that shadowy realm of childhood where each individual's fundamental perspective on the world seems to be established. Even if society dictates that men and women should behave in certain ways, it is fathers and mothers who teach those ways to children—not just in the words they say, but in the lives they lead. Much of what we become is powerfully determined by childhood experience; and if we are to change our lives, we need to understand these often hidden influences. Only then can we begin to alter the "rules for living" which we learned as children.

While sex-role conflicts form the dominant metaphor in this book, they constitute only one theme in the larger pattern of struggles between men and women. Our conflicts teach us that we are all loyal to our parents—to who they were, and to what we experienced at their hands. Even if we did not like what we saw in them, even if we hated what they did to each other and to us, we are still bound by them. As we begin to deal with this underpinning not only of marriage but of all adult life, the largest question of all becomes: "How can we keep the good inheritance our parents gave us, and go beyond them to a new kind of experience, a new kind of family? How can we balance family loyalty against growth and change?"

Such questions open us to the larger struggles of the human spirit, both now and in the past. At the heart of every relationship metaphor we examine, we will find this anguished struggle with the original architects of our experience. Whatever aspect of our lives we attempt to change, we will encounter the formidable influences of our parents—those loved, flawed people who taught us about the world, and to whom we are tenaciously and sometimes unwisely loyal.

We get married believing that we will create a family that is better and happier than the one we grew up in; and we deserve to accomplish that goal. In this interest, we would be wise to study and to confront our own histories, lest we repeat them.

So where do we begin? At the same place we hope to find ourselves in the end—only lighter, freer, less encumbered: the present.

1

Metaphors

EVERY NIGHT AT ABOUT eleven, I walk our beagle, and it is usually a supremely boring chore. One night, several years ago, as the dog and I made our way down our usual route, I found myself feeling deeply sad. It was spring, and through the newly leafed trees rose a full moon, so large and richly red that it seemed alive. Why was I so sad? And why, instead of my usual frustration and impatience with this ritual, did I feel so tenderly toward this little dog that sniffed its way here and there in the dark?

For some reason, I remembered a nighttime fishing trip I took with my father when I was a boy. It was spring, and there was a full moon; as I paddled our canoe down the river where we often fly-fished in the daytime, I realized that the usual sternness of my father's voice had vanished. He was relaxed and warm, and instead of criticizing my paddling, he reassured me that I was doing fine. Recalling the softness of his voice made me feel even sadder.

The dog, too, seemed a connection with my father. When I was four, my father left home to serve in the army in World War II, and on one of his infrequent leaves he brought me a dog, a beagle, which became my constant companion. I suppose the dog was a comforting link with my father during those four years when he was absent. I had in turn bought a beagle for my son,

1

who was now sixteen, and who, of course, usually forgot to walk him.

"But why now?" I asked myself. "Why these sudden memories of my father, and why with such sadness?" Then it hit me: the date was May 11. My father had died on just such a warm spring evening exactly twenty-three years before.

It is in this way that our reality is transformed. A cluster of circumstances awakens in us feelings that become so charged and intense that they literally change what we are experiencing. Walking down an ordinary street in our usual world, we find ourselves in a symbolic landscape which is laden with feeling. For a while we are living in a dream, one in which familiar people and objects call up feelings that are ancient, perhaps threatening, and very powerful.

During my walk, I was surrounded by a nexus of associations that pushed me back into memories of my father, and into my grief about losing him. The dominant theme in the memory was time itself—the anniversary of his death. But there were other elements, including the stimulus of having begun this book, which made me think about my own childhood. The spring night, the full moon, the dog—these were also figures in my waking dream.

Such "clusters of associations" also occur in relationships, of course; and the relationship that is the most vulnerable to such charged transformation is marriage—or any other committed love relationship which approaches the intensity and involvement of marriage. But marriage itself, legal and binding, is the relational landscape which is the most susceptible to this mysterious invasion of unruly, often frighteningly powerful feelings.

A couple was talking amiably while driving to their therapy appointment, when the wife, Joyce Olson, noticed a blob of tarry black asphalt on the floor mat of the car. She picked it up in her fingers and examined it quizzically.

"What's that?" her husband, Thomas, asked.

"Road tar, I guess," she said.

"Throw it out the window," he said.

The irritable, commanding tone in his voice annoyed her. "I don't want to," she said, half-humorously. "I'm looking at it."

"Throw it out!" he said again, commanding and impatient.

"No!" she said. "Don't talk to me that way."

"Listen, dammit, why won't you throw it out?" he went on, raising his voice to a yell. "You're going to get it on the car seat."

"Because I don't want to, you asshole!" she yelled back with uncharacteristic directness.

By the time the couple arrived at the office where Margaret and I practice marriage and family therapy, they were both absolutely furious, though they seemed confused about why they were having such a ridiculous fight. Margaret and I let the quarrel go on for a while, perhaps because Joyce was fighting back. But the conflict quickly became unproductive and repetitive.

Impatiently, I broke in: "I don't understand this fight—though obviously, Joyce, you didn't like the way Thomas spoke to you, sort of like a scolding parent."

"Absolutely," she agreed. "It made me furious; it always does when he speaks to me like I'm some sort of bad child." But that wasn't the only issue here.

"I'm puzzled about what started it," I said. "Joyce, you picked up that blob of tar and looked at it, and then you were reluctant to throw it away." I was implying that there was something symbolic about the tar, though I didn't understand what it was. I had a vivid image of her sitting in the car, holding tenaciously on to that little crumb of blackness while Thomas yelled at her to turn it loose.

"Something about letting go of a dark thing," Margaret said suggestively, abstracting the image to its basic form.

Suddenly Joyce's face began to brighten, and she chuckled. "I know what it is!" she said. Thomas, who looked rather stern and forbidding behind his scholarly beard, was disarmed. "We have begun to talk a little about Alan," was all she said. "And it's been difficult."

Though Margaret and I were still confused, Thomas seemed to know what she meant. Seeing our confusion, Joyce said, "Alan is the married man I had the long affair with." I recalled Joyce's brief mention in the first interview that she had had a previous relationship with an older married man.

Since Joyce and Thomas married when they were in their thirties, there was a lot of history to deal with. Now, as Joyce began, with relief, to talk about her relationship with her former lover, it was clear that she had indeed "held on to" her deep attachment to him. This was the "dark spot," a bundle of feelings that were both forbidden and compelling, and which she was having difficulty relinquishing. She loved her husband, but she had some unfinished business to attend to before she could really be "with" him.

More precisely, *they* had some unfinished business. Thomas's jealousy of this prior relationship, which he expressed in a critical, almost sanctimonious way, reminded Joyce of her mother's attitudes toward her, and it caused her to retreat from him. Before they could deal successfully with this issue, Joyce needed help with her guilt, Thomas with his older-generation criticalness and his jealousy.

This couple did not have a conscious plan to deal with this problem. The conflict emerged symbolically, and the "dark spot" was unconsciously chosen to represent their difficulty with this issue. It was a mutually defined metaphor, or symbol, for the conflict, and it was not until we all deciphered the meaning of the metaphor that we could get to work on the emerging difficulty in their marriage.

In its usual usage, a metaphor is a figure of speech that makes an analogy between two images or ideas, and its chief province is poetry. Unlike a simile, which makes the analogy explicit, as in "The tree was *like* a bare hand begging the sky's indulgence," a metaphor combines the two things being compared into a single identity: "The tree's bare fingers begged the sky's indulgence." In metaphor, the tree is not *like* a hand, it *is* a hand. The comparison is intimate; for a moment, the distinction between tree and hand is lost.

Metaphors also exist in everyday life. We experience certain events, certain people, even certain words symbolically; and we invest these "situations" with so much feeling that they are transformed into metaphors. As in poetry, the distinction between the metaphor and the "other reality" which it represents becomes blurred. For Joyce and Thomas, the blob of tar didn't represent a problem—it seemed to *be* the problem.

This process occurs, I believe, because we need it to. We need images, symbols, metaphors in order to cope with certain aspects of our private, internal experience—particularly the aspects of experience about which we are anxious or guilty.

One of the reasons this couple's fight emerged with such force was that they were on the way to a therapy interview, where they were free to suspend their usual self-restraint and to plunge into the unruly world of primary feeling. Margaret and I provided an "observing ego" to help them interpret the meaning of their conflicts, and we also supplied a cohesive element which allowed them to address their distress more freely. But while being in therapy may heighten the symbolic quality of life (a request to pass the salt can become an incendiary incident during the early months of therapy), this tendency to symbolize our experience is part of life itself.

Within each of us a vast reservoir of feelings—unexpressed, usually unnamed—clamors for expression, and for a response from the world. We all search for metaphors that can give these feelings form, and which will allow us to engage others in our personal drama. The institution of marriage is fertile ground for the creation of such metaphors. Like Joyce and Thomas, we are often anxious about our feelings about each other, and we need symbols to help us both express our conflicts and to protect us from knowing their full meaning.

A couple of sessions later, Joyce and Thomas described a fight that had occurred the previous weekend.

Thomas said, "Well, I was trying to do what Margaret suggested—negotiate this child-care thing with Joyce. I figured I would offer to keep Amy [their six-month-old daughter] on Saturday morning, and I hoped I would get to watch the football game that afternoon without Amy's being around crying and whatever. All I said was maybe Joyce would take Amy and go visit somebody—I suggested her mother—while I watched the game. I didn't mean anything by the suggestion, though I guess I was being selfish." Thomas looked angrily at Joyce, who was also clearly upset: "So I didn't understand when you left with Amy in the middle of the morning, and then came back in a huff during the middle of the game. You did keep Amy upstairs, but you stayed mad, and I didn't know why."

Joyce clamored to speak: "Didn't know why, when at nine o'clock that night you were still watching the damn game?"

"A different game," he said half jokingly, a glint of defiance in his eye, "and why shouldn't I watch football if you weren't talking to me?'' Then he spoke seriously. ''I never understood why you got upset in the first place.''

Joyce took a deep breath, as if she couldn't get enough air. Her face was flushed, and she seemed about to cry. Her words were halting, choked: ''It was the way you said it, Thomas.'' She paused, trying to regain her composure. ''Almost like,'' and she halted again, trying not to cry, ''you wanted to push me off on my mother.'' Tears now running down her cheeks, her breathing rapid. ''This is ridiculous, to be crying when I feel so angry!''

''Maybe you're afraid to get angry,'' I offered.

''That sounds right,'' Joyce said, smiling slightly through her tears. ''Afraid of feeling rejected again.'' Breathing rapidly still, her breath coming in jerks, she alternately laughed and cried.

''You don't have to pull yourself together,'' Margaret said softly. ''You were hurt by what Thomas said.''

''I was, I really was.'' Finally released by Margaret's permission, she cried, her chest moving in deep, breaking sobs. Eventually her breathing became more regular, and quieter; she opened her eyes, looking at Thomas. He seemed embarrassed, chagrined: ''Look, darling, I'm sorry. I . . .''

''I know I'm overreacting,'' Joyce said haltingly. ''It doesn't make sense.'' Then she smiled slightly and added, ''Of course it isn't the first time I've bumped into your football neurosis, or felt pushed away for that matter,'' and she looked at Thomas with a mixture of fondness and anger.

''What happened to your anger?'' I asked Joyce.

''I still feel it; it's like a burning in my chest. But I can't seem to get it out. I was angry as hell at Thomas that Saturday, but it took me this long to even talk about it.'' She seemed embarrassed about her inability to get openly angry.

''Do you think this could have to do with the childhood issue we talked about earlier?'' Margaret said suggestively. ''The feeling of being pushed off on somebody else, the fear of speaking up?''

''What do you mean?'' Joyce said, puzzled.

''Haven't you felt rejected in this way before? Especially in childhood?'' Margaret asked. She was recalling something that had come up in the initial interview.

Joyce hesitated, thinking. Her eyes focused on nothing; her face seemed vacant and sad. "This does sound like my struggle with my mother," she said finally. "I have definitely felt rejected by my mother."

"Do you remember what happened between you and your mother?" Margaret prodded her gently into recollection.

"Well, it's strange." She seemed to focus more, now looking directly at Margaret. "The family story is that I was the spoiled one, the baby of the family. My mother says it a lot, in fact—that my grandmother and Annie pampered me, and that my father did too. She makes a big point of it."

"I don't remember who Annie is," I confessed.

Joyce took a deep breath and sighed. "How long do we have?" I said that we had enough time to hear about her childhood. "Annie is . . ." Again she seemed overwhelmed by feeling, unable to continue. After several deep breaths, she began again: "I think Annie really loved me. There, I've finally said it." Then, realizing that she still hadn't identified her, she concluded: "Annie was the black woman who took care of me when my mother went to work."

"And your mother went to work when you were a year old?" Margaret said.

"Yes. I've recently learned more about it—from my father." Another pause as she thought. "Just before I was born, my grandfather died, my mother's father. My mother had been very close to him, and did not get along with her own mother. I don't know how the decision was made for my mother's mother to come to live with us—actually, I think my father encouraged it. He got along with her quite well. So there was always tension in the house between my mother and grandmother."

"And between your parents, it sounds like," I added. "Your grandmother and your father teamed up against your mother. Whose side were you on?"

Joyce said, "I must have been in the middle." After a pause, she continued, "There's more. You see, my father's business in the small town we lived in was failing—he owned a hardware store—and we had to move to Atlanta. He went to work for somebody else, and when I was a year old, my mother went to work as secretary to an executive. I don't think she really wanted to work, but she needed to. She once implied it was not just for the money, but to save her sanity. So my grandmother and Annie"—again her voice broke—"took care of me."

"Every time you mention Annie's name, you get tearful," I observed.

In a kind of reverie of recall, she went on, "I know. She was a big woman who would sing to me and rock me and tell me stories. She never criticized me; she just—I keep saying it—took care of me. But my grandmother also took care of me a lot."

"In a loving way," Margaret offered. Joyce nodded silently. "What happened to Annie?" Margaret asked.

Joyce looked up with panic in her face, as though she didn't want to speak about it. Finally she was able to continue: "When I was eleven—I suppose I was getting sassy with my mother, and I would turn to Annie or my grandmother when I was mad with her—one day my mother fired Annie; told her they couldn't afford her anymore." The room was very quiet as everyone, including Thomas, registered the enormity of this event in Joyce's life. She looked solemn, sad.

"After ten years of caring for you," Margaret said, a little angrily. "And it seemed to happen in conjunction with your becoming 'sassy.' No wonder you have trouble being assertive."

Joyce said, "What do you mean?"

Margaret explained, "When you got sassy, your mother fired this woman who loved you. On an unconscious level, you would have associated 'sassiness' with rejection and loss. So you would have become even more cautious about displeasing people."

"More cautious than I was already," Joyce said in acknowledgment.

"Yes," Margaret said. "I would imagine you were already quite worried about displeasing your mother."

"You are so right. I don't know what it is. She tries to be nice to me, says she loves me, all that. But then I will hear this tone in her voice that reminds me of ice water. A tone that says I've done something wrong. I've heard that all my life, and I can never figure out what I've done."

"Being loved by someone other than your mother, I suppose," Margaret said, musing.

"How is that wrong?" Joyce was perplexed.

Margaret said, "It isn't. But it created problems between you and your mother, and it sounds as if those problems started before you were born."

"I still don't understand. You think it had to do with my mother's relationship with her mother?" Now it was Margaret's turn to nod agreement as Joyce continued, "It's true they weren't close when my mother was young. As I said, she was her father's favorite."

I had been listening for some time, puzzling about Joyce's powerful sense of having been rejected by her mother. As I tried to visualize this person I hadn't met, I could see the vague image of a woman looking on in anger and frustration as another woman—sometimes her own mother, sometimes Annie—cared for her child. It was a scene both ancient and contemporary, full of regret and guilt. "What do you know about your mother's childhood?" I asked suddenly, startling Joyce. I had a fleeting image of the genogram, or diagram of the family relationships, which I had drawn in the first interview. "Do I remember that she had a younger sibling?"

"How did you remember?" Joyce said, looking vaguely disoriented. I had completely disrupted Margaret's dialogue with her, and Margaret looked slightly irritated. "My aunt Ella. She was my grandmother's favorite, and she and my mother didn't get along either."

I couldn't resist continuing: "So when your mother went to work and turned your care over to Annie and your grandmother, you became a symbol for your mother of her jealousy of her younger sister. Symbolically, you became the 'spoiled' youngest kid she had been jealous of as a child." Obviously confused by this new complexity, Joyce was silent. I wanted to be sure she understood what I was saying, so I repeated it, but a little more gently and more empathetically: "You are a youngest child, and you were being cared for by her own mother."

"So it did start before I was born," she finally said.

Margaret cleared her throat, and then smiled broadly at me. "As I was saying . . ."

"I'm sorry," I said.

Margaret turned to Joyce again. "I agree with Gus. Your mother got very jealous of your other caretakers. I think the real trouble—

or some of it—was between her and her mother: but she directed her ire at Annie. She couldn't fire your grandmother, though she probably wanted to."

It was these feelings of rejection—of being pushed away toward other people, other caretakers—that had surfaced in the interchange with Thomas; Thomas was now in the role of mother. The hurt, the anger—these were all focused on, and felt, in relation to him. It was Thomas who seemed not to love her, who seemed to want her to take her emotional needs somewhere else.

The unconscious mind is not precise: it recognizes vague outlines, familiar shapes; in this instance someone whom she loves and depends on seems to be pushing her away. Never mind that this is the present, that the person who is pushing her away is her husband, that the person she is being pushed toward is her mother. The little girl within Joyce sees the present "reality" through a haze of emotion; it is the "shape" of that reality that triggers these primitive feelings. When Joyce was a child, the same process was taking place in Joyce's mother's perception of her.

Of course, Thomas's cool, distant demeanor contributed to the problem in their marriage. He did seem defensive and anxious when Joyce wanted to be close to him, and he did often push her away. It wasn't the first time they had fought about his need for privacy and emotional "space," fights that seemed to center around his attachment to watching sports events on television, and around his involvement with his work. Thomas is a scientist, and his after-hours stints in the lab were a frequent source of argument.

"I want more attention, more time, more acceptance from you," Joyce said repeatedly. "I want to know about your feelings, and to be able to feel close to you."

"I feel crowded, and hemmed in," Thomas would reply defensively. And one could almost see him retreating visibly as he said it.

Thomas's defensiveness, and his typically male avoidance of closeness, were as deeply rooted in his history as Joyce's needs for intimacy and acceptance were in hers. Having grown up with a dependent and intrusive mother, Thomas was very anxious to maintain his autonomy

Thomas's aloofness reminded Joyce of her mother's coolness and distance; Joyce's efforts to get close reminded Thomas of his mother's intrusiveness. And so they danced around and around in a classical marital ballet with the woman in pursuit, the man in retreat. The more she pursued, the more defensive he felt: the more defensive he felt, the more she pursued.

Like the fight about the road tar, but at a much more significant depth, this pattern, which family therapist Tom Fogarty has termed a pursuit–distance dynamic, formed a symbolic "structure" in this relationship; it became a marriage metaphor, so laden with emotion that it seemed to flood their interchange, overpowering their rational selves. Both partners poured into the "dance" feelings that seemed to reach deep into their childhoods.

While we will return to this common polarization in marriage, Joyce and Thomas's conflicts raise a basic question: why does marriage become the target for such intrusive, irrational feeling? Rather than heaping these emotions on our partner, why don't we experience them in direct relation to the key figures of our childhood? Why are we so afraid of experiencing our anger at our parents, and so willing to be angry at our mate?

The answers to these questions are complex, but we can make a start here. Imagine Joyce as a child. She is two, and has had a perfectly normal outburst of temper. Sensing her mother's coldness, she feels danger. She does not understand this feeling in her mother, but for her it carries great threat. She does not know about the difficulty of trying to work and raise children, nor does she comprehend the conflicts between her mother and grandmother, or the problems between her parents. She only knows that her mother disapproves, and that mother's disapproval is frightening. She has been very anxious about her mother's absence of late, and puzzled by the fact that her grandmother and her father seem to be so much nicer to her than her mother is. She is angry with her mother, and hurt by her coolness; but she recoils inwardly, fearing the consequences of this anger. Mother is often unhappy with her these days; what if she were to leave her altogether? The human infant is an extraordinarily vulnerable and helpless creature—much less able to care for itself than in most other species; and this vulnerability is prolonged. Ours is not a society in which children can wander safely from family to family within a nurturant "clan" that takes collective responsibility for them. Not until she is nearly twenty years old will

Joyce be able to exist outside her family; her only security is her nuclear family and its network of "extended kin."

During that long childhood, Joyce is in effect a prisoner of the family, and is subject to its unconscious emotional "rules" (there may, for example, be unspoken prohibitions against the expression of anger, or against admitting vulnerability, or against even mentioning sexuality). She is also prey to the family's conflicts. If there are divisions or "teams" within the family, she will be helplessly drawn into them.

But it is not just the family on which she depends. Her life seems especially influenced by her relationship with her mother. It was mother who nursed her, mother who answered her earliest cries in the night, and mother who also seemed to know what she needed. In her case, however, it was mother who began to draw away from her: at first in going away to work when she was one; and, as Joyce began to be cared for by family members with whom her mother had conflict, her mother became cool and reserved with her. When something interferes with the mother-child bond early in life, it often has devastating consequences for the child. The threatened loss of her mother's approval was so frightening to Joyce that she "decided" at a young age to repress her feelings and to become a perfect child; and this strategy, of trying desperately hard to please, followed her into adult life.

The extraordinary importance of the mother-child bond in the life of the child is a highly problematic family dynamic: difficult for the emotionally burdened mother, and for both her girl and boy children. The unfairness of this arrangement, in which fathers are painfully, destructively absent from the inner life of families, will form a major theme of this book. But even as we question the wisdom of this traditional role structure, we must acknowledge its looming presence. Children are still, in the main, highly dependent on their mothers for emotional support, and in the very solitariness of that source, vulnerable to its loss.

How does a child deal with being angry at a parent over not getting her needs met—when that anger carries the terrifying threat of rejection? One temporary solution might be for the child to "split" her feelings about the parent into various parts, repressing the threatening aspects of the feeling. She could develop an image of a "good mother," including the parts of her mother that she cherishes and depends on; the parts of her mother that threaten and anger her would be focused on a "bad mother" image, which she would attempt to keep out of her consciousness. She might also divide herself into two such disparate parts, a "good self," consisting of those aspects of herself that are nonthreatening and compliant, and a "bad self," which she associates with the emergence of the "bad mother." In the self-focused logic of a child, she would blame her own "bad self" for the transgressions of the "bad mother." "I cause my mother to be unhappy," she might say to herself. She could then resolve to keep the negative aspects of her mother and herself hidden from consciousness in an effort to preserve her security.

These "split" emotions, particularly the negative ones, remain inside the child, undischarged; and they do not seem to dissipate with time. This deep childhood rage about the unfairness of life cries out not just for expression, but for reparation. It represents the child's yearning for justice in what frequently seems like an unjust world. But the power of these feelings remains latent, quiescent, like dammed water, or like the vast dispersion of electrical charge that creates lightning.

Later in childhood, children encounter another obstacle to open acknowledgment and expression of their feelings: they become aware of their parents' problems and frailties. As they mature, children not only learn about their parents' imperfections, but they are also pulled into these difficulties as "helpers." This involvement in their parents' emotional tangles—which will be the subject of extensive discussion here—creates in children a sense of bewilderment and frustration, and it makes it very difficult for these older children to admit even to themselves their feelings about their parents' failures. How can they be angry at these parents who gave them life, who did their best, and who are beset with their own problems? This sense of guilt, born of being angry at parents who tried, and whom they love in spite of their failures, often becomes more acute with time. The more one's parents become vulnerable, the harder it is to be disappointed in them.

Most of us enter adulthood with a vast reservoir of unexpressed emotion about the excesses and insufficiencies of our childhoods, but we are rarely aware of the power of this painful heritage. We assume that when we leave home we put all that behind us, and that when we marry we start fresh. Quite unconsciously, we bring to adult life, and to marriage especially, a deep yearning for wholeness, for approval, for all the things we deserved as children and didn't get.

In this culture, marriage may be the most popular form of psychotherapy. We all seem to believe that marriage will change our lives, will make us feel better about ourselves. This special person will make us strong when we feel weak, whole when we feel empty, comforted when we feel lonely. This is the magic union, the one that has the power to transform reality. We need only listen to the lyrics of popular songs to be aware of how widespread these expectations are.

This yearning for the magic partnership, which marriage is expected not only to be, but to be permanently, is, of course, modeled on the highly idealized "good parent" images of early childhood. We dream of a fused, symbiotic union in which we feel nurtured, safe, profoundly valued—and all-powerful. With this person "attached" to me, I can do anything.

Given the tedium, the frustration, the internecine combat of everyday life, the question is not whether this idealized relationship metaphor will fail, but when. For most of us, our failure to sustain this idealized union (and it may take us many years to face this failure, since dreams die hard) reawakens in us a sense of ancient injury; our disappointment with ourselves and our mate reminds us of our disappointments with ourselves and our parents when we were children. Our mate becomes the "bad parent," while we feel like a "bad self." All the rage and hurt of those early years may then pour out into our marriage.

This "displaced reenactment" of our early dramas is more likely to occur, I believe, because of the person we have chosen to marry; for we seem powerfully drawn to marrying someone who will help us recapitulate those early struggles with our parents. We may think we are marrying someone very different from our parents (and the intricate chemistry of this unconscious choice is to be the subject of further discussion), but the likelihood is that we will find ourselves forced to deal in our marriage with the core themes and struggles of our early life. If we grew up struggling with jealousy, or a sense of powerlessness, or a panic about closeness, or a sense of being unloved—those will be the issues in our marriage.

Why would we be so perverse as to choose to marry someone who will confront us with the most central and painful realities of our childhood? "Why would I happen to marry a man who has problems with jealousy, and who can be so distant and critical?" Joyce would eventually cry out in a mixture of humor and dismay.

Again, the questions are complex, but here is a beginning: as children, we are often injured emotionally; and that sense of injury causes us to retreat inwardly. Certain risks seem too dangerous; and so we wall off feelings, possibilities, alternatives. Part of us dies, or becomes dormant. Our sexuality, perhaps, or our anger, our playfulness, our creativity. We learn to live conservatively; we become experts at compromise.

That traumatized, injured, walled-off self yearns to reemerge, and to live fully—the way we were born to live, with all our spontaneity and vitality. The problem is how to manage this reawakening.

Marriage is an unconsciously motivated "experiment" in that direction. Part of the experiment involves recapitulating the circumstances that were so difficult for us as children—and we are skilled at finding someone who will help us do that.

But there is more to the experiment than reenactment. To simply repeat something, with no hope or expectation of change, would be terribly discouraging. So in addition to linking up with someone who inadvertently plays some of the familiar roles that we associate with our parents and our siblings, our partner also has the capacity to help us vary and change those dramas. This person, from a different family world, also represents newness and change. He or she *is* different from us, and from our parents. And he or she challenges *us* to be different, to rewrite our own script.

I think of myself here, and of one of my struggles with Margaret. My mother once talked about what she called my "personality change." I had been an extroverted, ebullient young child, full of talk and energy. "But when you were about nine, you became very quiet, and I never understood it," she said. Many years later, looking back, it isn't difficult for me to understand that change.

I was four in 1942 when my father left for the army, and I was at the beginning of that delusional Oedipal period when a boy routinely imagines banishing his father and marrying his mother. This normal and powerful fantasy is usually thwarted by the reality of a father who will have none of it. In the classic outcome, the boy puts away his crush on his mother, and sets to becoming like his father. In my case, however, fate contrived to grant me the illusion that my wish had come true. My father disappeared, and at four, I became what adults teasingly call "the man of the house." On an unconscious level, I took the fantasy of being my mother's "mate" much too seriously.

When my father returned, he and I seemed to be competitors. I remember one particularly painful scene which occurred during one of his leaves toward the end of the war. My mother had cooked a special breakfast—obviously for him—and had neglected to fry my egg to the consistency of shoe leather, the way she knew I liked it. All the eggs were pale and undercooked, the way he liked them. Feeling betrayed, I poked at the offending slippery substance with my fork.

"Eat your egg," my father said.

"I don't like it," I said. Becoming bolder, I flipped the egg petulantly with my fork, and, as I watched in horror, it slithered off my plate onto the fresh tablecloth. In a rush and a rage, my father, furious about the coalition which he sensed between my mother and me, came at me with his army belt drawn. I cringed in fright as the blows fell upon me.

This was about the time that I became, in my mother's eyes, withdrawn and shy, though she didn't associate the change in me with my father's return from the army. I obviously made an unconscious decision that my extroversion was dangerous because it threatened my father, and that I had to hide it. "Keep a low profile," seemed to become my motto.

I was still pretty shy and socially self-conscious when I met Margaret when I was a junior at a college in New England. While she had her own insecurities, Margaret was deeply involved with people. I was the poet, the loner; she was the social person, with a wide range of friends and other involvements. There were other elements in our attraction to each other, of course; but I was drawn to her social ability. I was also threatened by it.

Was I searching for that long-buried part of myself, which I saw in her? Probably. Was I hoping to trade on that ability, leaning on her for what I couldn't seem to do myself? Probably.

After we married, I became jealous of her friendliness and extroversion, and she had real difficulty tolerating my jealousy. After a while, I couldn't seem to endure being on the fringes of a social interchange, and she couldn't tolerate my kicking her under the table when I thought she was being "too talkative."

Obviously, I needed to hold my own with Margaret; rather than suffering and sniping, I had to learn to compete. And to do that, I had to reach deep inside for a part of me that I had lost touch with many years before. I simply had to grow. Margaret also had to learn to live with my occasional jealous outbursts, and, since she had grown up with a mother who was jealous of her, this turned out to be a very difficult task.

I believe that we all enter marriage with such unconscious "plans." While we inevitably repeat the dilemmas of childhood, we also want to change our response to them. We deeply yearn for these old dilemmas to come out better this time. We want reparation, justice, a "right" outcome. The person we marry is someone peculiarly suited not only to help us restage the original situation of our childhood, but also someone who is likely to provide us with a powerful "lever" (which is founded in his or her own family drama) for changing our role in that drama.

A central problem in marriage is that this amateur psychotherapy project is usually partially successful. Partial successes are dangerous, because our hopes are raised, and then we are disappointed—again.

Here we are, married to someone who reminds us in powerful ways of the struggles and identities of our youth, identities that have given our life shape, but also pain, and someone who seems to demand that we change those realities. The danger is that we will construct a kind of chrysalis in our marriage, a hardened and constrictive structure that feels like the strictures of childhood, and that we will direct at this "thing" between us all the frustration and rage left over from our childhoods. Our mate, of course, will not usually understand where this fury comes from, and will apply his or her own interpretation to it, often an interpretation that is based on similar distortions arising from the past.

We hope, of course, that our partner will see past our outbursts to the hurt and yearning within us; that he or she will be an ideal "parent." But because the past has been deeply learned, and so faithfully recorded within us, it inevitably becomes the basis for our predictions about the future. Even if we work strenuously to avoid a repetition of past events, our efforts are shaped by those very events. Like it or not, we predict that significant people in our adult life will act like the important early figures in our childhood; and we are extremely skilled in finding people who will confirm those expectations.

These volatile dynamics are responsible for the failure of many marriages. After battling with the "chrysalis" in our marriage for a number of years, it becomes easy to assume that we might have to "shed" the relationship itself in order to grow beyond its confinements.

When we become convinced that our mate cannot or will not change—and we are quite adept in approaching our partner in ways that make him or her resistant to us—it is easy to extend our theory to the next logical step: perhaps we need another "context," or another mate. And so begins the internal process that leads to divorce. It is frequently a process that is occurring in both partners, and, as I will explain in more detail, one that is "cooperatively" or collusively developed.

At times of high stress, it occurs to all of us that the way to resolve our problems and to change our lives is to leave this difficult person whom we have somehow had the misfortune to marry. While it may be absolutely necessary and desirable for some marriages to end, many marriages are dissolved unnecessarily while the ex-partners proceed to reconstruct with another mate a variation on the same set of problems. The difficulties, as it turns out, are not only between us, but also within each of us; and the experience of divorce does not resolve those deeply internalized struggles which we each brought into this marriage, and carry forward into the next.

It is quite possible for us to open our eyes to the fact that we are no longer helpless children, but capable adults, with many options and possibilities that we did not have as children. We can face the fact that our partner, while not wholly innocent, is someone surprisingly like us who has helped us construct a complex relationship metaphor in which we have cooperatively restaged the central issues in both our lives. Once we begin to see the origins of this drama between us, and the reasons for its existence, we can search for other ways of resolving these problems than through acting them out in our marriage.

If we are to break this marital hypnosis, however, we must first be willing to face its existence, and to feel its power in our lives. While the journey of this book will take us backward in time and will sometimes feel regressive, our goal is not to remain preoccupied with the past, but through encountering it to leave it behind us.

Our destination is to stand face to face, feeling the space around us, feeling our own powerful and unencumbered vitality, and sensing, across the abyss that will always divide us, this Other, who is present, important, and enough like us so that we have some chance of not being eternally alone; but different enough from us that we can never imagine him or her to be merely a part of us. We will discover our mate to be someone familiar, and someone forever new.

2

A Way of Working

MARRIAGE IS NOT A two-person relationship. Perhaps in the early "honeymoon" months we believe that there are only the two of us, but soon the many competitors for our loyalty to each other assert themselves; and thereafter we live in a tangle of conflicting obligations. Our ties to powerfully significant "others" begin to pull us away from each other: our parents (and their substitute caregivers), our siblings, grandparents, aunts and uncles, friends, employers; and, if we have them, especially our children—all these people command our time, attention, loyalty. When we look across at our mate, we see not just an individual, but someone enmeshed in complicated relationships with others.

The patterns created by these intricate ties can be troublesome, since they are likely to awaken in us the memories of similar relationship patterns in our childhood. Margaret's strong ties to her father, for example, may remind me of some of the jealousy I felt as a child when my father so rudely intruded into my special relationship with my mother. If we are to understand marriage, we must grapple with relationship patterns, for it is often a configuration of forces, rather than the individual personality of our mate, which causes us so much distress.

Albert Pesso is not a family therapist, but I have learned a great deal from observing his work with groups of individual clients, many of them therapists. An example of his approach to psychotherapy not only illustrates some of the ways the past is reactivated by our present relationships but also portrays a larger metaphor regarding the process of change.

In his groups, Pesso uses "role plays" to simulate historical situations in the lives of his clients; but these staged repetitions of history represent only one part of his efforts. I was recently in one of these groups, which consisted of ten other therapists. We all sat in a circle on the floor in a carpeted office. A young psychologist whose turn it was to "work" sat in the center of the circle. Looking very anxious, he addressed Al: "I am very self-critical," he said, "and I wish I could stop doing it. This tendency really inhibits my life, and I would like to change it."

Dressed in jeans and running shoes, Al sat cross-legged, facing his client. A trim, fit man in his fifties, balding, with an extremely kind face, he seemed strangely removed and skeptical. "I don't want to try to help you in that way," he said with gentle firmness. "I think it would be a mistake to begin by wanting to change yourself. The first thing we need to do is to admit who we are, to stand in the center of our truth, as it were. If we can do that, it will lead us somewhere. But if we start by trying to be different, it is like a self-negation."

"So what should I do?" the psychologist said, puzzled. "I don't know," Al said. A long silence, while the two men looked at each other. Al seemed in no hurry. "Wait until you feel something. I think it is a mistake to start with an *idea,* especially the thought of being different." Another silence.

The young man looked increasingly uncomfortable. "I feel like I am failing in some way, not doing it right."

"That may be your truth," Al said. "You are somebody who tries to do things right, and you feel you are failing."

"I guess that's me." His face seemed flushed, and Al noticed it.

"That's the first feeling I've seen," Al said. "Maybe we are on the right track."

"What can I do about it?"

"It's happening again," Al said, smiling. In the group, a slight rustle of amusement. After what seemed like an interminable silence, he offered, "I suppose you could pick someone in the group to role-play that critical voice."

Eager to do almost anything, the psychologist chose a man to role-play the critical voice, and, still seated on the floor, had the role player stand over him. "What is this voice saying to you?" Al asked.

"That I'm not doing things right."

Al turned to the role player and said quietly, "Say that—'You're not doing things right.'"

With a slight tone of sternness, the role player repeated the words. As he did so, the psychologist looked visibly disturbed. Again, his face flushed with feeling.

"That touched you," Al noted.

"It sounded very familiar," the young man said.

"Should he say it again?" Al asked the psychologist, who silently nodded agreement. The role player repeated the critical message. This time the psychologist winced as if someone had struck him physically. "You looked as if somebody had slapped you," Al said gently.

"It felt painful," he replied.

"Is this a voice from your history?" Al asked. "I notice you picked a man."

"It begins to sound like my father."

"Ah," Al said softly. "Let's let him be your father, then. I assume he's the negative part of your father." Speaking to the role player again, Al said, "Enroll as the negative aspect of his father."

The role player said, "I am role-playing the negative aspect of your father." The psychologist looked up at the man, who towered above him.

"You look frightened," Al said to the young man on the floor.

"I feel frightened. Like I have no defense against what he is saying."

"So that really is true, then. You feel that you have no defense against your father when he tells you you're not doing things right. What did he want you to do?" Al asked.

"Be a success. Be aggressive, good at sports. Make a lot of money, the way he did."

Being careful to pick the client's exact words, Al had the role player say, "I want you to be a success, be aggressive, be good at sports, and make a lot of money, like me." As the role player said these words, tears began to stream down the face of the young psychologist.

"That really wounds you, doesn't it?" Al said, watching the man before him very carefully. The psychologist nodded, unable to speak. "What's happening?" Al asked.

"I was hearing my father say, 'Instead of hanging on to your mother's skirts the way you do.' "

"Why don't you pick someone to role-play your mother?" Al suggested. Looking very distracted, the young man chose a woman from the group and positioned her, also standing, beside him. "She doesn't have a skirt," Al said smiling, "but you could hang on to the leg of her jeans." The young man did so, looking up at the role-play mother. "Now what do you feel?" Al asked.

"Like this is the way it was in my childhood." After a pause, he added: "Except she was sort of hanging on to me too, because he wasn't much less critical of her." Al asked the woman to grasp the client's arm. Son and mother now clung to each other. "This is right," the client confirmed. "This is the way it was."

"And this seems to be where you are stuck," Al said firmly.

"I feel like I hang on to my wife like this too," the young man said with a tone of embarrassment.

Al waited quietly to see in which direction the client's feeling would take him. The dilemma was clear; the question seemed to be whether the psychologist could change his situation in some way. "We could work on this issue with your mother, and the way it affects your marriage; but you keep looking up at your father. Right now, that's where your interest seems to be."

"I want to tell him that what he says hurts me."

"Tell him."

Looking up fearfully, he said to the father, "The way you talk to me hurts me!" Tears were streaming down his face.

Al quickly turned to the role player and said, "Accommodate." The role player registered the psychologist's words with a sound of acknowledgment: "Uh!" Seeing that his words had an effect, the young man was encouraged, adding spontaneously, "And you piss me off!" Again, the role-play father registered pain with a wordless sound.

The client suddenly looked fearful, as if he were afraid of retaliation. "He seems so overpowering," he said to Al. "I think it would help if I stood up."

"Go ahead," Al said warmly. The psychologist stood facing his symbolic father.

"What if he got on his knees?" Al nodded permission, and the role-play father knelt before his son. ". . . for a change," the son added ironically. The psychologist kept glancing at Al for guidance and approval, but, wary of being a controlling "parent," Al took his cues from his client's own initiative. Supported within the field of Pesso's keen and empathic vision, the young man seemed increasingly bold.

"You look very angry about the things he said to you," Pesso observed.

"I feel absolutely furious," he muttered.

"You could tell him how angry you are," Al said.

Released by Al's permission, the psychologist raised his voice. Suddenly, he was almost yelling: "Why the hell didn't you help me a little when I was a kid?! Why didn't you take some damn *interest*?" The role-play figure winced physically, and whimpered in pain. "You cared about your damn job more than me!" Angrily. "And then you have the nerve to come around and tell me I'm not pleasing you. Well, you didn't please me either!" The role-play father cowered on the floor, writhing in mock pain. The psychologist, his face still wet with tears, looked explosively tense.

"What's going on in your body?" Al asked.

"I feel very tense."

"Your leg is twitching," Al noted.

"I feel like I want to kick him, the way he kicked me with words."

"Let's see if we can allow you to do that," Al offered. Then he very quietly asked someone in the group to position a couple of thick cushions between the client and the role-play father, to protect the role player from the force of the kicks. Turning to the psychologist, he said, "Test it, to make sure it doesn't hurt the accommodator." The psychologist kicked the cushions several times, tentatively at first, and then harder, and the role player gave his permission for the work to continue.

Then, with mounting rage in his face and body, the man kicked the cushion with violent force. The "father" groaned in pain. Another violent kick, another groan. The psychologist repeated this act perhaps five times, each time with increasing force. Al checked with the role player again. "I'm fine. I can feel the kicks, but it doesn't hurt."

Finally the young man exhaled deeply, and stopped. He looked relieved. "What's happening?" Al asked.

"I feel better."

"There may be a lot more anger," Al said, "but that's all that seems to be coming out now." He waited, observing his client again. "You look sad now."

"That's what I feel. Regret, sadness." The young man looked down at the prostrate form of the role-play father.

"For what you didn't have with your father?" The young man nodded wordlessly. Having expressed his rage at his critical father, he seemed now to feel the deep disappointment of not having had a more loving, caring father. Al hesitated, waiting for some cue from the young man. Finally he looked up at Al, as if to say, "What else can I do?"

"Maybe you would like to experience what it could have been like with an ideal father," Al offered. The psychologist's face brightened perceptibly. "Why don't you choose someone to role-play an ideal father?"

The client looked around the group thoughtfully this time, until his gaze settled on his friend and colleague. He asked the friend to role-play an ideal father, and the friend assented readily.

"Position him," Al directed. The client sat on the floor, with the ideal father standing over him. The "real" parent figures still held their places silently, but they were now ignored. The room was very quiet. The young man looked up at the ideal father.

"What are you feeling?" Al asked softly.

"That I want him to help me, support me."

"Do you want to tell him that?" Al said.

"I want you to help me and support me," he said hesitantly to the new figure.

A practiced role player, the "ideal father" knew to repeat the client's exact words: "I will help you and support you," he said gently. With those words, the young man's face softened; he seemed deeply relieved.

"I want him to say that I am very important to him; more important than his work. More important than anything else—except maybe my mother."

As the role-player spoke, the young man sank back on his elbows, looking up at the new figure. The words were hypnotic and consoling: ". . . and you are more important than anything else—except maybe your mother."

Al interjected, "It sounds like we need a mother in here, so his attention to you doesn't come at her expense. Let's have someone role-play an ideal mother, and let's have her standing beside his ideal father, so he can see them together." As a woman was chosen and stood beside the ideal father, the psychologist looked relieved. "It's good to see them together," he said, looking intently at the "ideal" image.

Noticing that the client was leaning even farther back on his elbows, as if he were about to lie down on the floor, Al said, "You look like you need support. Would you like someone to support your back?" The young man nodded assent. Explaining that support was a function of good parents, Al suggested that the psychologist choose someone to role-play a physical "extension" of the ideal parents. When he chose a man, Al asked, "Shall we let him be an extension of the ideal father?" Again, the young man nodded in wordless agreement.

With some direction, this new role player sat on his knees behind the client, and the young man leaned back in this new person's lap. He now looked up at the ideal father, but could lean back on this other man, who was to be considered "part" of the ideal father. He now had a visible image of a strong father, by whom he could feel physically supported.

With a sigh, the young psychologist relaxed deeply, leaning into the figure behind him. For several minutes the room was very quiet. The client closed his eyes; he seemed very peaceful, his face deeply trusting and childlike.

Al said, "Would you like the ideal father to say something to you in addition to the physical support you are getting from him?"

"I would like him to say that he will support me and help me grow up."

Al said quietly to the ideal father, "Say 'I will support you and help you to grow up.' " As the role player repeated these words, the client relaxed even further. A sense of peace pervaded the room; the sound of birds could be heard outside the window.

"Take this in," Al said warmly, "this possibility. Let yourself 'memorize' the experience. You can call it back from memory any time you need to." After a pause he added, "Do you have a sense of what age you are at this time?"

"Five maybe. About to go to school." The alarm on Al's wrist watch, which he had set at the beginning of the session, chirped faintly. He ignored it.

After a long and serene silence, the young man slowly opened his eyes. He looked up at the ideal father, and smiled. "I'd like him to help me up," he volunteered. "Seems like a good way to end." Al smiled approvingly. The ideal father offered his hand to the psychologist, helping him to his feet.

Coming out of his reverie, the young man blinked, acknowledging his friends and colleagues. For a moment, no one moved. "Are you ready for them to de-role?" Al queried.

The psychologist smiled warmly. "Yes."

"Let's de-role," Al said matter-of-factly.

Rising from the floor, the "negative" father said that he was no longer playing the negative aspect of the father, and he said his own name. The other players went through the same ritual. When the ideal father reclaimed his own identity, he and the young man embraced spontaneously. As the psychologist returned to his seat, Al said to the group members, who had been absorbed in the work: "We can discuss the work if you like, but please speak only about your own feelings, and address your remarks to me. He needs time to absorb his work."

The therapeutic approach that Pesso was using is called "Psychomotor," and it was evolved by him and his wife, Diane. Both former dancers, they began experimenting with the therapeutic effects of movement in the early 1960s while on the dance faculty of Emerson College. While their philosophy and techniques were created in relation to dance and dancers, they soon began an innovative, grant-supported project at Boston Veterans Administration Hospital, where they spent five years adapting their approach to a psychiatric setting. The Pessos then moved to Boston's McLean Hospital, which created special staff positions for them, and worked there for eight years. They began to attract national attention for the exciting changes that their techniques brought about in their patients. Today, the Pessos operate a training and workshop center in rural New Hampshire, and Al leads numerous training groups both in this country and in Europe.

At the center of the Psychomotor approach is the belief that if we are to allow genuine expression of feeling, and if we are to bring about lasting restructuring of early childhood experiences, we must engage emotional issues on a primitive, bodily level, structuring, and then restructuring, these central issues of early life.

When Pesso speaks of the therapeutic process that he conducted with the young psychologist, he calls it a "structure." That is, he uses role-play figures to simulate actual relationship patterns, in the belief that this reenactment of psychological situations will help the client dredge up ancient and still troublesome feelings. His skillful observation of body language, his careful attention to the client's words, and his inventive positioning of role players are frequently successful in eliciting strong feelings, often associated with childhood experiences. Pesso is, in effect, fashioning a complex relationship metaphor, and he is helping the client restructure this metaphor in the way he or she would like it to have been.

Pesso's aim in this work is to allow clients to "discharge" some of the primitive anger and pain that they feel about their childhoods without having to assault their actual parents. But he is not fixed on negative feelings about the actual parents. In some instances, he would be working with a client's unexpressed love for a parent or unacknowledged grief over the loss of a parent; and he might even have the client choose two role players to represent the loved as well as the negative aspects of a parent.

But he is doing much more than allowing the discharge of accumulated feeling. He is also helping the client create an internal "model" of positive parenting. This brief structure does not make up for a whole childhood, of course, but it does allow the client a "sample" of the kind of experience he would have liked from his parents. The hope is that this highly charged, symbolic interchange will address the client's long-denied needs for certain key emotional experiences, thereby freeing the client to make more satisfying—and realistic—choices in present-day relationships.

As Psychomotor therapists talk about their work, the term "structure" keeps reappearing. When speaking about someone who is locked in a relationship conflict in "real life," they might say that this person is "in a structure." They mean that the individual is bringing to his or her present-day relationships some of the intensely charged feelings from childhood, and "acting them out" in these current situations.

A difficulty in using our marriage—or any other current relationship—to "work on" our childhood conflicts is that we are likely to keep repeating the same problems. Like the young psychologist, our very identities have been shaped by our early experiences, and these experiences form the basis of our predictions of what will happen in our current relationships. The young man expected male figures to be displeased with him; he expected to be in a clinging, dependent relationship with females.

Most of us are extraordinarily skilled at maneuvering others into confirming our expectations, particularly our negative expectations. Not only do we choose partners and intimates who have natural proclivities to play familiar roles in our historical family drama, but we can also be quite persuasive in capitalizing on whatever natural talent these actors possess. Let me give an example from my own marriage.

Margaret and I had not been married six months before I discovered that whenever I suggested that we were spending too much money, or that we couldn't afford something, Margaret bristled. Sometimes she would look frightened and intimidated by the suggestion; at other times she would get furious. While I didn't think of myself as an especially parsimonious individual when we married, I soon came to occupy that role in our marriage. Margaret would fail to balance her checkbook, and I would remind her to do it; she would want to buy an expensive piece of furniture, and it would fall to me to say that we couldn't manage it.

As this "issue" developed between us, I began to feel like both a victim and an instigator. Most of the time, I felt as though I were being drawn into a fight about money which Margaret insisted on having with me. Why wouldn't she balance her checkbook? Why wouldn't she think about the limits in our budget? Then, as I got to know her family, it became easy to see the origin of the role I was playing.

Margaret's mother had lost her father when she was six, and she and her two brothers had grown up on what their mother earned as an English teacher. Money had always been a struggle. Then, just as Margaret's parents married, the Great Depression descended on them, and her father lost all his savings in a bank closing. Though Paul was later very successful, Clora never forgot her early anxieties about money. She scrimped and saved, and constantly reminded her family to do the same. "Her stinginess was a dominant theme in my childhood," Margaret said later. "I think it made me feel unloved." I was clearly being seduced into playing the role of Margaret's mother, a process that family theorists call *role induction*.

But I was also an active instigator of these conflicts. I soon realized that if I were upset or anxious about something, I could get Margaret instantly upset by bringing up the subject of money. Even if she were in a good mood, I could spoil it for her by raising the issue of our budget. It wasn't that I set about to do it consciously; but the sequence was embarrassingly predictable—I would be worried or upset; I would start to talk about money; Margaret would get upset; and I would feel better. Unconsciously, I seemed to use her vulnerability to this issue in order to "transfer" some of my own discontent from myself to her.

As I thought about these fights, I also realized that I had my own history of anxiety about money. My father's career reversals had kept our whole family on edge financially; it was my English-teacher mother's salary that had often sustained us through difficult times. In some respects, I was like Margaret's mother—someone who grew up worrying about money. I suppose I was also angry with my father about not earning more, and about not managing better what he earned. All these anxieties and frustrations were being focused on Margaret.

In trying to understand and solve our marital problems, these are some of the problems we face:

The "structures" or metaphors we create in marriage are invariably two-sided. Not only am I a role player in Margaret's family drama, but she is a role player in mine. My anxiety about money reminds Margaret of her mother; her rebellious attitudes about managing money (which I interpret as irresponsible) remind me of my father. I confirm her negative expectations; she confirms mine. Unlike the cooperative role players in our example, who know that they are mere stage props, each of us takes personally the other's expression of frustration and anger; and the fight is joined.

Because we are reluctant to look at our own problems and our own histories, we will tend to focus on our mate's contribution to the problem. Of all the temptations which we face, this will be one of the most difficult to counter. We will find ourselves incredibly insightful about our mate's difficulties with his or her family of origin, and we will have innumerable helpful suggestions about how these problems can be solved. We must learn to resist such temptations, for they only lead to more difficulty!

Because our identities have been shaped by our early family experiences, and because we are unfamiliar with other alternatives, we will tend to keep repeating these familiar patterns. Having created certain "issues" between us, we will hurl ourselves at each other repeatedly, each confirming the other's expectation of disappointment and frustration. We are often in the same position that the young psychologist would have been in if he had stopped his work with the expression of anger at his father: he might have felt relieved at having "expressed some anger," but he also would have felt incomplete, unfinished, let down.

A central problem, then, is that we have great difficulty imagining, and creating in our relationships, the positive outcome, the more satisfying "ending." We will need to remind ourselves again and again that the past need not dictate the future. Whatever the metaphors in our marriage, and in our other relationships, we *can* reshape them. Perhaps it will help to keep before us the image of the young psychologist as he first allows himself to visualize what he wants to happen, and then finds a way—with outside support—to experience this new reality. In our own way, we can follow the same process.

In our search, we would be wise to follow Pesso's initial advice to the young psychologist. We should begin with what is true about us, rather than what we want to be true. We also need to look especially carefully at the sources of our emotional "excesses" in relation to one another. It is, of course, important to learn to be less threatened and defensive in the face of our spouse's feelings, and to respond more positively to him or her; but we will never manage this worthy goal if we cannot be aware of and accept our own feelings.

Most of us learned long ago to mistrust our own turbulent emotionality. Sometimes we wish that our negative feelings— particularly our anger at the person we love—would go away. But this uncomfortable current within us is a wellspring of vitality, a source of energy and life. Distress and pain are friends to growth. They tell us that something needs to change, and often they provide us with a motive and a direction for making changes.

An initial task, then, is to recognize when we are in an emotional "structure," or an important relationship metaphor. The following cues should arouse our suspicions:

1. Every time we are in a particular type of situation, we get upset. For example, if a friend doesn't return our call for a couple of days, we get depressed. Later we make a sales call and don't get an order, and again we get depressed. These incidents are metaphors through which we express our sensitivity to rejection.

2. Our response is out of proportion to the situation. "Why am I so upset by such minor matters?" we ask ourselves.

3. Despite the efforts of others to reassure us, and our own efforts to be more rational, the feelings persist. We wonder to ourselves, "Why does this keep happening to me?"

If we are open to learning from these troubling and repetitive experiences, they almost always lead us to a significant life issue, often one originating in childhood. Here are a couple of examples, one from my life, one from a client's.

Around the time we moved from Wisconsin to Atlanta, I became acutely aware of the deficiencies in my relationships with my children. Margaret wanted more support in raising our kids; and I too was unhappy with how often my preoccupation with work had interfered with my enjoying them more. I also resented the exclusiveness of Margaret's relationship with them, and wanted a more primary and intimate involvement.

It was mid-July, unbearably hot and close in Atlanta, but cool and refreshing at the mountain cottage we had rented for two weeks. "I'll have lots of time to be with the kids," I said to myself.

The first few days of the vacation were pleasant and uneventful, but toward the end of the first week, I began to reexperience a distressing pattern in our family. When something interesting happened, the kids turned to Margaret to talk about it. It was she they joked with at the dinner table, she they pushed off the raft at the lake. When I was alone with one of the children, we had things to talk about; but when we were all together, I felt strangely separate. I struggled against this feeling of exclusion, but it persisted.

Then came a rainy afternoon, with no television to distract us and nowhere to go. Someone suggested that we play Monopoly, and after some resistance from Julia, who was then only six, we all sat around a rickety card table and began.

Bold buying, complaints about the roll of the dice, jokes about place names, teasing prods, borrowing and lending; and amid the tedium of waiting for a turn, idle chatter. For a while I felt part of this familiar weave of family activity, but gradually I began to withdraw, and more and more of the conversation took place between Margaret and the children. It was pleasant enough for a while just to sit and feel the life of the family flowing around me, but soon I began to feel distinctly sad. Vowing to reenter the conversation, I started to say something, but Sarah, always eager to talk to Margaret, interrupted me. Should I challenge her? That seemed childish. I took my turn silently. Minutes later I began to say something else, but this time Mark was teasing Margaret about landing in "jail." Then Julia took her turn ahead of me. "Hey," I said angrily, "I'm still here!"

As the game wore on, I felt more and more isolated from the family. "It's as if I were invisible," I said to myself. No one seemed to notice my dilemma. Margaret and the kids were having a good time, and I was dying inside. I wanted someone—Margaret, obviously—to see my distress, and to come to my rescue. I wanted to speak up and intrude into the merry mix, but I felt helpless to do it. I was angry by now, and I knew that anything that I said would appear defensive and ridiculous. Why did I feel so isolated and alone? Why couldn't I just be part of the trivial, easy ebb and flow of the family's chatter?

Inside me was a frantic churning, a mounting desperation. Finally someone took my turn again. My heart beating wildly, I rose from my chair and said angrily, "If one of you ignores me one more time—"

"Gus, what is going on?" Margaret said, shocked.

"I'm tired as hell of feeling ignored in this family," I blurted out.

"'I don't know what you're talking about!" Margaret said, growing angry herself. And that was all I could take. I bolted from the room, plunging into the woods in the gentle afternoon rain. From inside the cottage I could hear Julia say "Daddy! Wait!" but I went on, too upset and embarrassed to turn back.

Once out in the quiet of the woods, I felt better. Sitting down under a tree that offered some shelter, I waited. In the distance, I could hear Mark calling me. Suddenly the absurdity of my reaction hit me. The family had been playing a game, and in the midst of it I had mysteriously stormed out. I had to go back and face them.

After the apologies to my very upset children, I had to face Margaret, who was furious. Why was she so angry? However ridiculous it seemed, I had been in a lot of pain. But the most important question was—why had I gotten so upset?

My puzzlement about my overreaction persisted, and I was still thinking about it when we returned to Atlanta a week later. I guessed that this panic was related to my feelings of isolation in my family of origin, but my overwhelming sense of aloneness and isolation simply did not fit my conscious memory of myself in my family. Yet the incident had awakened some new awareness in me. Perhaps at some time I had felt much more alone than I now remembered.

My parents were both dead, and my only sibling, my sister Jane, lived in New Mexico. A bit sadly, I turned to my childhood scrapbook. Where to look? After flipping through the pages at random, I was finally drawn to the year we moved to Spartanburg, South Carolina, the year my father came home from the war. In most of the pictures our family looked happy—and why shouldn't we, since we were all together again? Then I noticed a particular photo, taken at a state park where the family had gone camping. We were all clustered around a brick grill, where my mother was cooking breakfast. She was kneeling, tending a frying pan of scrambled eggs, and my father sat on the edge of the brickwork beside her; my sister—four years younger than I—was sitting on his lap. I stood slightly to the side, looking vaguely unhappy, and physically close to no one.

As I looked intently at this picture, I could recall—vaguely at first, but more clearly as I focused my memory—the sense of acute loneliness that I had felt at that moment. I hadn't said it to myself in so many words, but I must have been thinking, "Where is my place in this family?" The memory was of the empty space around me, of a painful void in my life. But what was the void?

"Of course," I said to myself, recalling the incident in which I had been beaten by my father. While my father was away, I had undoubtedly occupied a special place in my mother's life. When my father returned, and experienced me as a rival, my mother probably distanced herself from me—not deliberately, but unconsciously. My father had related warmly to my mother and sister, but not to me. Between us there was tension, and quiet competitiveness. So, at twelve, I felt quite alone.

Once I began to feel the power of that sense of aloneness, I could remember a series of such experiences: being alone in our house, and feeling depressed when Jane and my mother went grocery shopping together; being unhappy at school for no apparent reason; having trouble sleeping at night, and staring out my window at a blinking red light on a radio tower, thinking, "I see it, but it doesn't see me." Here was another picture: my sister sitting proudly on my mother's lap, while I looked on.

Why now? Why had these memories of feeling isolated within my family come flooding back with such poignancy? Then I realized that Mark was about the age I was when my father had returned. I had been "tracking" myself while following Mark's growth, and this process—probably coupled with some midlife anxiety about aging, which produced an acute desire to break out of old patterns that were inhibiting me—had led to this moment. My isolation in my childhood family had been replicated in an experience in my present family, and out poured this long-buried grief about an old sense of injustice. During the game of Monopoly, I was certainly in an emotional "structure."

Most of the time, our mate participates in these situations of emotional overload. Not only was I panicked by how alone I felt, but my way of dealing with my alarm—leaving the scene—provoked at first anxiety and then anger in Margaret. These two-sided panics can easily feel out of control for both parties; and unless someone manages to calm down, they can escalate wildly.

"Why," I asked myself, "was Margaret so angry?" Embarrassed by my own behavior, it took me a while to ask her the question, and she had to think a while before she could answer it.

Finally Margaret said: "I know part of the reason. When I was a girl, and my parents got into a fight, my father would always threaten to leave. He would storm off to work with his overnight bag packed and say that he was going to spend the night at his club. He usually came home, but occasionally he didn't; and I was often terrified that he was going to leave." After a pause she added: "I guess I also overreacted."

In acting out of my own distress about being an outsider in my family during a certain period of my childhood, I apparently assumed the role of Margaret's father. Had she, out of a need to confront her feelings about her father's leaving, unconsciously participated in provoking my panic? Probably.

This is how we learn about ourselves—particularly those hidden and vital truths that our childhoods hold. *We should listen for what upsets us, what feels out of proportion to the situation, what feels embarrassing and repetitive and excessive.* If we pay attention to such experiences, this kind of "excessive" emotion almost always leads us to an important discovery about ourselves.

We can also listen to our words, especially those words that seem to state themes of discontent, and that seem to be spoken with a kind of peculiar "underlining."

Sam and Linne Aberg are bright, outstandingly nice people. He is a successful attorney; after being a prominent community volunteer and raising three almost grown children, she has recently taken a job as a full-time fund-raiser for a local museum. As the last of their children prepares to leave home, they are faced with the bleak facts of their marriage: they have sex infrequently, argue often, and rarely feel close or loving. They seem to care about each other, but there is little joy.

As their household routines change, Sam is making an effort to do his share of the housework. While Linne is at a meeting, Sam washes the dishes, but "forgets" to do a couple of dirty pots. Linne focuses on the unwashed pots: "Why would you do a nice thing like that and leave part of the job undone?" The word "why" is high-pitched, almost anguished, and sounds vaguely out of place. Sam feels unjustly criticized, and retreats. Then Linne gets upset about his retreat. "I can't help but feel angry when I see that martyred look," she says.

They are driving to a party; Sam takes a wrong turn, and they get lost and are late for the party. "Why would you do that when you know how upset it makes me to be late?" she asks, and again the pleading "why" speaks of some mysterious injury which seems far more serious than Sam's mistake warrants. She is not just angry at Sam but seems to feel betrayed by these seemingly minor transgressions.

Finally, after about the fourth minor incident that has elicited this bewildering cry—high-pitched, anguished and sibilant, saying "How could you do a thing like this?"—we begin to press Linne about the origins of this mysterious pain. She can't remember feeling betrayed by anyone. She felt her parents loved each other, and that she loved both of them. But she looks sad as she says this, and her voice is thick with pain.

I persist. "Did one of your parents do something damaging to the family, or to you?" Still she can't think of anything terribly significant. Her father, a successful businessman, had been in a battle with the president of his company, and had lost the struggle. He died of a coronary in his mid-fifties, after several years of forced "retirement." Linne was obviously sad about her father's death, but her grief seemed muffled and unexpressed. She had felt close to him, was his favorite child, and his life had ended tragically.

Sam caught my eye; then he spoke to Linne: "I don't want to interrupt, but wasn't there something that happened when you were in college—about the time we met?"

"Believe it or not, I was just starting to remember that," she said softly. "I guess I had forgotten it."

"Can you share it now?" Margaret asked gently. Linne paused, as though wondering if she dared. Her face was changed; it showed the anguish that previously had been revealed only in her voice.

"Well," she said, drawing in a sharp breath, and then releasing a long and melancholy sigh. "When I came home from college during my sophomore year, I discovered that my father was having an affair, and that he had a serious drinking problem. Both had apparently been going on for some years," she went on, "since the beginning of the battles with his boss." She paused, recoiling from the memories. "My mother told me about the affair and the drinking, and I can still see her pained, martyred look, as though she had to endure it all passively. But I was just shattered. I had idealized my father; as far as I was concerned, he hung the moon." Another wait, as she looked sadly and vacantly ahead of her. "And then, while I was still angry at him, before any of it could be resolved, he died. We never even talked about it."

And so we had found another part of the work that needed to be done. Linne's feelings about her father were blocked—she was unable to feel her grief because she was so angry at him, and unable to feel her anger because of her love and grief. Confused by this cross-current of emotion, she had repressed much of her feeling about her father; and it was this mixture of anger and pain that had been directed at Sam. Sam wasn't innocent, of course, but he was the object of some of his wife's unexpressed feeling about her father.

When he retreated in the face of Linne's anger, Sam also became the target for some of her anger at her passive, martyred mother. Here the dilemma for Linne was much the same: how could she be angry at her long-suffering, "good," victimized mother? One has a right to such feelings—wishing that a parent had been stronger, more assertive, a more complete person. But one feels terribly guilty about feeling this way. How can you be angry at a victim? Again unable to allow herself to feel such "unacceptable" anger at a loved parent, Linne repressed her anger at her mother; and it emerged in her relationship with Sam.

Many of us share Linne's problem in dealing with a painful part of the past. We often fail to recall events, and the feelings associated with them, that involve disappointment with our parents. Our tenacious loyalty to our parents leads to our repressing or denying the negative side of our feelings for them. If we are to gain access to these facts about our lives, we simply must be willing to endure some of the pain of feeling disloyal to these loved, and inevitably imperfect, people.

There are, fortunately, some avenues of approach to these issues that allow us to feel less angry, and less guilty about our anger at our parents. These involve understanding something about the formative events in our parents' lives—because they obviously had parents too. This way promises not only understanding, but, ultimately, forgiveness.

As we explore our histories in our search for self-understanding, it will of course be helpful to talk directly with our parents about their perceptions of us during early childhood—particularly in the years before six, which most of us recall poorly. We will also want to know something about what was happening in the family's life during that time. Where did we live? Were there any particularly stressful times during those years? Were we separated from either parent when we were young children? If we encounter resistance and defensiveness in our parents—and I will discuss techniques for dealing with that possibility—family photographs are a wonderful avenue for learning about ourselves. Look carefully at the positioning of family members. Who has his or her arm around whom? Who looks satisfied, who unhappy? Who is absent from certain photographs? Why is he or she absent? Looking at photos with our parents or siblings can be an excellent way of assembling a more coherent view of our childhood, since the photograph prompts recall in everyone, and gets us talking.

Another way to learn about ourselves as young children is to observe our parents interacting with our own children. Often they will say to our children some of the same things they said to us, and they will give us advice that they followed. Of course, all parents change with time; and we can be fairly certain that our parents are more relaxed and mature as grandparents than they were as our parents; that change can make us feel envious of the warmth and care that they can extend to our children.

Our foray into the past is not undertaken in an effort to avoid responsibility by blaming our problems on our parents. On the contrary: through insight into our histories, and through a more direct experience of long-repressed feelings, we hope to free ourselves of these hidden and subtly intrusive influences in our daily lives, and thereby to gain self-control and autonomy.

Our initial challenge will be to take seriously the notion that our mate's behavior is not the primary source of our unhappiness—even though it often seems to be. If we clear that hurdle, and dare to ask questions about our histories, we can not only learn a great deal about ourselves, but we can acquire more self-possession. While we may have been unable to change our mate, we can learn to alter our own responses to certain difficult and potentially entrapping situations in our relationship. If we can change our own behavior, this highly interdependent relationship system—our marriage—*must* change. If we are different, our partner cannot remain the same.

I should acknowledge that there are risks in such an undertaking, and potential losses. If we brave the encounter with our own origins, our mate is likely to lose a certain power that he or she has held in our imagination. We stand to lose someone to blame, someone to idealize, someone who promises that it will be all right. In giving up our childlike dependency on each other, we lose the sense of having a symbolic parent beside us. We must then face our fundamental aloneness in the world; we must learn to take care of ourselves.

What we gain is a sense of ourselves as at least marginally competent to bear the bruises and assaults of the world, and of having a fellow traveler to share the struggle with. Our mate becomes someone like us—often scared, more than a little crazy inside, and a very human mixture of assets and liabilities. We love this person, but sometimes we hate him or her too; we feel cheered when he or she comes into the room; somehow we always find something to talk about. This is someone who will endure our irrational outbursts and our jokes, and who often knows what we are going to say. This body is a comfort to us in the night, and though sex with this person may be less thrilling than it once was, it has more of the full power of our *being together*—angry, lustful, tender, melancholy, playful. When we finally realize that this other person has stayed with us, just that "staying with" begins to permit more and more risk. Maybe I can finally let myself love, and be loved back.

So there are things worth looking forward to, worth fighting for. It is in this little knot of people—our mate, and the children who become the physical embodiment of our relationship—that our life faces its most difficult tests, and finally has its real meaning. The exciting thing is that we can shape that meaning, and that outcome. We can't do it just with our intellects, but if we learn to trust and to team with that powerful wellspring of unconscious emotion which is just below the surface of our lives, we have a vital advantage, a purchase against fate.

3

Finding a Theme

ONE DAY, IN THE anxious early stage of my private practice, I was conducting an initial interview with a couple. Within a matter of minutes they proceeded from a mild argument to a screaming fight. As they leaned forward in their chairs, their faces contorted, their voices raised to an anguished pitch, I suddenly realized that I did not know what their fight was about, nor did I understand why it had escalated so rapidly. Every remark by the wife incensed the husband, and his replies had a similarly incendiary effect on her. It was as if they spoke in a kind of code about ancient and unforgivable injuries, and I did not know the code.

As the couple fought, their tones began to convey an entreaty: "Please help us out of this agony," they seemed to ask. Before me their words formed a screen, a wall, an impenetrable mystery. All I could think of was the Tower of Babel, and about how my family was going to starve in the coming Wisconsin winter if I didn't do better than this.

Eventually I said something about their blaming each other, and I wondered whom else they blamed when they were growing up. My having spoken at all seemed to calm them down a bit, and somewhat miraculously, they later scheduled another appointment.

In nearly twenty years of working with couples and families, first interviews have gotten easier; but they are still tense moments for me. The couple or family is usually in crisis, and their difficulties are not only deeply embedded in their histories, but thoroughly covered by layers of confusion and misunderstanding. Even if a couple says, "We fight about money" (or sex, or their in-laws), these issues are more like summary metaphors. Because the deeper issues are more painful and threatening, the real sources of their distress remain hidden behind a veil of repression and denial. Sometimes, only the agony is visible.

In an effort to provide the reader with a beginning framework for examining his or her own marriage, let me cite a few instances from a therapist's "cookbook," that reassuring set of notations which reminds us where, over the years, we have learned to look, and what we have learned to look for. Again, the couple is Joyce and Thomas Olson. Though we have already heard part of their story, a look at their initial interview will fill in some background issues, and allow us an overview of their marriage.

First impressions are always intuitive, and invariably significant. As Joyce and Thomas filed into our living room–style office for their first interview, Joyce led the way, talking. Six-month-old Amy was not present that day, though later in the therapy she came many times.

"Well, we found your office without any trouble," Joyce said cheerily. "Your secretary gives very good directions. Wouldn't you say, Thomas?"

"Yep," Thomas replied matter-of-factly, taking his place at one end of the sofa, while Joyce sat at the other. I was struck immediately by the disparity between them. Joyce was attractive, slightly plump, with a soft, vulnerable quality, her voice subtly musical. She seemed lively, animated, determinedly cheerful. I was reminded of Julia, who is always cheering us up, and of Margaret, who had that role in her family.

Thomas seemed much cooler, more contained and reserved. An attractive man also, he had thinning gray hair and a rather pale complexion; his serious, almost stern appearance added to an impression of age and authority. I thought to myself that he seemed solitary, and vaguely angry. "So this is what a family therapist's office looks like," he said, a broad, rather boyish grin emerging on his face. "I thought maybe you had couches for everybody."

"I don't think they are going to put us into analysis," Joyce said, looking at Thomas with an expression that was both embarrassed and slightly condescending. It was then that I first noticed that subtly parental quality in Joyce—a kind of primness, an aura of rectitude that was almost matronly. It was not congruent with her vulnerability.

"At least Amy's safe," he said. "For today, anyway."

"He doesn't seem to want to be here," I noted to myself.

"Before we begin, let me get a few facts, if you will," I said. The note-taker in our partnership, I had a yellow pad in my lap, and on it I had drawn a simple genogram of the nuclear family.

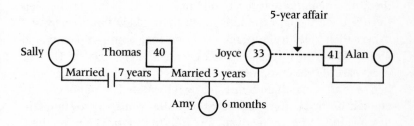

At the beginning of therapy, simple, factual information is vital. Once, during an initial interview, I asked a divorced mother—who had brought her troubled teenager for therapy—where she (the mother) grew up, and she told me quite calmly. Then I asked if she had been born there, and she dissolved into tears. She had, as it turned out, been adopted at eight months after being in a neglectful foster home, and this "fact" had had profound consequences for her, as well as for her daughter. So we ask questions, and listen carefully.

"How about your ages?" I addressed the couple.

"Are you older than Joyce?" Margaret said to Thomas.

"Is it that obvious?" he replied defensively.

"I'm sorry," she said genuinely. "I didn't mean to offend you."

"It's okay," he said. "Seven years." That broad, guarded smile again. "I'm forty."

"So you're thirty-three," Margaret said to Joyce, who nodded.

I thought to myself, "They are pretty old to be having a first child." I also noted that Thomas was at a decade "marker," and wondered how he felt about being a father at forty, and why he had waited so long. Nor did I comment on the age difference between them, though I wondered if it meant that Thomas was something of a father-substitute for Joyce. Such age differences are always significant in some way.

The question of age also raised an important issue: of what "generation" was this couple a member? If they had been in their fifties or sixties, we would assume that they were brought up with traditional family expectations, and in many cases would expect their role definitions to be traditional. If they had been in their twenties, we would assume it much more likely that they would expect their roles to be egalitarian, and that both partners would anticipate having careers. Like Margaret and me, Joyce and Thomas were part of that group of couples in their thirties and forties who had a traditional upbringing but who entered adulthood early enough in the changes associated with the women's movement to be powerfully affected by them; and thus to feel torn between these old and new patterns.

Time itself forms a dimension of significance in our inquiry. Not only are we powerfully shaped by our generation's collective experiences, but we are each caught in our own unique struggle with time. In the background, we hear the omnipresent ticking of our biological clock, and this solitary, individual awareness of time periodically intrudes into the hypnotic togetherness of marriage, confronting us with the imperatives and limitations of the body. At thirty-three, Joyce was undoubtedly feeling the pressure of being in the last decade in which she could "safely" bear children; at forty, Thomas too seemed to feel the pressure of time.

Every marital crisis is importantly related to time. "Why now?" we therapists ask ourselves as we puzzle about the causes of the present problems. What in this couple's life has brought them to therapy at this time?

There is always an immediate source of stress, and sometimes it is quite visible—a job change, a recent move, a serious illness in the family. Frequently, the family is dealing simultaneously with several such stresses. While such "external" pressures may explain the timing of a marital crisis, the conflicts usually involve a more fundamental life-stage transition. They are a young couple trying to master living together for the first time, or an older couple coping with the changes brought on by retirement. Frequently, the crisis is precipitated by the birth or maturation of children, those powerful engines of change who pull us through all manner of new experiences. In Joyce and Thomas's case, Amy's recent birth seemed the likely "precipitating event." Her parents were probably having difficulty reorganizing their marital "system" to meet her intense demands.

Whatever the current stress, it inevitably has a deeper significance in the partners' lives. Something in the shape of the recent events has touched old, painful scars, bringing forth pain that is mysteriously intense. This is particularly true of those changes associated with having children, since our deep attachment to them pulls out of us our own embedded memories of childhood. Our children awaken the hidden children within us.

From our telephone conversation, I knew that Joyce worked outside the home, but I didn't know what her job was.

"I'm a supervising nurse at a cardiac care unit," she said confidently, in response to my question.

"That's a demanding job," I said. "Very stressful, I would imagine."

"Yes," was all she said. Then Margaret asked the question about child care, and Joyce sighed deeply. "We have a full-time housekeeper. She's the daughter of the woman who took care of me when I was a child." Margaret asked about the sigh, and Joyce said: "I have a lot of conflict about leaving Amy, because I know I resented my mother's working when I was young. I feel very guilty sometimes, so I try hard to be available to her." Then she hesitated, as though considering whether it was a good time to go further with this area. "That is one of the reasons I wanted to come to therapy, because I don't think Thomas understands the kind of stress I am under."

"Could we come back to this issue, then, when we have a little more information?" Margaret said. Joyce looked relieved.

We learned that Thomas was a chemistry professor at a local university. "I have a lot of pressure too, but it's different. My stresses have to do with faculty politics, the difficulties of getting money to do my research, that kind of thing. I don't think she understands mine very well either." He had not mentioned his role as a husband and father, which probably meant that Joyce "carried" most of the responsibility for their home and their child.

"How long have you been married?" I asked.

"Three years," Joyce answered. "We've survived that long!" Then looking at Thomas with a smile, she added: "Though it seems much longer." Again, the complexities of time. The stage of marriage they are in is somewhat out of phase with their years.

"Why is that?" Margaret queried.

"Because we've known each other for a long time, since before . . ." and again Joyce glanced at Thomas.

"She means before my first marriage." He completed her sentence.

"And before my long relationship with another man," she added.

Noting to myself that they finished each other's sentences, I had no doubt that this was a very "involved" couple. "Actually, it's no small accomplishment, making it to your third anniversary," I said, "since a quarter of all divorces occur in the first two years of marriage. So congratulations."

"I'm not sure we're ready to be congratulated," Joyce replied quickly. "I'm certainly not happy with things the way they are." The majority of couples who enter therapy do so because of the wife's complaints; having gotten Thomas this far, Joyce didn't intend to minimize their problems.

I assured Joyce that we needed to hear about all their concerns, but added, "I am curious about how you met. You said you knew each other before—"

"Thomas's marriage," Joyce said, avoiding mention of her own relationship. She turned to Thomas. "Do you want to explain it?"

"Sure." He had a mischievous smile this time. "Her mother introduced us." A pause. "After I graduated from college—I must

48

have been about twenty-three—I worked in an office one summer, and her mother was my boss. I met Joyce when she came by to see her mother at the office; and then her mother had me over to dinner a couple of times, and Joyce was there."

"So what attracted you to each other?" I asked. Thomas seemed to want to talk, and I felt relieved. The more we could engage him, the better.

"I was in love right away. She was—" glancing at Joyce "and is, beautiful. But she also had this cheerful, sprightly sort of way about her that appealed to me. She was also independent and—how to say it—elusive. She was a bit of a tease, then." He paused, searching for words. "The problem was, I felt like a dirty old man being attracted to this sixteen-year-old who had this great figure." Another glance at Joyce.

She responded, smiling: "You notice that he said 'had.' I suppose that's also an issue I'm concerned about, my weight." She was only slightly overweight, and I was suspicious of moving to such an "individual" issue. The challenge of the first interview was to define the *couple's* problems, and to engage them both in working together on solving those problems.

"Is her weight a problem to you?" I asked Thomas, trying to keep focused on the relationship.

"A little, maybe," he said with a sly smile, "but she still has a great figure." Joyce sighed. Despite her effort to be cheerful and upbeat, I kept hearing that sigh. I made a note to myself that she was undoubtedly depressed; that her overweight was probably related to her depression; and that her depression was at least partly caused by her situation in her marriage. But what situation?

"We're back to your being a dirty old man." Joyce rebounded with a smile, turning to Thomas.

"That's me, I guess. I did feel guilty about being attracted to Joyce when she was sixteen, so I kept quiet about it. But I really liked her, and I looked for chances to see her."

"Come to think of it," Joyce interjected, "my mother actually encouraged you, didn't she? I hadn't realized that until now. Maybe that's why I resisted."

Thomas looked directly at Joyce: "Did you know how much I liked you?" A bold move. They hadn't been prepared to talk about the beginnings of their relationship, but they were clearly interested in doing so.

"I don't think so," Joyce said. "I did have a crush on you, of course, but I thought of you as this handsome, worldly *man*. It never occurred to me that we could have had a romantic relationship."

"So what happened?" I asked eagerly.

Thomas said, "I took her out a number of times over the next few years, and it was always very platonic. Then she went to college." He turned to Joyce. "I remember that time we had lunch before you left. I was really hurting inside. I wanted to say 'Don't go,' but I didn't do it. So we just talked about trivia, and you left. I was really depressed for quite a while."

"But you got over it," Joyce said. "I mean, you got married to Sally just a few years later."

"I didn't get over you." A short laugh of realization. "Obviously!" Now he turned to fill us in. "I met Sally some time after Joyce went to college. Come to think of it, she was also a lot younger than me. Anyway, I always had doubts about her." Then he turned back to Joyce. "Do you remember that time we had dinner together? I think you were a junior. I was dating Sally, but we weren't that serious. I remember wanting to start seeing you, but you started talking to me about that jerk you were involved with. Remember that? You were upset that you were having an affair with a married graduate student, and wanted to talk about it. I guess I didn't show it, but I felt really hurt, like all I was was a father confessor, or a friendly uncle. So I said to hell with you. It was about six months later that I got engaged to Sally."

"I didn't know some of this," Joyce said softly.

"How long were you married?" I asked Thomas.

"Seven years."

"Did you think about Joyce while you were married to Sally?" I asked.

"Yes. A lot. I tried not to, but I did anyway." A thoughtful silence in the room.

"What happened to your first marriage, Thomas?" I asked.

"We did all right for a while. But we got into some kind of struggle where she was very rebellious toward me—maybe it was because I was older and had different ideas about how to do things.

Then she became very silent and secretive. Eventually she had an affair with her damn tennis coach, a kid, really. She came in one day and said she was leaving."

"A very painful thing to face," I said.

"You could say that." He clearly didn't want to talk about the end of his marriage, and for the moment, I decided to let the subject drop. But I noted to myself that he had had a dramatic and painful rejection, and that he would undoubtedly be worried about its happening again. This fact could account in part for his reserve.

"How did you finally get together?" Margaret wanted to know.

Joyce said, "I got the courage to break up with Alan, the man I was involved with. After I finished my master's degree, I realized that that relationship was never going anywhere, and I just left. I moved back to Atlanta and got a job."

Thomas smiled again. "I heard from her mother that she was back. I had gotten divorced by then, and this time I made up my mind that I wasn't going to let her get away. So I really pursued her."

"Swept me off my feet," she said with a slightly ironical, song-like inflection. "Actually, I was hurting—and here he was. He was very persistent, and attentive. I also realized that we were—how should I say it?—friends. That we liked each other, had a lot to talk about." She paused thoughtfully. "It was strange to feel myself falling in love with somebody I had known for so long, but that's what happened."

We were particularly curious about the beginnings of Joyce and Thomas's relationship, because in their description of their initial attraction, we hoped to hear something about the strength of their original emotional bond. Some couples get married casually, almost circumstantially; there seems to be no real "electricity" between them, even during their courtship. Other couples marry in the midst of the thunderstorm of a larger life crisis, and thus feel forced into marriage as a refuge. Still other couples experience a deeper and more complex magnetism, a force that is not produced by extreme emotional need but by a uniquely strong "join" of lives which has been, and continues to be, very difficult to describe.

It is this "depth" or "intensity" dimension which we were listening for, and it is perhaps the most critical aspect of any marriage. "How intensely involved, how deeply connected, how 'bonded' was this couple in the first months of their relationship?" we asked ourselves. "Was there some craziness, some of this special magnetism between these two?"

This "depth" dimension does not refer to the degree of emotional satisfaction in the relationship; if there is real intensity between two people, there will also be pain and anger. The question is whether this relationship exposes, catalyzes, brings to the forefront the deepest issues in these lives. The real issue is *involvement*.

As we examine this area, we have in mind a number of questions: If there was an intense involvement at the start of the relationship, what has happened to this emotional investment over the years? When did their relationship begin to feel troubled? What was happening in other areas of their lives—family-of-origin crises, career difficulties, health problems, the birth of children—at around the time their marriage became an area of conflict? Is the couple just experiencing conflict, or do they question their basic commitment to the marriage? Are both partners distressed, or is only one person complaining? Often, one partner has become a "specialist" in voicing positive feelings for the marriage, while the other "carries" the negative feelings for both of them.

As I saw Joyce's fond, anxious, frustrated glances at Thomas, witnessed her eagerness to get him into therapy, heard her melancholy sighs, I had no worry about her involvement with Thomas. Nor any question either about her unhappiness with him. Thomas's coolness and reserve, and his boyish leer, troubled me. "Does he love her?" I found myself wondering. Then, as he described his early longing for Joyce, I felt reassured. "I think he does," I said silently to myself. Answering one question raised another: "Why doesn't she feel it?"

Joyce had apparently been thinking about the same issue. "It's good for me to hear that you had those feelings for me," she said somewhat skeptically, "because often I don't really feel cared about. A lot of the time I feel pretty alone." I wondered what had happened to Thomas's pursuit of her.

Thomas turned toward us. "I don't understand that. I love her; and I tell her that I do. It's as if she doesn't believe me."

Margaret interposed, with a slight smile, "It takes more than words sometimes, Thomas. I know that for me, Gus's behavior is often much more significant than his words."

"I think that's it," Joyce said enthusiastically. "It's his behavior."

Thomas was looking very uncomfortable, and I was concerned about his feeling blamed. He was reluctant enough already about being in therapy. "Can you be more specific?" I asked Joyce.

She sighed. "Well, I think one area is what happens when I am tired and stressed, and trying to do something that needs to be done. Like the other day. For once, I got off from work a few minutes early, and I realized that I could swing by and pick up Thomas's dry cleaning on the way to the grocery store. It's the kind of thing I often do for him. Then I got home and started fixing supper, and Amy was fretting, so I went and played with her for a while. After supper was over, I went back to the kitchen, and I was standing there fixing our lunches for the next day, feeling like I was going to drop. He didn't notice how tired I was, or what I was doing, or anything. I think he was reading; Amy was in her crib, fretting again. When that kind of thing happens, I feel terrible inside, as though I were invisible."

Relieved to get to talk, Joyce was feeling angrier. She looked at Margaret as her voice rose in pitch: "I just want some sense of being noticed! I mean, I work full time, I do most of Amy's care, most of the cooking, and I'm exhausted all the time. He does help with the housework and cleanup, but the worst part is that he doesn't seem to notice what's happening to me." It was an issue I recognized in a very personal way.

"Can you respond to what she's saying?" I prodded Thomas.

"This is news to me. She doesn't tell me this at home. I appreciated her getting the dry cleaning, and I admit she does a lot of things like that for me; but I didn't know she was that tired. I would have helped if she had asked me. I had washed the dishes, and I was sitting in there resenting the fact that she was spending so much time in the kitchen. I wanted her to just let some of it go, and come in and spend time with me and Amy!" This issue, which was essentially about equity, and which is so common between dual-career couples, was obviously important, but at the moment I was less concerned about the content of the issue than I was about the process that was occurring between the couple. Thomas was feeling accused, and was responding defensively.

"You're feeling blamed, I assume," I said to Thomas.

"I *am* being blamed."

"Joyce is complaining about your behavior," I conceded. Then I decided to shift the focus. "Thomas, I assume that Joyce is responsible as you are for many of the problems in your marriage, and we need to look at her contribution to this problem too. But if you only respond to her by defending yourself, she will feel unheard. So assume we are addressing only part of the problem, and addressing it from her perspective. The immediate issue is: can you respond to her in a way that gives her some hope that her feelings can be heard?"

Looking slightly scolded, Thomas said dutifully, "I'll try."

Margaret addressed Joyce. "I think it would help, Joyce, if you would talk more clearly about your feelings, and less about Thomas."

"I don't know what you mean," she said.

Margaret said, "Try this. 'Thomas, when I feel tired, the way I did the other night, and you don't notice, I feel ignored, I feel hurt. I feel very discouraged.' You should describe the situation you are in, but you should also describe your experience in that situation."

Joyce brightened. "It's true. When he does that—"

"Tell him," Margaret urged, gesturing toward Thomas. Joyce looked more anxious now as she looked directly at Thomas. He sat straight, as if he were being tested.

"When you don't notice how I'm feeling when I'm very tired and have done a lot for the family, I do feel . . ." and she couldn't continue. Her face was flushed; she seemed on the verge of tears. Finally, she managed to say hesitantly, ". . . hurt." Then she recovered. "You do it all the time, it seems to me."

Margaret said, "It's hard to stay focused on your own feelings, isn't it? It's much easier to talk about him. Try again."

Again Joyce looked at Thomas: "I do feel all that she said—hurt, ignored. And I don't feel loved."

She had done it. Now Thomas stirred, aware that he needed to respond. "I'm sorry, but you don't let me know what's going on— what you feel and what you want. I thought I was doing the right thing by staying with Amy." He seemed strangely panicky about Joyce's vulnerability, as though he were trying hard to avoid that part of her.

"Thomas," I said as reassuringly as I could, "if, when she takes a risk and exposes her feelings, you then reply by justifying your behavior, she will, as I said, feel even more ignored. Remember that she said that she felt alone? This is one of the reasons." Thomas still looked defensive. I plunged on. "You're going to need to get over being defensive." A pause, while he regained his composure. "Now," I resumed, "look at Joyce." He did so. She was still teary, and seemed even more vulnerable. "What do you see?"

"She seems . . . sad."

"Keep looking at her, and think about what she said earlier. When she is doing something for you or for the family and is very tired and you don't notice it, she feels ignored, unnoticed, and unloved. Can you understand how she could feel that way?"

"Of course." Warmer, softer.

"What you need to do is acknowledge that to her, let her know that you see what she feels, and accept her feelings. Just that much." Thomas looked as though he were struggling valiantly to keep from defending himself again.

"I do see that . . ."

"Speak to her," I urged.

Embarrassed, he looked at Joyce, who was crying silently. "I understand how you would feel ignored, not supported. I understand you feel that . . ." He hesitated, as if he didn't know what else to say, then added, ". . . because maybe I do that. If I do, I'm sorry." His words registered in Joyce with an almost physical impact; she visibly relaxed. They had probably been through their predictable cycle hundreds of times—Joyce trying to present her needs to Thomas, often indirectly, and Thomas replying defensively, pulling the focus back to himself. As small as it might seem, the shift in Thomas's response was significant. Thomas could not resist continuing, however, and I was afraid he was about to undo what he had accomplished. "But if I could—"

"Stop," Margaret cautioned him. "Leave it there." She then turned to Joyce, and asked, "Did that seem different to you, Thomas's responding like that?"

"Very different. It seemed uncomfortable, almost."

"That's because you are both breaking your 'scripts,' as it were. You can get used to it," Margaret said firmly.

55

I spoke to Thomas. "If you want to add something, you could add: 'Is there anything I can do to make this problem better?' " Still trying hard, Thomas repeated my words to Joyce.

For a moment, Joyce looked blank. "I don't know what to ask for," she finally said.

"You don't know what you'd want Thomas to do differently?" Margaret asked.

Again, Joyce seemed confused. "It's such a strange thing, to think about what I want. What would I want from him?" She mused. "I'm so accustomed to thinking about what he wants."

"Come on," Margaret urged, "you can think of something."

"I guess I would like him to notice when I'm tired, and offer to help with cooking, or with Amy, or with whatever it is I'm doing."

Margaret summarized the request. "First, he's going to notice when you are tired; then offer to help." She looked at Thomas. "Thomas, would you agree to do that?"

"Sure I will," he said pleasantly. He seemed relieved to have something more specific to do than acknowledging Joyce's feelings.

Margaret then addressed Joyce. "Joyce, you said you were standing there working at the counter, feeling like you were going to drop. You have a difficult time asking for help, for support. You're having trouble with it right now. This is an area that I have struggled with mightily, so I know how difficult it can be. But you need to learn how to ask for support, and expect that you can get it."

"I know it's difficult for me," she acknowledged, "and I don't understand why."

"We can get to the why eventually," Margaret said, "but you might start out by trying to do some systematic 'contracting' with Thomas. Think of the situations where you want help or support from him, and come in here and ask for them. We'll help the two of you negotiate—because he's bound to have things he wants too." She paused, then said with concern in her voice, "You look very tired. You're undoubtedly doing much too much."

Joyce looked deeply relieved that someone had seen the depth of her fatigue, and named it. "I am," was all she said. "I really am." Another of those registering, listening silences.

The issue the Olsons had raised is of course a terribly common one today, and it defines another major "dimension" in marriage: interpersonal equity. In our work with them, we were dealing with two different aspects of the same issue. On one level, we were hearing about Joyce's sense that the "workload" in their marriage was inequitably distributed; and no doubt it was. But rather than focus on the "content," we decided to emphasize the communication process between the couple, hoping that we could help them develop skills that could be applied to other areas in their marriage. We would later come back to the workload issue and deal with it in more detail.

In the "process" between them, there was also a kind of inequity: when Joyce talked about her feelings, Thomas became defensive and immediately refocused on his own dilemmas, leaving Joyce feeling completely unheard and unsupported. This communication pattern reflected a larger set of emotional "rules" in their relationship which encouraged Joyce to be helpful and self-sacrificial while Thomas was allowed to be rather narcissistic and self-focused. Not only did Joyce "cater" to him and try to please him, but when she tried to talk about her needs, he felt attacked; and in defending himself, he again brought the focus back to himself. We explained to the Olsons that whatever their personal histories, they were battling many centuries of male and female role conditioning; and we assured them that we too had struggled hard with these issues.

The underlying question in the crucial dimension of interpersonal equity is: whose feelings, whose subjective experience, whose emotional needs are most valued and receive the most attention. In the simplest terms, who is the "giver," who is the "taker"? While women are often in the giving role, this is not always the case.

I glanced at the clock. Only thirty minutes left, and much ground to cover. We hadn't heard much about their prior relationships, knew very little about their families of origin, and had an incomplete outline of their current struggles.

"This feeling of rejection," Joyce said, shifting the focus, a note of perplexity evident in her voice, "is something I feel a lot with Thomas." She seemed persistently interested in talking about her individual difficulties. I was suspicious about this willingness, since it tended to take the heat off their conflicts; and it could be part of her tendency to be self-sacrificial. She clearly needed to be able to be more confrontational with Thomas; but for now, there was a reason to relieve him of some pressure. He had taken quite a bit.

"I always seem to be chasing him, as it were, for his attention. And he always seems to be wanting to be more separate; he usually has something to do that seems more important than talking to me." She waited, as if searching for the point she wanted to make. "I don't quite understand why I am so sensitive to feeling rejected, though."

And we were into another "dimension," one that we have already seen operating in Joyce and Thomas's relationship: the perpetual marital struggle over emotional closeness. This dimension is of critical concern, for it tells us how the couple handles the degree of interpersonal "space" between them. As I attempt to visualize this pattern, I see it being enacted on the horizontal plane— a to-and-fro contest over how close, or how separate, the partners' lives are to be.

There are couples who insist on always being together, and who exert great effort to maintain a kind of closeness that many of us would consider smothering; and other couples who live perpetually at arm's length, never really getting very intimate. Most of us, however, engage in a constant and often-shifting joust over this issue. While the most frequent pattern is the one the Olsons were in, with the woman in emotional "pursuit," and the man engaged in emotional "distancing," there are a number of variations in this contest.

At the time of their initial interview, Joyce's needs for closeness, and her sensitivity to rejection, were all focused on Thomas, and it seemed useful to inquire into the origins of some of these feelings in her childhood.

"You are wondering if you have an underlying vulnerability in this area," Margaret offered. Joyce agreed that she often felt too wounded, too easily hurt. It puzzled her.

"Let's talk about your childhood," Margaret suggested. "Who was in your family?"

Joyce began to describe the cast of characters of her early years:

the grandmother who came to live with them, the loving house-keeper, her parents, her siblings. As is often the case in first interviews, her discussion of her family of origin was matter-of-fact. It was not until later in therapy, when her trust in the process was higher, and when her insight into the role of historical issues had been heightened, that she described the same relationships with much more feeling. As she talked, I made notes. In a very few minutes, the genogram looked like this:

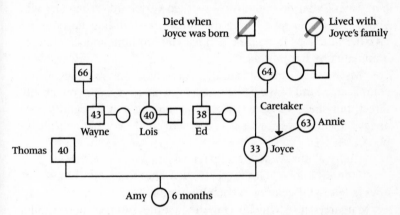

As I outlined her family relationships, I placed the oldest sibling on the left, as is the custom, proceeding in chronological order toward the right. Joyce's older brother Wayne was, like Thomas, a chemist. "He runs the laboratory of a large chemical company," Joyce said, "and I guess he's the family star, the achiever." As she talked about him, it was clear that she liked him, but didn't know him very well. Her feelings about her older sister Lois were more ambivalent: "Lois is so conservative and straight; she's a good person—maybe too good for my taste. She goes to church regularly, stays home with her kids, all that." She became pensive. "I don't know, we just don't see things the same way. She is very close to my mother."

Her closest sibling in age, Ed, a high school teacher, seemed to be the family loner, the outsider. "He's a lot like my father," Joyce said warmly. "Quiet, easy to get along with, does his own thing. I spent a good bit of time with him when we were kids, but when he was a teenager, he sort of pulled away from the family. Then, pretty early, he married Patti and they moved to Knoxville." The other kids had remained in the Atlanta area. As she described her siblings, I was listening to the possible roles each played. I guessed that as the youngest, Joyce had perhaps had difficulty separating from her family, a guess that turned out to be accurate.

"How about your father?" I asked. Joyce also spoke warmly of him, saying that he had always worked very hard. When she was young, he would take her to the hardware store that he ran, and give her little jobs to do. She had felt close to him, and saw him as dominated by her mother.

"My mother runs our family," she said, "but she does it in a complicated kind of way. She's never openly angry, or even terribly direct; but she is extremely skilled at making you feel guilty. I've always felt that way with her, and I've tried very hard to please her."

"Guilty about what?" Margaret asked.

"I don't know," Joyce said. "It's the strangest thing—I've always felt like I've done something wrong."

Margaret said, "Quickly, say the first thing that comes to mind that you could have done wrong."

Joyce looked blank. Then her face emptied of its color. "What jumped out at me immediately were the words 'Being born.' " After what seemed like a long silence, she added, "I can't believe it's that bad."

Margaret's response was reassuringly confident. "That must mean you were born at a time when your family was quite troubled. What was happening in your family when you were born?"

At that point, Joyce did not know a lot about the history of her family during her early years. She knew her father's business had failed when she was young, and that her grandmother had also come to live with them before she had any clear memories. "I know there was a lot of tension between my mother and father when I was young, and between my mother and her mother. And I always felt I was involved in these tensions, but I didn't understand them." She also knew that much of her daily care was done by the house-

keeper, Annie, and by her grandmother, and she spoke very lovingly of both these people.

Margaret urged Joyce to try to learn more about the situation
in her family during her early years. "Whatever the tensions were,
you would have been aware of them on some level; you may
have blamed yourself for them." Then Margaret glanced over at
my notes, and asked to see them. "I thought so," she said. "You
are around the age your mother was when you were born, and
you have a daughter." Joyce looked startled. "No wonder these
issues would be coming up for you now.

"I can assure you, though," Margaret said confidently, "that
your being born did not cause whatever problems your family had—
even though as a young child you may have thought you were to
blame for those tensions."

Joyce looked thoughtful, and vaguely troubled.

Even at that initial interview, it was evident that the sources of
Joyce's insecurity centered around her doubts about her mother's
love. The fact that her mother had gone to work full time when she
was quite young seemed to be part of her insecurity; but the family
politics into which she was born were also complex and difficult.
Joyce seemed to have decided at an early age that her safety in life
lay in trying to please everyone in her family, but especially her
mother. She would make herself cheerful and optimistic, would be
independent and resourceful, and would always be helpful, never
demanding.

When she had difficulty as an adult owning and advocating her
own needs, it was partly because of this early—but entirely
unconscious—decision to deny the "needy child" aspect of herself. It
was partly, of course, the result of her social conditioning as a woman,
in which self-sacrifice and helpfulness were expected of her.

Thomas seemed to depend on Joyce's seeking him out, on her
helpfulness, and on her eagerness to please him. As we had just
seen, when she became more openly needy, he was threatened,
and attempted to bring the focus back to himself and his needs.

There was little time left, and I realized that we knew almost
nothing about Thomas's family. Moving to engage him, with a few
questions I filled in his side of the genogram.

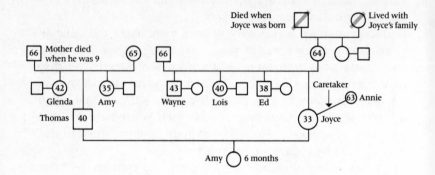

I was surprised to learn that Thomas was a middle child, surrounded by sisters. Let me explain the surprise. As I saw Thomas look at Joyce, I kept seeing a stern, rather parental expression; and that critical, demanding part of him was even more in evidence later in therapy. He was at first glance so clearly the dominant partner in his marriage that I expected him to be an oldest child, having grown up exercising authority and power over his siblings. "He did have a younger sister," I thought to myself. "Five years younger."

"My older sister, Glenda, is the strong type, and I guess you'd say she 'mothered' me when we were kids. I resented it sometimes, but I suppose I was also spoiled by her. Amy, who is our Amy's namesake, of course, was the one who could do no wrong in our family; and I have to admit she was a charmer, still is. She's really a lot of fun. I always felt she looked up to me as a big brother." Some of his expectations of being catered to were beginning to be understandable.

As Thomas talked about his family, I realized that my interest had shifted. The inquiry into Joyce's family was in the interest of learning what led her to be an emotional "pursuer," easily rejected and insecure enough to be very indirect about her needs and constantly trying to please. While I was curious about Thomas's "side" of their struggle over closeness, I had become more interested in the power aspect in their marriage.

This is, of course, another critical dimension in any marital struggle—the one-up, one-down aspect of the relationship. Some marriages seem to avoid the issue of power altogether—there is never an open contest; other marriages are in a constant uproar over who is to be in control. Most relationships live with an intricate and sometimes shifting state of compromise. While it is tempting to think of power in terms of arm-twisting and coercion, power is also exerted in relationships through caretaking, or through any activity that is typically older-generational—teaching, advising, criticizing.

"Why does Thomas stay so stiff, so in control?" I asked myself. "It's not as if he wants to dominate Joyce by force," I went on silently to myself. "He wants to see her as strong; in fact, he ignores the vulnerable part of her. But he wants her to wait on him, try to please him, take care of him." Then I realized what that meant: "He wants her to be like a strong, good, self-sacrificing mother—to him." And Joyce *was* maternal with him. Then the obvious thing hit me. "He wants this to happen without his having to be open about his needs." Not once in the hour had he admitted a need, a wish, a personal vulnerability. A final, cynical remark to myself. "Like many men."

Margaret had asked about his parents. "They are very traditional, the father-knows-best kind of family, I guess. My dad was a truck driver and away a lot when I was young; and then he gradually bought several trucks and eventually ran a small trucking company. My mother stayed at home—she had to, she doesn't even drive, if you can believe that." Thomas seemed willing to talk, but he didn't know what to talk about. He rarely thought about his family.

"What did you feel about your father?" I asked him.

"Scared of him, I guess. My mother would tell me he was going to punish me when he got home, and sure enough, he would." Asked how he was punished, he said, "He'd yell. Sometimes he would spank us." Then he added, "He was also very strict and stern about religion." The judgmental, critical part of Thomas, which he had incorporated from his father, was beginning to make more sense.

"Was he that way with your mother?" Margaret asked.

"That's the strange thing. With her, he was sort of like a kid. He often told me I had to try to please her, not upset her. I think he was the one who was afraid to upset her, and he seemed to do whatever she asked." After a pause, he added, "The thing that bothered me most about my father is that he would often cry when anything sad came up—on a TV program, or whatever. Sometimes, on holidays, he would cry at the table when we said grace." He sounded contemptuous of his father's vulnerability; it was a painful mixture of feelings to have for a father—fear and contempt.

"Why do you think he cried?" I wondered. "Did something extremely painful happen in his life?"

"Yes—I'd forgotten about that. His mother died when he was nine, and he was raised by his father from then on. His father was a very stern, strict fundamentalist. I never liked him very much." I was thinking about how often children grow up to be like one of their grandparents; there, at least, was the deeper origin of Thomas's critical side.

"His crying at sad parts in a TV show, or at holidays, makes more sense, then," I said, "though you wouldn't have understood that as a kid."

"I had never thought of that connection," Thomas said somewhat vacantly, but thoughtfully.

"What was your relationship with your mother like?" Margaret asked. We were getting very short of time. Seven minutes left in the hour.

"I'm not sure I know. I didn't like the fact that she couldn't drive. When I was a teenager, I'd have to do it. Other than that, and the fact that she calls a lot and implies that I'm some kind of criminal for not visiting more often, I don't know."

Joyce cleared her throat in an obvious attempt to get our attention. "Could I offer an opinion?"

"What do you think?" I asked Thomas.

"Be my guest," he said, with a half smile. He was still thinking, probably about his father.

Joyce smiled as she spoke. "His mother is, I think you could say, possessive. I mean, there is a lot of pressure on him to come back home, and do things for his family—especially from his mother. And she and I do *not* get along."

Margaret suggested, "You're the one who stole Thomas?"

Joyce said, "I think that's it."

I was struggling to see something definitive and insightful about Thomas, straining to see the family he grew up in, his role in that family, and the influence they had on him. Like many men, he clearly needed to stay adult, in control of himself and his emotions. He was critical of, even frightened by, Joyce's needs, especially her dependence. Yet he seemed to need to be pleased, to be taken care of himself. I thought about his father—harsh, critical, yet very dependent on his wife. And his mother—she too sounded rather helpless, and controlling. She seemed to have leaned on Thomas. "His parents sound needy," I thought to myself. "And Thomas seems . . ." the words that came were ". . . unparented, unnurtured—except maybe by his older sister." Finally, "No wonder he is frightened by Joyce's needs—they remind him of his needy parents. And no wonder he wants her to be maternal and take care of him."

I could not think of a way to say this, nor did I think it was particularly appropriate to broach all this complexity. There would be time.

Margaret said, warmly and directly, "Thomas, I'm touched by your description of your family, particularly by what you did not get from your father. I can see how you would have been put off by his neediness—it would have been very confusing for a kid." Thomas felt her empathy for him; his face seemed open, and a little softer. "But I'm concerned that your fear of being like your father leaves you cut off from your own feelings and needs." He seemed to have the same problem many men had, only for a different reason; his father was more open about the little-boy side of himself than many men. Margaret waited, letting each statement register. "I'd like to help you find a way to pay attention to your own feelings without worrying that they would be humiliating or embarrassing to you." She then added: "It may sound unlikely, but if you could do that, you would also find yourself more able to respond to Joyce's feelings and needs."

I was a little jealous that she had said it so well; but neither did I want to end with the focus on Thomas, so I added, "Joyce, let me offer you one caution. If you're right about Thomas's mother—and I suspect you are—you should be careful about 'interpreting' his problems, because he will feel it as intrusive, and parental. And you don't want to remind him too much of his mother." I saw that the time was up. "We've got to stop," I said.

Amused, Margaret smiled broadly at me. Then, seeing the couple's perplexity, she explained, "He likes to get the last word."

"Do you want to schedule another appointment?" Margaret said, still smiling. Thomas and Joyce looked at each other; Joyce looked worried that Thomas might not want to continue. Realizing that they needed to talk privately, and aware that it was a very serious issue, Margaret added, "You don't have to decide now. You can think about it, and call Paula."

"That sounds good," Thomas said, looking relieved that the hour was over.

The question of whether they would take on the difficult and anxious job of changing their marriage was palpable, visible; it hung before all of us. There had been no doubt from the first moments of the interview that Thomas was the reluctant party, the restraining force in their relationship. The final dimension in our diagnostic survey, one that had run throughout the interview and had emerged as a crucial issue, was flexibility. The capacity to adapt, to bend, to yield. Flexibility is a central issue in any relationship, and in any life.

We are all born with the impulse to act, to move, to seek what we want in the world. Powerful forces impel us forward. But as we are bruised by life, we learn to be cautious, to restrain ourselves, to hesitate. These internal tensions—between impulse and restraint—also get built into relationships. Some relationships are dominated by one force or the other: a couple may be so careful and cautious that they never take any risks, and approach change with great skepticism; another couple is so impulse-ridden that they are forever in hot water. Most of us get polarized around the issue of how flexible to be. One person becomes a "yea-sayer," the other a "nay-sayer"; and we may even specialize within certain areas of the relationship.

Like many women today, Joyce wanted change in their marriage; and like many men today, Thomas was reluctant and skeptical. It was easy to guess that he anticipated losing something valuable to him if their marriage changed any more than it already had—probably Joyce's caretaking, her "mothering." They had done fairly well in the just-we-two phase of marriage; but now that Amy was demanding her share of parenting, Thomas was already anxious about how much of Joyce's time and attention went into Amy's needs. It was probably one reason he wasn't more helpful with the parenting process; like many men, he felt competitive with his own child for his wife's attention.

Would he be able to see that there were benefits for him as well as for her in changing their marriage? It is, of course, the question in so many marriages today. We guessed that unless Joyce made an issue of their being in therapy, he would still be uneasy about such a project. But we expected she would make an issue of it.

After Joyce and Thomas left the room, and as I slipped my notes into a folder, I said to Margaret, "Thomas is a reluctant customer, isn't he?"

"I don't blame him," Margaret replied. "Joyce is pretty angry at him." Then she added, "But I think they'll be back."

Later we discussed the couple's difficulties in more detail, and I added some notes to the folder. We had managed to at least touch on the six dimensions through which we usually evaluate couples:

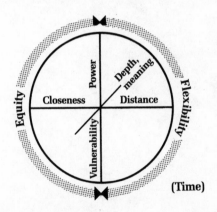

My notes concluded with the following remarks: "This couple seems basically committed to each other. The most obvious current stress involves the birth of their first child into a traditional relationship structure in which husband is at least superficially dominant, but within which he extracts considerable caretaking from his overfunctioning wife, who has a stressful job as well as many family commitments. Her self-sacrificial, helpful stance leaves her constantly fatigued, raising childhood issues around feeling unnurtured and unsupported.

"Major issues are around interpersonal equity, closeness–distance, and power and vulnerability. Immediate strategy: to get Joyce to be more open and direct about her needs for support, and to help Thomas learn to be more nurturant in relation to her. Don't question his position of power in the marriage for now, but help him to be more supportive of her. As he struggles to meet her needs, he will experience some of his own deficits in early parenting. Be alert to these deficits, and encourage him to turn to the therapists for support, not to Joyce. Help both contract a rescheduling of household responsibilities, especially around Amy's care. Bring Amy next meeting."

4

Metaphors of Equity:
An Experience

SILENCE. AT A TIME when we would usually be talking nonstop about our day, only the sound of the traffic was heard as we rode home together that evening after the initial interview with Joyce and Thomas. "What's wrong?" I asked finally.

Margaret stared ahead unresponsively. "I guess I'm tired; it's been a hard day."

Two hours later, after we had stepped into the swirl of demands of our kids' need to talk, after a dinner that Margaret cooked, and after Mark and I had washed the dishes, she was still silent; and looked even more tired. "Something is wrong," I said when we were finally alone. It was ten o'clock, and we were standing in our bedroom.

"The interview with Joyce and Thomas was hard for me, Gus. The issues are so close to ours, and I guess they brought it all back. I know things have changed, that you are trying hard; but in some ways we still have a long way to go."

I knew, of course, what she meant; the interview had also made me uncomfortable. Later we would tell the Olsons that we too had struggled with similar problems, but a first interview hardly seemed the time to do that. I could see that my confident advice to Thomas must have sounded a little hollow.

This time, I saw Margaret's fatigue, her discouragement, and I said, "You look very tired. Why don't you go to bed and read?"

"I think I will," she said. "Would you fix me a cup of decaf?"

"Yes," I answered with relief.

For a good many years, I managed to avoid thinking about the issues of equity or fairness in our marriage. I thought Margaret and I had an equal if somewhat traditional relationship. Not until we moved to the South did I finally begin to see the underlying structure of our partnership. By then, I didn't just see this structure; I collided with it.

I raised the issue of our moving away from Madison—at first tentatively, and then, as I realized how distressed I felt about my career, more and more insistently. The critical issue was my relationship with my mentor, Carl Whitaker, though other factors also contributed.

For a number of years, I enjoyed being the protégé of a powerful and widely respected man. The envy of most of my colleagues, I had constant and easy access to a brilliant man who helped found the field in which I worked. For someone whose father had been often absent and largely unsupportive, Carl's strength and availability met a deep need.

As I approached my mid-thirties, however, I began to feel concerned about my dependence on Carl. If I got into difficulty with a family, it was easy to call him in as a consultant. If I needed advice about anything—personal or professional—he was there. I couldn't seem to resist leaning on him, and he didn't offer me much incentive to change.

My colleagues also saw me as his protégé. Most of my professional papers were co-written with Carl, and though I often contributed original ideas to these papers, they were presumed to be his. Why couldn't I develop a separate professional identity? Part of the problem was the depth of his helpfulness. He sent me a steady stream of clients; some of the workshops I led were the ones he couldn't do. Many of my ideas about family therapy also came from him—he was really my only teacher. In addition to leaning on him, I was deeply indebted to him.

Quite unconsciously, I decided to repay this debt by writing a book about my work with Carl. When I was thirty-five, I began *The*

Family Crucible, a fictionalized account of a family's treatment; it took most of my spare time for several years. As it neared completion, and as I neared forty, I began to have thoughts of leaving Madison. Though I didn't know it, I was in the phase of male development that developmental psychologist Daniel Levinson—whose research contributed heavily to Gail Sheehy's *Passages*—terms "Becoming One's Own Man." The disciple in a mentor relationship feels a powerful urge to "individuate"—to develop a separate professional identity—and this task often necessitates a break with the mentor. The same forces seem to operate in the female mentor relationship, though they have been less extensively studied.

As the idea of our moving surfaced, Margaret and I began to fight. She didn't like the Wisconsin winters either, but she didn't want to leave. She loved the school, her friends, our house by the lake. Psychologically, I had lived like a student, while she had established deep roots in Madison. But Margaret also didn't like some things about our lives: my overworking, the level of stress in my work, and the lack of time in my life for our children. As we fought, a compromise began to take shape. If we moved, would I change this traditional male pattern? Would I work less hard, and be more involved with our children? Would I help with the housework, and the maintenance of our household? Would Margaret be able to work more or less full time as a therapist? Could we live at a slower, more satisfying pace? Saddened at the thought of leaving Carl, the house, our friends, the lake, but deeply excited by the possibility of moving, I said yes.

I did not realize then how much Margaret was giving up; I especially did not see how deeply meaningful the school was to her—those special teachers, those happy kids, that vital community she had helped create. But perhaps I did see it, and was threatened by her success; or saw it and chose to make my own needs more important.

We chose Atlanta ostensibly because it was a large city where I could teach family therapy as a private practitioner, because we had some contacts who would be helpful in starting our practices, and because it had a good climate; but I think it was really because I had roots there. Atlanta was where my parents had begun their marriage, where I was born, and where my parents had returned late in their lives, after my father had lost his job. Both my parents had died there. It was also where Carl had lived before coming to Wisconsin; and where, as the reader will see, I first met him. So it was a complicated choice, one laden with memory and meaning.

In families, a move is often like a marriage, a birth, a death—it can represent a major change in the direction of one's life. In return for what Margaret was giving up, I promised to change my role in our family. I had not reckoned with how difficult that job would be—for both of us.

The immediate problem was in getting established in a new city. *The Family Crucible* was widely read by therapists, ministers, physicians, and others in the "helping" professions, and soon after we moved into our rented apartment in Atlanta, the phone began to ring with requests for me to do workshops, give lectures, and be a consultant to agencies. We needed the money, the connections, the access to a new city, and I also wanted to try my wings away from Carl. So again I said yes, yes, yes. Soon I was busier than I had been in Madison.

Margaret, on the other hand, had left her large support system, and she did not have a book to introduce her to Atlanta. She was Gus's co-therapist, and at Paideia, the progressive school our children attended, she was a newcomer in a well-established community. Since I was so busy, she was left with buying the groceries, finding a pediatrician, and taking the children to their activities—all the things she had done in Madison. Only now Sarah's dance class was across a large and traffic-ridden city, Mark was playing soccer, and Julia was only in school half-time.

Nothing had changed for me. I was working harder than ever, while Margaret had lost all her support outside the family, all the recognition she had had; and the demands on her were increased. She began to plead with me. "Gus, I need your help, your support. I'm not doing very well. I'm spending all my time in the car or on the phone, trying to find this or that. When I do get over to Paideia, I feel like a nobody." She began to look gray, tired, depressed.

I tried to think about her situation and her needs. I listened attentively; intellectually, I saw the dilemma she was in. But I didn't really feel it. Eventually I would turn the conversation back to my stresses. I was worried about a workshop, and I needed help with a certain family. Would she see them with me? And my writing. I wasn't getting any done. Could she help me make some time for it? I was very skilled at getting the focus back on my problems. Finally, Margaret would sigh and give up.

One of the difficulties I had in understanding Margaret's dilemma was that most of the time she was so cheerful and competent. She seemed so strong. Later we would both realize the extent to which she was playing a role taught her by her family, one that demanded that she be optimistic, strong, and helpful. I wasn't conscious of this at the time, but I was implicitly saying to Margaret, "You are not allowed to be vulnerable; I need you to be the way you are."

It is painful to listen again to some of those conversations, hearing the little-boy quality in myself that said, "I need you to be strong to help me," but also hearing the bullying, demanding sound in my voice that commanded, "I won't let you be any other way." Painful, and embarrassing.

Now I can see that I was in a dependent, but highly controlling, position. I was like a kid trying to please his mother by making good grades in school, and addicted to mother's praise and reassurance. So why was mother complaining? I was trying hard to do what I thought I was supposed to do. Wasn't it enough that I was working sixty hours a week at a very difficult job, and having trouble coping with all the demands being made of me? What did she want? I was an experienced male martyr and knew my lines well.

Margaret, of course, wanted me to see her vulnerability, her need for support. Partly because she had trouble revealing her needs, I experienced her as demanding and controlling. She began to seem like the classic nag. The harder she pulled on me for support, the more resentful I felt. At times she seemed like an overpowering tyrant herself, intent on controlling every aspect of my life. But rather than confronting her directly, I dodged, I promised, I fought in subtle, unconscious ways—like forgetting to do the grocery shopping. As I dodged, Margaret felt more and more alone.

She persevered: trying to get connected with Paideia, doing most of the car pooling, all of the grocery shopping, supervising the renovation of the house we bought, doing co-therapy with me. She also tried to make friends; and everywhere she encountered established relationships, like the ones we had left in Madison. I was too busy to notice that I didn't have friends. We were into the second year, and there was no turning back.

Our fights, which became increasingly circular and repetitive, were usually about some detail of daily life—the housework, the grocery shopping, a car pool. Margaret kept asking me to do more, and I kept promising and trying. I would agree to shop once a week, and I often forgot. Sometimes I wouldn't show up at a car pool, and the other parents would complain to Margaret. I helped grudgingly, and I had to be reminded.

Margaret began to be very tough on the husbands in the couples we saw together, and I sometimes overheard her making angry, disparaging remarks about men. She and Mark also began to have difficulties. If Mark refused to do something Margaret asked him to do—a chore, say—she would get furious at him. Then she would ask me to discipline him, and I would come down on him hard. How could he be so unfair to his mother?

At the time, we didn't see what we were doing to Mark, but he had clearly become a focus for the barely submerged anger between us. Margaret was blowing up at him for not doing a household chore for her, and I too blamed him—for the very things I blamed myself for. Mark's anger at us for using him as a scapegoat began to come out at school, where he was often in conflict with other boys. Vaguely sensing that we were the cause of his difficulties, we worried about him.

One morning in the fall of our second year in Atlanta, I decided to leave for work an hour early. Maybe I would do a little of the interminable paperwork of private practice. As I was leaving, Margaret asked me to call Mark's soccer coach and find out where a postponed game was to be played. All I said was, "Would you mind doing it? I'm running late." Standing by the back door, my hand on the doorknob, I glanced at Margaret; she looked very tired, very discouraged. She wore a bathrobe, and I was dressed in a coat and tie. There was a steely, distant look in her eyes.

"Yes, I would mind," she answered, her voice a commingling of resignation and resentment. Then her face and her voice toughened. "I would mind very much."

"What do you mean?" I asked. "I have to get some letters written and I have to look at the accounts."

"It's always something," she said bitterly.

"What do you mean?" I sensed something coming, and I half-welcomed it. I felt angry too.

"I mean you always have something to do that's more important than what I want you to do." She turned to leave, a hard expression on her face. I felt the open door pulling me toward work, but I hesitated. The distance between us seemed immense.

"Well, I do have a lot to do this morning, but I'll make the call to Mark's coach for you if you want me to." Resentful, helpful condescension. Margaret turned back toward me.

"For me?" She sounded angrier. "How about for you? Don't you have any responsibility toward him?"

"Of course I do."

"Well, if that's true, why haven't you done anything about getting in touch with his teacher about the fight he got into after school with Adam? Is that my job too?"

"All right, I can do that." I was beginning to get angrier.

"*If* I remind you and stay in behind you."

"Look, what is the point of this? What else are you mad about?"

"Try last night." She spoke tersely, that glint in her eyes again.

"What about last night? You had a committee meeting. I stayed with the kids."

"And when I came home, the house was a mess, the dishes were unwashed, and the kids were all upset. Julia had a cut on her forehead because she and Mark had been roughhousing, and Sarah cried when I came in because you had forgotten to pick her up at the ballet studio. She waited for you for half an hour." She paused. There was obviously a lot more.

"Look—" I began apologetically.

"I know, you have plenty of excuses. You had an article to work on, you didn't notice the kids fighting, and you just forgot about Sarah." Her voice was getting angrier. "But what galls me, really *galls* me, is that you had the audacity to be critical of me for coming home late from that meeting. One little committee that I chair, the only thing that really seems like mine, and you are critical when I am an hour later than I planned to be." She couldn't stop. "Not only do you punish me for having that meeting by screwing up what I asked you to do—or by not doing it at all—but you are critical of me for being late!'' She was shouting now. ''Do you know what that does to me?! *Do you*?'' No opportunity to answer, but I was hardly tempted. ''It makes me want to quit. Just walk out and leave you with the kids and the house and the whole thing.''

We had been married for sixteen years, and for the first time it seemed quite possible that Margaret might leave me. I had always presumed that her caring, her commitment, her involvement with me were immutable and unconditional. Now, suddenly, I could see her upstairs packing a suitcase—a horrifying image.

Margaret wasn't finished. ''You make it very difficult for me to be involved with Paideia. Next week I'm likely to forget to make a critical phone call, or I'll set somebody up to be angry at me.''

I knew that I was guilty, but I also knew that the problems weren't all mine. ''Just because I said one thing critical? Dammit, I don't take all the responsibility for what you do.'' I could feel myself becoming defensive, and I was about to launch into my argument about how I was the only one who worried about money and how she never balanced the checkbook and how she didn't give a damn about my stresses; but I realized that I had better not do that this time. This fight was different. We were on the edge of a cliff.

''Look,'' I said, backing away from my defense. ''I admit what you're saying. I know I'm having a problem supporting you.'' I paused, ''I *am* trying. And I'll try some more. But would you tell me again what you want? Maybe I don't understand it.'' This time I was pleading. It was as though I was groping for the first time to really understand the person I was married to.

We were still standing by the door, the cool fall air moving between us. Margaret looked up at me, her face less angry now. As she spoke again, her face softened, tears in her eyes. She was trying not to cry. ''Gus, I need your support. I want you to see me as I am, not the way you need me to be. I'm not always that strong. I need your help.''

''What kind of help? I know you've said it before, but say it again.''

''With the kids, the house, the logistics of our lives.'' She waited, thinking about the problem. ''You will do things if I ask you to, but you wait to be reminded. I want you to take the *initiative* to see the problems and to share them with me. You could take a lot more initiative in helping Mark with the problems he is having with those boys at school. You could notice when the groceries are getting low. You could look around you at the house and see what needs picking up." Another wait. "I mean, it's as if you don't identify with what we all need, other than money."

I knew she was right. I loved her; I loved my children. But I was too preoccupied with my own struggle, my own mission in life; and it was a preoccupation that was cheating this family. I nodded acknowledgment.

"Gus, you have to stop being subtly critical of my involvement with Paideia. It makes it so much harder for me. I mean, it's difficult enough as it is. They hardly know me there, and when you are critical of my being there, I sacrifice myself in some way. I find myself pulling back."

I felt like crying too; I also fought against the impulse. My voice dropped apologetically. "I know I make it harder. I guess I'm threatened. Maybe I'm afraid I'll lose you." Saying it made it seem ridiculous. How could a grown, successful man be threatened by his wife's involvement in a career separate from his own?

"Well, you have to come to grips with that. You couldn't live in Carl's shadow, and I can't live in yours." There wasn't anything I could say to that.

Our fight seemed to be over. Maybe something had happened. Maybe I had really heard her. We stepped outside the door into the cool morning. Then I noticed the stone steps which I had just descended from the house to the parking area. They seemed hard, immense; the thought of climbing them again, and of reentering my own home in some new fashion, looked enormously difficult.

In the days following that confrontation, I felt confused and disoriented. It was as if the entire structure of our relationship, all the patterns of living that I had relied on for sixteen years, were in question. Though Margaret's words rang in my ears, I still did not fully grasp what she wanted. I knew, of course, that this was a fight about equity, though at the beginning of Margaret's confrontation I only heard her impassioned cry that something in our relationship was unfair. With time, I began to distinguish more specific problems.

A central issue was the distribution of the workload in our

marriage. Like many husbands, I had been granted the "right" to a stimulating, interesting job. While Margaret had my official sanction to have a career, her many other obligations made it very difficult for her to find the time and energy to develop her career. As we talked further, I began to see just how many responsibilities she had: grocery shopping, cooking, supervising the cleaning of our house (we all helped with that area, in addition to having some part-time outside help); and the major responsibility for our children. It was the last area that weighed most heavily on her shoulders.

Not only did Margaret monitor our children's needs, and carry out hundreds of necessary practical tasks for them—car pooling, taking them to the doctor, seeing that they had what they needed for their lunches, following their school progress, and on and on—but she also *worried* about them. Even though I made an effort to "help with the kids," I functioned more or less as her assistant. The ultimate responsibility for their welfare—and the stress and anxiety attendant on that role—had always been hers; and I had not realized how emotionally burdensome that responsibility was. If she was ever to have the energy to develop her life outside our family, I apparently had to do more than "help"—I had to take emotional as well as practical charge of half the workload that had been hers, and to take an active initiative in fulfilling that responsibility.

But apparently there was a subtler and more pervasive inequity in our marriage. My emotional experience, my feelings, tended to receive the most attention. Like many couples, we had created an "interpersonal inequity," an imbalance in the vital determination of whose experience, whose feelings, had the most "importance." As is often the case with men, I was the narcissistic partner, the emotional "taker," while Margaret shared with many women the job of being the emotional "giver," or the self-denying partner.

I kept hearing Margaret say, "I have for years thought about what you wanted, what you needed—cooked the meals you liked, made love when you wanted to, accommodated to your schedule, moved to cities you wanted to move to, helped make your life easier. I have cared deeply about what you wanted and needed. Have you done that for me? Do you know what I need, what my day feels like, what would make me happy? Do you even think about my experience?"

I had to admit: I thought mainly about myself, and about my career. It wasn't that I didn't care about Margaret, or about my family; but I thought of my responsibility in relation to them as a kind of "performance." Like most men, I worried about how I was doing in the larger world; that was my way of being a good husband and father. I simply wasn't accustomed to thinking directly about Margaret's experience. Nor was she accustomed to telling me about her needs. Time and again, she would mention something she wanted from me, I would miss the cue, and she would sigh and do it herself. Her self-sacrifice was certainly part of the problem.

The roles that encourage male narcissism and enforce female self-denial are of mythic proportions: they loom large through history, and they are communicated to us in subtle and not-so-subtle cues which we begin to absorb from our earliest days. Males have a right to get what they want, while females must deny and sacrifice their needs. Though the women's movement has awakened in many women—as it did in Margaret—a profound need to assert their power and to proclaim their worth, these primordial stereotypes are still firmly in place. A recent study of classrooms, for example, revealed that boys are called on in class far more frequently than girls, even by women teachers who consider themselves feminists. And even though she may be quite successful at work, the woman executive who rushes home to tend to children and household, while her husband does far less than she, has of course not escaped the self-sacrificing aspect of her role. In fact, when it comes to finding time and energy to devote to her own personal needs, she may have to contend with an even higher level of self-denial than did her mother.

Patterns of narcissism and self-denial do tend to be sex-typed in marriage, but the self-centered partner need not be a man. Margaret and I are currently working with a couple in which the wife has a long history of narcissistic self-preoccupation, the husband an equally long record as a self-sacrificing caretaker to women. "What irritates me," the husband says, "is that my wife always expects me to be attentive and supportive, while she rarely gives the same to me. The day that I lost a large ad account, she insisted on going to a party we'd been invited to. She hardly noticed how down I was; she was worried about who was going to be there, and how she looked."

One way of conceptualizing this kind of giving/taking relationship dichotomy is to think of each individual as a *subjective*, feeling, experiencing entity, with many physical and emotional needs. The individual tries to meet his or her needs by finding others who become the *object* of these needs. In a simple example, I experience (subjective) sexual needs, and Margaret becomes the target (object) of these needs. I *use* her to satisfy my needs.

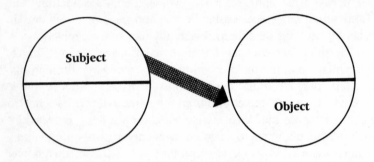

This kind of "usury" is not necessarily bad: it simply means that we need other people to satisfy certain needs. In the healthy relationship, each partner can be a "subject" (someone whose experiences and needs are important), as well as the "object" of the other person's needs. In the sexual metaphor, I use Margaret to satisfy my needs, and she also uses me in the same way.

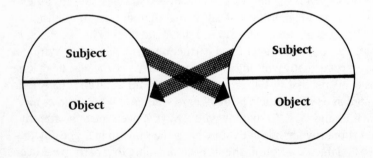

Of course our experiences, our moods, our various needs are not identical. I want to make love, and, for whatever reason, Margaret doesn't. If our relationship is healthy, we will each voice our own preferences, and then find a compromise that will meet both sets of needs. Since most of what transpires between people is either an expression of need or a response to another's need, every relationship contains a continuous, intricate, largely intuitive process of negotiation.

In order for a relationship to remain balanced and equitable, each person must be able to advocate his or her needs assertively *and* be able to respond sensitively to the other person's needs. As simple as it sounds, this is not a simple accomplishment: valuing myself, promoting my own welfare, *and* looking across at my partner and seeing him or her as equally valuable, equally important—not just for what he or she can do for me, but because I recognize this individual's inherent worthiness as a separate, equal person.

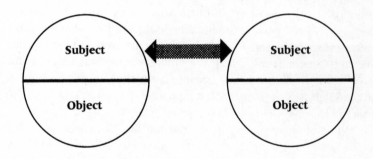

Though it is important in marriage to be able to negotiate, to trade, to "deal," the highest form of equity transcends such mechanical exchanges. We need the other's experience to be as valid as our own. There is probably no better definition of love: to be able to cradle the other's experience within our own compassionate understanding. In this empathic exchange, each values the other not just as a rewarding "object," but as a separate, equally valuable "subject." The theologian Martin Buber has called this kind of bond the "I–Thou" relationship, and it is one in which each identifies in the other the most cherished aspects of his or her own personhood. While I will explore this difficult-to-define qualitative distinction in more detail, perhaps the essential element is a mutual appreciation of the Other's emotional life, morale, "spirit."

So much can interfere with the creation of this delicate balance between the value of the self and the value of the other. We all have an inherent tendency to "objectify" the other person—to incorporate them into our own private set of needs. In the stress of facing the work world, I needed to feel supported and taken care of; and I was tempted to see Margaret as the "object" of this need. Internally, I wanted to experience her as my caretaker. Without realizing that I was doing it, I made her a symbolic person, someone who would subordinate her own needs in the interest of helping me. In at least part of our relationship, I wanted her to act in ways that my mother did.

Since Margaret's life experience as a woman and as a caretaker in her family of origin made her typecast for the role I wanted her to play, it was almost inevitable that she would be drawn into that role. The "objectification" of our partner can be so pervasive that the "objectified" partner can literally disappear from our consciousness as a separate person. That is what is meant when we say that we take someone for granted. We simply incorporate them into our own world view; and they become a function, a role, a kind of psychological convenience. That, apparently, is what I had done to Margaret.

While the narcissistic partner in a marriage does take advantage of the self-sacrificing partner, matters are never quite that simple. A strong, competent person like Margaret, who gives far more to others than she gets in return, has inevitably grown up in a family where that approach was adaptive. We had not seen our respective roles in our families of origin very clearly at the time of that first bruising confrontation; but as we explored our histories more carefully, it became clear that Margaret had had as much training in being a "giver" as I had in being a "taker."

This stance—learning to gain importance, value, and security within the family by helping others—is, of course, extremely familiar to women. Not only is it related to the experience of learning to give to children, but it is tied to centuries of living in societies that gave women little official power. The power of women has often lain in their hiding or suppressing their needs, and in creating indebtedness in others through helping. And, to a certain extent, this way of living is effective: we men do feel obligated (and guilty) when our wives sacrifice themselves for us; and we are all bound to the women in our lives through their giving to us. While it has also been possible for women to gain satisfaction vicariously, through the successes of their children or their husbands, women today are finding these indirect satisfactions increasingly frustrating.

The origins of the narcissistic pattern are also complex. While males are conditioned to be more self-focused than females, there are also particular forces within the family that create narcissistic children—who, of course grow up to be narcissistic marriage partners. Two types of experience have this effect on children: emotional neglect, and its opposite, "overparenting" or infantilization. Neglected children grow up to be self-focused adults because they attempt to meet in their adult relationships the needs for nurturance and support which were unmet in childhood. Such people are emotionally "hungry," and they depend too heavily on their friends, their employers, and especially their spouses. Other kids have the opposite problem: their parents gave them too much, helped them too much, thereby conditioning them to be "reassurance junkies," unable to stand alone, and largely unaware of the needs of others. Self-sacrificial parents who are unable to address their own needs directly, but who "project" these needs onto their children, whom they overparent, often fail to train these children to think of others' needs.

As I later learned about myself, many kids grow up with a confusing mixture of overindulgence and neglect. We may be ignored by one parent and infantilized by the other, or we may be the object of a confusing blend of inconsistent treatment by both parents. I believe that male children are often treated with such inconsistency. Our mothers often do too much physical caretaking of us, but we also struggle with a kind of emotional neglect which we carry with us into adulthood. Margaret's confrontation was my initial introduction to these and other problems in men, problems that unfolded with distressing clarity over the next several years.

One of the dangers in this pattern of interpersonal inequity is that over time, the polarization between the partners can become more and more extreme. The drained, exhausted "giver" gets angrier and angrier, and after a while she becomes cynical about ever getting her emotional needs met. She does not know how to ask for support, understanding, help. Like Margaret, she approaches her partner in a demanding, often critical manner, saying, "*You* aren't doing things right; *you* aren't helping me!" The needy child within her cries out for attention; but because as a child she learned that adult support came only when she was strong and helpful, she still unconsciously assumes that it isn't possible to reveal her vulnerable, "child" aspect.

The emotional "taker" (and remember, either sex can play either role) responds anxiously to his partner's irritable approach as if it were, in fact, an attack. Like Thomas and me, he becomes defensive. Defensiveness creates a great many problems in marriage, and it is especially common in men. Learned in childhood, it is a natural response to feeling threatened:

"I didn't do it," we said when accused. "She did."

"I'm sorry, I won't do it again."

"You do it too!"

"I'm doing the best I can."

As kids, we may have felt genuinely overwhelmed by our parents' often subtly communicated needs or by their demands, criticism, or attacks. In these encounters with our parents, we felt cornered, trapped, helpless, inadequate; and so we learned strategies of self-protection that were adaptive—at that time. Perhaps we used verbal strategies like those just mentioned, but we may also have learned to withdraw, to placate, or to use a host of other defenses.

Unfortunately, we carry these defensive strategies into adulthood, reacting to our spouse as if she or he posed the same threat to us that our parents did. When I hear Margaret's irritable, demanding tone of voice saying, "You don't . . ." I begin my intricate, repetitive defense:

"I do pay the bills!"

"I am so stressed with work, I can't add anything else."

"You don't balance the checkbook either."

"I'll do better next time."

"I'm doing the best I can."

How ancient is this dilemma: a man, threatened by his partner's needs, becomes defensive, and in the process of defending himself, leaves her feeling lonely, unseen, and burdened. Of course, we see in these anxieties in a man the looming shadow of his mother's emotionality, and the childhood situation he was in with her. We will spend time exploring the childhood origins of these male dilemmas; but we should not neglect his wife, who has also brought to marriage her own unmet needs, which she hurls at her husband in increasingly repetitive, anguished fury.

Margaret and I soon discovered that while it was helpful to have these issues out in the open, and to have some insight into them, changing our behavior patterns was extremely difficult. Margaret tended to see what needed doing around the house, and do it. Then she would find herself feeling depressed, and realize that she was back in her strong, self-sacrificial mode. I, of course, would have allowed this to occur.

The same thing happened when we tried to share responsibility for the children's needs. I agreed to help both Mark and Sarah with their math homework. I would start to work with one of them, and suddenly Margaret would appear in the room with suggestions. I would get irritated at her for "interfering," and before long I would drift away while she took over. I began to accuse her of wanting help with the kids but not wanting to share control. As I slipped away from responsibility, I blamed her.

I consistently had difficulty taking a more active interest in the kids' lives. I loved them, enjoyed my time with them, tried to do the things Margaret asked me to do with them, but I seemed unable to translate my concern into a kind of enduring attention. What was Mark's experience at school like? Who were his friends? How was Sarah doing in math? How was she bearing up under the strain of being in a highly demanding dance company? When were their dental checkups scheduled? In the same way that anxiety about money seemed to "belong" to me, this bundle of anxious responsibility belonged to Margaret. While she seemed to have much less ambivalence about sharing the grocery shopping ("I get tired when

I *see* a grocery store," she said emphatically), she had more difficulty shifting to me some of her sense of responsibility for the kids; and I had great difficulty assuming it.

But another intense struggle involved my accepting Margaret's having a strong commitment that was not only outside our family, but separate from me. Here was Paideia, a school very much like Wingra; and she was trying to make a place for herself there. "Isn't it enough to be a therapist?" I asked. "Why is education so important to you?"

"Because I love schools," she said definitely. "It's a chance to shape the experience of kids in ways that are exciting to me." Then she added: "It's also something that belongs to me entirely. I don't share it with you." I suppose that was what made it difficult for me: this was an interest that took her away from me.

I made an agreement to enable Margaret to have the time and energy to devote to her interest in education. As Paideia discovered how talented and energetic Margaret was, she began to have more evening meetings. On those nights, she would cook dinner, spend a few minutes with the kids, and leave. The kids and I would clean up together, and I would be on call for homework consultation. Gradually I began to feel more comfortable with the kids' needs, and to enjoy being able to help. But I found myself strangely uncomfortable with Margaret's absence; and when she came in, tired but excited, I continued to find little things to be critical of. Had she forgotten to do something during the day? Had she been later than she said she would be? My criticisms were not substantive; they constituted a kind of low-key harassment. Her being away made me feel vaguely anxious, and in spite of my resolve to be more grownup about this whole thing, I continued to express my anxiety through subtle, insistent criticism.

Finally, Margaret confronted me again. "Dammit, Gus, what is going on? Every time I'm away, I get this veiled attack. And it gets to me. I begin to question my right to do this. I begin to feel like I should give it up."

"I am anxious; I know I am," I admitted. "It's ridiculous." Ridiculous or not, my anxiety was embarrassingly persistent. Was I worried that she would get involved with another man? Perhaps I was. She now worked frequently with a number of interesting men who served on the Paideia board of directors. Yes, now that I thought of it, when she came in late, I had fleeting thoughts of her standing in a dark parking lot, talking to a man. Maybe that was it.

After another of these late-night scenes, I finally revealed my fantasy. "I know you're unhappy with me. Are you getting involved with some man on this board?" Margaret smiled, an open, honest smile.

"I'm fond of several of these men," she replied, looking straight at me, "and I respect a couple of them a lot. But I'm not involved with anyone else, and I don't intend to be. I *am* trying to do something for that school." The anxious fantasy I was having is not uncommon for a man whose wife is entering the world outside the family, away from his influence and control—but in our case, it was largely my own invention.

I continued to be anxious; Margaret continued to be sensitive to my jittery criticism. In my more rational moments, I approved of what she was trying to do, and said so; but on an unconscious level, I apparently felt differently. In spite of my intentions, I persistently communicated my disapproval of Margaret for "leaving me," as I seemed to anticipate would be the ultimate result of her activities. It was these largely nonverbal messages to which she responded: "Every time you attack me like that, I do something to compromise myself, Gus," she complained. "You've got to stop it!" While some of the sources of our difficulties continued to be hidden, some of them began to be evident. It was soon clear that Margaret did not really have "permission" from her family of origin to be doing what she was doing.

As they enter the job world, women frequently fail to get encouragement from their families of origin. Often it is mothers who send their daughters subtle messages of disapproval. "How are the children?" a mother asks suggestively. If the woman indicates any problems, she will encounter the implication that her children's difficulties are caused by her being away so often. Some mothers give verbal approval, but send confusing nonverbal messages. A woman psychologist said, "When I got my Ph.D., my mother seemed very proud; but my graduation present was—you won't believe this—a Mixmaster!"

Even if a woman's mother isn't opposed to her having a career, the fact of the mother's lifetime example exerts a powerful influence. "I look at my mother's life in relation to my own," one woman said, "and I usually feel guilty. I see what she hasn't experienced, and I feel that I am leaving her behind. I also feel alone in what I'm doing. How many times have I wished that she could understand my problems and give me some help with them."

Whenever we attempt to break with the life-pattern of our parent of the same sex, we have a difficult struggle. Margaret's mother was a talented and intelligent woman: an active community volunteer, an excellent bridge player, and a skilled homemaker. She didn't openly oppose Margaret's having a career, but she offered her little active support.

Margaret's father was another matter. Having lost his own father around the time he was born, Paul grew up feeling responsible for his mother; and he was fiercely protective of his wife and his daughters. Over the phone, Margaret sometimes made the mistake of telling him how busy she was:

"Well, be careful," he would counsel. "You know you're a sucker for anything that needs doing, and you know how you can get run down. If you lose your health—"

"I know, Dad," she would say quickly, with irritation. "If you lose your health, you lose everything."

Margaret had heard this warning since childhood, and she had learned that it could have an insidious, almost hypnotic effect on her. "Whenever he says that, I begin to question whatever I'm doing that he seems to disapprove of. It's amazing how powerful it can be." After one of these conversations with her father, Margaret was extraordinarily alert to any sign of anxiety or disapproval from me about her activities outside our family; and if she found what she anticipated, she exploded. "Why don't you yell at *him* for his unfair tactics?" I countered. "He's part of the problem too!"

"He's an old man, and he wouldn't even understand what I'm talking about," she would reply angrily. "You do understand what you're doing."

"I'm not sure he's so innocent," I argued. "He certainly knows how to get to you."

Whatever part Margaret's father played, I could not deny that I was having difficulty complying with the range of things she was asking of me. Phrases from our arguments kept drifting back accusingly:

"See my vulnerability, my needs. I'm not superhuman."

"Please give me support in doing things outside this family, the way I've supported your career all these years."

"These are your kids too. I want you to take as much responsibility for them as I have."

As we struggled, I became more and more aware of how deeply challenged I felt. What sentient man would not agree with her right to the things she asked for? But forces greater than my rational intent seemed to be prevailing.

I knew that a large part of my difficulty was in my own history, and increasingly I felt the looming presence of my father. Like most traditional fathers, he had not been the kind of husband and father I was trying to become.

"When you were young, your father wanted you kids dressed and fed and ready for bed when he came home," my mother had said once. "He would play with you for a while, and then I would put you to bed, and the two of us would have dinner together. That was what he expected."

As in most traditional families, my father's expectations were a powerful determinant of what happened in our family. He expected to earn a living, and to make the major decisions. When he was home, he helped with the household chores occasionally, but my mother was clearly delegated to raise the children. He was also away a lot: except for a few wonderful furloughs, he was gone for four years during World War II; and for about ten years he was a salesman, home only on weekends.

As I struggled to be a more involved father, and a different kind of husband, I reached for some example to follow, some pattern to lean on. At those moments I felt a great emptiness, a deep sense of absence. The absence of my father. I remembered missing him during the war years, and during the years when he was a traveling salesman. But, like so many fathers, he was not just physically absent. My father was often preoccupied, self-absorbed, emotionally withdrawn; and though sometimes he was simply tired, or worried about his business, his increasingly serious struggles took him away from his family.

Psychological absence of the father is the norm in our culture, and it is often paralleled by physical absence as well. We think there is nothing wrong with a father's being gone during the week on business, or with his being in his study working on his computer when he is home; but his absence from the intimate life of the family does quiet violence to the possibilities for that family, and it ultimately leaves a silent wound in the children who experience that absence. I will describe some of the effects of this legacy in all of us. When men like me decide to try to be more involved fathers, we encounter this vast emptiness; we learn about the father who was not there.

I also began to be aware that I was strangely loyal to the father I had. My pattern of self-preoccupation, of absorption with my work, of inattentiveness to my family's inner life was his. As I attempted to change this pattern, I sensed not only a certain awkwardness and anxiety about this new role, but also a deep resistance to changing the one I knew. In spite of his faults, I still loved my father, and I held on to him as he was.

Puzzling over this struggle with myself, I recalled a time when we were living in Wisconsin. Our children were in elementary school, and I was terribly overextended—doing private practice, teaching, writing, and leading workshops on family therapy around the country. These workshops not only involved travel, but were stressful and draining. One night before a training session, I awoke in a motel room in a small town in Iowa. Outside I could hear the moan of the winter wind, and against the window the quiet hiss of driven snow. Before me was the looming presence of an anxious day, and around me the vast extent of the dark, midwestern winter night. I seemed almost totally alone, bereft, solitary. Then I thought of Margaret, our children, our house. I ached to be at home. Why was I in a motel room in Iowa in the middle of winter? Why was I doing this? Suddenly I thought of my father, and of the years when he had been away from our family. Was this the way he felt when he woke up in an army barracks, or in a motel room? Thinking of him, and of his experience, seemed to help me. He lived through something like this; so could I. At the time my father had been dead for nearly ten years, but I felt strangely close to him. Then I realized that I too was a kind of traveling salesman, out in the hinterlands selling family therapy.

"Why are we loyal to patterns in our parents' lives which we wish had been different?" I asked myself as I thought about this incident. "Why do we repeat again and again some of the most painful aspects of a difficult past?" As we attempt to forge new roles in our lives, these are important questions for both men and women; but since women are being more successful at breaking with their mothers' patterns than their husbands are in altering their fathers' examples, I believe they are especially important in relation to men. Why are we men having such a difficult time changing the role definition, the "life script" that was written by our fathers? Though one could argue that we are not eager to change because we have the advantage of greater power in marriage, and in the society at large, I believe that more complex forces are at work within us. The greatest impediments to changes in our traditional roles seem to lie not in the visible world of conscious intent, but in the murky realm of the unconscious mind. As Margaret and I struggled, it was that anxious, fearful child-within-the-man who seemed to rise within me with such insistent force, and who seemed to hold the answers to the questions which troubled me; and it is that eternal child-person in both of us, men and women, who presents the greatest resistance to change.

As family therapist Ivan Boszormenyi-Nagy has taught many of us through his pioneering work, *Invisible Loyalties*, we are intensely loyal to our parents. In spite of the pain we experienced at our parents' hands, we cling tenaciously to their views of life; and their examples of what it is to be a man or a woman follow us throughout life. Acknowledging the power of our loyalty to them, and especially our loyalty to our same-sex parent, is only the beginning of our journey to improve upon their model; but it is at least a first step.

The sources of inequity in marriage are of course much more complex than the patterns of narcissism and giving that I have described in this chapter. We need to examine a number of other topics that are related to this area, among them that difficult to define but critical variable, power. But we also need a deeper look beneath the visible patterns in marriage to the forces in the childhood family which prepare and coerce us all to play the parts we play. Our aim is to develop what family therapist Norman Paul has called "gender empathy," or a kind of informed compassion for these old and often painful postures of humanity which we name male and female.

5

Metaphors of Closeness and Distance

ONE EVENING AFTER SHE had put their daughter Amy to bed, Joyce Olson asked her husband, Thomas, "Would you like some coffee?"

"Sure," he answered, looking up from the easy chair where he was watching a basketball game on television. "Decaf?" he added routinely.

A few minutes later Joyce returned with a tray bearing two cups of coffee and a plate of cookies. "Shall we sit over here?" she asked cheerily, putting the tray down on the coffee table by the nearby sofa.

"Just a minute, hon," Thomas said vacantly, continuing to look at his game. "It's almost half time."

Joyce sat down on the sofa, poured milk in their coffee, and folded her arms. After maybe a minute, she sighed loudly. "It's getting cold," she said with a trace of irritation.

"It's almost over," Thomas repeated. Joyce sighed again, and began drinking her coffee.

Finally, after what seemed to Joyce like several minutes, Thomas rose from his chair and joined her on the sofa. The television set was still on, and as he sat down, Thomas glanced at it. Joyce sighed again.

"Thomas . . ." she said, with definite annoyance.

"All right, all right. I'm sorry," he said defensively. "It's a very tight game."

"I just wanted us to talk," Joyce said.

Opening his arms demonstratively, Thomas smiled, "I'm here. Let's talk."

"Funny." Joyce smiled also. "How long do I have?"

"All of half time," he said. "How was your day?"

Deciding to ignore her increasing distress, Joyce said, "It wasn't the best day I ever had."

"What was the matter?" he said.

Joyce took a deep breath. "Sarah wasn't there—she was sick—and I had to do some things I don't usually have to. She had forgotten to order some I.V. needles, and I had to get them in, and there were also some equipment problems. When you are responsible for these very sick heart patients, you shouldn't have to take time for that kind of thing. I know when she comes back and I mention it, she will get very defensive and feel like I'm picking on her, but . . ." Thomas had glanced back at the television set, where a coach was being interviewed. "Would you mind if we cut that thing off for a while?" Joyce said, feeling annoyed again.

"Then I won't know when the game comes on again." Realizing that was the wrong thing to say, Thomas quickly changed his mind. "Okay," he said, going over to the set and turning it off. "I'm sorry."

Still fighting her anger, Joyce tried again. "Where was I? Oh, Sarah's absence. I don't know what to do with her; she's so prickly about criticism." Thomas still seemed distracted. "You seem preoccupied," she said sympathetically. "Is something wrong?"

"No, not really," he said without conviction.

"You're sure?" Joyce prodded. "It must be something other than this game."

"Well, maybe it is. Work too, I suppose. You know, the same old issues." He didn't seem inclined to continue.

"I'm not sure what those would be," she said hopefully.

"Money. What else do I worry about?" He seemed slightly irritated at her questioning.

"How would I know? You don't talk about it." As Thomas felt Joyce's pressure to talk about his worries, he seemed guarded.

"What is there to talk about? I have a big grant application pending, and several of my research positions are dependent on it. I'd hate to let some of those people go."

"Thomas, how would I have known that you were worried about that? I was feeling angry because it seemed like the game was so damned important." She was trying to be understanding. "If you would only tell me what's going on . . ."

"Look," he said, "watching a game on television is one way I can avoid thinking about things I can't change." Joyce later recalled feeling that at that moment a door slammed shut.

Having failed to get Thomas to listen to her dilemmas, or to talk about his own, she didn't know where to turn. She decided to try one final avenue. "Could I change the subject?"

"Fine with me."

"Did you notice that Amy was fretful tonight? I'm concerned about her."

"And?" Thomas still seemed distant, and he was now irritated.

"I'm just worried about her, that's all. She spends so much time with Annie. I was a lot older when my mother went to work, and she didn't have the kinds of hours I do." Joyce sighed. "I just wish that I had more flexibility in my job, or fewer hours, or that *something* would give me more time with her."

Thomas recognized the issue instantly. Joyce would work the conversation around to the fact that his schedule was more flexible than hers, and she would want him to come home earlier and take over Amy's care. The very thought of that possibility raised his anxiety. He needed the late-afternoon time to meet with his research team; he wanted somehow to dodge this conversation. "Look, I'm sorry you're worried about her. I really am. I wish we could do something about it." Thinking about the game, he glanced again at the television set.

Seeing the last of her efforts fail, Joyce sighed and said, "You're thinking about the game again. Maybe you'd better watch it."

"I'm sure half time is over," he said apologetically.

Rising from the sofa with the tray, Joyce felt a roil of tension in her chest, and though she didn't pause to name the feelings, they were a mixture of hurt and anger. As she walked to the kitchen and began putting the dishes in the dishwasher, she could see Thomas through the open door to the family room. For a moment it seemed that she was watching someone else's husband. He seemed hypnotized, enclosed in his own life; she was an outsider.

As she climbed the stairs to their bedroom, Joyce felt the fatigue come on, a great hollow heaviness. By the time she reached the top step, her legs seemed barely able to oppose the great weight that bore down upon her. With a final effort she moved down the long, narrow hall, stopping at the door to Amy's room. In the soft glow of the night light, Amy seemed infinitely tender and valuable, the slight rise and fall of her breathing coming in gentle waves. Just seeing Amy loosened something in Joyce's chest, and walking over to her crib, she felt her own breathing come easier. For several minutes she stood over Amy, loving her, watching her sleep. Then she felt the sadness of their situation: the morning coming, and the other needy ones lying there in that tense nursery of tubes and monitors, waiting for her. She put her hand very gently on Amy's head.

Going into their bedroom, Joyce undressed slowly in the dark. Then she turned on the radio beside the bed, feeling grateful for the music that surrounded her. Was it Mozart, or Haydn? She lay there for a long time, not really listening, thinking that she should go to sleep.

In the family room, Thomas tried to reinterest himself in the game, but his attention wandered. Joyce's words kept drifting back; as he heard them, he felt increasingly guilty. She had tried to talk to him, and he had been difficult. He could have spent some time with her—listened better, at least. Why did he have such difficulty doing that? If only he wouldn't get angry when she tried to get him to talk.

With a vague sense of foreboding, Thomas realized that he had heard this kind of complaint in the past. Before she became so quiet and withdrawn, his first wife would also try to draw him out. Then he thought of Sally's affair, and of the catastrophic end of their marriage. Suddenly he felt anxious about what had happened between him and Joyce. With a wave of tenderness for her, he wondered if she were still awake; if there were some way to repair the evening.

When Thomas entered the bedroom, he thought that Joyce had fallen asleep. After quietly undressing, he turned off the radio. Then, lying in bed, he felt her stir beside him. "You awake?" he said softly.

"Yes," she replied distantly.

"You okay?" he asked.

"Not really."

"What's wrong?"

"Just feeling blue about things." Then, after a long silence, she added, "Would you hold me?"

"Sure." Cheerily. Joyce wondered if his team had won.

Thomas moved over beside her, and enclosed her in his arms. Feeling the warmth of his familiar embrace, for the first time that evening she felt hopeful. Maybe now, like this, she could sleep. Maybe she wouldn't think of that benign, awful bell that meant that one of her patients was at the edge of dying.

Then Thomas shifted an arm from around her and folded it against her chest. Slowly, he moved his hand across her breast. Disbelieving, she stirred uneasily. He then moved his hand, and put it with unmistakable pressure between her legs.

Without warning to herself or to him, Joyce began to sob—great, heaving, undeniable sobs that rose in waves from the deepest part of her.

"I don't understand," was all Thomas could manage.

At the next interview, it took us some time to reconstruct this story, which was not unfamiliar to us. Almost every couple experiences a version of this pursuit–distance agony. A great many women would like to have greater verbal intimacy with their partners. They would like the men they love to listen to their feelings, or talk about their own, or both. They would like to do with men what they can often do with their friends: sit down face to face and open up their lives, diving into a warm and enveloping atmosphere of honest talk. Their hopes, fears, fantasies, prohibitions, angers—with the best of friends, it all comes out. And having immersed themselves in each other's lives, they both feel better.

When women try to do this with men, they are often greeted by the kind of stubborn resistance that Joyce met in Thomas. Not only is he too preoccupied to hear her dilemmas very well—he may give her some well-meaning advice, but little else—but when she asks about his feelings, he balks. Why is he so resistant? Does he really believe that the best way to deal with his problems is to try to forget about them, or to think about them while he works at his work-bench or at his computer?

Women who encounter this resistance to verbal intimacy in men are usually puzzled at first, then hurt, and finally enraged. It usually takes women several years to reach rage. Along the way, their almost inveterate helpfulness exacerbates the problem.

As soon as they see the problems their partners are having dealing with their feelings, many women try to teach their recalcitrant charges about communication. "It's simple," they say in many different ways, "all you have to do is sit down, face each other, and say what you feel." Like Joyce, they set the stage properly, and assume that with a little encouragement, their partners will respond.

When their partners balk, many women just try harder. They explain in more detail, and they apply more pressure. "Surely if I can do this, he can too." Scheming to create ideal conditions, they plan their words carefully; they may even leave books on communication in conspicuous places.

When a man's wife begins a systematic campaign to teach him about his feelings, he smells a trap. The words she uses, the stance she takes (helpful, didactic), the pressure she applies—all identify her to his unconscious mind as a member of the older generation. He may not be able to give words to his fears, but alarm bells sound: they signal *mother*. And so he resists.

The forces that cast men and women in these tragically antagonistic roles are not produced entirely by social norms. While it is true that from an early age males in our culture are discouraged from revealing their vulnerability, and that females are encouraged to be emotionally open and disclosing, certain dynamics of the childhood family also contribute powerfully to these dilemmas.

THE PURSUER   In all outward respects, this individual is unremittingly enthusiastic about emotional closeness. Like Joyce, she talks about wanting an intimate relationship, and is forever strategizing to achieve this goal. She is expansive, and wants to cross emotional boundaries between herself and others. In addition to desiring closeness, she also fears rejection. Because her efforts have met with disappointment, her anxious, irritable approach to her partner partly engenders the very response which she fears.

Not all pursuers are women. To my knowledge no one has surveyed a large number of couples to determine the percentages of men and women who occupy this role, but a significant proportion of men are in the seeking, pursuing position in their marriages.

Nor does all pursuit take place in the verbal, conversational realm. In most marriages, there is a sexual pursuer: someone who frequently attempts to initiate sexual activity. Just as "verbal" pursuit is more common in women, sexual pursuit is more common in men. We later learned that Thomas's ill-timed advance was not an isolated incident. While Joyce pressured him to be verbally intimate, he constantly pressured her to be sexually responsive. And each stubbornly refused to give in to the other.

The Pursuer often grew up in one of two family situations:

As an "overhelped" child. This person is the "reassurance junkie" who expects to be hovered over and constantly attended to. In marriage, this kind of pursuer is simply expressing his or her addiction to attention.

As a rejected child. Most pursuers are in search of the emotional support that they did not receive as children. Many different family situations can produce this neediness, but the common result in adulthood is the kind of anxious pursuit which contains the inherent prediction of defeat. "I want closeness, but I fear rejection." We certainly had plenty of evidence of a rejection issue in Joyce's childhood.

Many women struggle with both sets of dynamics. They may have been overinvolved with their mothers, and, based on that relationship, may expect an unrealistic level of intimacy in marriage. They may also have had traumatic rejection experiences. A great many women have deficiencies in their relationships with their fathers, and bring these emotional needs to marriage.

THE DISTANCER This individual seeks separateness, autonomy, and containment. He seems to enjoy solitary experience, and may be focused on work and on dealing with physical objects. He values boundaries, and may constantly place them between himself and his partner. In the classical cartoon image he reads the newspaper at the breakfast table while his furious wife attempts to circumvent this thin but impermeable barrier. Today he may be absorbed in his computer, or, like Thomas, in television.

Just as the pursuer fears rejection, the distancer fears invasion. He is keenly sensitive to emotional intrusion; but his very fears contain the prediction that it will occur. In fact, he sometimes seems to cultivate the intrusiveness he abhors.

Some people remain emotionally distant out of habit. They grew up in families where there wasn't much closeness, and they are uncomfortable when their partner attempts to be close to them. Intimacy simply seems alien.

Other distancers grew up with an emotionally intrusive parent. They avoid closeness because when they were children it came at a high price. "If I let my mother know that I was upset about something," one man said, "it was like inviting an ambulance into your house. She would come roaring in with all kinds of help. I soon learned to keep my problems to myself." Another man spoke about his mother's interest in his romantic life when he was a teenager: "My mother was too interested in what I did with girls. She would find out I was dating someone, and before I knew it she had met the girl's parents and was tracking my every move. After a while, I kept my interests a secret. I suppose I began to live a double life."

Many men struggle with a difficult combination of rejection and intrusion in their early relationships with their mothers. They do not feel genuinely "understood" by their mothers, and they also feel subject to periodic invasion by their mothers' emotional needs, a situation that is ideal for producing a need for, but also a fear of, intimacy.

In the days that followed Joyce and Thomas's painful encounter, they barely spoke. Joyce retreated, going woodenly through her daily activities. Now it was Thomas who tried to get a conversation going; but it seemed too late. "Am I going to get divorced a second time?" he asked himself. By the time they arrived for their next appointment, Thomas looked very worried, and Joyce sat passively in her chair: pale, distant, deeply discouraged.

Our first task was to try to restore the couple's morale. As we listened to the story, we pointed out that both had felt the disappointment and the hurt. We also said, "This 'dance' may have met certain needs in your lives in the past, but it has clearly become so unsatisfying that you have made it apparent to yourselves it must change." The implication was that they had unconsciously "scheduled" this bruising experience to dramatize the need for change.

"I don't understand how this kind of thing could meet anybody's needs," Thomas said skeptically. Joyce looked vacantly out the window, saying nothing.

"Not the fight," I said a little defensively, "but the pattern. Joyce's pursuing you for closeness, and your retreating." Deliberately ignoring his sexual pursuit of Joyce, I assumed we would deal with it later.

"What do you mean?" Thomas was still puzzled.

"The pattern gives Joyce a familiar way to make contact with you. She knows how to reach out. It also gives you, Thomas, the sense of being needed, of being sought out." I knew I would not be believed.

"What I usually want is to be left alone more," Thomas protested.

"Consciously, yes. I know that." In this kind of pattern, we assume that the couple's overt behavior does in fact meet a need in both partners. Thomas complains about Joyce's pursuit, but part of him needs her to do the very thing he objects to. She protests his distancing, but relies on it. This open, acknowledged conflict engages them in ways that are familiar, if painful; it also protects them from facing hidden issues that are more difficult for both of them. At the moment, however, there was no point in trying to convince either of them on this issue.

"What you need to know," Margaret said, "is that the pattern has already begun to change. Thomas has been seeking you out, Joyce."

Joyce stirred, a flicker of expression in her face. "If I have to go through *that* to get him to pay attention to me, it's not worth it."

"Of course not," Margaret countered. "There is an easier way."

"I would like to know it," Joyce said flatly.

"Well, you may not like it, because it involves your doing some work," Margaret said with a smile.

"If you ask me to try to get more response from Thomas, I can't do that." There was a note of defiance in her voice.

Margaret smiled. "It's the opposite kind of task." Thomas looked curious.

I recognized the tack Margaret was taking, and it is one most therapists who work with this pattern have learned to take. As I moved to join her, I borrowed a strategy from family therapist Phil Guerin who—in collaboration with his colleagues at the Center for Family Learning in New Rochelle, New York—has written most clearly about the treatment of this dilemma.

Margaret said, "What if you assumed that for the time being, Thomas needs emotional space in his life. If you agreed to give him that distance, at least he wouldn't feel pressured, and you wouldn't be constantly disappointed."

Joyce was still impassive. "How would that be different from the way it is now?"

Glancing at me, Margaret continued, "We would try to give you support in changing your step in this complicated dance. We think you would be happier if you got a sense that you could control more of what happens to you. Right now, you probably feel that a great deal depends on how Thomas responds to you."

Joyce nodded affirmatively. "It does depend on him."

"Can you see the position that puts you in?" Margaret said.

"Yes, a dependent position." A thoughtful silence. "So how can I change that? What would you like me to do?" she said a little warily.

I volunteered, "We would like you to stop doing anything to pursue Thomas. You wouldn't try to set up situations for the two of you to talk; you wouldn't approach him in any way for intimate contact." Then I added, "Instead, you would turn to other things to occupy yourself—do jobs around the house, read, attend to your work; and if you get lonely, which you will, you should rely on your women friends for support. If it gets really bad, you can call us."

"I think I can do this," Joyce said a little bitterly. "I certainly don't feel like chasing him anymore."

"Good!" Margaret said enthusiastically.

"Do I have to do anything?" Thomas asked.

"No, you get a break," I said. "For a while, at least, you get what you've wanted." Thomas looked relieved at the thought of not having any more "intimate conversations," but he remained worried about the breach between him and Joyce. I assured him that this change would help Joyce feel better about him and about herself.

In assigning this "homework," we were attempting to alter their marital system by helping Joyce learn to control her own compulsive pursuit of Thomas. We were also following a maxim laid down by both Phil Guerin and Tom Fogarty: "Never pursue a distancer." If we had teamed up with Joyce and put pressure on Thomas to be more open and intimate, he would have resisted us in the same way he was resisting Joyce.

At the next session Joyce looked less depressed, but somewhat perplexed. "It was a good week in some ways," she said seriously. "I felt relieved at not trying to get anything emotional from Thomas, and it was helpful to know that I could call you. Actually, I did call a friend a couple of times. I was surprised at how difficult it was to stop chasing him. Often I would catch myself about to suggest that we talk, or something like that. When I tried to resist doing it, I got very anxious."

"Do you know what you were anxious about?" Margaret asked.

"I was afraid that if I didn't reach out to him, there would be nothing between us. A great void."

Margaret said, "How did you deal with the anxiety?"

"A couple of times I slipped. I did try to get him talking to me. Then I caught myself, and went and took care of Amy, or did something else. But the urge to pursue Thomas was very strong."

"When you think about this anxiety," I said, "does it make sense as a larger issue in your life—the feeling that if you don't reach out, work hard, try to please others, you will be alone, with no support?"

"I suppose so," she said thoughtfully. "It must be what I decided as a child: that I had to do the work if I was going to get anything." This was exactly what we had hoped she would see.

I continued, "So if you don't constantly seek support, you will get nothing. That's your theory about people."

"Sounds silly, doesn't it?" she laughed nervously.

"It wasn't silly when you were a girl," I said, feeling empathy for the child who had made such a decision. "You need to learn now, however, that you aren't helpless the way you were then." Joyce had replicated in her marriage that sense of helpless, frustrated dependency which she had experienced as a child; and in encouraging her to learn to take care of herself, including turning to others for support when she needed it, we were essentially saying to her: "Things are different now. You can control your own destiny." This exercise was a therapeutic metaphor for taking adult control of her life.

For the remainder of that session, we encouraged Joyce to continue her strategy in creating more autonomy from Thomas; we also checked in with him. Though he encouraged her, he sounded worried about Joyce's efforts.

At the next session, Joyce again seemed depressed. "It really helped when I called you," she said to Margaret. "I was feeling that panic again, as I said, and just talking to you calmed me down. I guess I lost it. I thought I was doing pretty well, but all of a sudden I was back at my old routine, begging Thomas for attention. And of course he started watching television, right on cue."

"Were you able to stop pursuing him after we talked?" Margaret asked.

"Yes. I'm a little worried that I may be using Amy as a security blanket," she added. "But it really helps to have her to take care of."

"I would be concerned if that were a long-term solution for you," Margaret said confidently. "But right now it's all right. In fact, it's an apt metaphor. You really are learning to take care of the child aspect of yourself, and taking care of your literal child isn't a bad way to symbolize that goal."

Both partners get anxious when they begin to change a pattern, and they often revert to their old habits. We simply encouraged Joyce to continue her efforts.

At the following meeting, Joyce seemed calm and rather cheerful. "It was a good week for me," she reported. "I got caught up on some paperwork, and spent more time with Amy."

Thomas, however, did not look at all happy. He sat dejectedly at his end of the sofa, saying little. "You look depressed," I said.

"I am," was all he offered.

"What's the matter?" I asked seriously.

"I don't know. Work is shitty; we didn't get the grant; there's nothing going on at home for me." He didn't seem inclined to continue.

"What do you mean, 'nothing going on at home'?" I asked.

"Well, Joyce is doing great. She goes out with her friends; she calls Margaret when she is upset. I never see her."

"That's not true, Thomas," Joyce countered. "I went out with Ann once for a glass of wine. You and I do see each other."

"For what reason do we see each other?" Thomas said with a tone of irony. "There's nothing happening when we do."

"How do you feel about that?" I asked matter-of-factly.

"Bad. It's lousy. It's like living with a stranger."

Not only did Thomas look depressed, but he seemed angry as well—a muffled, pouty anger.

"I'm worried about him," Joyce said solicitously. "I can tell that what I am doing is affecting him, and I feel guilty."

"Yeah, I guess I am upset about all of this. I'm having trouble sleeping at night, which never happens to me."

Margaret addressed Joyce: "You're tempted to try to take care of him, aren't you?"

"Yes," Joyce said sheepishly. Another of those convergences, Margaret obviously seeing in Joyce her own temptations.

"It would be a mistake," Margaret said resolutely.

I spoke to Thomas. "Thomas, I think I understand what you are going through. You probably feel abandoned by Joyce."

"I suppose I do, though I hadn't thought of it in exactly those words. I certainly do feel the distance."

"And what do you think you are trying to do about the distance?" I asked.

"Live with it, I guess."

I smiled. "If I know anything about this situation, and I think I do, I think something else is going on. I think unconsciously you are trying to get Joyce to give up her new behavior—to feel sorry for you, and to get her to start seeking you out and trying to please you again. There is a little-boy quality in your reaction. Can you feel it? Can you hear yourself saying, 'Please feel sorry for me'?"

A thoughtful silence. "I suppose you could be right. But why would I do that?"

"Because you have relied on her pursuing you—maybe more than you realized." He seemed exposed, embarrassed. Then I saw that vacant, absent expression that he sometimes got, as if he were totally alone, unnoticed and unnoticing. It was what Joyce called his "tuned-out look."

"I sometimes see this expression you have now," I said to him. "You look as if no one notices you."

"I suppose I sometimes feel that way," he said resignedly.

"Is it a familiar feeling from childhood?"

"Yes, I guess. I did feel at times that I was not noticed." I remembered his being a middle child, between two girls, with a critical, absent father. I had an image of myself at about fourteen, wandering alone in the woods with my dog and a rifle, feeling lonely.

"And at other times your mother was quite intrusive, possessive?"

"It seemed to be one or the other," he said. "And I think the possessiveness came later, when I was a teenager. As a kid, I spent a lot of time alone."

"See," I said, "I think you have needed Joyce to seek you out—because you didn't get enough nurturant parenting as a kid. It is understandable that you have relied on her."

"But embarrassing," he said.

"Well," I said, "the way to change it is not by this kind of manipulation to get her back into her old role. You need to work on your needs for parenting with me and Margaret, and to begin in adult ways to reach out to Joyce." It is something he would not have heard several weeks previously. Now he seemed to be listening.

"How do I reach out to her?" It seemed like a genuine question. "I'm not used to doing that."

"I know you're not," I said sympathetically. "And it carries a feeling of risk, of possibly getting rejected. But you need to try it anyway. Find out what she would like, and begin to do it." Then I added: "You could do some of the things she has done in the past—set up some circumstances in which there could be more intimacy between you. Get tickets to a concert, and invite her to go. Take over putting Amy to bed, then fix her a cup of coffee and invite her to sit down and talk. When she shares something, just listen to her feelings; don't give her advice."

"It sounds like a big order," he said with a sigh.

A long, thoughtful silence. "What are you thinking?" I asked curiously.

"About the subject of intimacy between us." He seemed reluctant to continue.

"What about it?" I said.

"Well, see, I have suggested several times that we get a sitter for Amy and go away for a weekend at a hotel somewhere, and, you know, have a romantic getaway. I thought this was reaching out to her, but Joyce resists doing it."

Margaret had been silent for a while, and she now responded to Thomas. "I would guess she resists because this kind of weekend brings up the sexual area of your relationship, and introduces those problems."

"Exactly," Joyce said. "What that says to me is 'Let's go somewhere and have sex all weekend.' "

"What's wrong with that, I want to know?" Thomas said angrily.

"Thomas," I intervened. "You are introducing a whole new issue. We can work on your sexual relationship, but right now you are bringing it up as a way to resist looking at and changing your behavior."

He looked chagrined. "I suppose you are right."

I continued, "Later, when Joyce is less angry, a discussion of your sexual relationship will go better. If you are more attentive to Joyce, she will be much more responsive to you sexually."

"When other things improve between us, I would be glad to work on our sex life," Joyce said. "I'm not happy with it either."

As we ended that session, we encouraged Joyce to respond to any nonsexual initiatives by Thomas. For the time being, they were to put off trying to change their sexual relationship.

The couple's progress was not smooth. In the following weeks there was further conflict; and several times they reverted to their old pursuit–distance pattern. But there was improvement, especially as Thomas began to rely on Margaret and me for advice and support. He got season tickets to a concert series, and he and Joyce began going out to dinner before the concerts. He also took over Amy's bedtime, and he and Joyce would then settle down and watch television together. We encouraged them to sit close to each other on the sofa, which pleased Thomas. For the time being they seemed much happier.

In every marriage, both partners are anxious about intimacy, and both unconsciously "cooperate" in regulating the quality of togetherness. In Joyce and Thomas's marriage, she "specialized" in promoting verbal intimacy, while he "took charge of" promoting sexual intimacy. Some couples alternate positions in this dance. As long as one person is unavailable, the other will pursue; but as soon as intimacy begins to develop, the pursuer will turn and run, as the distancer becomes the pursuer. This dance can move back and forth in rapid oscillation; the only constant is that someone is always moving away. Carl Whitaker has said, "The marital temperature rarely changes; we just alternate turning the thermostat down."

But in attempting closeness with someone we care about, we all encounter the same dilemma: intimacy involves being vulnerable. In an intimate exchange, we risk revealing the hurt, angry, needy, lustful, tender, affectionate, emotional "child" aspect of ourselves. Our first and primary model for intimacy was created in the profoundly vulnerable and unequal parent-child relationship, and we intuitively fear repetition of the injuries that this "child" experienced at the hands of our parents. The major dangers were two: that we would be abandoned or rejected; or that we would be overwhelmed and swallowed up in closeness, and lose our identities. These two fears, of rejection and intrusion, account for most of our caution.

It was several sessions before the question of sex came up again. Thomas had been working hard to be more attentive to Joyce, and was succeeding. He was fathering Amy more effectively, and doing some of the cooking. As he began to face some of what he had not been given as a child, he also had several bouts of depression; but he had been able to lean more on Margaret and me for support during such times. And Joyce was battling effectively against her addiction to emotional pursuit.

"I can't complain," Joyce said one day, smiling. "He's doing great."

Thomas smiled back, but said nothing. "What's the matter?" I asked him. "Can't you take a compliment?"

"It's not that," he said hesitantly.

"What is it, then?"

"It's that I can't return it. I can't say I'm that happy." After a pause, he added: "I'm glad we're getting along better; don't get me wrong. But some things haven't changed as much as I'd like. They're better, but not good enough for me."

"Are you talking about sex?" I asked.

"Yes."

Joyce looked anxious.

"Would you agree to talk about this now?" Margaret asked Joyce.

"I suppose so," she said reluctantly.

Thomas outlined his complaint. "The thing that bothers me the most is that I am always the one to initiate; and often as not, Joyce says no. Sometimes she doesn't say anything; she just pulls back physically, and I feel like some kind of, I don't know, brute."

"Do you feel rejected then?" I asked. He agreed that he did.

Joyce seemed extremely uncomfortable, as though this area were "her problem." "The difficulty for me, Thomas, is that you are always ready to have sex; or it seems that way to me. If we hug, I feel guarded. The next moment you are going to be feeling me up, and the minute after that we will be in bed—if I let it happen. It's a constant sense of pressure. I feel that if I let down, you will just move in."

"And I feel that if I don't keep trying, nothing will ever happen."

Margaret turned toward Thomas. "You don't think that if you waited, she would eventually approach you?"

He looked askance at Joyce. "How many times does it happen? I think I could count the times on one hand."

"I never got the chance, Thomas." Joyce was irritated.

As in the couple's other pursuit–distance pattern, each occupied an entrenched position. Thomas was constantly searching for any indication that Joyce was willing to make love; and feeling crowded and pressured, Joyce usually kept her defenses up. Another classic dilemma between women and men, and a difficult cycle to change.

In addition to the discharge of tension through orgasmic release, sexual experience provides a deep immersion in body contact. This body-to-body meeting—which often involves several forms of oral contact—leaves both partners feeling literally swaddled in physical warmth. For a few moments, at least, we are able to return to some of the primitive sense of nurturance which we experienced as infants. Certain aspects of adult sexual experience, then, form an "experiential analogue" to being nursed, held, and securely protected.

This beneficent regression is especially significant for men, who have often been denied—for a variety of reasons—certain dependency needs. Men have learned to focus some of these needs on the sexual experience. Not many men dare to say to their wives, "Please hold me," but they do risk saying, "Let's go to bed."

Even then, this entreaty is ambivalent. Like Thomas, many of us approach our partners with rough, too-eager hands that predict and partially engender the very rejection which we fear. Some of our ambivalence is about sex itself. Some of the anxiety is also about nurturance. Secretly fearful of rejection, we have learned to predict it. When we get rejected sexually, it really hurts. Just as our needs for emotional support are focused on sexual satisfaction, our vulnerability to rejection is expressed around sexual turndown. "Unfair!" we cry out, and the echoes of this cry resound through many areas of our lives.

Sex, then, is for many of us a kind of addiction. Like alcohol—which also produces a euphoric, boundaryless sense of being swaddled in warmth, and which men abuse much more frequently than women—it is a compulsive, indirect way of meeting a more basic need. In this case, for acceptance, nurturance, support.

"Thomas," I said. He looked at me dubiously. "Can you see the problem in the way you are approaching Joyce? It sounds as if you come at her in a way that is almost designed to turn her off, or at least to put her on the defensive."

"Like making a pass at me when I'm trying to take care of Amy," Joyce interrupted.

Margaret's tone was slightly critical. "Joyce, you're rescuing him. Let Gus deal with this."

"I'm sorry," Joyce said.

I began again: "Thomas, when I do something like this—push Margaret too hard, or at the wrong time—it's usually because I am anxious about sex."

"I'm anxious about not getting it," he said with a smile. I decided not to argue with him about his sexual anxieties, since Joyce's reluctance in effect protected him from being more aware of them. Until she felt freer to approach him, he would continue to believe that the anxiety was all hers.

I said seriously: "You have the same problem with feeling rejected that Joyce has, only you experience it in a different area of your relationship."

"True," he answered rather flatly.

"If you'd like to change this pattern, I can suggest a way," I said. "It involves your doing some work."

"What do I do?" he said hopefully.

"I would suggest that you back off from exerting *any* pressure on Joyce sexually. That you turn over all control, all initiation of sex, to her." After a pause I added, "For the time being."

After a moment of silence, Thomas said warily, "I don't think it will work, but I'm willing to try it."

"Not just try it; do it." Firmly. "Wait for her to approach you."

Turning to Joyce, Margaret said: "Your part of the agreement would be to begin to move toward him—at your pace, using your own timing. And if you feel anxious about anything that is happening, say so. You would have the prerogative of stopping at any time. And I would suggest that you exercise that prerogative if you feel uncomfortable."

"So she is completely in control," Thomas said with that sly smile again. "Think I'm safe?"

"Making a joke of this sounds like anxiety to me," I said to him.

"I'm sorry," he said, changing his tone. We spent the remainder of the session coaching the couple on making this shift in their pattern, and I told Thomas that the success of the experiment depended in large measure on his honoring his part of the agreement. He was to give Joyce total control.

At the next session, which happened to be two weeks later, Joyce looked very upset. After the initial pleasantries, Margaret asked her what the matter was.

"It went well at first. Thomas was very good. He just backed way off, and I began to feel much more relaxed. We had some heavy petting sessions, which were fun. It was a little like being in high school again, where I did feel very much in control." A pause, during which she looked at Thomas for reassurance. He smiled, a warm, caring smile for a change. "Then I decided to get more adventurous, and make a real pass at him. Seduce him, as it were." Another wait.

"And?" Margaret encouraged her.

"I had a terrible anxiety attack. I couldn't breathe; I thought for a while I might die. It was really awful."

"I'm sorry," Margaret said. "Do you have any idea what happened?"

"I haven't the foggiest. It just came out of nowhere."

The room was quiet, Margaret and I wondering to ourselves how to deal with this development. Fortunately, Thomas was not saying "I told you so." He looked genuinely concerned about Joyce.

"Have you ever had anxiety attacks like this before?" Margaret said gently.

"From time to time. And they usually are associated in some way with sex. Maybe the issue is my taking the initiative." Thinking, turning inward for reasons. She seemed apologetic for having this difficulty.

Margaret began to probe. "When you think about what you learned about sex growing up in your family, what kind of attitude do you think was communicated about a woman's taking the initiative sexually?"

"I don't remember anything being said about it. Nothing was ever said about sex in my family. Nothing." Still thinking. "My mother was very proper; I suspect she never did that—take initiative."

Margaret said, "Do you think your father felt frustrated sexually?"

"I would certainly guess so. In fact, he said as much to me."

"He talked to you about his sexual relationship with your mother?" Margaret said with concern.

"Yes. It made me very uncomfortable."

"How old were you when that was happening?" Margaret queried.

"Thirteen, fourteen." Joyce seemed troubled by the thoughts she was having.

"That was unfair," Margaret said gently.

"It felt unfair," Joyce said, looking anxious. "I often had the distinct feeling that I had to set the limits with my father. I don't think I ever let myself think about what worried me, but the feeling was, If you don't set the limits with him, something bad could happen. I guess it was his flirtatiousness with me, his talking to me in that confessional way."

Margaret said, "And did anything really inappropriate ever happen?"

Joyce hesitated for a moment, then said definitely, "No, it didn't."

I said to her, "So as a young teenager, you couldn't play that usually harmless game of learning to flirt with your father. That's how many girls practice their sexuality; and if the parents have a good sexual relationship, it's not a problem. But your parents didn't have that."

"No, they didn't," Joyce said sadly.

Margaret looked skeptically at Joyce. "Joyce," she said, "when I asked if anything inappropriate had happened with your father, you hesitated. Why do you think you did that?"

"I was thinking," she said defensively, "trying to remember."

"Are you sure you weren't remembering something?"

Joyce looked as though Margaret had struck her. Her face was pale, her breathing shallow. After a long and extraordinarily uncomfortable silence, she sighed a long breath of resignation. "I've never been sure it really happened. It seemed so unreal."

Margaret said, very warmly, "If you can't talk about it now, I could meet with you separately, Joyce."

"No," Joyce said, again with resignation. "I want to get it over with." There was a wait as she thought. "When I was about sixteen, I went with my father to look at a piece of land that a friend had offered to sell him. It was way out in the country, and the friend had to leave early." Another pause. "We were walking in the woods, and my father put his hand on my breast. That's all that happened."

"What did you do?" Margaret said.

"I said, 'Daddy, what are you doing?' and he apologized as if he

113

hadn't realized what he had done." Another sigh, this one of relief. "There, I've told it."

"Is there anything else you didn't say?" Margaret said hesitantly.

"No, that's it. The strange thing is that neither of us ever spoke of it again. It was as if it hadn't happened." She added, as if it was an afterthought: "But that was when the anxiety attacks began. I had the first one that summer."

"It's no wonder you have difficulty taking the initiative sexually with Thomas," Margaret said. "What happened to you was very unfair."

"Yeah, keeping my guard up seems very familiar." She was crying.

We of course worked further on Joyce's early trauma, which was really only the most overt incident in a long history of subtle, sexualized pressure from her father. Just talking about this history provided Joyce with some immediate relief, and allowed her to make some progress with Thomas. Just as Thomas had to struggle to overcome his anxieties about verbal intimacy, Joyce had to muster her courage to delve into her own fears of sexual closeness.

The tasks that we assign in this "behavioral" stage of therapy sometimes produce rapid change in a couple's interaction, but they also point to the deeper issues that have created these patterns. As these problems come to light, they lead us to work which is more serious, and more ambitious: the job of rewriting history.

6

Metaphors of Power and Vulnerability

DOES ANYONE NOT REMEMBER the joys of that improvised, splinter-ridden fulcrum of Saturday pleasure, the seesaw? The delight in finding someone roughly our own weight, and after getting the board balanced between us, practicing sending them up into the sky, and then being pulled ourselves up to the same dizzying height, then down, then up again, augmenting and amplifying these movements by synchronous pushes until we made the board bounce? Then practicing the subtleties: balancing precariously at dead center; sliding treacherously forward as we let our partner crash with a thud to the ground; sliding suddenly back on the board to leave him stranded in the air; learning the precise leverage necessary to ride with someone heavier than we. And, most critically, learning that sustaining this almost sexual ecstasy required both our efforts. Once we got stranded in one position, the fun was over.

So it is with marriage: if we get trapped in one psychological situation, the fun is over. In the realm of power and vulnerability, we have a strong tendency to become immobilized in our respective positions.

When we were children, almost all of our safety and protection came from the profoundly unequal relationship with our parents, but especially from the bond with our mother. As adults, we tend to deal with some of life's insecurity by structuring our relationships hierarchically. John, a middle-aged client, describes a recent visit to his family of origin: "When I saw my brother at Thanksgiving, my older brother, that is, he said . . ." Noticing my smile, he smiles back, and resumes his story. What amuses me is that John's "older" brother is his identical twin, born twenty minutes before he was. I understand John's need to see his brother as older—he had an absent father, and was himself a parental kid who felt responsible for his mother—but I am struck by the strength of the need.

There may, of course, be a genetic basis for the pervasive human habit of forming relationship hierarchies. But there are undoubtedly emotional bases for this tendency; and marriage is powerfully subject to them.

In order to recreate some of the sense of being nurtured and protected which we experienced as children, we not only choose a mate who reminds us of one or more figures in our family of origin; but we may also learn to behave in a "parental" manner with our spouse. In seeing our mate as a "parental" figure, we of course endow him or her with all the associations we acquired in living with our parents: their capacity to wound us, to abandon us; their rules about sex, anger, and love.

In addition to our needs for protection and safety, we also have profound needs for autonomy and independence. These needs require that we be in an equal and separate relationship with our partner. The tension between these needs—for safety and protection, and for independence and autonomy—is fundamental to human life itself; and it is never "resolved." But the way in which we deal with this struggle in marriage vitally affects the quality of our lives.

We may enjoy leaning on our mate for leadership and strength, but spending all our time on the downside of the seesaw eventually begins to feel degrading and limiting—a bit like perpetual childhood. While we may initially like being strong and in control in our marriage, staying precariously perched on the upside of the seesaw also begins to tire. We sense the awful burden of responsibility, and the strain of having to give and give.

In the healthy marriage, we can experience power *and* vulnerability. We can be strong and give support; we can be needy and receive it. But support is different from "parenting," a distinction that will require some elaboration. We can also be vulnerable together, sharing feelings of tenderness or sadness (perhaps this is that delicate teetering moment on the fulcrum when neither sends the board up or down). But we should also be able to be simultaneously powerful, confronting each other, or trading ideas forcefully (and here we bounce the board up and down vigorously as we test the limits of our own strength). If we dare, we can ride this sexy board for all it is worth.

There are many obstacles to this best of all possible marriages in which we can be both powerful and vulnerable. Most of these obstacles are the result of our having grown up in imperfect families, where we learned that in order to feel loved, we had to limit ourselves. Each of us needs to know how we developed these inhibitions; we need to understand where, for us, the seesaw gets stuck.

A commonly accepted definition of power is that it is the ability to produce intended effects on the behavior of others. That may include the capacity to keep others from changing their behavior, a stance in which many men today find themselves in relation to their wives. So power is the ability to get others to behave in ways that you want them to. Surprise, surprise.

As they have attempted to place their fragile calipers on this elusive dimension, researchers have approached the problem from different vantage points. In a widely quoted book, Cromwell and Olson describe several "domains" of family power:

POWER BASES (OR RESOURCES)   Those personal qualities that allow someone to exercise power and control. What is it that makes someone powerful? Does being male always confer power? Does the person with special expertise or ability have more power? The pursuer or the distancer? Is the person who earns more money always dominant?

POWER PROCESSES   The way a couple expresses power. How do they negotiate? What communication patterns do they engage in: supportive and friendly, or challenging and hostile? Are certain communication styles associated with higher power? With greater satisfaction? Studies of this area have tended to be based on direct observations of couples' discussions.

POWER OUTCOMES The results of decision-making. When a couple must make a decision—which movie to attend, whose parents to visit—who prevails? Over time, does one partner win the greater share of decisions? Do they alternate decisions, or negotiate each one jointly? Studies of this area often rely on the questionable practice of asking couples to describe their decision-making.

PATTERNS OF POWER

In a review of scores of research reports, psychologists Bernadette Gray-Little and Nancy Burks asked: "What is the relationship between marital satisfaction and marital power?" Though Gray-Little and Burks voiced technical concerns about a number of the studies they reviewed, certain trends emerged repeatedly from these studies. These findings also agree in large measure with our clinical experience.

For the purposes of research, social scientists have classified marriages in three basic patterns of power, and these patterns form the basis for Gray-Little and Burks's comparisons:

EGALITARIAN MARRIAGES Within this type, some consider there to be two subgroups: in one, the couple negotiates all decisions jointly; in the other, each has a separate "territory" within which he or she makes decisions. According to Gray-Little and Burks, in study after study, *egalitarian marriages proved the most satisfying in which to live*. This finding occurred in a variety of cultures.

HUSBAND-DOMINATED MARRIAGES These traditional partnerships claim second place in the marital-satisfaction sweepstakes, and in several studies they were not far behind egalitarian marriages. In a few studies they were reported as more satisfying. Some analysts point out that these first two groups are somewhat confused, maintaining that "separate but equal" egalitarian marriages are really traditional, male-dominated partnerships.

WIFE-DOMINATED MARRIAGES   Gray-Little and Burks found that in almost every study, *this pattern was by far the least satisfying for both men and women*. This finding held regardless of the method of study, and was confirmed in a number of different cultures. Social scientists are not sure why these marriages—which occur less frequently than the other two patterns—are so universally unhappy; but I will later hazard several guesses about the origins of distress in this and other problematic patterns.

The other clear finding in these studies is that *marriages in which the partners engage in a high level of criticism or coercion are almost universally unhappy*. Some researchers feel that the style of communication, or the way in which power is exercised, is more important in determining marital happiness than the pattern of power itself.

Gray-Little and Burks admit that classifying marriages as egalitarian, husband-dominated, or wife-dominated is probably too simplistic, and I would agree. As Margaret and I begin to examine the issue of power in a marriage, we look at power somewhat differently from the researchers, and we ask the following questions:

Are the partners in SYMMETRICAL or ASYMMETRICAL power positions?

In symmetrical patterns, both partners are on roughly the same "level," and exhibit similar behaviors. For example, both may be assertive, forceful, and openly powerful; or both may be quite unassertive and timid about exerting power. The crucial distinction is that one partner is not clearly one up or one down to the other. They are peers, or in the same "generation."

In asymmetrical patterns, the partners seem visibly and obviously unequal. One partner is in a more dominant or "parental" position, the other in a more submissive or "childlike" position. Because such terms sound blaming, many therapists use Murray Bowen's description of the "dominant" spouse as *overfunctioning*, the "submissive" spouse as *underfunctioning*. These less pejorative terms are descriptive, in that the overfunctioning spouse in a marriage often does carry more of the emotional burden of the family, while the underfunctioning partner gets away with doing far less.

All of these patterns can be relatively satisfying, or highly distressing, depending on a number of factors, which we will explore.

What is the covert pattern of power and vulnerability in this marriage?

All couples are engaged in a constant attempt to influence each other, but many of these attempts are carried out covertly, and often unconsciously. Obvious patterns are often deceptive. The seemingly strong, dominating spouse often masks his or her insecurity; and the seemingly weak and intimidated spouse may exert a great deal of influence through subtle, indirect means.

I will never forget my formal introduction to the covert use of power in marriage. I was a graduate student, studying the marriages of four student couples, and the marriages of these students' parents. In my interviews with Tim and Dora, I had heard a lot about Tim's intimidating father—his booming voice, his temper outbursts, his physical bulk. "I hate to say it, but he's sort of a bully," Tim admitted.

When I went to interview Tim's parents, I was anxious about meeting this man. Sure enough, he greeted me at the door, and with a loud, friendly voice, invited me in. Calling his wife, he pointed to the chair where I was to sit. As I faced this six-foot-four, two-hundred-and-fifty-pound owner of a tire store and his rather quiet, plainly dressed wife, he said, "So, what do you want to know?" making it clear that he was going to answer my questions. The first questions were factual, and he did answer most of them, though his wife occasionally and politely corrected him. No, they hadn't met in 1940; it was 1941.

When I asked about how they made decisions, he said with a laugh, "Well, we talk about them." A pause. "And then I make up my mind." He added with a finality that I had no reason to question: "I make most of the decisions around here." Glancing at his wife for her opinion, I realized that she seemed slightly irritated, but not at all cowed. I felt confused.

At that moment, the phone rang. This quiet, seemingly compliant woman turned to her husband and said with a dead-certain flatness, "Answer that." It was a command if I had ever heard one.

Without the slightest protest, Tim's father rose from his chair and trotted like an obedient puppy to fetch the phone.

"It's your Tim," he boomed. "He wants to talk to his mom."

"Tell him I'll call him back," she said curtly.

Returning to his seat on the sofa, he said, "Where was I? Oh, our decisions." Then I noticed his wife's ever so slight smile.

Later, Tim would recall the times his father lost jobs because of his temper; always his mother would take over and help find him another one.

We family therapists assume that the covert realities in marriage need to become overt. The partner with hidden vulnerabilities needs to be able to expose those insecurities, and the partner who has been forced to communicate his or her power indirectly needs to do so directly and openly. Tim's father was indeed an insecure bully, and his wife had been forced to live in his shadow; she needed to exert her considerable strength and intelligence in indirect ways.

What does the quality of the couple's communication tell us about the way they deal with power?

Communication patterns in marriage inevitably reveal the underlying emotional structure of a relationship. As we begin to work with couples, we listen for two major problems:

Hierarchical communication. The overfunctioning spouse is easily identified by "older-generational" language: helping, teaching, analyzing, explaining, or directing messages tell us that this person plays a "parental" role in the marriage. The underfunctioning spouse is identified by compliant, pleading, "mistreated child" (or victim) messages that betray a one-down position in the marriage. We begin almost immediately to try to help couples change these one-up or one-down communication patterns.

Blaming, responsibility-denying messages. When spouses place blame on others, they reveal an undeclared dependency. "You are why I am unhappy" is not simply criticism; it identifies the speaker as someone who has handed responsibility for his life to his partner, and blames the partner for not meeting needs that are inevitably left over from childhood. This denial of responsibility for self must be addressed before the couple can begin to make constructive changes.

A look at several of the most common patterns, and the ways we work with them, beginning with symmetrical marriages:

SYMMETRICAL MARRIAGES

In that the partners are thoroughly committed to being peers, the *egalitarian marriage* is of course symmetrical. What goes into making such a relationship, which is clearly the most satisfying one for both partners? This is a question to which we will add information as we proceed; but we can make a start here.

Egalitarian, working partnerships are earned. Few of us begin marriage with such a relationship. Most of us didn't see our parents make decisions equally, cooperatively, and jointly; and we cannot model our marriage on our always unequal relationships with our parents or our siblings. Often, our friendships form the model for this kind of partnership.

Egalitarian marriages are created through constructive conflict (a process that is treated in more detail in Chapter 16). In early marriage, we all discover that if we let it happen, our spouse will quite inadvertently use us, dominate us, subjugate us to his or her ends. The only way to escape slavery in marriage is to demand equality. This is a distressing fact, but it is a fact. We are all preoccupied with ourselves, and must be constantly reminded that there is another psyche over there somewhere upon whom we are impinging. *In every healthy marriage, both partners have found a way to advocate for their own needs, and to deal openly and constructively with conflict.*

One of the most critical problems in marriage is that certain childhood experiences prevent us from asserting ourselves in situations of conflict. Why can't we demand our fair share? Defining and learning to deal with the hidden vulnerabilities that prevent us from being capable self-representatives in conflict is one of the fundamental aims of this book.

The married partners accept compromise. In addition to being able to be assertive, egalitarian partners have come to grips with the sad fact that in order to gain the benefits of another's support and good will, we must make certain surrenders of wish and will. We must come to grips with our narcissism.

They respect individuality and separateness. Egalitarian partnerships are built by two whole people who can stand on their own, take responsibility for themselves, deal with life autonomously—and who respect the autonomy and individuality of others.

They require maintenance and work. Egalitarian partners spend a lot of time together solving problems; and they talk about everything—the kids, the bills, their sex life, the daily news. Talk—lots of it—may be the one common denominator of the successful marriage.

They seek both mutual and individual pleasures. These couples find ways to please themselves *as couples*, both in and out of bed. They circumvent competitiveness by learning to nurture the relationship through a continual process of mutual enjoyment, such as weekly dates and shared hobbies; but they also allow separate activities and interests.

They have a way of breaking the hypnotic appeal of conflict, often through a sense of humor. They can step back and say, "Isn't this ridiculous?"

Their relationship is underlaid by an intangible quality of trust. At the worst moments, they believe in hanging tough.

Some symmetrical relationships, however, are decidedly less healthy than the egalitarian pattern:

THE EMBATTLED MARRIAGE   One in which the partners seem equal enough but have a constantly challenging, highly conflictual style. Often, each is fearful of being dominated by the other, and their efforts to prevent this from happening make them guarded and aggressive. They may fight about every decision, and have great difficulty acting jointly.

Embattled couples have histories that make compromise difficult. Sometimes it feels dangerous. In one couple we saw recently, each spouse saw their same-sex parent, with whom they sympathized, brutally dominated by the other parent. He saw his father retreat into depression in the face of his mother's constant criticism; while she saw her mother physically abused by her father. Since each was fearful they would meet the same fate as their same-sex parent, they engaged in a constant, vigilant defense.

Some embattled partners had parents who attacked and

dominated them when they were children, and they are fearful of being treated in this way by their partner. In an effort to defend themselves, they become mutually intimidating to each other.

Often, these partners had roles in their families of origin that make it difficult for them to share decision-making. Two eldest children, for example, may be accustomed to being leaders, and to dominating their siblings. Because they have not learned to compromise and negotiate, they continually feel challenged by their partner's style. Some recent clients of ours were doubly vulnerable, in that he was an only child, and she was an eldest; and both had highly critical, controlling mothers. They could turn the simplest issue into a control battle.

Beneath the tumultuous surface of these marriages, such partners are often deeply dependent on each other, and fearful of being "swallowed up" in this dependency. Though at a high cost, their battles serve the purpose of keeping them psychologically separate. These defensive partners may also have sexual problems which they avoid through their constant conflicts.

Embattled couples first need insight into why they are so threatened by each other's efforts to exert influence and control. They then need to learn how to give in to each other, to learn to do what the other wants. As they begin this seemingly risky process, they discover the magic of reciprocity. "If I please her, she doesn't overwhelm me and demand more, she does things to please me!"

We also teach these couples to "make trades," and to bargain: "If I take out the garbage, will you wash the dishes?" It may also help these couples to contract for separate areas of control, or to alternate having control of certain activities. One contentious couple alternated control of the checkbook and bill-paying, with periodic conferences to discuss major decisions. Another couple alternated all major decision-making regarding household activities on a weekly basis. We try to make such exchanges gamelike, with encouragement to see power-collisions coming, and to defuse them with humor if possible.

Because they are so threatened by an underlying fear of togetherness, some embattled couples benefit from a temporary separation during the therapy process. As soon as they begin living separately, these couples often calm down and learn to negotiate more reasonably.

THE PSEUDOMUTUAL MARRIAGE   In dramatic contrast to the embattled marriage, these spouses never seem to fight about anything. First described by family therapist Lyman Wynne, "pseudomutuality" is a state of forced, false pleasantness, and it is motivated by a fear of anger. These partners may be together constantly, and may seem highly cooperative; but beneath the surface they are very angry at each other.

The histories of such couples are likely to contain rejection or loss experiences. Since conflict is seen as leading to a repetition of the loss, it is seen as dangerous: "If I get angry, I will be rejected." They work very hard to please each other, denying their frustrations and angers.

Their tranquillity comes at a cost. Couples who come into therapy saying "We never fight" usually have very serious problems. They may have a scapegoated child who has become the target of their aggression; one or both may be seriously depressed or have psychosomatic problems, because they turn their anger against themselves; or the anger may have erupted openly, and they may feel that getting divorced is the only way to contain and deal with this fearful volatility.

In working with pseudomutual couples, we try to help them see how much they need and depend on each other, and, somewhat paradoxically, we support their togetherness. This support for their marriage often allows them to be more aware of, and to voice, their suppressed anger. But these partners need to have insight into their fear of loss, and to see the impact this fear has on their dealing with anger.

Anger needs to be normalized, and again humor can be lifesaving: "If Gene raises his voice, are you really going to leave him? Will you reject him if he doesn't like oatmeal?" We eventually give both spouses homework assignments to make a certain number of assertive statements each week. We praise them for having even minor fights. Margaret and I talk about our own disagreements, and may even recount them blow by blow.

As in other dilemmas, pseudomutual couples may not solve

their problems until the underlying childhood issues have surfaced, and have begun to be resolved.

ASYMMETRICAL MARRIAGES

I believe that asymmetrical power relationships in marriage are usually problematic. Though a traditional couple may be able to avoid certain conflicts by establishing a hierarchy in their marriage, and by dividing their territories into "his" and "her" realms, each gives up vital aspects of personhood in making such agreements. This kind of role specialization is basically an expression of dependency: each depends on the other to be the part of themselves that they don't dare be. Though they may afford certain benefits to both men and women, I do not believe that traditional, male-dominated gender patterns are healthy; and wife-dominated marriages, which will be considered in the next chapter, are often very unhappy.

THE HUSBAND-DOMINATED MARRIAGE   This is the marriage pattern many of us have been brought up to think of as "normal," and it is still the most common motif.

"Joan, would you come here?" The voice was her husband's, and his irritation was unmistakable. "What have I done?" she wondered anxiously. "And where is he?" she puzzled.

She had been standing in the kitchen, tending to the roast she was cooking, and as she walked into the hall, she realized that the basement door was open. "I'm down here," Eric's voice rose with a hollow echo through the stairway.

Stepping quickly down the recently carpeted basement stairs, she could see Eric standing near the foot of the stairway, leaning against the wall. "That again," she said cynically to herself, her breathing tighter.

"I'm sorry to disturb you," he said politely. "I know you're busy."

"Does he have to always be so damn polite about it?" she said to herself, catching the glint of Eric's steel-rimmed glasses. As she walked up beside him, his large, muscular frame seemed, as it often

did, intimidating. "What's the matter?" she asked pleasantly, knowing what was coming.

"The phantom has struck again. The basement thermostat is
turned off. I'm just afraid the place is going to mildew." After a
pause he asked, "Do you think Deborah did it?" Joan winced
silently. Their sixteen-year-old daughter was always the culprit
when something went wrong; why couldn't he let up on her?
Seeing Joan's silent displeasure, Eric continued, his voice becoming
sterner: "We've *got* to get her to stop doing things like this." After a
further wait, he said, "Will you speak to her about it?"

Joan felt an anxious fluttering in her chest. Behind Eric's mad-
dening politeness she heard that stern, fine edge of anger, saw the
steely glint in his eyes that frightened her. Why wouldn't he let
Deborah alone? Why was he always after her? She sighed. "All
right," she said compliantly.

"Do you disagree with what I am saying?" he said, a slight note
of hurt in his voice. That was the strangest of all, her capacity to hurt
him—just by disagreeing.

"No, well, yes. I do disagree." She had said it. Why couldn't he
relate more directly to the children, rather than using her as his
lieutenant? "I wish you would talk to her yourself, for once." It was
the kind of thing she couldn't have said a year ago, and she knew
it was because of the job. Low pay, part time, but a start. Her heart
was beating wildly.

"All right," he said flatly. "I will." Knowing that he was displeased, she started up the stairs, worrying about what he would say
to Deborah, and how she would take it. There was no way out of
this.

They did not speak again before dinner, though it was difficult
to know whether he was angry; and as always, she tried to be
pleasant. The dinner table was lively. Reserved, scholarly Anita,
eighteen and a senior in high school, sat across from her talkative,
popular best friend, smiling as the friend described the school play.
Deborah sat next to Stacy, her punk friend who had mercifully left
off her white makeup. As the rest of the family talked, Deborah and
Stacy occasionally whispered to each other. "If you are going to
talk, please share it with us," Eric said firmly, but pleasantly enough.

"Sure, Dad. Sorry." Joan thought how compliant both their kids were; how lucky they were not to have a really rebellious child like Stacy. They liked Stacy, but Deborah's friendship with her concerned both parents. It was not, however, the only thing about Deborah that worried them. Her grades had recently gone down, and she had seemed sullen and withdrawn; not at all her buoyant, spunky self.

At the beginning of the meal, Eric presided: carving the roast, addressing each person as he served it. He was pleasant to both guests, and he reminded Deborah about putting her elbows on the table. As the meal progressed, however, the talk increasingly flowed between Joan and the girls. Joan knew their teachers, the other kids they talked about, and some of the gossip. It was easy, friendly, companionable conversation, and Joan enjoyed it. Glancing at Eric, she realized that he seemed rather stern and solitary, and felt a moment of concern. Later, he made an effort to steer the conversation toward politics, a topic he wanted the girls to be more informed about; but, as usual, they were soon back to the latest movies and an upcoming rock concert. Joan was worried that he would bring up the thermostat, but he didn't. "Would you two"—indicating Deborah and Anita—"make sure the dishes are done?" he said firmly at the end of the meal, and both girls moved routinely to comply.

It was nearly ten o'clock when Joan heard the argument, which seemed to be coming from the family room. Both the friends had left, and Deborah, who had recently gotten her license and looked for every opportunity to drive, was about to go out to buy cosmetics at an all-night drugstore. "I tell you I didn't do it!" Deborah said loudly. "How many ways can I say it, Dad? Why won't you believe me?"

"Anita says that she didn't, and I know your mother didn't. Who else would have done it?"

"What about Selma?" Deborah countered angrily. "Have you interrogated her?" It was later discovered that the cleaning woman had indeed been turning the furnace off.

Though Joan knew he was furious, Eric's voice remained calm: "What is bothering me now, Deborah, is the way you are talking to me. I'm trying to be reasonable with you, and you—"

"So why do you always accuse me, Dad? Why is it me every time? Huh?" The last syllable was said with a lunge of provocative anger, and it registered in Eric like a body blow.

"Listen, young woman, until you can learn to talk more politely to me, you are *grounded.*" Joan had rarely heard Eric so angry; she wanted to walk in, to defend Deborah, but she was afraid of making it worse.

At that moment Deborah exploded, simultaneously yelling and crying. "Is that so, Dad? Well why don't you ground me for a month, two months, six months! Why don't you lock me in my room and throw away the key!" Then she turned and walked out the back door, slamming it behind her. As the car roared to life in the driveway, Eric made no effort to stop her.

It was not until three o'clock in the morning that they located Deborah. She had driven around for hours, then finally gone to Stacy's house. Over the phone Joan tried to coax Deborah into coming home, but, weeping and saying that she was afraid to, that she never wanted to come back, Deborah refused. It was the sound of Deborah's crying that gave Joan the courage to turn to Eric.

"Eric, I cannot accept this." Something told her, "Be calm," but she just couldn't. Before she realized what she was saying, the words were out: "You are just like your father. Living with you is just like living with him must have been. Everybody is frightened of you, Eric! Don't you realize what a bully you can be?"

The words hit Eric like a well-planted knife. He could feel them going in and in; he seemed to have no resistance to them. "This is not happening to me," he said to himself. A vivid image of his father beating his mother flashed before him, and he fought it away. It could not be true; he had built his life on trying to be different from his abusive father—trying to be rational, calm, responsible, good to his family.

"If I am like him," he was finally able to say, "I won't stay in this family. I *won't* be like him; that's all there is to it." In his chest he felt a really terrible pain.

Eventually they both calmed down a little, and were able to talk. Out of that talk, which lasted the remainder of the night, came an agreement to get some help. A week later, after Deborah had been away for three days, we met with the Strand family for the first time.

The opening sessions were tense and difficult. The pressures of this authoritarian, husband-dominated family had been building for a long time, and they felt explosive. It seemed apt that the emerging conflicts had surfaced around the innocent symbol of the furnace control, which seemed to represent the issue of control itself. With mother and daughter acting in unconscious collusion, Eric's leadership of this tightly hierarchical family was under siege. Deborah's maturation and the beginning of her separation from the family developed in synchrony with her mother's increased courage, derived in part from her new job as a substitute teacher. In an intuitive coalition, they had defied Eric's authority.

As Joan admitted to her unhappiness with their marriage, the focus shifted sharply away from Deborah. "Yes, I do admit wishing I could talk to you more boldly, like Deborah can," Joan finally said. "There's a lot I'm unhappy about." Joan could see that she had subtly supported Deborah's rebelliousness, had in fact unconsciously cheered her on. She knew that she needed to learn to be more assertive.

Eric was not relieved to have a public hearing for their troubles. A proud and private man, he was resistant to being in therapy. He knew he was too stern sometimes, but he would work on that. As is often the case with such men, we were torn between trying to build a relationship with him and having to confront him about his behavior.

The older of two children (his sister was three years younger), Eric had learned to be a leader in his childhood family when his executive father was often away for long periods of time. "It was when my father came home that the trouble started, often on the second night. I think he began the abuse—in his own mind, at least—because my mother turned him down sexually; at least that's all I can guess. Mostly he would yell and scream at her, but sometimes it got worse and he would hit her. I was frightened when I heard this going on in the night, and I was afraid for myself too— though he never beat me. When I was sixteen, I was the same size I am now, and one day I couldn't take it anymore. I don't know how I did it, but I told him that if he touched my mother again, I would kill him. And it never happened again—physically. The yelling continued though, and all of it took its toll on her."

Eric looked very sad when he talked about his family. His father had died several years previously, and his mother was in a nursing home. "She was never the same after those beatings," he said. Eric had in fact vowed as a child to be different from his father: to be strong but rational, and to always be helpful to women. He had not realized that in spite of our conscious intentions, we are all unconsciously identified with the parent of the same sex, and are bound to be like him or her in some respects. Eric's quiet domination of his family did have a punitive aspect, and when he was confronted by this fact, he was horrified.

Eric's strength was part of what attracted Joan to him initially. He was, in effect, the father she didn't have. Her own father had been a chronic depressive who was in and out of mental hospitals and had died early. After the father's death, Joan's mother, who had been the strong parent, became an alcoholic; and Joan in effect became the family's "parent," caring for a younger brother and for her mother. Eric was really the only man she had ever been able to depend on; and as an adult, he was her major source of emotional support.

Asymmetrical marriages are often founded on an "unconscious contract" between the spouses—a concept introduced by family therapist Clifford Sager—in which one is "parent," the other "child." Although they may appear so on the surface, such agreements are rarely one-sided. As we got to know the Strands better, it was evident that Joan was a quietly strong person who frequently "mothered" Eric; and it was perhaps the threat of losing this aspect of his relationship with her that made him anxious about her becoming more openly independent. But on the surface, he was not only dominant, but inappropriately so.

During childhood, overfunctioning men like Eric often identified with the more dominant parent. That parent may have been another dominant father, as in Eric's case; but it may also have been a dominant mother. One of the most absurdly intimidating men I have worked with in recent years was a very busy physician whose wife was his office manager, and who ruled every aspect of her life. He was the oldest child in a family in which the father, a chronic alcoholic, abandoned the family, leaving the tough, anxiously controlling mother to run it single-handed.

This man had felt controlled and intimidated by his mother, and because of his father's failures, he also had an intense desire to be successful. His solution was to adopt his mother's way of dealing with people. This aggressive stance allowed him to feel forceful in relation to women, and to compensate for his father's weaknesses. He practiced what Freud called *identification with the aggressor*, becoming like the person he was intimidated by. The terrible bind for him and his wife was that he was very threatened by her attempts to be stronger and more autonomous. If he risked being less dominant, he was unconsciously fearful of being controlled by a woman again, and of being weak like his father. It was only through showing him the terrible toll his frenetic overfunctioning was taking on his health, and on his family relationships, that he began to change; and he did not really respond to his wife's distress until she had consulted a lawyer about divorce.

An imbalance in power in the previous generation is extremely important in determining an imbalance of power in the present generation. When we were children and looked at our parents' struggles, we made unconscious resolutions to change the pattern of injustice which we perceived in their generation. The ways in which we limit ourselves or make demands of ourselves in our own marriages depend in large measure on how we identified with our parents—whom we saw as the victim, and whom we saw as the aggressor. A clear example is the many women who remain one down in their marriages because of their sympathetic identification with their one-down fathers.

As we attempted to get Joan to be more assertive, we encountered strong resistance; she kept saying, "I can't be like that." One day, in an attempt to learn more about how she saw her parents' relationship, we asked her to imagine her parents sitting in two empty chairs, talking to each other. When she tried to do this, Joan began to cry. "I see a very sad process. My mother is saying hard, critical things to my father, and he is just sitting there, cringing. He can't seem to fight back." In what might be called "identification with the victim," Joan had, in effect, identified with her father's plight; and part of her difficulty in being more assertive was that she did not want to be like her critical, attacking mother. Her fear of "being like that" made it difficult for her to be normally assertive. Many women who had such harshly critical mothers are severely limited by their fear of repeating their mothers' patterns.

There are other, less "personal" power bases in marriage, the most widely studied being that intimately related trio of income, education, and occupational prestige. In all of these areas, men have had, and still have, the advantage.

The control of money is the most visible aspect of male hegemony. A great many marital conflicts are about money, and while this summary metaphor—only sex exceeds its universality as a focus of conflict—can symbolize many issues, including love and security, it most often represents control and power; and it is a vital fulcrum in the marital seesaw.

The research on power bases is extensive, and the results seldom surprising. The power of men in their marriages varies according to their socioeconomic resources (income, education, occupational prestige). Not only are men who earn healthy salaries and have prestigious jobs more powerful in their marriages than are more hard-pressed men, but they are also less likely to get divorced. A man's status and income may provide his wife with benefits that compensate for her lack of power within the marriage.

Eric was the head of a large accounting firm, and for most of their marriage Joan had been a housewife. Though she was attractive and very talented, Joan was profoundly conscious of her economic vulnerability. "When Eric says, 'I can't live in this marriage if you accuse me of being like my father,' I feel terrified. I don't know what I would do if we divorced." For many women, the stark facts of their economic disadvantage, and the difficulties they anticipate in remarrying, make them fearful of confronting their husbands.

Of course, as women have had more access to jobs, and especially to well-paying jobs, their power within marriage has increased. Even Joan's brief, part-time employment helped her be bolder with Eric. Unfortunately, women's new economic power has often led to increased conflict within marriage. In a sad commentary on the easily threatened male psyche, marriages in which the woman earns more than the man are much more likely to end in divorce than marriages in which the reverse is true. Many researchers speculate that the increase in divorce in recent decades is directly related to women's employment. Women who have the option of supporting themselves are simply less willing to endure unsatisfying marriages.

Children also affect the power balance in marriage, though the evidence here is conflictual. Some studies seem to indicate that having children increases a woman's power within the family, while other studies reveal that the needs of children limit women's access to employment, and thereby limit their power. Most studies show that as women age, their power in the family increases. Deborah certainly had lent support to her mother, and her increasing independence may have created a crisis in Joan's life.

While there is much to learn from the research on the economic and social influences of marriage, I am convinced that the fundamental opponents to a more equal marriage lie in the shadowy realm of childhood experience, aspects that are often unconscious. What is it in the childhood experience of males that makes them as adults unable to support their wives in being strong, independent, and autonomous? What is it in the childhood experiences of females that makes it difficult to insist on those prerogatives when they become women?

In the Strand family, these forces made Eric resist the therapy process. While he came to the meetings, he was defensive and guarded, and Joan was hesitant about challenging him. When I tried to talk to Joan about her feelings, Eric interrupted me. He tried to cooperate, but he didn't want a stranger toying with his family.

Joan also engaged in a kind of surreptitious campaign against Eric, drawing the kids into her anger at him. Several times she subtly encouraged Deborah to complain to her father about some issue which turned out to express Joan's own anger at him. Joan was embarrassed to admit to such guerrilla tactics, but she had difficulty changing them.

In spite of these resistances, we made some progress. Eric relaxed his pressure on his kids to be perfect, and he was gentler with both girls. Joan was a little more assertive with Eric, and learned to take a firmer stand with Deborah. We even encouraged Anita not to be such a hard-driven achiever. Then, with relationships improved but fundamentally unchanged, the family stopped coming.

About six months after we had last seen the Strands, Margaret was standing at the appointment desk looking over her day's schedule when she noticed that Paula had scheduled her for an hour with Joan Strand—alone. "What's this about?" she asked Paula.

"I don't know," Paula said. "She wouldn't say." After a moment's hesitation, she continued, "I know you usually only see couples together, but she wanted to do this, and she was very reluctant to meet with Eric. I guess I should have talked to you."

"No, that's all right. I'll see what it's about," she said.

That evening after dinner I was reading in our study, and Margaret sat down beside me. "I have to talk to you about Joan Strand." She looked tense.

"Okay," I said, putting down my book.

"I saw her alone today, and it may have been a mistake. I now know a very difficult secret."

"Which is?"

"Deborah is pregnant."

I felt stunned. Then I remembered that it was a secret. "You mean Eric doesn't know?"

"That's right," Margaret said tersely. "And I do."

"What are Joan and Deborah planning to do?" I asked, afraid of what I was going to hear.

"Joan is planning to take Deborah on a 'shopping trip' to New York, where Deborah is going to have an abortion." Margaret's lips were drawn into a tight, thin line.

"Does Deborah agree to this?"

"She's sixteen, Gus. She does *not* want to have this baby. But she is terrified that her father will find out, and she has convinced Joan not to tell him."

Still incredulous, I asked, "And Joan has agreed to do this without telling him?"

Margaret said, "She is also afraid of what he will do. Her fear is that he will get very punitive with Deborah, and that if she defends her, the conflict will end their marriage. She's forty-nine, with very little job history, and she's frightened." Imagining Eric's wounded fury, I could well understand her anxiety. The looming presence of an angry man seemed to permeate our conversation.

"But does she understand what this kind of secret could do to Deborah, and to the family?" I asked. "I would worry that Deborah would feel so guilty that she would unconsciously do something really self-destructive. Getting pregnant is already a huge step in that direction. I think a secret like this would be tremendously divisive in the family. It would split it right down the middle." We had both seen the terrible effect that major secrets can have on families. Not only do they produce guilt, but on some level this kind of secret is always "known," if only half-consciously. Sooner or later, Eric would become aware that something mysterious and powerful separated him from Deborah. We assumed that the family itself would eventually force the secret out into the open, and it would likely be in a way that was even more destructive than what had already happened.

"I said all of this to her, almost word for word." Margaret sounded irritated.

I sighed, a long, frustrated sigh. "What in the hell should we do?"

"I wish I knew," Margaret said.

"How did you leave it with her?" I asked.

"I said that I had to talk it over with you, and I scheduled a time for her with the two of us the day after tomorrow."

"Alone?"

"Yes."

"When is this 'shopping trip' scheduled?"

"In one week. She's already six weeks pregnant."

We thought in silence. Could we give our tacit approval to a minor's abortion without the knowledge of that child's other parent, when we believed such a step—if taken in secret—might have serious negative consequences for the child? On the other hand, could we put pressure on Joan to reveal something that might result in this child's being severely punished, and that might force her mother to take a stand that could end her marriage? To complicate the situation, all the members of this family were our clients; we had responsibilities to each of them.

"I wonder why she told you?" I asked aloud. "Why didn't she just work it out on her own?"

"I guess she wanted support for her decision," Margaret said flatly.

"Maybe she wanted help in telling Eric," I mused.

"That's not what she said."

"I have an idea." I smiled. "Let's get a consult from Carl."

In this instance I meant Carl Johnson, who is our group's rational decision-maker. He not only gets us to pay our bills on time, but he somehow manages to stay cool when the rest of us are upset. Over the phone that evening, his calm voice was reassuring: "I think the mother told you about this because there is some kind of unconscious plot afoot to confront the dad, and to get the family to face its underlying tensions. I think you should put pressure on the mother to tell her husband, and just assume that he isn't as fierce as she thinks. Given a chance to deal with this, he might be more human than anyone predicts."

Margaret and I both thought to ourselves, "He doesn't know Eric," but maybe it was good that he didn't.

The session the next day with Joan was painful and difficult. "We think you should tell him," Margaret said, and again she explained the reasons.

"I can't do it," Joan said plaintively, and she repeated her fears.

Again Margaret voiced her concerns for Deborah, and for the family. Again Joan said that she could not tell Eric.

After about half an hour of frustratingly circular discussion, I began to feel angry. "Joan, we can't force you to do something that you don't want to do. And I don't know exactly what we will do if you refuse to tell Eric, but I do know that we cannot work with you or any member of your family if we are party to this kind of secret. Either the secret comes out or we resign."

Now it was Joan who looked stunned. "But Deborah is going to need some counseling when she goes through this abortion."

"We would be glad to help her. But Eric must know about this dilemma that affects his child. We really need to help the two of you help her together." I felt irritated that she could not see Deborah's vulnerability in having to live with such a secret. "And if you will tell him, we will help you confront him with the fact that his family is frightened of his anger. We will also confront him."

"I have to think," was all she could offer. Margaret and I ended the session feeling troubled, with nothing settled. As she left the office looking gray and tired, Joan did not say goodbye.

Late that evening we got a call from Joan. "Eric is asleep," she said softly. "I have decided to tell him. What should I do?"

Having thought about this question, we suggested that she make up whatever excuse she needed in order to get the whole family to our office at six the next evening. "Say it's for you, say anything you need to."

"Anita too?"

"Anita too." Then I said, "Tell the whole story, every bit of it, including Deborah's fear of her father, and yours too. We will help you do it."

Joan, with dread in her voice, said, "I won't sleep a wink."

Margaret tried to comfort her. "I'm sorry you are having to go through this, Joan. I really am."

"I am too," I said, and meant it.

Our last appointment is usually at five, and we are tired by that time of day and often running late; adding a six o'clock, particularly one like the Stands', felt a bit much. But here we were, facing four fragmented views of a family. Eric and Anita seemed puzzled about the nature of the meeting. Deborah seemed both depressed and fearful; and Joan almost paralyzed with anxiety.

I began. "Margaret and I suggested this meeting, because we felt there were certain things that needed to be discussed by everyone."

Sensing immediately what was coming, Deborah spoke sharply to Joan, who had apparently promised not to bring up her pregnancy. "Mother?"

Eric looked quizzically from mother to daughter. "What is—"

Before he could finish his question, Joan took a deep breath and launched in, addressing Deborah first. "I know I told you I would not tell your father, but Margaret and Gus feel that I should, and I guess I agree with them. I know you are going to be upset."

Terrified and enraged would have been more accurate. Deborah rose from her seat and started toward the door. "I'm leaving," she announced. "You liar!"

"Please don't, Deborah," Joan pleaded. "It will just make it worse if you do. It is too late now to turn back. It has to come out."

What stopped Deborah was Margaret's voice, which was both firm and compassionate. "Deborah, stay five minutes. Just give it a chance to work out. Then you can leave."

Deborah paused, saw a small chair near the door, and took it. Sitting hunched over, clasping her arms to her sides, she looked bleak with despair and utterly abandoned. Margaret walked over and squatted beside her chair, putting her hand on her shoulder. "It is going to be all right," she comforted. "I really believe it is."

"How could it be?" she said angrily.

"Let the adults try. Just give us a few minutes."

"Five minutes," she said grudgingly.

"Will somebody tell me what is happening?" Eric said with irritation as Margaret returned to her chair.

Joan took another deep breath. "I'll tell you." Another breath. "Several weeks ago, I noticed that Deborah had been sick a couple of mornings in a row. I suspected she was pregnant, and it turned out I was right. She is. Six weeks pregnant." No sound in the room, not even breathing. "Deborah and I talked. She was afraid for you to know, Eric, for fear that you would be very angry and punish her. She and I worked out a plan to take her to New York where she would get an abortion, which is what she said she wanted. That's what the shopping trip was about. It was an abortion trip." After a significant pause, she concluded, "I guess I lied to you for the same reasons she did, because I was afraid you would punish her, and that if I stood up to you, it would mean the end of our marriage. But Gus and Margaret persuaded me to tell you; and I am relying on their advice in doing this. But I'm still frightened."

After what seemed like a long silence, Eric said, "Let me see if I understand this. Who . . .?"

"Jeremy." Deborah blurted out the answer before her father could ask the question.

"I assumed as much," he said coldly.

Then he turned to Joan. "And you didn't tell me because you assumed what? That I would punish her? How would I punish her?"

"I don't know, Eric," Joan said apprehensively.

"That makes me angry, Joan," he said. "I feel that you are reading these things in, that I am being seen in a way that I am not. I am not angry at her; I feel sorry for her for having to deal with such a thing at sixteen. But I'm angry at you for lying to me."

"Didn't you say that you were frightened of your father?" Joan turned to Deborah.

"Terrified would be more like it, Dad. You can be scary the way you get that tone in your voice, and the way you yell."

"You are exaggerating," Eric said even more angrily to Joan. Margaret intervened. "This is degenerating."

The next move seemed to be mine. "Eric, you are doing what they predicted you would do—reacting angrily, and blaming. Maybe you don't hear it, but I do." Now I took a breath. "I know that inside, you are hurting with the fact that your daughter is in a jam, and that your family is afraid to turn to you. I know that hurts you, makes you feel bad about yourself." I waited a moment for this statement to register. "But you are not showing them any of this human vulnerability. You are showing them your coolness and your anger. And in revealing only that side of yourself, you don't allow them to really know you. You stay a stranger to your own family."

He looked as though he had been struck—not just by my words, but by the entirety of the present situation. His face flushed, and he became silent. I suddenly realized that he was fighting against the impulse to cry. I went one step further. "It would be the best thing for this family if they could know about this tender part of you."

It was the last thing anyone, including me, would have expected of him, sitting there red-faced and silent as tears streamed down his face. His large chest expanded to take in a jagged breath, and then he calmed himself and said, "It does hurt to feel that my family is afraid of me. It hurts a great deal. And I'm sorry if that's the case." Sitting amid his amazed family, he was crying silently now, but crying. "I'm sorry, I can't help it," he apologized. "It's all too much."

"No need to apologize," I said to him.

There was, of course, much more to do. Margaret turned to Joan and pointed out that when she was angry at Eric she habitually leaned on her kids, especially Deborah, for support; and Margaret challenged Joan to learn to stand up to Eric without using the children. But the major confrontation with Eric was accomplished. So stunned was he by his sudden awareness of his family's fear of him—and its cost to Deborah—that he committed himself to being in therapy, and on a much deeper level this time.

There was much work to do with Deborah: helping her get prepared for the abortion, helping her through it. We met a couple of times with Deborah and her boyfriend, and several times with her individually. She had the abortion locally, and both parents were with her. The family is still in therapy, though most of the meetings now are with Joan and Eric. Deborah is doing well.

The usurpation of power exercised by dominant husbands is, I believe, largely unconscious. Most men want to be supportive husbands and fathers, and when they are confronted forcefully about their punitiveness, or their insensitivity, and helped to change, they usually respond positively.

But there is that frightened "child" aspect of such dominant men that resists being vulnerable, and that fears—in a quite irrational way—sharing power and control with their wives. The trappings of the male role are rewarding enough that many men are unwilling to risk facing their internal demons unless they are forced to.

Women like Joan are indeed vulnerable. Our society does not yet offer enough opportunity and support for women so that they can challenge their husbands as readily as their husbands can challenge them. But those circumstances are changing. As women gain more power in society, and as they exercise that power at home, we see the emergence—even in men like Eric—of the child within the man. We men are indeed threatened by our wives' newfound assertiveness, and we may react to this quality in a variety of childish ways, from regression into depression to outright intimidation.

Male fearfulness of female power, of course, has its origins in childhood, and we must understand this fear better; for while it is not the only enemy of equality in marriage, it is one of the most formidable.

As we attempt to help women like Joan confront men like Eric, we find ourselves saying over and over again: "You have more power than you realize, and more than you are using." It is true, but knowing it doesn't take away the risk.

The other type of asymmetrical marriage, of course, is the wife-dominated partnership, and since it seems to be such a problematic pattern, it merits a more extensive example.

7

The Wife-Dominated Marriage

JACK AND VICKI GORDON, a couple in their thirties, came into therapy because Vicki was acutely unhappy with their marriage. "I'm exhausted all the time," she said. "And I don't feel that I get much help from Jack." Her husband seemed to be another of Vicki's responsibilities, which included two children, their household, and a full-time job. When she wasn't worrying over one, she was worrying over another. It was immediately evident that this was a marriage in which the wife was overfunctioning, and dominant.

They had been in therapy for only a few weeks when an incident occurred that brought their problems into excruciatingly clear focus. The episode was significant enough that we spent some time with them reconstructing it, and looking at the part each played.

The minute she saw Jack's slumped shoulders, Vicki thought he had had a difficult day. When he sighed a long, discouraged sigh as he laid his dirty denim jacket across the back of an easy chair near the door, she knew that he had. Responding to a tightening in her chest which she could have labeled anxiety if she had allowed herself to, she said, "What's the matter, hon? You look bad." It wasn't really a question; she already knew what the problem was.

"He underbid again." After another sigh, he went on, "We have two weeks to do the job, and I somehow have to make it work. That son-of-a-bitch." The foreman for an electrical contractor, Jack Gordon was always having to deal with the errors in judgment of his scattered, marginally competent boss. Vicki could feel herself getting angry, and could hear herself about to give her usual advice about quitting this frustrating job. Deciding on another tack, she said warmly, "Well, go wash up and help me set the table. Dinner is almost ready."

Making his way tiredly toward the downstairs bathroom, Jack felt a familiar tension in his stomach. "I'm in the door for one whole minute and already she's telling me what to do," he said to himself.

Vicki stood at the stove, listening for the boys upstairs. Amos, seven, and Ben, nine, had been playing together quietly, but she was now suspicious about the silence. She tried to call to Jack to check on them and realized that he couldn't hear her. As she felt the steam from the boiling pot of spaghetti on the stove rising beneficently into her face, Vicki realized that she was very tired. Every night the fatigue seemed to be in a different place; tonight it was in her arms, and her eyes too. "I should be thankful I'm not in the fix those women are in," she said to herself, thinking of the welfare mothers who were her clients, and whose sad, imploring faces kept appearing before her. Aware that she felt vaguely put upon, she dismissed the feeling, remembering guiltily someone she had turned down for food stamps.

Jack came into the family room which adjoined the kitchen and slouched into the easy chair. With a slight irritation in her voice, Vicki said, "Jack, the table."

"Oh, sorry," he said absently, rising slowly.

"Would you call the boys?" Vicki asked. As she walked into the dining room and set the steaming plate of spaghetti on their new Danish modern table and stepped back to look at the meal, she realized that as usual, Jack had forgotten to pour the milk. Upstairs, the sound of roughhousing. The dinner was getting cold, and he was playing with the boys. "Jack!" she yelled angrily up the stairs. "It's getting cold!"

"Your mom's on the warpath," Jack said to Amos as they filed into the room. "Watch out for her," he added, with that infectious grin he sometimes mustered.

"You forgot the milk," Vicki said crossly.

"See what I mean, kids?" he countered, still smiling. "Watch out for her."

"I'm glad to see you smiling again," she said to Jack, realizing that she didn't like his rebellious way of teaming up with Ben and Amos. Sometimes she thought she had three sons, and she had even said so on occasion.

For much of the meal Jack was silent, and the talk was entirely between Vicki and the children. Several times she glanced anxiously at him, wondering if he was angry at her for what he called her controlling the conversation. Tonight he seemed lost in thought, and quite depressed. Trying to remain cheerful for the children, she said to herself, "I have enough to do without worrying about him."

At the end of dinner Amos and Ben began to tease each other, and Vicki knew exactly why. In a moment one of them would complain that he couldn't do his chores because he had homework. "Would you take charge of this?" she said to Jack.

Raising his considerable bulk out of the chair, Jack strode over behind the two boys and grabbed each by the back of his shirt. "I certainly will. I will put one in the dishwasher, and one in the washing machine. Then you and I will watch a little television." With both boys screeching in mock pain, he muscled them into the kitchen, knocking over two chairs in the process.

Vicki thought cynically, "Why do I have to constantly remind him?" Then she added, "And he does everything halfway. He never does it right." As the noisy process of dishwashing got under way, Vicki wondered if she should do the laundry or start on the bills. "Some choice," she muttered half out loud.

It must have been nearly ten o'clock when she went into the family room to find Jack watching television. With a flash of irritation, she realized that she had been working nonstop since six-thirty A.M. "Wrestling?" she said in amazement. Then she realized he wasn't really watching. "What's the matter?" she said solicitously, feeling guilty about being angry with him.

"I guess I'm just tired," he said with a slight tone of self-pity.

"You sound depressed," Vicki offered. She knew this path well, and approached it with a sense of apprehension.

"Yeah, I guess. What's new."

"You want to talk about it?"

145

"What's there to talk about?"

"I don't know. I'm concerned about you." Vicki could feel that tightness in her chest again. Jack did not seem to want to talk; but he did seem to want something from her, and she didn't know what it was. She never did. "Did you get into a fight with him?" she asked.

"No, he avoided me. He knew what he had done, and he knew what I felt about it." His flat, depressed tone frightened her.

"Jack, I wish you would quit this job. You could get a much better one." Even though Vicki fought it, she realized that a slight edge of irritation had crept into her voice. It was true, of course, and Jack knew it. Not many of his classmates with electrical engineering degrees were working in construction. Still, he hated the pressure from Vicki. "From the moment I walked in the door—" he said to himself. Then aloud to her he said, "Vicki, I know that." She did not understand his relationship with John, his boss; she never would.

Vicki sighed. If she had stopped to think about it, she would have realized that she felt vaguely panicked about Jack's depression, and extremely frustrated with him because he wouldn't do anything about his situation. "Then why won't you do it?" More irritation; this was all so familiar.

"Because I have ten years of my life in this company, and I own part of it." He sounded angry too.

She knew she shouldn't but something compelled her to say it anyway. "I don't think that's it. I think it's because he's just like your father, and you can't face abandoning him." The youngest of three kids, Jack had grown up with an alcoholic father who was the family albatross; and he was the only one who still lived near his family. His older brother, a successful chemist, lived in California; and the middle child, a sister who also had a drinking problem, was in Florida. It irked Vicki that Jack was always going over to his parents' house to deal with some crisis. It often seemed to her that he was more committed to that family than he was to their own.

Jack felt a surge of anger, then a wave of shame and helplessness. "That's not true," he said plaintively. He knew she was right, but he hated her for saying it. "Besides," he said firmly, "it's my damn business."

Vicki did not know just what in Jack's reply angered her so, but suddenly she felt furious. Perhaps it was that mixture of helplessness and defiance which seemed so exasperating, and so familiar. He seemed to want help, but he resisted everything she said. "God-dammit, Jack, it *is* my business. You come home and mope around all night while I work myself into exhaustion, and then when I try to help you, you tell me it isn't my business. Well, it is, Jack!"

"It isn't!" He had raised his voice too, though he looked vaguely frightened. "Dammit, Vicki, how is it I come home depressed, and you wind up yelling at me? What have I done to deserve this?" A doleful plea.

Vicki felt a sinking inside. How could she, in fact, fight with Jack when he was down like this? It was another familiar moment, one in which she would usually feel guilty, back off, and make up to him. Then *she* would feel depressed. But tonight she was so exhausted, and felt so stymied by Jack's obdurate helplessness, that she plunged on.

"Jack, you've always got an excuse." And as if that weren't enough, she added, "There's always some reason why you can't hack it."

There was a moment of stunned silence. Neither of them could believe she had said it. Jack sat upright and still, like an animal mortally wounded by gunshot and not yet falling. He rose in one enraged motion out of his chair, and towering over the small wiry frame of his wife, stood red-faced and unable to speak. Then something in him loosened, and he bellowed the words, "*WELL YOU CAN GO STRAIGHT TO HELL, YOU GODDAM CONTROLLING SOCIAL-WORKING BITCH!*"

The sight of Jack looming over her, and the immense wounded blast of his voice, was simply overwhelming. Though she had courted it, his anger was so surprising that she was not able to answer it in any way. Vicki drew back, frightened. Blind with pain and rage, Jack had absorbed too much for too long. "*YOU CAN TAKE YOUR FUCKING HELP AND SHOVE IT!*" He yelled, his words pouring over Vicki with overwhelming force.

As she sometimes did as a child when her mother turned on her with her withering, scornful anger, Vicki burst into tears. Suddenly she felt like a very small, brutally punished kid. Unable to stand this cataclysmic diminution, she turned and walked out of the room, sobbing.

"Oh my God!" Jack thought. "Now I've done it." For a moment, rage and remorse battled within him. He could still hear Vicki's awful words, but even more alarming now was the sight of her retreating in devastated hurt. She had been trying to help; she was right in many ways about him. And now he had blasted her. "I should know better than to get angry," he scolded himself, moving toward the kitchen where he could hear her crying.

Vicki was standing at the sink, her head down, trying to calm herself. Standing beside her, Jack put his hand on her fragile, bony shoulder. Most of the time he thought of her as so strong; now her slender body seemed small and vulnerable. He felt guilty, tender, strangely loving. "Vicki," he said softly. "I'm sorry. I'm very sorry." She drew back from him, and his hand fell to his side.

"Leave me alone," she said through her sobs. "Just leave me alone."

"I will," he said sadly, realizing that there was no immediate remedy for the immense space that yawned between them. As he stood there, Vicki's crying diminished somewhat, and after a moment she turned and went upstairs. Jack wondered if his shouts had wakened their children. Feeling devastated himself now, and helpless to undo anything that had happened, he walked back into the family room and sat down. The wrestling was still on. With an angry punch he turned the set off and sat in the silence. Maybe after a while he would try again; maybe she would talk to him then.

When Jack and Vicki came for their next appointment a couple of days later, they were both still feeling bruised and distrustful, and it took a while to get them working productively again. We were concerned that the fight might have been caused by the therapy process; but apparently they had periodically had fights like this since the early months of their thirteen-year marriage.

The wife-dominated marriage, or the couple in which the wife is an overfunctioner, is indeed often unhappy. In several surveys of our appointment rosters, approximately two thirds of our clients fall in this category.

That is not to say that husband-dominated (or husband-overfunctioning) couples are not unhappy; I believe that they usually are, though the women in these marriages may be less verbal about their discontent, and sometimes less conscious of it. We family therapists are also likely to see fewer husband-dominated couples because the wives have more difficulty getting their husbands to come to therapy. Since any change in the marriage is likely to be threatening, dominant men are usually resistant to being in therapy; and their unhappy wives may be forced to seek out individual therapists who attempt to give them support in dealing with their situations. Husband-dominant marriages may also provide women with the compensations of being able to rely on their husbands for a certain amount of protection and financial support.

In wife-dominant marriages, both partners may feel critical of themselves because they fail to conform to the husband-dominant social stereotype, but each person must also deal with the stresses of his or her own difficult role. Though these partners seem very different, and though they deal with their needs in different ways, both bring intense emotional needs to the marriage.

While almost every woman who works outside her home today could be called an overfunctioner, some women are particularly vulnerable to becoming overextended because of their childhood histories. Vicki's problems are common in such women, and they are rarely simply situational. Vicki's job was demanding and her family responsibilities imposing, but her family history made it difficult for her to set limits on the extent of her indebtedness to others. She was thus prone to becoming more and more overextended.

Overfunctioning women have several characteristics in common: they often seem strong, organized, and competent; but inside, they feel emotionally starved and unsupported. These women tend to be out of touch with their dependent or "child" needs; often they are not even aware that they feel emotionally needy. Instead, they focus on the needs and problems of others, and they work very hard to please the people who come to depend on them. They are compulsive workers, often driving themselves to be perfect at whatever they do.

Since such women unconsciously encourage others to depend on them, they frequently marry dependent men who have difficulty functioning both at home and at work. These women play "parental" roles in their marriages, roles that are extensions of similar roles which they filled in their families of origin. Having grown up as "miniature adults," they have long since forgotten how to get their own needs met directly; instead, they take care of others as a way of feeling valued.

Overfunctioning women feel ambivalent toward their husbands. On one hand, they encourage the dependent nature of this relationship by being directive, helpful, and often psychologically interpretive; they also resent the position they find themselves in. Their helpfulness is often so habitual that they are unaware of it. In an early session with the Gordons, Vicki denied being parental with Jack, but we pointed out five instances in that hour in which she had quite unconsciously assisted him. Twice she had offered "interpretations" of his problems; once she had moved the focus away from him when he looked uncomfortable; and twice she reassured him.

Helpfulness is habitual for many women; and while it is an immensely valuable trait, it also causes much difficulty in marriage. It casts the woman in an "older-generational" psychological stance, allowing her mate not only to depend on her as a parent-surrogate, but setting her up as the inevitable target for her husband's anger at his controlling or rejecting mother.

Her helpfulness is in many respects a trap for both partners. The underfunctioning man may benefit from being dependent, but he also feels devalued and one down. Because he doesn't feel confident, he often communicates his anger indirectly, by failing to keep his promises, and in other "passive" ways. Since the overfunctioning wife gives much more than she receives, she eventually begins to feel used and drained. While she may encourage him to be dependent on her, she also resents the process. She may express her resentment subtly, through being anxiously, critically controlling. This indirect "attack" is in part a disapproval of the dependent part of her partner, and it may contain a number of emotional components:

- ☐ She is angry at the dependent part of herself, and focuses this anger on her dependent spouse.
- ☐ She is angry at the parent in childhood who depended on her, and for whom she felt responsible; and again she transfers this anger to her husband.

□ She may be angry at a younger sibling in childhood who (as her husband does now) received more support than she did.

□ She is inevitably angry about the inequity of her situation.

Vicki was the classically overfunctioning wife. The oldest of four children—she had two younger brothers and a younger sister—she had grown up as the "parental child" who helped raise her siblings and was heavily involved with both her warring parents. Vicki's relationship with her mother was complex, and it took us some time to sort it out. Her mother was sometimes very anxious and critical, and at other times depressed. Vicki seemed to try hard to please the "critical mother," while she felt responsible for taking care of the "depressed mother." She played a more "companionate" role with her father, in which she frequently listened to his difficulties with Vicki's mother. Her role with her father was also subtly sexualized, a fact that did not make it easier for Vicki to please her mother.

No wonder Vicki had difficulty being aware of and seeking support of her emotional needs. Having grown up feeling responsible for others, and with little attention being paid to her needs, she was vulnerable to becoming the wife of a man like Jack. Jack's depression, of course, reminded her powerfully of both her parents' neediness, and in the face of Jack's demands, she habitually shelved her own needs and fell to taking care of him.

Underfunctioning men are also ambivalent about their marriages. While they invite caretaking from their wives, they also resent it. Often these men had controlling mothers who were over-involved with them. This was certainly the case with Jack, whose overfunctioning mother took emotional care of her alcoholic husband. Her relationship with Jack was one of the few bright spots in her life, though she periodically directed at Jack some of her intense frustration with Jack's father.

"My mother did this 'poor Jack' routine on me as long as I can remember," he confessed. "She thought I would get hurt if I played football, so she wouldn't let me do anything like that. It's a wonder that I grew up at all. Of course she didn't like the girls I dated either, including Vicki." But periodically, Jack's mother would also turn her anger on him. "Several times a year, my mother would lose it and just start screaming. I caught it sometimes because I was handy,

I think. I used to dread these outbursts, and would try to get out of the house when I saw them coming." Vicki had been "induced" to play Jack's mother's role—she was alternately caretaking and attacking.

Some underfunctioning men had absent or rejecting mothers, and their search for a caretaking spouse is an effort to compensate for this early childhood deprivation. Many men approach adulthood with unmet dependency needs, and they inevitably bring these needs to marriage.

Underfunctioning husbands often had absent, weak, or inadequate fathers. They have difficulty being strong and reliable in their marriages because they did not have models for such strength in their families of origin. Jack's father had been alcoholic since Jack was in early grade school; and since he was at home as the father's drinking worsened, he was exposed to a very weak and depressing example of manhood. Vicki was right: Jack's dependency on his inadequate boss was a perpetuation of his relationship with his father. Just as Jack wanted to be a stronger mate, he wanted to leave his dysfunctional work "family." In neither instance did he seem to have the strength to do so.

If ever there was a vicious cycle, it is in the wife-dominant (or wife-overfunctioning) marriage. Feeling emotionally starved and unsupported, Vicki pursues Jack in a critical, irritable manner; and feeling attacked and pressured, he defends himself by withdrawing or counterattacking, leaving her still more unsupported. And around they go.

In trying to interrupt this cycle, we have learned not to encourage the person in Jack's role to stand up for himself and "fight back"—at least not right away. The last thing Vicki needs is a husband who is acting like a rebellious adolescent determined to defy her. The first step is for her to stop trying to change Jack, and to admit her need for emotional support.

Margaret said, "I know this may sound strange, Vicki, but in a way this fight between you and Jack went in the right direction."

"What do you mean?" she said incredulously.

"Well, it wound up with your feeling very vulnerable, and with Jack's comforting you. That's what I mean about the right direction."

"There must be a better way for me to get a little comforting," she said bitterly.

"Absolutely," Margaret concurred firmly. "That's what we need to help you and Jack find." We believe this often happens in such cataclysmic fights—they represent a couple's way of raising the stakes until some needed shift takes place in the relationship. In this instance, Jack needed to be stronger and more empowered, and Vicki more able to be vulnerable and to accept support. They somehow managed to achieve this "existential shift" during the fight, but at too great a cost.

We had already begun to point out to Vicki that she had difficulty knowing what she felt and needed, and difficulty asking directly for support. "We are going to propose some homework," Margaret said to her, "which will move you in a new direction."

"What we would like you to do," I offered, recognizing this assignment, "is to practice thinking about your needs and asking for support for them."

"How would I do that?" Vicki asked tentatively, shifting her gaze in my direction.

Margaret glanced at me, then smiled. I started to apologize for interrupting her, but she nodded for me to continue. "Between now and the time we meet next week, we want you every day to make one simple request of Jack. The request should address a personal need—something that would help you in a direct way."

Vicki looked understandably skeptical. "Give me an example, please."

" 'Jack, would you please sit down and just let me ramble on for a few minutes about my supervisor at work?' " I offered. "Or, 'Jack, would you give me a neck massage?' "

Vicki smiled. "How did you know I liked those?"

"You work at a desk," I said. "Try 'Jack, would you put the kids to bed and bring me a cup of tea? I'm very tired.' "

"I like the sound of this," she said. Then she paused. "But you know, I think this will be hard. I like the things you suggest, but I can't think of a single thing on my own. It's very strange."

"That's how unpracticed you are at being aware of your own needs," Margaret said. "I have the same difficulty, Vicki. I usually know what other people need, but I have a blind spot with regard

153

to myself." Then she added, "Let me make a suggestion. When you ask for something, let Jack know that you are making your 'special request,' so that he will know that you are not just asking him to set the table as part of the usual routine. He needs to know that you are taking a risk in making this need known."

"And your role, Jack," I offered, "is to try to respond to these requests. Try not to see her as directing you, but as risking revealing her vulnerability. This will be hard for her, but she needs to learn that she can *ask* for what she needs."

Margaret addressed Vicki. "Try to let your vulnerability show— your fatigue, or your loneliness, or whatever you are feeling. That will help Jack know that you are not ordering him."

"One of the benefits for you, Jack," I said to him, "is that you will learn that you can feel connected and valued as a strong, helpful person. Your mother's 'poor Jack' routine trained you to think of yourself as a victim, and your father's example didn't help much either. But you need to learn the benefits to both of you of your being stronger and more empowered." After a short wait, I smiled knowingly. "I think you will find there are many rewards for you in making this shift."

As we explained the dynamics of their relationship, we cast Jack as "addicted" to being a depressed, one-down "victim" who was accustomed to getting attention from this needy, helpless position. We cast Vicki as similarly addicted to being helpful. We said that each faced a real battle in order to change his or her own pattern, and each would need our support.

Our references to "addiction" were not casual. As is common in families with a history of alcohol abuse—and very few families have not been touched in some way by this widespread problem—adult children of alcoholics always reveal emotional scars from having grown up in such families. Jack's older brother, for example, reacted to his father's alcoholism by being a "heroic" overachiever, driving himself to compensate for his father's failures. Jack's sister repeated the father's pattern. And Jack "transformed" the literal addictive pattern into one of chronic depression and dependency.

Vicki played what addiction specialists call the "co-dependency" role, or that of the spouse who—out of his or her own problems— supports and allows the dependent spouse's behavior. That is one reason we began to ask her to change first, because if she did not find a way of getting her needs met directly, she would unconsciously undermine any changes Jack made. Of course Vicki was also in the same psychological position as Jack's mother.

As we ended the hour, I noticed that Vicki's lean, intense expression had softened. She already seemed more vulnerable, as if she were somehow protected by a new atmosphere of possibilities.

At the next session, both Vicki and Jack seemed hopeful. "It was very difficult," Vicki said with a sigh. "At first I couldn't think of *anything* to ask for. I forced myself to keep trying, and as the week went on, it went a little better. After a while I realized that if I focused on a single half-hour in the evening, I was better at asking for something for myself. If I became too global, I got very anxious."

"That's because asking for support is so unfamiliar for you," Margaret said authoritatively. "Your unconscious mind assumes that there is no one there for you." She smiled broadly, concluding: "It will get easier, I assure you."

I asked, "How did Jack do?"

"Fine, generally," Vicki said. "A couple of times he seemed absent-minded, and a little slow on the uptake, but he did all right."

"It was a relief to hear her talking about her needs," Jack said, "and much easier to respond to them than when she is telling me what to do." This was something I also experienced as Margaret learned to tell me about her needs.

Knowing that this kind of change is usually ephemeral, we made the same assignment for the next week; and at the next session there were indeed more complaints. Jack felt "ordered" again, and several times Vicki forgot to make her requests. Again, we brought the focus back to Vicki. "Why do you think you had difficulty?" Margaret asked her.

"Because I have done things on my own for so long," she said with a sigh.

"And because you don't have an internalized model for getting your needs met," Margaret added empathically. When Vicki asked what she could do about that, Margaret said, "You can begin to construct an image of yourself in a situation where you do get your needs met. You can do some internal practicing, as it were."

"How do I do that?" Vicki said.

I volunteered, "Let me make a suggestion. Try to imagine an ideal mother—we can start with a mother—who would be attentive and supportive. We can let Margaret role-play the voice of such a mother." I glanced at Margaret, who nodded assent.

Vicki looked anxious: "I'm not sure what you mean."

I repeated, "I'm suggesting that you rehearse what it would be like to have a parent who would be able to meet your needs. In order to be more open to receiving support in the present, you could let yourself experience what it would have been like to have had such a mother in childhood."

"I'll try it," Vicki said, looking frightened. "Tell me what to do."

I turned to Margaret. "Why don't you enroll as the voice of an ideal mother." Margaret said, "I will enroll as the voice of your ideal mother." Then she looked warmly at Vicki, who smiled back at her.

"And you could just close your eyes," I said to Vicki. Sitting stiffly upright, her eyes closed, she looked small and solitary. "Let yourself imagine the face of an ideal mother, someone who would be whatever your own mother wasn't."

"I keep seeing my own mother," she said worriedly, her brow furrowed.

"Let yourself think of the mother you wanted instead." She looked so alone that it was easy to speak warmly and softly to her, and as I did so, she seemed to relax a little.

"I see someone like my friend Karen," she said. "Only older."

I said that was fine. Then I asked her what that mother would say to her. As I asked that question, Vicki frowned again, and tensed her shoulders. After a long pause, she said quietly, "She would say that I don't have to try so hard to please."

Looking at Margaret, I asked her to repeat Vicki's exact words.

"If I had been your mother when you were a child, I would tell you that you don't have to try so hard to please me." Vicki softened visibly at the sound of Margaret's words.

"And that it doesn't matter if I make mistakes."

Margaret repeated the words: "It doesn't matter if you make mistakes," and again Vicki seemed to relax in the presence of this imaginary mother.

A long pause. Then with a deep breath, Vicki added, "I will love you no matter what you do."

This time Margaret's voice was very accepting: "I will love you no matter what you do." With these words, Vicki began to cry silently, her tears gleaming in the light from the nearby window.

I suggested to Vicki, "How about 'And I will support you and take care of you no matter what you do'?"

"That's good too," Vicki said, and Margaret repeated those words as well. There was silence, and a feeling of peacefulness and completion.

"Is there anything else you want to hear?" I asked.

"I don't guess so," Vicki said. But after a moment of thought, she added, "She could say that she would not be jealous of any attention that I get from my father."

Margaret said, "I would not be jealous of any attention that you get from your father."

I volunteered, "How about if she said, 'Since your father and I have a very good relationship'?"

"Yes," Vicki said enthusiastically.

"Since your father and I have a very good relationship," Margaret said. And with that statement a broad, warm smile emerged on Vicki's tear-streaked face.

"We should stop there," I said. Vicki breathed easily in the silence, savoring the image before her. After a long pause, I said quietly, "Begin to open your eyes slowly."

As Vicki did so, she and Margaret exchanged smiles.

"I need to de-role as the voice of your ideal mother," Margaret said. "I'm Margaret."

In ending that session, I suggested that for the time being, Jack and Vicki discontinue their assignment. "I'm worried that if you ask for support from Jack right now," I said, "you will be too disappointed. Let's work some more on helping you believe in a positive outcome for yourself, Vicki. Then we can go back to your relationship."

This fantasy technique, which is a kind of informal hypnosis, borrows heavily from Pesso's work; but since in couple therapy we don't have the luxury of group members to role-play real or ideal figures, we often work in fantasy, using our own voices to reinforce the client's images. There is, of course, some "transfer" of our clients' feelings about their parents—both real and ideal—to us, and we must sometimes be cautious in suggesting such "experiments."

Following this exercise in fantasy, Vicki began to feel very sad. While she had acknowledged on an intellectual level some of her childhood deficits, this experience brought home to her in a much more personal way what she had missed; and it began to open up the possibility that she was not consigned to a life of self-sacrifice. Margaret's role-play participation in this fantasy also opened a bridge between her and Vicki, a span over which there would be increased travel in the months ahead.

In trying to change the structure of a relationship, we all encounter the resistance derived from our having spent so much of our lives in our respective roles. In the couple with an overfunctioning wife, the woman must first give up being the helper, the rescuer, the facilitator of others' lives. Once she has initiated this process, the way is open for her husband to begin to confront his own difficulties.

As Vicki learned to take better care of herself, and to rescue Jack less frequently, he felt bewildered. "I know this is crazy," he said, "because I do like our relationship better, but I also know I'm trying to get her to be the way she was." Awareness of this tendency didn't keep Jack from trying: he forgot his agreements, he complained and whined, he was so depressed he couldn't sleep. With Margaret's support, Vicki held firm.

Underfunctioning men have much to learn. For one, they must be able to be assertive and to confront their wives when they relapse into their habitual controlling, parental mode. They must also learn to be less self-focused, and to offer genuine support to their spouses and children. They must learn that being helpful and strong offers them real rewards. Many underfunctioning men must also confront their difficulties in dealing with the world outside the family, transferring their newly learned skills of assertiveness and strength into the occupational realm.

In all these efforts, they need models. Most underfunctioning men are emotionally tied to their wives, and they must be encouraged to reach out to other men, cultivating friendships and peer support. They especially need contact with men who are strong and assertive themselves.

But many men need the continuing support of a therapist (or a pair of therapists, in our approach) in examining the childhood script that consigned them to a one-down role; and they require continuing support in changing that script. As we settled down to longer-term work with the Gordons, I felt confident about being able to help Jack. I had had an alcoholic father and knew well the sinking despair about that problem; and I had also spent ten years with a very tough and strong mentor at whose hands I had learned a great deal.

In an indirect way, Jack reached out to me. After about the tenth session, he began taking quick, sniping shots at me as he left the interview. "How late should we be next week, Gus, so that we don't have to wait for you too long?"

After about the third such parting snipe, I got angry. "Dammit, Jack, if you are angry with me about something, tell me. But I don't like your oblique criticism. If you want to fight, let's fight."

Jack was silent for a moment, and then he replied, "It does make me mad when you are late. I feel unimportant."

Then it occurred to me what was happening. "Jack, are you worried that I will be weak like your father?"

"I suppose I am," he admitted.

I said with a smile, "Let's try something." Then I stood up, and taking my shoes and socks off, braced myself strategically. "Why don't you get up and come push against me."

Jack looked skeptical, but he had a slight smile. Then I noticed how solidly built he was. Jack put the palms of his hands against my shoulders as I instructed him, and the two of us squared off. As our wives watched, Jack tried repeatedly to push me over, but because I had practiced this exercise many times and kept my position low, he couldn't manage to topple me. The harder he tried, the more firmly I dug myself in. After about ten exhausting minutes, Jack gave up, and with a great sigh of relief, sank down on the sofa. "You're stronger than I thought you were," he said with a broad grin.

"We'll need to try this again," I offered. "You still probably don't believe that you can let yourself depend on me, or on any man." It was an anxiety that I knew well.

There are two critical moments in the life of the wife-dominant couple: the first comes when the woman begins to accept support; the second occurs when her husband begins to be appropriately assertive. It was two years later when Jack finally came in one day and said, "I had a revelation today. It may seem small, but it felt important to me." We listened as he described the early stages of what might have become a major conflict between Vicki and him. "Then she told me in that directive voice what she wanted me to do. I could feel myself getting angry inside, and all of a sudden it occurred to me that I didn't have to do it. I didn't have to make a big scene, but I didn't have to do it. So I said, 'Vicki, I can't do that right now. Maybe later, but not now.' That's all it was, but it felt like freedom to me." It wasn't the first step or the last, but it was perhaps the most significant moment in his growing consciousness of his power.

Changing a major relationship pattern like the skewed power balance in which the Gordons found themselves is a difficult feat. It often takes years of work. But such changes are possible; and the journey toward a more equitable marriage is worth all the effort it demands.

In many marriages, both partners feel dominated by the other. On closer examination, we find that each partner has a sphere of influence within which he or she acts in a dominating manner. I may criticize Margaret's driving, for example, while she directs my activities with our children. This two-sided parental behavior allows us both to feel "taken care of," though of course we also resent being criticized and controlled. Learning to give up both our needs for a resident parent-substitute and our predeliction to be such a figure to our mate is an anxious prospect, but it is the way toward freedom and equality in marriage.

8

Players: The Insiders

IT IS A GAME I remember playing on those soft summer evenings when our neighborhood congregation of kids, giddy with fatigue, was trying to ignore the impending call to supper. I must have been about six years old. We called it "sling the biscuit," and dim light and a flat lawn gave it a certain credibility. The "slinger" would grab someone by the arm and, turning rapidly on his heels, begin to pull him in a tight circle, straining against the increasing outward-pulling force of the other as these two gyrating dancers built momentum steadily, until finally the slinger could hold on no longer and would release his victim, who would career drunkenly across the lawn, coming to rest finally in a position that was half-chosen, half-forced, but inevitably contorted. Other players would take their turns, and finally we would all be splayed across the lawn like strange broken sculptures. We would proudly hold our positions until we began to ache and sweat with strain; then someone would move, and with a delicious sense of freedom we would be released. After we decided whose position was the best, we would start over again.

Even as children we sensed that we were being coerced—by the looming presence of our parents, by the intense gaze of our peers, and by the tyranny of schools—into psychological stances that were awkward, difficult, and ultimately painful. In this metaphoric game, at least we got to choose some aspect of the postures we assumed; and when we could stand it no longer, we could break free of our confinement. In our daily lives, we rarely had this sense of choice.

Because the family was our most critical support, its influences were by far the hardest to resist. In this charged field, we began to be twisted and bent according to the family's largely unconscious but extremely forceful collective will. Early in life, we settled into *roles*, psychological postures which became over time both rigid and limiting. Caught in the family's need for us to play certain parts in its drama, rarely did we question the rightness of those needs.

Most of us are still playing the same parts we learned as children. If we are to understand the underlying issues in our marriage, we need a working knowledge of the "dramatic structure" of the family we each grew up in—particularly the roles we assumed, and how we came to occupy them. The reader may find it implausible that the roles we played in our childhood families are repeated in our marriages, and are also passed down to our children; so I will illustrate how this occurs. In this chapter and the next, I will describe a family's treatment in order to outline several common, problematic family roles which influence our choice of a partner, which shape the marriage that we create, and which powerfully affect our children's lives. We will also examine the dynamic interplay of these "role players," both past and present. Without a sense of the flux and flow of the family drama *over time*, we are likely to miss some of the most interesting aspects of our own history. First, the naming of characters; then the progress of drama itself.

I have a dilemma in deciding at what moment in the family life cycle to begin the story of its drama. Partly because it is such a turbulent era for the entire family, I choose adolescence, that period when a child begins to emerge from the family's inner boundaries. Not only is this a critical moment in the life of the family, but it is a time in which it is often easy to see the roles that these "separating" children occupy. While our position in our family might have been obscure at four or five, by sixteen or seventeen the roles we played were often clearly visible and painfully delimited.

None of us played just one role in our family of origin. In all likelihood, we each took several roles; and some of us occupied several roles in relation to a particular person. These "players," then, should be seen as ways of describing our *function* in the family we grew up in; and we should be careful not to oversimplify the complex and often changing matrix of connectedness within the family.

Colin and Stephanie Land were worried, conscientious parents. They had assembled their family of five with considerable difficulty, flying Audrey in from North Carolina, where she was a college freshman; persuading Bert, who was a junior in high school, to miss basketball practice; and dealing with the resentment of their youngest, Laurel, a freshman in the same high school, who thought that family therapy was ridiculous. Not to mention the imposition on their own schedules: Colin ran a busy insurance agency; Stephanie was the principal of an elementary school.

A highly verbal, hardworking "Protestant ethic" family, they seemed preoccupied with intellectual achievement; and while they appeared to be involved with each other, they did not talk about their feelings easily. In fact, until the conflict with Audrey emerged, it was difficult to find much emotion at all, or to guess why they had come for therapy.

Then Stephanie admitted that she had found a letter. It was from one of Audrey's professors, and Audrey had left it in her room on a visit home. Unable to resist reading the letter, Stephanie learned that her daughter was undoubtedly having an affair with her philosophy teacher.

Even before Stephanie mentioned the letter, there had been a great deal of tension in the room—as if everyone somehow knew what was coming. "I can't understand this," Stephanie said coldly. "Nothing in my experience has prepared me for it." Then she asked, "Is he married?" When Audrey nodded, Stephanie began to cry.

"I'm sorry, Mother." Audrey recoiled defensively. "I didn't do it to hurt you. I'm sorry it does hurt you."

"It feels like we have failed you in some way," Stephanie said in a tone that accused both mother and daughter.

"I don't consider either of us a failure, Mother. Having a relationship with Herb is complicated, but it doesn't make me a bad person."

Stephanie could not be consoled, and she began to engage her daughter in an angry, anguished pursuit. "Why are you doing this?" she repeated over and over. "Will you agree to stop seeing him?"

"No, I won't," Audrey said firmly. "I won't." It was the kind of stand which Audrey had apparently never taken before, and it left her mother feeling distraught. At the beginning of the session, the tall, slender, intense mother seemed to tower over her daughter; now the younger woman's gritty toughness revealed itself as she braced her small, wiry frame against her mother's anger.

A rather short, slightly built man, Colin Land had an intensely focused, scholarly composure. Though his wife often led the discussion, one sensed in him a subtle intellect, and a kindness that was both tentative and strong. As the tension between Audrey and Stephanie became more and more vocal, he finally spoke. "I wonder if we are making too much of this, Stephanie. After all, she's eighteen."

"That's my point, Colin," Stephanie said curtly, in the first visible schism between the couple. "You would defend her."

Audrey's siblings had sat in shocked silence as the conflict emerged; but while Colin and Stephanie looked angrily at each other, Bert engaged them. "This is the way it goes, doesn't it? Mom fights with Audrey, and Dad sticks up for her."

"Am I fighting with Audrey?" Stephanie said in amazement. "I guess I am; I thought I was just trying to talk to her."

"You're more forceful than you think you are, Mom," Bert said. "What needs to happen is that Dad needs to stand up to her, and you need to give her a break."

"And you, young man, are a family therapist," Margaret teased Bert. Handsome, athletic, and very serious, he seemed worried that his parents might disagree with each other. The youngest, Laurel, looked worried too, though she said nothing.

Every family has its battle lines, and of course the most critical schisms are between the parents. In some families marital conflict is hidden, even from the partners, who are too threatened by their disagreements to be consciously aware of them. Instead, beneath the surface of the couple's politeness there is a deep, vaguely felt tension, which is often expressed through the vacant spaces and vital omissions in the marriage.

Couples who cannot deal directly with anger, who cannot confront each other about their grievances, are at a great disadvantage. The methods they use for avoiding conflict—repression, and denial that conflict exists—leave them isolated from each other, and from their own feelings. Inevitably, the couple's children are drawn into this superficially cooperative, uneasy situation. They become pawns in the undeclared battle.

At certain junctures in their history, every couple encounters serious marital difficulties. Many of these conflicts are of long standing; they lie dormant until they are exposed by a particular stress (an illness, a death, a job loss, a move) or by a certain stage of development. Often it is time itself, and the demands that its changes place on the partners, which exposes their problems. So when someone in the family is having difficulty, we assume a background struggle in the marriage—though sometimes it is in the foreground. The question is what the conflict is about, and what roles the various family members play in it. While we are peering intently into the nuclear family, trying to grasp their particular pattern of warfare, we are also attempting to see the families that loom over the heads of these parents; trying to see each one as the child he or she was, and to some degree still is.

Stephanie was almost hysterical. She sounded as though her daughter's affair had inflicted in her a mortal wound. "I can't understand this," she kept repeating. "It is inconceivable to me that you could be involved with a married man."

A bit confused ourselves, we asked about the history of Stephanie and Audrey's relationship. "I would say it has been very close," Stephanie offered. "Wouldn't you?" she asked her daughter.

"Yes and no," Audrey said tentatively. "We have done things together—especially around the house and with the other kids. I think I have helped a lot as well."

"I would agree with that," the mother said. There was a strangely clipped, almost indignant tone in her voice, as though she were still incredulous about the conflict with her daughter.

"Well—" and Audrey stopped. After a moment of reflection, she resumed. "Sometimes, I think I have done too much."

"Helped too much?" Margaret asked.

"Yes. I realize that Mother has had a lot to do, and not a lot of support from Dad, especially with the kids. But there were times when it seemed a big imposition on me. I would want to have a date or go out with my friends, and she would want me to take care of Laurel." A quick, warm smile in the direction of her sister. "I didn't mind, but then again I did." Another hesitation. "It wasn't so much what I had to do, but something"—acknowledging her mother again—"made me feel guilty about having my own life. I don't know, maybe I'm making too much of it."

"Maybe not," Margaret said. "Anything else you've been angry with your mother about?"

"The picture, I guess. The big framed one in the entry way."

"I don't understand," Margaret said blankly.

Audrey looked embarrassed, and hesitant about going further. "I don't like it," Audrey said. "It's of me when I was about six years old, and I am in a frilly white smock. Whenever I look at it I get very uncomfortable. I think it reminds me of something I also feel with Mother."

"Which is?" Margaret asked.

"That that is the way she wants me to be."

Margaret said quietly, "Sometimes your mother treats you in a way that makes you think she wants you to stay a little girl."

"Yes."

"Anything specific that she does? Or is it just a vague sense?" Margaret asked.

"It's a kind of hovering, a way she tries to help me too much. I don't know." Seeing her mother's hurt expression, she seemed to be losing heart. Then she said, "I know I'm not being consistent, but sometimes I don't think Mother and I are close at all. I think she sees the things in me that she wants to see, but that she doesn't see the part of me that is different from her."

"And adult?" Margaret offered. This time Audrey nodded. These were confusing crosscurrents. She felt tied to her mother as a "helper," and also fearful that her mother wanted to keep her a child. And she had never talked about these issues.

"How about your father?" I asked, trying to take some of the pressure off Stephanie. "How do you see your relationship with him?"

Audrey looked surprised that I had asked, as though she had

never questioned her bond with her father. "I guess I would see us as close. We talk a lot—even now, when I have an academic problem at school, sometimes I'll call him. He's very good in math, and we both like philosophy." Then she smiled broadly, realizing that she had also chosen a philosopher as her lover. I smiled back at her, and, with no reference to the content, she added, "I had never thought of the parallel."

"Ever have the same sense that your father was having trouble letting you go?" I asked.

"No," she said after a moment's thought. "No, he's not like that. It's as though anything I want is all right with him."

"So, in a way, it's too easy to please him," Margaret said, "and too hard to please your mother."

"True. I often feel Mother is criticizing me, in a subtle way."

"And maybe your dad isn't firm enough, doesn't offer you a sense that he is in the older generation," I said.

As we begin to look at roles in families, I am often reminded of the work of the German family therapist Helm Stierlin, whose book *Separating Parents and Adolescents* offers an incisive commentary on this period of family life. I have leaned heavily on Stierlin's typology of roles here, though I have added several modifications that are derived from my own experience.

Stierlin, who also enjoys metaphors of physical motion, contends that some families are dominated by "centrifugal," outward-moving forces. These are loosely organized families, whose members are not closely tied to each other. When tension in the family rises, they turn loose from each other all too easily. Some therapists call these families "disengaged." Other families are tightly tied to each other, and tend to pull their members inward. These "centripetally" dominated families, who tend to be "enmeshed," have great difficulty letting their children separate from them.

Most families live with a complex mixture of these forces, and each family member feels them in a different way. Audrey was clearly strongly pulled toward her mother; she also felt close to her father, though he seemed better able to let her separate from him. As we look at each child's (or adolescent's) role in the family, we try to determine what role or roles that child plays in relation to each family member—but particularly in relation to both parents.

We are particularly on the lookout for coalitions between parents and children that seem problematic for the children. Family therapist Jay Haley maintains that the central problem in disturbed families is that the coalitions across the generations are stronger than the coalitions between the married partners. Ties between the parents and their children are closer than those between the parents. Of course, these inappropriate teamings across the generations often extend back a generation: many adults have not been able to separate from their own parents, even though they are married and may have children themselves. Later we would ask about the relationships between the adult Lands and their parents; but initially we needed to see the pattern of teaming within this nuclear family.

At the start of therapy, then, we not only ask, "Where are the teams (or coalitions) in this family?" but we are also curious about the way in which these coalitions function. That is, if a child is "tied" to a parent, *how* is he or she bound to the parent?

THE BOUND CHILD

Kids who are held tightly by their parents and who are pulled toward the center of the family are called *bound* children by Stierlin, and they constitute a major category of the family's players. In a departure from Stierlin, I prefer to categorize these kids according to the generational "level" at which they are bound to their parents.

Parental kids function as parent surrogates in the family, sometimes working alongside their parents, sometimes actually parenting the parents. Such kids are "promoted" upward by two generations! Carl Whitaker would often tease these kids about their tendency to be prematurely adult. "You know, if you mother your mother like that, it makes you your own grandma."

Marital or *companionate* kids function as peers with their parents. Like parental children, they are pressured to be much more adult than is healthy for them. The "marital" child is of course a protagonist in the classic "Oedipal triangle," while "companionate" kids become their parents' friends.

Dependent kids are infantilized, or held in an exaggeratedly childlike position. Unlike parental children, they are encouraged to be much less mature than they are capable of being.

Most parents want their kids to be able to leave home successfully, and to have separate, autonomous lives. But because some parents need their kids so badly, they unconsciously set up obstacles in the way of this "individuation" process. The parents' resistance to their kids' separation is often communicated in a subtle and indirect manner; but because bound kids are so loyal and so sensitive to their parents' needs, they respond strongly to their parents' anxieties about their leaving. As we see in Audrey's struggles, these kids' normal developmental transitions often create turbulence in the family. Audrey wanted and deserved independence; but her choice of an "unacceptable" lover both created a barrier between her and her parents, and it drew her back into the inner circle of the family's politics.

THE PARENTAL CHILD Without question, Audrey had been a parental child. Within this group of kids there are, however, some important distinctions. Like Audrey, many parental kids are drafted at an early age to help with the functional, practical part of parenting. Oldest girls are especially vulnerable to becoming "assistant parents"—helping with cooking, housework, and child care. As long as the burdens aren't too heavy, this isn't a bad role to occupy. In the past, girls learned their mothers' skills, and they learned to be industrious. They also developed a sense of companionship with their mothers. Boys, too, can play such roles: in the past many boys left school early to earn money for the family, and of course they often worked beside their fathers on farms and in small businesses. In poor families, these financial pressures still weigh very heavily on young males.

Some parental kids carry far too much of the practical responsibility for a household, and they assume too much of the emotional responsibility of parenthood. This is particularly likely to occur when one parent is physically absent; but as we learned later in the therapy with the Lands, it can also occur when a parent is psychologically absent.

This is Audrey, speaking in a subsequent individual session. "I suppose it happened partly because Dad was always so preoccupied with his business, but I really had a lot of responsibility for our house. Mother got her first teaching job when Laurel went to school, but even before that I did a lot for her. It got really bad for me when I was eleven or twelve, and Mother would want me to stay with her in the afternoons after school when I would want to be with my own friends. I would do it, but I think I sometimes took out my anger on Laurel. Later, when I began to drive, Mother would always have something that needed doing—the grocery shopping, or taking Laurel to piano lessons, or something like that. That's when I really began to feel angry about all she depended on me for. But it wasn't just the everyday things I did. I also worried a lot about Laurel, and when she would get depressed or upset, I felt helpless and confused about what to do. Sometimes it seemed as though I was her parent instead of Mother.''

These practical helpers are often precociously competent. Everyone, including the kid herself, assumes that she is strong. Parents frequently say about such children, "She is so independent, she doesn't really seem to need us." The unfortunate fact is that the parents need to see this child as strong. Inside, she feels deprived and empty; and the only way she knows to meet her needs is by helping. That is her way of "connecting," and of feeling close; and while this role affords her a valued place in the family, it also sets her up for later difficulty in life.

Other parental kids' burdens are not so practical. They don't work beside the parent they help; they literally nurture one or both of their parents. Here is the voice of another parental child:

''I could tell when my mother finally gave up on my father. She just stopped caring about him. He had retired early and lived on his trust fund, and my mother became very scornful of him. He started to drink more heavily then, and I would worry a lot about him. In the afternoon when I came home from school, I would see him looking depressed and would go in and try to cheer him up. Sometimes I would even make up stories to make him laugh.'' At age nine, she had made a conscious decision to "parent" her own father; and her concern for him formed a dominant theme in her life. As an adult, she had married a very dependent man whom she also felt responsible for and worried about constantly.

A large number of families have at least one dysfunctional parent, and the children in these families are usually drawn into care-taking roles with that parent. If a parent is seriously depressed, alcoholic, or mentally ill, the other parent is often preoccupied with the family's practical survival—and angry at his or her "failed" spouse. It falls to one or more children to "caretake" this wounded adult; and the experience of doing so forms in these children a primitive, often lifelong fear: *"If I don't take good care of others, something terrible will happen."* That "something terrible" may include the fantasy that without his or her help, the parent would die; and beneath that fear there is a yet deeper one: that the child would not survive the loss of this parent.

There is a third type of situation in which a child learns to be parental. In this instance, the child is perceived by the parent *as if the child is literally the parent's parent*. The parent looks at the child and somehow manages to see an image of his or her own parent. This is obviously a disturbed process, but it is extremely common.

According to family therapist Ivan Boszormenyi-Nagy, who introduced the concept of "parentification" in his influential work *Invisible Loyalties*, this primitive process is responsible for much child abuse. The needy parent "loads" expectations on the child, and when the child cannot live up to them, he becomes the target of the parent's anger at his or her own parents.

I learned about this bewildering phenomenon when my son reached the predictably belligerent age of two. As Mark had the usual stormy outbursts of a "terrible two," I began to feel strangely frightened. "He's going to run over me," I said silently to myself, and soon I was being very tough on him about his rebelliousness. I knew that my response was exaggerated, but I couldn't help being threatened by his seemingly powerful anger. After several weeks of being much too punitive with Mark, I had a flash of insight. I recalled how angry my father had gotten at me when he came home from the army, and how overwhelmed I felt by his temper. Suddenly my fears that Mark was going to overpower me made sense: I had "parentified" him—and was reacting to him as if he were my father. The fact that he was male and was angry was all my unconscious mind needed. Deeply chagrined by the unfairness of my response to my diminutive son, I resolved to change my behavior.

Sometimes parentification occurs in a relationship in a much more persistent way. Several years ago Margaret and I worked with a family in which the son, a senior in high school, was engaged in some minor delinquency. It quickly became apparent that mother and son were highly involved with one another, while the withdrawn father was preoccupied with his job. After some initial work in helping the parents place more emphasis on their own relationship, the son began to improve. As his graduation approached, however, his mother became increasingly agitated.

One day she came to a session extremely upset. Almost immediately, she burst into tears. "I don't know what's happening," she said, bewildered, "I can't stop crying. I've been crying all weekend." After she had calmed down a bit, she continued, "I know I should be glad that my son is doing so much better, but instead I feel terribly sad. I wonder if I am losing my mind."

After some further exploration of her history, we learned that this woman's father, whose favorite she was, had died when she was thirteen, and that her childhood was never happy again. Her mother and sister were very close, and she felt excluded from their relationship. She had eventually married a man who was somewhat parental toward her, but whose coolness reminded her of her mother's emotional distance. So in her adult life, this boy, who resembled her father, had come to replace him. It was not that the son acted in a parental way, but his mother laid on his shoulders many of her positive feelings for her father. When her son began in earnest to leave the family, his imminent departure awakened in her a long-buried grief.

Certain children are particularly vulnerable to becoming "parentified." Because they have so many opportunities to be helpful, eldest children are often drawn into parental roles; and because of the ubiquitous expectations placed on them to attend to the needs of others, all girls are more likely than their brothers to occupy such roles.

☐ Parental kids grow up very aware of others' needs, and are often unaware of their own. Since their emotional safety comes from their being competent and helpful, they become adults who seem strong.

- ☐ Parental kids often work much too hard for their own good. Since they occupied "adult" roles and couldn't depend on an adult to say, "I'll take care of that; you don't have to worry about it," they have trouble setting limits on how much they are responsible for. Some parental kids are "omnipotently helpful."

- ☐ Often described as "good" people, parental kids may be self-righteous, since as children they gained status through their identification with their parents' roles.

- ☐ Cut off from the angry, needy, emotional "child" aspects of themselves, they need to associate with others who have access to those parts of themselves.

- ☐ As adults, these kids frequently choose partners who are underresponsible, or who seem to need help. They tend to occupy dominant positions in their marriages, and to become critical of their dependent "charges" (on whom they project their dislike of the dependent part of themselves).

- ☐ Parental kids are often caring, competent people who do far more than their share of the world's work. While we all depend on them, they are at risk for being exploited by others.

As we worked with Audrey, it became clear that although she had been trapped in just such a parental role in her family, she was also rebelling against its constraints. "You're being irresponsible!" her mother would repeat; and though Audrey had difficulty defending herself, we tried to help her see that there was a healthy impulse in her rebellion.

But there were other issues in her struggle with her family, one of which involved her alliance with her father. Again, at a later individual session, she said, "It never occurred to me that there was anything wrong with the way it happened, though I do remember feeling vaguely uneasy. Many times on summer evenings, my dad and I would sit out on the porch, talking. We would talk about just anything, but often our conversations would be about philosophy or religion. Sometimes the talk would go on and on, and Mother would come to the screen door and ask if Dad wanted to go to bed;

and he would say, 'In a minute.' Then we would realize suddenly that it was midnight, and I would wonder if Mother would be angry. There was never anything sexual or inappropriate between me and my father, though often I wondered why he and my mother couldn't talk the way we could."

THE MARITAL OR COMPANIONATE CHILD The second type of bound child only has to stretch up one generation to reach a peer relationship with the parent, but that "stretch" is difficult enough. This is the marital or companionate child. Even if the needs are expressed quite indirectly, when kids are pressured to meet a parent's sexual needs, or their needs for friendship or companionship, these kids are bound to the parents in unhealthy ways, and their lives are seriously compromised.

The Companionate Child. We all need friends: caring peers with whom we can share our struggles and our joys. When adults lack peer adult support, and particularly when that quality of comfortable sharing is absent in a marriage, those adults' children are often called on to meet this basic need. The companionate child is such a person.

This kind of intimate peership, which is extremely common between mothers and daughters, is not problematic unless the parent depends on the relationship too heavily. A woman friend speaks of her relationship with her daughter: "Diane and I were always talking. When she was in high school, I couldn't wait for her to come in from school. We would talk about her day, her latest boyfriend, the gossip of the other girls; and though I tried not to lean on her too heavily, I'm sure I often talked about myself, and I complained about the frustration of being a housewife. But we also had a lot of fun. We could laugh at the same things, and enjoyed doing things like shopping together, and even housework. We just enjoyed being together."

Fathers and sons also form companionships, though they are often oriented around joint activities: hunting, fishing, playing sports, working on cars. But while father and son may joke together and may share a kind of nonverbal warmth, they don't usually talk about their feelings. Since men often have difficulty forming intimate friendships, the father who does develop a deeper level of closeness to his son is likely to depend heavily on that relationship.

Of course companionate relationships also exist between fathers and daughters, and between mothers and sons. Audrey and her father were intellectual and "spiritual" companions. They had an easy, comfortable ability to talk together that Colin obviously depended on—and that made Stephanie jealous. When parents have dissimilar values, or have few interests in common, and when one parent leans on a particular child to fill these needs, the child not only has to deal with the other parent's jealousy of this "platonic affair" but also with the burden of trying to be a parent's friend.

Such children are cheated of the experience of being able to lean on a strong, authoritative parent—someone they can "test the limits" with, learn to fight with, and ultimately depend on. Companionate kids are flattered to be their parents' friends, and they rarely notice the sense of betrayal which they feel. If Audrey could articulate her dilemma, she might say, "Instead of my being able to lean on my father, he leans on me."

Like all bound adolescents, companionate kids also have difficulty breaking away from the parent who depends on them. Again, my friend speaks about her daughter. "Every time I think about her senior year in high school, I get a little teary. We started to fight about halfway through the year, and it got worse and worse. We fought about everything—her boyfriend, her studies, her choice of college. She opposed me at every turn. Then one day we both broke down crying, and I said to her, "We're separating, aren't we?' After that, we both realized what was happening, and we could talk about it."

The loss of the companionate child through the normal process of growth is a serious problem in many families, particularly for the mother who does not have enough companionship in her marriage, or enough meaning in her life outside her relationship with her children. But many men don't have satisfying friendships either, and the departure of a companionate child can also create in them a deep sense of loss.

The Marital Child. While we joke good-humoredly about mama's boys and daddy's girls, and while in the healthy family there is indeed much to enjoy in the harmless flirtation between mothers and sons, and fathers and daughters—indeed, this game is a useful rehearsal for adult sexuality—this "game" can have grave consequences. In troubled families, adult sexuality may be channeled inappropriately into these parent-child alliances.

Such ties almost always occur because the other parent is physically or psychologically absent, or because there has been a serious breakdown in the relationship between the parents. Even if there is no overt sexual overture on the parent's part, the child feels the psychological pressure of the parent's need for an intimate heterosexual relationship. Family therapist and incest specialist John Bailey calls this kind of constant, sexualized emotional pressure "subclinical incest." "It's terribly damaging," Bailey contends, "because the kid must constantly defend against this subtle, invasive 'presence' in her environment. She feels vaguely untrusting, unsafe, and eventually she is exhausted by a process which she may not even be able to name."

A remarkable number of women have had an invasive, physically abusive sexual experience at the hands of an older male. The "perpetrator," as such males are called by child-abuse experts, may be an uncle, a grandparent, an older brother; but often enough, he is father or stepfather. This experience may consist of a father's putting his hand once on his daughter's breast, or coming into her room repeatedly when she is undressed, or parading in the nude before her in a way that makes her anxious; but it may also involve repeated fondling and even intercourse. As common and as damaging as such acts are, the subtler forms of sexual invasion are even more common, and may be seriously injurious.

Audrey, for example, did not perceive her relationship with her father as sexualized. She thought of her father as her "pal," and indeed there was a strong component of companionship in their relationship. But as she later learned more about herself in therapy, she had another view. "I suppose there was something about those times when we would talk so late into the night that made me uneasy, and it makes me uneasy now to mention it. There was a tone of confidentiality, of conspiracy almost, between us, and I suppose that is what made Mother angry. Maybe it was just too intimate." Audrey also eventually realized that it was not coincidence that she was involved with an older man: "As embarrassing as it seems in retrospect, Herb *is* a little like my father." Audrey had "acted out" the hidden dynamic in her family—her coalition with her father; and her mother's intense distress about her relationship with the teacher was partly an expression of her largely unverbalized feelings about the father-daughter bond. At least in regard to Audrey's literal affair, she could be legitimately outraged.

Of course mothers also sexualize their relationships with their sons, a process that is probably even more common—though usually subtler—than inappropriate father-daughter ties. Since fathers are often absent from the home for various reasons, boys are especially vulnerable, not only to their mothers' needs, but to their own grandiose fantasies of replacing the absent father. This "father-absence dynamic" is a central problem in the family, and we will return to it in a later chapter.

Today, kids in divorced and remarried families are especially at risk. Divorced fathers are often much more absent from their sons' lives than in intact families, leading these boys to be strongly overinvolved with their mothers; and girls are especially vulnerable to abuse at the hands of stepfathers.

- ☐ Marital kids tend to fear engulfment and intrusion; but since the overinvolved parent is always "unfaithful," they also fear rejection.
- ☐ These kids feel drained or fatigued because of their sense of obligation to the overinvolved parent; and in addition to generalized feelings of inadequacy, they often feel sexually inadequate as well.
- ☐ While they may be warm and friendly toward the opposite sex, they may have difficulty trusting their partners.
- ☐ They are often competitive with same-sex friends.
- ☐ They may act out sexually and be exploited by others; or they may be flirtatious and exploitative.
- ☐ The marital child usually grows up to marry another marital child.

Companionate kids have many of the same issues, but to a less extreme degree. For example, they also feel drained and inadequate from having tried to meet a parent's companionship needs, and they are unconsciously mistrustful of the parent who uses them in this way. They are also vulnerable to rejection, and to feeling intruded upon.

THE DEPENDENT CHILD   A child can also be bound to a parent through the parent's excessive helpfulness or attentiveness. In this case, the child is systematically, if unwittingly, taught by the parents to feel helpless or weak. Such parents communicate that the world is a fearful place, and that this child needs special help and protection, thereby keeping the "infantilized" child unnecessarily dependent and immature. Youngest kids are especially vulnerable to this unconscious "strategy," as are girls.

In the Land family, both Audrey and Laurel complained about being treated in this way. In Audrey's words, "I know that it only happens sometimes, but it really annoys me when you treat me like I am a little kid, Mother. I mean I'm nineteen, for God's sake, and you sometimes call me up and ask me if I have been to the doctor when all I have is a cold! But it's not always that specific. Sometimes I just feel hovered over, worried over, in a way that makes me feel small." Laurel did not voice them at the beginning of therapy, but she too had the same kind of complaints about her mother's treatment of her.

To some degree, the overprotection of girls is a cultural norm. Margaret's father often said to her, "If you had been a boy, I would have had to treat you differently. But because you are a girl, there are things I don't have to teach you." The implication was that she didn't have to learn to fend for herself; that a man would look after her.

Another young woman, complaining about the same phenomenon, said, "When my parents talked about my childhood, they always described me as 'like a doll.' And they—especially my father—somehow managed to convey to me that I was delicate and fragile. He would try to help me with everything, especially with my music. He wanted me to play the violin with him, but when I had trouble, he was all too willing to help—so I felt inadequate and never got really competent. My mother did the same thing to me, but she was also very critical. Not until I was an adult and my parents started calling me with all these vague complaints about their lives did I realize how needy *they* are, and how threatening my independence is. They tend to blame Arnold [her lover] for all the tension between me and them, but it is really my independence that makes them upset."

As this young woman discovered, parents who infantilize their children often got little support themselves as children. They may seem like adequate adults, but internally they remain emotionally deprived; and it is this deprived "inner child" which they project onto their literal child. In overhelping their child, they are indirectly attempting to meet their own needs, trying to be for the child the kind of parent they wanted for themselves. Always attentive and solicitous, they not only fail to see their child's need for independence, but they establish habitual dependency in the child. The child becomes, in effect, a prisoner of helpfulness, a reassurance junkie. In adult life it is so difficult for this child to find a replacement for the parent(s), that he or she may repeatedly return to the parental nest. In the worst case, the infantilized child can be bound for life.

"You baby the kids," men often say to their wives. Indeed, mothers are often guiltier than their husbands of infantilization of their children, but for a complex set of reasons for which they hardly deserve blame. I believe that in this culture, mothering is a profoundly lonely activity; most mothers feel stressed, alone, unsupported—especially by their husbands. Often they must give much more emotionally than they receive. In the "emotional vacuum" of their role, women gain emotional closeness through caretaking their children. They are tempted to project onto their girls their own unmet needs and, as a result of this intense identification, to overmother them. When women have husbands who are emotionally absent, they are also sorely tempted to infantilize their sons as a way of keeping them close to them. It is as if they say to their sons, "I don't want you to leave me the way your father does."

While women have been blamed for binding their children to them in this and other ways, the pathology of father absence lies behind many of their dilemmas. If a mother were not so alone, if she did not need support so badly, she would be much less likely to restrict her children's growth in unhealthy ways.

Many of us had a self-sacrificial mother who gave more than she received, and who bound her children to her in a kind of angry sympathy. As Boszormenyi-Nagy has pointed out, if a parent has sacrificed too heavily for a child, that child feels indebted (and bound) until that debt is repaid. A parent who refuses to allow the child to repay the debt, and who continues to be self-sacrificial, produces a continuing guilty tie between parent and child.

These helpful, self-sacrificial mothers—of which mine was one—create difficulties in their adult children's lives, and they make very difficult mothers-in-law. My mother learned this approach to life as an oldest (of four) parental child who was responsible for too much of her siblings' upbringing. She was also her father's favorite, and very intent on pleasing men. I inherited some of that effort, which was expressed in her doing all manner of things for me which I could have done for myself. She also overhelped my sister, Jane, who is four years younger.

It was not until recently that Jane and I realized another component in the origins of this overdriven compulsion to help. It is the dilemma of a woman who is asked to give too much too early, and to keep on giving. Angry at the situation she is in, and guilty about feeling angry at her children for needing her, she reverses the direction of her feelings, concealing her anger in exaggerated helpfulness.

I suppose I owe the survival of my marriage to my mother's younger sister Dorothy, who apparently said to my mother one day when I was about six, "If you don't stop doing so much for that boy, no woman is ever going to be able to stand living with him." Margaret has always liked Dorothy.

- ☐ Dependent children are highly conscious of needing others' support, and in relationships where they feel safe, they are often warm, friendly, and loyal to those they depend on.
- ☐ Fearful of jeopardizing this support, they have difficulty expressing anger. They may communicate anger subtly and passively; they may also turn it inward and become depressed.
- ☐ In an effort to gain sympathy, they may "script" themselves as others' victims.
- ☐ When they marry, they are sometimes drawn to other dependent kids; but they usually seek our parental children who promise to take care of them.

Being in therapy can sometimes worsen such an individual's problems, especially if the therapist fails to understand that this person needs to be confronted about his or her "addiction" to dependency. Most of all, they need to see that they have been "hypnotized" into believing that they are much less capable than they are. Support in becoming independent and assertive is the major need.

When the conflict between Audrey and her mother emerged, their struggle dominated the room and the session. Because she was so relentlessly unaccepting of her daughter's decisions, so doggedly persistent in pressuring her, and spoke with such coolness and scorn to Audrey, it was difficult not to be angry at the mother. Sounding strong, tough, and righteous, she would not yield. As the session wore on, Audrey became increasingly silent and withdrawn. I worried that she would not come back, that she might even feel suicidal. As she began to address Stephanie, I sensed in Margaret the same concern:

"Stephanie, I find myself feeling angry at you." The room became silent. "I know you are distressed, and my kids have certainly done things that have distressed me." Her words were firm; her voice contained an edge of tension. "But there is something else going on here. You seem to me to be overreacting; you are driving your daughter away." Margaret looked momentarily at Audrey, who seemed almost defeated.

"I believe I am doing what is right," Stephanie said defensively. "I believe she is making a mistake."

"She may be," Margaret said, waiting as she thought. "But it is her mistake, her life. I think that's what you're missing."

"It's also my life; my feelings are involved too."

"Too involved, I think," Margaret countered. "That's what puzzles me."

"What do you mean?"

"I wonder where all the extra emotion is coming from in you. I think there is another way to approach this—if you could be a little calmer, try to help Audrey a little more, support her more. But something is blocking that." She paused again. "This is a guess, but what if we introduced your mother into this drama?" Margaret glanced toward an empty chair directly across from Stephanie. "I know she died several years ago, but if we could imagine her sitting in this empty chair, I wonder what she would say about this situation."

Stephanie looked startled, almost frightened at the prospect of her mother's presence in the room. For a moment, it seemed as though she would refuse to continue. Then she said more softly, "My mother was deeply religious. She would say that what Audrey is doing is wrong. Very wrong."

"And what would she say about you for having a daughter who would do such a thing?" Margaret probed.

"She wouldn't *say* anything negative to me. She would sympathize with me. She once had to deal with something like this herself."

"All right," Margaret said, hearing the emphasis on the word "say." "What would she think?"

"I'm afraid she would think that I failed her." This was spoken in a low, hushed tone, as if she were trying to keep her mother from hearing.

Margaret's voice warmed perceptibly. "So in a sense she is here, now, and you feel that you have disappointed her."

Stephanie said nothing; she was crying. Though there were many issues that needed attention, the hour was over. Margaret went over beside Stephanie and put her hand gently on her shoulder. While the family watched awkwardly—they had probably rarely seen her so vulnerable—Margaret talked to her quietly. As the family filed out of the room, Margaret walked with her, still touching her arm.

9

Players: The Outsiders

I FELT RELIEVED WHEN Audrey appeared at the next session, though she hardly looked happy to be there. Settling her slight frame into a chair, she folded her arms defiantly. Stephanie looked intently at her daughter; Audrey's eyes flashed angrily away. "I see that not much has changed," Margaret said. The other members of the family looked apprehensive.

"There has been no communication between us," Stephanie said firmly. "Colin made all the arrangements for this meeting."

"Well, let's get to work," I said.

"I'm still thinking about how we ended." Margaret addressed Stephanie, who was confused by the remark. "I felt a lot of empathy for you after what you said about your mother. What you were talking about seemed important, and I was sorry we didn't have time to go on—though you may have another agenda today that you want to work on." The mother seemed irritated at being distracted from her preoccupation with Audrey. "I was also puzzled by something you said," Margaret continued.

With a sigh, Stephanie finally relented. "What was that?"

"You said your mother had to deal with something like this."

Stephanie sighed again. "It was my sister." The words were

clipped and angry, though I wasn't sure whether she was angry at the sister or at Margaret.

"What happened to your sister?" I asked. Stephanie clearly did not want to talk about this subject. "I don't see the relevance of it," she replied in her efficient manner. Another sigh; that made three.

"There may not be any," Margaret said matter-of-factly.

Still looking irritated at being distracted from her fight with her daughter, but beginning to seem increasingly pensive, Stephanie was silent for a long moment. With still another sigh, she said, "When my sister was a senior in high school, she began going with a wild crowd. One boy in particular my mother didn't approve of." Another pause, as though she were dreading her next statement. "Just before she graduated, she got pregnant." There was sadness in her voice and face.

Margaret said, "What happened when she got pregnant?"

"My mother was very religious, very dedicated to the church. She was terribly hurt by it, as if my sister had done it to wound her. My mother's world just fell apart." Stephanie looked absently into space.

"How did the family deal with this crisis?" Margaret asked.

"There was a very tense situation between my mother and my sister. Our family had never had anything like this, of course. We were a respected family in our community. My mother did not insist that my sister get married, but because my sister knew how devastated Mother was, she did. She didn't graduate from high school, and there she was, seventeen with a baby and a husband who worked at the textile plant. The marriage lasted about six months, and my sister moved back home with the baby." As Stephanie talked, her own daughter softened perceptibly, her anger giving way to curiosity.

"I didn't know any of this," Audrey said. "I didn't even know Aunt Kathryn had been married to somebody before Don. So who is Charles's father?"

"Amos Lauder," Stephanie said with some embarrassment. "You wouldn't know him. He was killed in a car accident a few years after that."

"My God," Audrey said blankly.

"Could you go on?" Margaret urged. "Tell the rest of the story?"

Stephanie said wearily, "It was an awful situation for years. My sister kept running around with 'unacceptable' men, and my mother had most of the care of the baby. She and my sister fought a lot: my mother would say she was irresponsible, my sister would say Mother was interfering in her life; but then she wouldn't get out either. My sister finally got her degree and got a decent job and moved, but the conflict between my mother and sister went on for at least ten years. She was about thirty when she met Don, the man our kids know as her husband. They later had two children."

"What is her situation now?" I said.

"She lives in Charlotte, where my parents lived—and my father still does. She's divorced from Don, and has a good job. She is finally doing all right."

"But she had a terrible time breaking away from your mother," Margaret said.

"That's what I feel so sad about," Stephanie said seriously.

"How have her kids done?" I said. "Especially the first boy—what was his name?"

"Charles. He's not doing at all well, in fact. He's a young alcoholic."

"A fatherless kid," I said. "And the family could not talk openly about all of this."

"My mother saw to that. She was just so ashamed," Stephanie said. "Because she and I were close, she would talk to me about her struggles with Kathryn, but most of the time my sister's problems were never mentioned."

"Was your mother close to Charles?" Margaret said curiously.

"That's one of the things they had conflicts about. My sister said that my mother kept interfering with his life, and I suppose she did. But then my mother took care of Charles when he was young."

Margaret said to Stephanie, "I see the similarity between this story and the struggle between you and Audrey." For a moment, Stephanie seemed startled by the remark.

"I know I said something about their being similar," she finally said, relief mingled with embarrassment, "but I had never really thought about it, if you know what I mean."

"I do know what you mean. There is a difference between sensing something, and being fully conscious of it. One problem here is that you are in the very difficult role your mother played," Margaret added sympathetically.

Stephanie thought quietly, and as she did so she seemed softer, more forgiving. "It's strange if that is happening, because what she did to my sister is one of the few things I feel at all angry with my mother about. But I guess I also feel angry at my sister for what she put my mother through."

Margaret said, "Sounds as though you felt torn between them."

"Exactly. When I think about it, I still feel a kind of wrenching in my chest."

"You still have very strong feelings about that time in your family's life," Margaret said tenderly. "And Audrey is playing a role in recapitulating that situation."

"As my sister?" Stephanie inquired.

"Yes," Margaret said firmly. "But it seems more complicated than that. How did you see yourself in your family?"

"I suppose I'm a typical eldest kid," she said with the first smile of the hour. "Bossy." There was a pause. "I guess I'm also hard-working, responsible; boring things like that."

"How about the 'bossy'?" I asked Colin, who had been quiet throughout the session.

"I would concur with that, at least at times," he said good-humoredly.

"Oldest of how many kids?" Margaret asked. Stephanie described a brother two years younger, who was a physician; a sister, married to a lawyer, who was two years younger than the brother; and the rebellious Kathryn, now a real-estate broker, the youngest by three years. Stephanie's father had been a successful farmer who later owned a store in the small town where she grew up. Her mother had always been a housewife.

As she talked, we began to see Stephanie's origins more clearly. "When I was a young child, I felt very close to my father. He would read to me, play with me. I can still see the size of his large, rough hands as he held a book, and I can feel this immense arm that would be draped over my shoulder. I don't know what happened in my relationship with him, but we were not that close later on. Maybe he got too busy—I don't know." She sounded almost melancholy. "There were also financial stresses. I sometimes remember his losing his temper, and I felt afraid of him then. But I never questioned his love for me, or mine for him. In those later years, he seemed to be at a distance, as if he had left the raising of the kids to my mother."

She described her mother as a slight woman, private, quiet, extremely hardworking and serious. She was also often sad. "A lot had happened in her life. Her father had had an affair when she was young, and she saw her mother hurt by it; so I don't think she really trusted men. She certainly loved my father, but she didn't really lean on him, if that makes sense. She relied on herself, and I suppose on me." Another of those thoughtful pauses, as if deciding whether to continue.

"I also remember my mother's reading to me occasionally, but I suppose she was often preoccupied with the other children. I knew I had to help her, and I suppose a lot of our relationship involved my doing things with her that had to be done. But I never resented that. I loved her very much; I still do." There was a quality of mysteriously intense compassion in her description of her mother; it was as if this relationship were sacrosanct, unquestioned.

Stephanie was plainly a parental child. Except for the very early nurturance by her father, all her sense of closeness seemed to have come out of her teamed, companionate helpfulness to her mother. Having grown up worrying over her mother, and functioning as her "assistant parent," she had transferred her anxious overresponsibility to her own three children, and to Colin. Though Colin was a successful businessman whom she often deferred to, she also "parented" and fretted over him as well. "And, like her mother, she also doesn't rely on him for support," I said silently to myself.

The more I heard about Stephanie's almost joyless, enduring strength, the more concerned I felt about her. Where in her life was there pleasure, nurturance, and relief from responsibility? I knew that Margaret heard this issue especially clearly.

In examining Stephanie's family of origin, we were not only attempting to understand her role in that family, but trying to decipher the pattern in which all the members of her present, nuclear family were influenced by that original family experience. Because we have such powerful feelings about those key people in our past, and because our feelings about them are usually unexpressed, our conflicts with them unresolved, *we tend to recreate in our children aspects of those original players*. Our spouse, of course, is involved in this process. Not only do we marry someone whom we associate with the member of our family of origin—a process which we examine in the next chapter—but that spouse is also engaging in the same kind of recreation of his or her history. Our children, then, grow up in a maze of psychological complexity, in which they frequently trigger feelings in us that are related to our pasts. They too act out roles in our "structures."

Though she was a bound, parental child, we also heard other issues, and other roles, in Stephanie's description of her family of origin. The other group of family roles defines the family "outsiders," the children who are subject to the outward-pulling, centrifugal forces in the family dance. These children are not held as close as their bound siblings; they live at a certain distance from the family center.

"Before your sister began her struggle with your mother, what was her relationship with your parents like?" Margaret asked boldly, and, judging from Stephanie's reaction, irrelevantly.

"She was, I suppose, the favorite child," Stephanie said blankly. "She got along with everyone."

"She got a lot of attention from both your parents?" Margaret prodded.

"From everyone, including me."

Margaret said, "Do you remember seeing that attention being given to her, and feeling jealous of it?"

"I suppose I must have felt that way sometimes, but not often," Stephanie said meditatively. "Why do you ask?"

"I assume it was hard for her to break away from the family because your parents needed her, and that it would be natural for you to have a lot of jealousy about your parents' overinvolvement with her, that's all," Margaret said.

THE REJECTED CHILD

When we were kids, we sometimes stood off to the side of life, feeling rejected, blamed, ignored. Maybe we played a good basketball game, and nobody from the family was there to see it. Maybe no one in the family spoke to us in a friendly tone for several days. Maybe we had a fight with one parent and he or she was deliberately cool for what seemed like weeks, but was in fact hours. Maybe we repeatedly asked a parent to do something with us and were put off until later.

Most of the time, someone would say, "You look unhappy. What's the matter?" Or they would apologize for slighting us, or criticizing us. Reinvited into the circle of love and light, we would feel better.

For some kids, this is not a temporary experience. They spend much of their lives feeling attacked or rejected; and they learn to live on a psychological island. At least in solitude they feel moderately safe, if desolately alone. Unlike the bound child, who fears closeness because it carries the threat of being pulled in too deeply, the rejected child keeps himself separated—sometimes for a lifetime— because he fears a recapitulation of the original rejection.

Stierlin considers the rejected child a major role player in the family; but even if it does not form the major theme in our lives, we are all touched in some way by the experience of rejection. Since the dynamics of rejection are so complex, I can only describe a few of the situations that create these dilemmas.

THE UNWANTED CHILD   She is a fretful, fussy six-month-old who seems to resist her mother's efforts to care for her. When the mother tries to hold her, she struggles irritably; and the harder the mother tries, the more contentious the child becomes. It is as if mother and daughter are wrestling, the mother trying to force the child to love her. What the mother does not see is her own tension, her own rough touch, her own impatience—which the baby senses, and fights. The mother is too young; like my mother and Stephanie and many others, she had too much parental responsibility as a child, or not enough mothering herself; she has an unsupportive husband; there is financial stress or another life crisis in the background. This child was not planned or wanted, and on a fundamental level she knows it. By the time she is three she will whine constantly, and when she becomes an adult, she will not know why she struggles with depression. Perhaps she will say something like this woman, a thirty-three-year-old accountant:

"It took me a long time to be willing to think about the circumstances of my birth. Then one day, about a year after Hal and I started therapy, I realized that I was born when my mother was thirty-eight, six years after my brother. 'I was an accident!' I said to myself. Then I asked myself, 'Did my parents really want me?' That was frightening to think about. What I came up with was mixed. I think my mother didn't. She was just beginning to work full time, and she quit her job. I guess that's why my relationship with her has always been strained, and why I try so desperately to please her. But I think my father did. He spent a lot of time with me, and I felt close to him. Of course I guess he owed me something, since I kept mother at home for him."

These troubled beginnings lie in the shadowy times before memory, and their effects on us—black moods, bleak days—seem as mysterious as they are undeserved. Perhaps our parents learned to love us later, or the crisis abated, or the mood in the family changed; but this sunless season left its deep imprint on our lives, and it stays with us.

AN EARLY LOSS "Why is she so desperate to please her husband?" I asked myself as I began working with a couple in which the husband seemed to be a tyrannical taskmaster. "Why can't she stand up to him?" Then I learned about the fact that when she was four years old, she had spent six months in a specialized hospital in New York for treatment of a rare illness. The treatment had been successful, but the scars of the lengthy separation from her parents were evident: a profound sense of insecurity, and an inability to risk displeasing people on whom she depended, especially her husband.

We have learned to inquire carefully about this kind of occurrence; and if we suspect such an event, we often send our patients home to their parents to get more information. Separations from father have their own traumatic effect; but because she is the primary caregiver, *almost any but the briefest separations from mother in the early years of life can leave a lasting impact on a child*. This may seem like an extreme statement, but it is supported by many years of clinical experience. So many times we have wondered why an individual had persistent difficulties with depression, felt easily rejected, and had problems being assertive—only to discover this kind of early separation from the mother. Often, the incident has not been remembered.

Whether it is a brief separation at a critical stage of development, or a major loss through divorce or the death of a parent, the category of traumatic loss of support of a parent is such a major one, and affects so many of us, that we will need to return to it; for such losses leave us with shaky emotional foundations, and they have a drastic impact on our capacity to deal with conflict in marriage.

CHRONIC NEGLECT Sometimes the loss of parental support is not traumatic, but chronic, and it occurs in the slow, unnoticed omission of care and attention. Here is Hal, a thirty-year-old stockbroker: "I spent a lot of time alone as a child. I would go up in the attic and rummage through old things, looking for something—I didn't know what. Or I would read. Later, when we got a television, I became attached to it. I realized now that my mother was so involved with her mother that she was often over at her house; and of course my father worked two jobs and was never home."

This is Margaret, speaking of her own childhood: "Many times I remember coming home from school and finding the door locked. My mother would be playing bridge, and she would just forget about me. Sometimes I would go to a neighbor and call my father's office, and he would send someone out to let me in. Or she would be supposed to meet me at dance class, and would be half an hour late. I would stand out on the street, afraid to look up. I'd look at people's feet, watching for my mother's shoes."

Such experiences communicate powerful things to children, but they are so much a part of everyday life that they don't seem out of the ordinary. They set up emotional "rules" about what kind of support these kids can expect.

In some instances, neglect occurs in the midst of the family. That is, the parents are physically present, and they may be highly involved with some of their kids, but they simply don't "connect" emotionally with a particular child. In one family of five children, I began to ask about coalitions. Each of the children reported being on the mother's or father's "team"—except the middle child. He was also extremely depressed.

CHRONIC CRITICISM OR ATTACK Being habitually criticized or attacked verbally is one of the most common, and most damaging, experiences of childhood. For some kids, their only link with a parent may be through that parent's criticism. "When I come home in the afternoon," a teenage boy says, "before she even says hello, Mom asks me in this mean tone of voice whether I have any homework. She almost always talks to me like that." Such kids internalize the parental criticism, and it becomes an integral part of their self-concept. They learn to be critical of themselves, and they tend to seek out partners who replicate this pattern.

Parents are critical for a wide variety of reasons. This boy's mother was furious at her alcoholic husband, and directed her anger at her son. But parents are almost universally critical of children of whom they are jealous. This mother was also highly disapproving of her beautiful eighteen-year-old daughter—because the father was overinvolved with this daughter. Somewhat paradoxically, some parents verbally attack children for whom they have half-conscious sexual feelings. Guilty about having these feelings, they attack the child who provides the stimulus for the feelings, blaming the child for their own transgressions. Still other parents blame their children because they remind them of a disliked parent or a sibling in their own family of origin, or of a disliked aspect of themselves. We tend to be toughest on the child who reminds us most of ourselves.

Whatever its origins in the parent, chronic verbal attack (and of course physical attack is also extremely damaging) leaves the child feeling misunderstood and rejected. Although a child may eventually say to himself, "I must have done something to deserve this," on the most vulnerable level he feels hurt and abandoned.

PARENTAL BETRAYAL "When I was a kid and was at home with my mother during the day, she would be very warm and friendly with me. We would play all these fun games, and I felt close to her. Then my father would come home, and everything would change. She would become cool and distant with me. I could not understand it. I was the same, but she pulled away from me so dramatically that I felt really hurt. I know that must have been why I acted up; and of course then I would get punished by my father."

This is the classic family triangle. This child first feels honored, loved, flattered by the parent's special attention, and takes it very seriously. If the same-sex parent is habitually absent, this child may develop grandiose ideas about replacing this parent; especially if the parent's absence occurs during certain developmental periods, as when my father was absent during the classical Oedipal years (ages four to six). When the absent parent returns, the child feels cast aside. Boys who grow up in single-parent homes with divorced mothers are especially vulnerable to this sense of rejection. When the mother remarries, or becomes involved with another man, these boys often feel quietly devastated.

The traumatic shift of a parent's allegiance can occur in relation to a sibling. Here is a young woman who has had a lifelong struggle with rejection. "As the oldest, I was always my mother's helper. I knew my mother didn't have much to give me, and I didn't expect it from her. But I was special in the eyes of my father, and I really counted on him to support me. I don't know exactly when my relationship with him began to change, but I think it was when my younger sister was about nine or ten. She is the great beauty in our family, and when my father began to pay a lot of attention to her, I was extremely hurt. I never showed it, but I felt abandoned by him. I know that is why I worry so much that a better-looking woman will come along and take Ralph [her husband] from me."

That simple, almost universal anguish: sensing that our brother or sister possesses what we most covet, the love of a particular parent. How often have I heard parents say "We love our children equally." They want this to be true, but often it is not. What is it about a certain child that captures a parent's heart, and sometimes the heart of both parents? Physical attractiveness? A companionate slant of mind? A resemblance to a loved parent? A particular talent? While parents will deny "partiality," it exists, and everyone in the family sees it. The child outside this special bond inevitably feels rejected, particularly if he or she is not "teamed" with either parent. But even if we feel deeply loved by one parent, our need for the other parent's approval can be extremely intense.

Sibling order has a strong influence on the amount and kind of attention given to children. Every sibling position is, each in its own way, vulnerable. Because parents are so anxious about their own performance in the early stages of family life, eldest kids are subject to being controlled and directed in a very anxious way; and since parents are trying so hard to be responsible themselves, eldest kids are constantly told to "be responsible." Later, as parents relax and become more confident, they are more tolerant of their kids' needs, and may be more openly loving. Eldest kids see this "loosening up" occur, and they often feel envious of younger siblings.

The experience of feeling "replaced" by a younger sibling is the most common and the most underestimated trauma of childhood. Seeing one's rival cuddled, nursed, swept up in the love we have recently lost is so painful to children that many literally feel murderous toward the sibling. We laugh about sibling rivalry, but to children it is not funny.

Middle children—and children in the midst of a larger number of children—are vulnerable to rejection because they are neither the cuddly youngest nor the achieving oldest. They also escape some of the be-responsible messages, and may be fun-loving and creative. They are tempted to get in the middle of family conflicts, and to become mediators.

Youngest kids are, of course, the most likely to be infantilized by their parents; but if the parents' marriage deteriorates over time rather than improving, or if the parents have been exhausted by a series of other kids and other responsibilities, these kids may get the leftovers. They may be rejected kids. Or they may be alternately rejected and infantilized.

I am convinced that a disproportionate number of males are rejected kids. Not only do boys frequently feel abandoned by their preoccupied, psychologically absent fathers, but they are also subject to the anger of their unhappy mothers. There is a good deal of sociological evidence that points toward rejection's being a central issue in males: from the higher incidence of alcoholism and substance abuse in men, to the much higher incidence of suicide, to men's general emotional isolation.

Rejected kids have these characteristics in common:

☐ Though they may have trouble revealing it, they have a fierce need to please others, and to prove themselves worthy.

☐ They have a tendency to be self-blaming. If rejected, they believe it is because of their own failures.

☐ Because they have difficulty expressing anger, or in doing anything to "rock the boat" in a relationship, they are vulnerable to depression and to being passive.

☐ They have difficulty forming stable, committed relationships.
They may overcommit to others, and find themselves being continually rejected.
They may keep their distance, withdrawing when a relationship becomes more intimate.
They may drift casually in and out of relationships.

☐ While rejected kids may marry each other, they are also often drawn to parental kids, who of course promise to be the parents they didn't have.

It seemed clear that within Stephanie Land—the parental child, the responsible mother, the successful principal—there was a rejected child who had been envious of her parents' attention to her younger sister, and who had wanted a kind of intimate support which she dared not ask for. Part of Audrey's difficulty with her mother was that she was female, and in her mother's position in the family. On one level, Stephanie expected Audrey to be like her—responsible, hardworking, extremely moral; and she "projected" this set of expectations onto her daughter. But she also seemed to project onto Audrey her own needy self. "Mother sometimes seems to want me to be a little girl," Audrey complained.

Audrey was, then, the target of confusing forces that impinged on her from both her parents. To better understand these forces, we need to examine two final "types" in the family's cast of characters. I am again influenced by Stierlin's typology of roles, though I have recast them somewhat to fit my own clinical experience.

While bound children struggle with being overincluded in the family's inner circle, and rejected kids must turn to others outside the family for support, another group of kids live in an ambiguous borderland where approval is granted only if they perform in a certain way. Often, these kids must do something in the world outside the family to earn the attention they need.

THE DELEGATE

This child lives to please others, often by doing things that are socially approved. He or she makes good grades, gets elected to office, stars in sports, or is in some obvious way a credit to the family. This is the child the parents talk about proudly when they call the folks back in Boise. Though few would guess it, this kid often feels lonely, insecure, pressured, and unhappy. For the family's delegate can rarely do enough to feel loved and secure.

Bert sat quietly through most of our early sessions with the Lands, and it was not until much later in therapy that his problems came to the forefront. But it was evident to us from the beginning that he was a lonely, isolated kid who lived for his basketball team, his grades, and his secure but joyless position as the family's delegate. He was the boy all mothers wanted their daughters to date; but he didn't date at all. The other thing he did was worry over his mother; and we of course presumed there was some relationship between his concern for his mother and his lack of involvement with his peers.

Some delegated kids are under fierce and obvious pressure by their parents to perform. The parents teach them to read at four; they appear at school conferences to ask anxiously why their third-grader is not being taught a foreign language; they cringe on the sidelines when their child makes a mistake on the soccer field; they begin their child's preparation for the SAT in junior high; and they make sure he or she does lots of volunteer work for their college applications. In an age dominated by performance anxiety, these driven parents and their joyless kids are legion. Few parents realize there is something wrong with these kids, or with the orientation to life which they have been taught.

Other delegated kids respond to implicit needs in the family, and often they apply the pressures to themselves. These kids see an injustice, a deficit in the family; and they dedicate their lives to righting it.

As I prepared to go to college, I was vaguely aware that my father's career was in trouble. Nothing explicit was said, but something in my mother's hovering, anxious attention conveyed to me,

"What you are doing is very important. Don't fail me . . ." Later, the evidence of my father's drinking would accumulate, and I would see him struggling with a terribly traumatic job loss. Then I would add the concluding phrase which my mother had not spoken but had implied, ". . . like your father."

By the time Margaret and I met, I had transformed my mother's message into my own words: "I must not fail." This injunction seized me with a fierce, icy grip; it rang in my ears; it owned much of my loyalty and my life. I would feel its desperate imperative whenever I read a book, took a test, had a thought about the future. While I deeply resented its tyranny, I could not seem to resist it.

This "heroic" response to an underfunctioning father is common in males, and it puts great pressure on the child, and on the man he becomes. He must essentially live two lives: one for the father, and one for himself.

A great many women grew up seeing their mothers feeling depressed and demoralized in their roles as housewives, and these women delegates feel the same kind of fierce determination to live out the potential which their mothers never realized. They too must live a kind of double life, often subordinating their own needs in the interest of their mission.

Psychologically, delegates resemble parental children: they seem strong, self-sufficient, competent; and they too have difficulty being aware of their feelings and needs, especially their dependency needs. Oriented toward the future, highly conscious of time pressure, they are driven by impossibly high goals for themselves. Rarely do they allow themselves simple daily pleasures, including friendship.

What distinguishes the delegate is the focus on pleasing others through performance in the world outside the family. While the parental child earns approval through caretaking, and is quite capable of transferring this ability to those within her immediate family, the delegate lives for applause—from the original family. There is a lonely narcissism in the delegate, a "look-at-me-now" quality that cries out for recognition; and because the delegate may have felt loved only through this kind of reward, he or she can work terribly hard for a few words of praise. Beneath the competent surface, there is often—if one takes away the recognition for achievement—a rejected child.

We delegates are difficult to be married to. We want our mate and our kids to accommodate to our needs to be successful; and our heart is often in our job or our outside-the-family projects. Often, we ignore the emotional needs of those around us because we have never addressed or admitted our own.

Delegates tend to marry parental children, or rejected kids who will accommodate to their needs.

THE RULEBREAKER

This is a complex and often courageous kid. She may get pregnant; he may drive too fast; he or she may skip school, fail classes, and yell at adults. He won't take out the garbage; she won't clean her room. Called by a variety of names—the black sheep, the rebellious kid, the family scapegoat—this child constantly pushes the limits, and tries the patience of everyone. Beneath the surface of this family revolutionary there is a strong, gutsy kid who is worried about the family.

The rulebreaker senses trouble in the marriage, and is willing to take the heat—often at considerable sacrifice. "Hey, look at me!" this child cries out, as he or she maneuvers to distract the parents from their struggles with each other. This usually unconscious self-sacrificial response seems to be almost innate in kids. So many times I have been working with a young family and, as the parents began to touch on a sensitive subject, their toddler would act up in order to draw the parents' attention. The need of children to protect their parents' relationship may be as fundamental as the parents' need to protect their children.

According to Stierlin, the rulebreaker is a kind of "negative delegate," in that he or she senses an unacknowledged, unexpressed impulse in the parents, and acts it out. For example, the parents may have sexual difficulties, and be unable to face them. One of the parents may be tempted to have an affair. Sensing these problems, their adolescent acts out sexually, presenting the parents with a metaphoric "screen" onto which they can project their forbidden impulses, experiencing them vicariously with minimum risk to themselves.

Sometimes the rulebreaker expresses angry, defiant impulses for one or both parents. A family may come into therapy because they have an aggressive child who fights with his peers and is belligerent with his teachers. When we meet with the family, the parents often reveal a peculiar kind of sympathy for this child. "Johnny's teacher [whom Johnny has just kicked in the shins] is very difficult, and we think she is unfair to him. The other kids also gang up on him and mistreat him." While these parents may punish their child when he gets into trouble, they also subtly encourage his defiant attitude, teaching him to blame others for his difficulties. These parents are angry conformists who would like to be able to break society's rules, but don't dare. Their child is the ambassador of the family's aggression.

Of course childhood misbehavior is a very complex subject. Some disruptive kids release at school anger that is daily being heaped on them at home.

Frequently, the rulebreaker defies his or her family's own rules. One parent may be stern and heavy-handed, and may intimidate the entire family, including the other spouse. The one-down spouse "officially" agrees with the dominant partner about the family's rules and restrictions, but covertly would like to defy them. In ways that may be very difficult to see, this parent "signals" the rulebreaking kid that it is permissible to defy the rule. The signal may be as subtle as a wink, or a slight inflection of voice.

"You would take her side," Stephanie said to Colin when he expressed sympathy for Audrey. Stephanie had faced the coalition between father and daughter before, and she resented it. Indeed, Colin was clearly one down in their marriage, and gave implicit "permission" for Audrey to defy her mother. Most rulebreaking kids are in coalition with the one-down parent, whose anger they are expressing, and whom they are unconsciously attempting to "liberate."

Rulebreaking kids take it on the chin. They not only get punished by the parent whom they defy, but they may be betrayed by the parent with whom they are in coalition. A teenage boy who often fights with his domineering and punitive father says, "I'm always in trouble with Dad, and Mother never defends me. I wish just once that she would stand up to him and say that something he is doing is unfair."

Of all the kids in the family, I have a special fondness for the rulebreaker. She takes a stand against the forces of conformity and coercion in the family; he declares fearlessly, "I don't care what you think of me!" Whatever the life force in the two-year-old that makes him say "No!" to his parents with such authority, and which returns again and again over the years in waves of self-assertion, culminating in that child's leaving home for the larger world, that birthing force toward a progressively more complete selfhood—is expressed in the family rebel. These kids often do what their parents can't: they stand up, they speak out; they declare themselves.

Rulebreaking kids fill a complex and difficult space:

- They have a keen sense of injustice, often siding with the underdog.
- They have problems with authority, and often seem angry.
- Because there were two discrepant levels of communication in their families, they tend to mistrust what others say.
- Since they have been blamed by their families, they learn to blame themselves, and are prone to depression.
- Frequently creative, strong, and courageous, they also make good mediators.
- They often marry parental kids whom they then rebel against.

No individual can be described by a single role. Most of us play several parts, sometimes within one relationship. Audrey was bound to her mother in ways that were alternately parental, companionate, and dependent. She also felt rejected by her mother; and she acted out impulses that forced her mother to face old dilemmas in her family of origin, and which exposed deficiencies in Stephanie and Colin's marriage.

One way to use this typology is to examine the roles one played in relation to each family member. It is also important to examine patterns over time, since roles frequently change as the family changes. For example, while Audrey was the rulebreaker at the beginning of therapy, both Bert and Laurel later went through periods of confrontation and conflict with their mother as they reached late adolescence. But the rulebreaking role is not the only one that rotates among family members. Parental roles may also be passed from child to child. They may also be subdivided among the children, with one child playing "assistant mother," the other playing "assistant father." Changes in the family's situation may also alter a child's role quite suddenly: the youngest child may be infantilized by both parents, only to be psychologically abandoned when they divorce.

The sex of a child is of course a powerful determinant of that child's role in the family. Girls are more readily drafted into parental and dependent roles; a disproportionate number of boys are delegated and rejected kids. The other roles are more gender neutral. As we will see, our roles in our family of origin have a strong influence on our choice of marital partner.

We circled the dilemma, seeing it with increasing clarity. At first we could not quite believe what we were hearing, but with each repetition, we became more convinced that Stephanie meant it when she said to Audrey, "If you continue this affair, I can't stand it." She didn't say, "I will reject you," but the coldness in her voice said it for her. Stephanie's insight into the parallel between this struggle and the one in her family of origin had given her only slight pause. Faced with such a choice, Audrey was clearly enraged. She was inclined to keep her problematic lover, and to sacrifice her relationship with her family.

"I can't seem to help feeling this way," Stephanie said sadly but determinedly.

"You mean you would give up your relationship with Audrey?" Margaret said incredulously.

"I would see her, if that's what you mean. She would be welcome in my house, or I would try to make her welcome."

Margaret said, "But you would be cool, like this?"

"That's what I can't seem to help," the mother admitted.

"Who would want to be around this kind of attitude?" Audrey asked. Not just anger now, but a bewildered, uncomprehending hurt. "It's like she would always be saying that I'm dirt. I couldn't live with it."

"You could change; you could give him up," Stephanie said angrily.

"So could *you* change, Mother," Audrey replied, also angrily.

Margaret addressed Stephanie, looking at her aslant, as if she herself could not understand a mother's making this response to her daughter: "It should be possible for us as parents to love our kids, and to accept them, even when they do something we wouldn't dream of doing."

"I know that," Stephanie said pensively. "I wish that I could. I really do."

"I believe you," Margaret said, peering intently at the mother.

I had been trying to visualize Stephanie's own mother, wondering what she was like, trying to grasp the power of her hold on her middle-aged daughter. It really did seem as though Stephanie's mother was sitting there disapproving; and that Stephanie was so loyal to her that she could not oppose her stern morality. "How could loyalty to a dead mother take precedence over a living daughter?" I too asked myself.

"What if we imagined your mother sitting here?" I said quietly to Stephanie, glancing toward an empty chair. "Because it seems as though she is."

"What would that accomplish?" Stephanie asked skeptically.

"At least it would help us understand more of what is taking place within you," I said.

She looked at the chair, and as she did so, an expression of great complexity entered her face: sadness, anguish, guilt. "You look sad when you look at her," Margaret said, "and guilty."

"I feel guilty," Stephanie said to us.

"What if you said it directly to your mother?" I suggested softly. Stephanie again looked at the chair, tears sliding slowly down her face.

"I feel guilty, Mother, that I've failed you." This was the point at which we had stopped before.

"And what would she say back to you?" I asked.

"She would say, 'It's all right, honey,' or something like that." I repeated the words as if the mother had said them, and they had a visible impact on Stephanie. Her face was wet with tears.

"You seem very sad," I said to Stephanie.

"I miss her," she said, her voice pleading.

"What if you said that to her?" I suggested.

Stephanie looked fearfully at the empty chair, and uttered the words: "I miss you, Mother." With the words she took a deep, jagged breath, and began to cry. Her crying was muted, restrained. Margaret sat beside her on the sofa, putting her arm around her shoulder. For several minutes Stephanie cried, relaxing against Margaret's shoulder. Gradually, as she began to absorb some of the support she was receiving, her crying softened, became rhythmical and relieved. The feeling in the room itself seemed gentler and more benign, as though the coldness between mother and daughter had been dissipated.

Finally, Stephanie looked up at Margaret, and smiled. "It's been very hard to say goodbye to your mother, hasn't it?" Margaret said.

"Yes," Stephanie said, sadly again, looking away. "I think of her every day."

"I know it's always hard to lose a parent," Margaret continued, "but has there been a complication in your relationship with your mother that has made it especially difficult?"

I had been thinking the same thing. It was evident that something had impeded the normal process of grief and separation following the mother's death. Even though her mother had been dead for three years, internally, Stephanie had "held on" to her. And since she couldn't separate psychologically from her dead mother, she couldn't allow her daughter to separate from her. Even now, she was pulling away from her grief, cutting it off.

"We were so very close," Stephanie said. Then she added, "And she gave up so much for me."

I said to myself: "She is so guilty about being separated from her mother that she cannot be conscious of her anger at her." With Margaret sitting beside Stephanie like a kind of "ideal mother," I wondered if Stephanie might now be able to experience greater separateness from her mother.

"Could you also say that to your mother?" I suggested, again looking at the chair. "That you acknowledge how much she gave up for you?"

Stephanie looked at the empty chair, her face full of desolation. When she said nothing, I asked, "What is happening? What are you seeing?"

"When I imagine her, I see her looking very sad and alone. She seems small, unhappy." I glanced at slender, diminutive Audrey, wondering if daughter and grandmother resembled each other physically. Stephanie resumed: "So much happened in her life."

"Something you haven't mentioned before?" I queried.

"Yes." She was beginning to sit up straight, pulling away from Margaret's support. A long sigh. "When I was about nine, I had pneumonia. It was before penicillin was available, and they thought I was going to die. My mother prayed for me, apparently, and promised God that if I lived, she would tithe faithfully, and would dedicate her life to the church. When I did live, she kept her promise. For the rest of her life, every time the church door opened, she went in it. And we gave ten percent of our income to the church."

"What was the problem in that?" I asked.

"My father was not as religious as she was. He resented the time she gave to the church, and the money. It caused a lot of tension between them; and I felt that I was the cause of it." With dismay, I realized that she may have felt guilty enough to consider sacrificing her relationship with her daughter in recompense for her mother's sacrifice. "Every time the subject of the tithing came up, I cringed. My parents really couldn't afford it."

"What a difficult dilemma for you," Margaret said. Positioned so close to Stephanie that it was difficult to talk, she moved to a nearby chair, sitting now between mother and daughter. "That situation was not your fault."

"There's more," Stephanie said. "I think it was also very difficult for my mother, because of something that happened to her as a child." She kept the link with Margaret, speaking now to her. "When my mother was about twelve, her parents went to visit relatives in the next county. They left my mother at home in charge of the two younger kids. It was in the early spring, and still cold. The youngest, a girl who was I think about seven, tried to cross the creek on their farm, and fell in. By the time my mother's parents got home—they were only gone a couple of days—the girl had pneumonia; and she died about a week later." The event being described, and its link with the present, registered in every face in the room. The silence of sudden comprehension. "I don't know if my grandparents blamed my mother, but I think they did. I certainly know that she blamed herself."

Margaret said, "So when you got pneumonia, and got well, your mother probably felt that she had earned a chance at forgiveness."

"At a cost," Stephanie said sadly. "She had to keep earning it."

"And her efforts to do that bound you to her in a very guilty way. It was as if you inherited the guilt," Margaret said.

"Every time I saw my parents fight, I felt terribly guilty." Contemplative silence, and a kind of peacefulness that often comes when a dilemma is understood.

"My worry," Margaret said, "is that you would feel that if Audrey insists on doing something which your mother could not accept, your guilty ties to your mother would require that you sacrifice your relationship with Audrey." After a brief pause, she added, "That would be *your* sacrifice."

Stilled by the insight, Stephanie finally said, "I would hate for it to have to be that way."

The other members of the family had been silent throughout this exchange. At first Audrey had seemed confused by what she heard; now she looked relieved. Bert, always worried about his mother, came forward: "There has to be a way out of this problem, Mother. There has been enough suffering in our family." Colin remained quiet, as though he did not know what to offer. I wished that it had been he, rather than Bert, who had made contact with Stephanie.

"We have made a start, just talking about this history," I said to Bert. "But there are other things we can do as well." Had Stephanie's mother been alive, we would have brought her into the therapy. Without her, we would have to work symbolically, trying to imagine and then to improvise important fragments of a different kind of childhood history for Stephanie. But once more, there was not time for that today.

"Can I say something?" Brooding, small, and angular like her mother, Laurel had not spoken once during the hour.

"Of course," I said.

"I think Audrey ought to apologize to Mother for putting her through this, and stop dating this old geezer." Before Audrey could interrupt her, she continued, "And I think Mother ought to stop trying to run Audrey's life. As long as Mom is doing that, there will be a fight about something."

"I agree with you," Bert interposed, not to be displaced as the family therapist. "But I think it would be easier for Mom to back out if Dad was more involved with all of this. He does leave Mother kind of alone with it." Glancing at his father, he looked anxious about what he was saying. "It's true, Dad." Both kids were taking the focus away from Stephanie's very painful history.

Colin looked guilty himself, and a little embarrassed. "I am involved with all of this," he said defensively. "Your mother and I talk about it all the time."

The time was gone, and new issues swirled around us. "I have to agree with the kids," I said with a smile to Colin, "that your support is critical for Stephanie if she is to stop being so intensely caught up in the lives of your children. But she probably has trouble leaning on you emotionally, because her mother couldn't do that with her husband either. So she may need some practice asking you for support; and you may need practice in learning to give it." I knew that he had been a youngest kid, and rather neglected by his own father; so that he would need work in being a stronger husband and father.

"But there is a way we can work symbolically on the problems between Stephanie and her mother. And we should do that too."

"Hey, you guys, we've run over." Margaret called time.

We grow up in the turbulence of the past. From our earliest moments, its agonies and injustices impinge on us, shaping our destinies. But we feel the forces of the family history with particular sensitivity in those delicate years when we are trying to leave home. One foot is in the family, the other in the larger world; and we are off balance. At exactly the time when we are trying to start afresh, we are vulnerable to being caught in the past's unfinished business; and as we reach out for a partner, we inevitably form a continuing link with history. But in the mixing of these two lives, both attempting a new kind of family world, there is in fact the exciting inevitability of change.

We are ready to look at that moment of reaching out, that voyaging of the spirit which leads toward marriage.

10

Choosing

WE MEET IN A thousand different ways: at school, through friends or relatives, in bars, at work, through newspaper ads or computerized dating services, with the help of professional matchmakers, walking the dog, or buying groceries; and always by chance. But the chances are not casual. Especially when we are young, we are all intently searching, high-stakes gamblers hoping to find a special person who will supply the missing something in our lives. Call it the biological imperative to produce another generation; call it i rpersonal attraction or mate selection; call it love; call it magic; call it life's yearning for itself. However it is defined, we can be sure that the process of choosing a mate is so bewilderingly complex that no one fully understands it. No one.

But we can hazard an educated guess about some of the forces involved in the decision to marry. However faulty such decisions may seem to be, I believe that they represent a highly creative, unconscious attempt not only to solve some of our most difficult problems, but to fulfill our potential as people.

The initial choice of a partner occurs when most of us are in our early twenties. During this time we are crossing that treacherous and turbulent channel between the port of home and the open sea: we are moving out, going away, beginning to try to make it in the great Out There. Though we work hard to pretend otherwise, we are all terrified about facing the world outside the family; and we have no idea about how to deal with a harsh and competitive society. However brave we may sound, the choice of a mate is made against this background of existential terror. We aren't just attracted to each other; we need each other, often badly.

Even then, there is great variety in our stories about the decision to marry.

This is Jonathan Ames, who is in therapy with his wife Estelle: "I remember thinking out the decision to marry Estelle. I realized that we had a number of interests in common, and that it was easy to talk to her. I was also attracted to her physically." Glancing at his pretty blonde wife, he smiles uneasily, "As I still am. Our getting married seemed like a good idea."

The critical word is "idea." This couple's decision—Estelle's description was similar—was made intellectually and rationally. A surprising number of people get married in this sensible, passionless way. They have been together for a long time; their families like each other; everyone thinks they are the ideal couple. Her roommate is getting married and she worries that she might never get asked again. The time, the place, the circumstances seem apt; all the pieces fit together logically.

Such decisions, which I call *underdetermined choices*, are usually made by cautiously reserved people who mistrust emotion. One or both may have been raised in cool, logical families; or they may have been brought up in turbulent, emotionally destructive families. Whatever the origins of the decision, both are committed to living sensibly.

This isn't necessarily a bad way to get married—no type of decision to marry guarantees a happy marriage—but in working with such couples, one often wishes for more of that messy passion in which many become entangled. These rational couples eventually realize that in their preoccupation with doing the proper thing, in their panic about not getting out of step, they have missed something. Often enough, they search for it in other relationships.

Another type of choice contains all too much emotion. Peter Baron, who is in therapy with his second wife, Laura, speaks about his first marriage, which took place when he was just out of high school: "Jessie was one of the 'bad girls' in my class, though you didn't have to be very bad in the fifties to get labeled that way. Anyway, my mother didn't approve of the relationship from the start. The strange thing was, the more my mother disapproved, the more determined I was to go out with Jessie." An only child of divorced parents, Peter rarely saw his wealthy father, who left him to struggle single-handedly with his anxious, highly controlling mother. Peter's choice of Jessie was determined partly by his mother's opposition to her; and this "rebellious" relationship was part of his struggle to create a separate identity for himself.

"Jessie got pregnant the summer after I graduated; otherwise I don't think she would have considered marrying the kind of person I was. We were never really a match—the bookworm from the wealthy family and the bad girl. I'm surprised we stayed married long enough to have a second child before she left me."

This is the *overdetermined choice*, a marriage made in the midst of emotional storm and strife. Such choices are full of background anxiety; and often the source of the stress is a family crisis of some kind. Peter Baron's choice was overdetermined by his struggle with his mother over his right to make his own decisions in life. His choice of a partner was not made independently, but was strongly influenced by his mother's disapproval of Jessie. This rebellious reaction to parental attempts to control, sometimes called the "Romeo and Juliet effect" by researchers, is common in precipitous marriages.

Other emotional stresses also distort the process of marital choice:

☐ *The psychological absence or disability of a parent.* It is a quiet kind of crisis, but growing up with a psychologically absent or disabled parent creates a deep sense of need in us, and the pressure of that need can severely distort the process of choosing a mate. Joan Strand said, "I know that I was attracted to Eric partly because he seemed strong and in control, and was so different from my father in that respect. I loved my father, but he was so ineffectual that it felt in some ways as though I didn't have a father."

Another client, Teresa Simpkins, made a similar decision. "My father was an alcoholic, and I suppose I was the one who functioned as his 'replacement' in our family. At least I was the one my mother relied on. I know now that my decision to marry Sam [who was her high school band director] was partly an attempt to find a father." Sam was twelve years older than Teresa, and she had always felt so controlled and one down in relation to him that she had trouble believing she could be his peer. After several years of therapy in which they struggled hard with this issue, the couple divorced.

☐ *Sudden loss of a parent or other significant relationship*. Choosing a mate soon after the loss of a parent, or the loss of a spouse or lover—either by death or through rejection—is fraught with danger. If one chooses a partner because of his or her ability as a "therapist," the choice may seem specious when the "patient" who suffered the loss begins to feel better.

☐ *Pregnancy*. Imagine young Deborah Strand trying to make a successful marriage with her seventeen-year-old high school lover. Her pregnancy was so overdetermined by her conflicts with her family that the decision to marry would later have seemed psychologically "owned" by her parents, and almost entirely the product of her conflict with them. In order to define her identity as a separate person, she would probably have sacrificed her fledgling marriage.

In one large study of marriage, one fourth of the brides were pregnant at the time of the marriage. This is a startling figure. While we know that marriages of the young and pregnant are notoriously fragile, all couples who marry while dealing with the pressures of pregnancy are more likely to divorce than couples who marry without these problems.

Many different situations make young adults feel desperate to find safety from the storm of instability at home. These "lifeboat" marriages usually turn out to be unsuited for the long and arduous passage ahead.

In overdetermined marriages, the stresses of these life crises interfere with the delicate process of intuition in which each person responds to the other's uniquely individual attributes. Peter Baron's need for someone to help him fight with his mother made Jessie a kind of "object," symbol of his rebelliousness. In the same way, someone who has recently lost a lover may use the next partner as a therapist. This kind of "objectification" eventually makes one or both partners question the validity of their choice of each other.

Intense emotional pressure, whether it comes from external situations or internal need, overrides our sense of choice. We all want to feel married out of our free choice. It is the only way we can trust our own caring, and trust that we are cared about. Any decision to marry that feels as though it was made under duress will eventually be called into question, often through the unconscious creation of a marital crisis. This "testing the relationship" crisis may come early or late in the marriage cycle, and it may not result in divorce; but it can only be resolved if both partners reaffirm their commitment to each other.

There is another kind of choice, one which is made with a great deal of feeling, but is not driven by crisis. Why not call it falling in love? If one wanted a more technical term, one might name this version the *integrated choice*. While a wide range of experiences— from the frankest lust to the most abject infantile need—are called "falling in love," this kind of choice clearly meets more than these primitive needs. This once-or-twice-in-a-lifetime experience is bound to be a thoroughly mixed bag—part desperation, part sexual hunger, part calculation—but it also contains something so intricately complex that we are struck dumb by it. I do not pretend to understand it fully; but I believe in its inherent wisdom, its creativity, its affirmation of life. Perhaps it is life's yearning not only to perpetuate itself, but to improve itself.

After years of listening to people describe the experience of falling in love, the only common characteristic I can identify is *confusion*. Some people know each other for years before it hits them; others see each other once and feel it immediately. A close friend described it this way: "I saw Marion [to whom he has been happily married for thirty years] when I was walking to class at the university. All of a sudden my head started spinning, and I didn't know what was happening. So I started following her, and imme-

diately it occurred to me, 'That is the person you are going to marry.'
I followed her to her dorm, but I didn't have the nerve to talk to her
then. It took me a couple of weeks to meet her." Marion also turned
out to be an art student at this large state university; six months
later, they were married.

But I can best describe this experience autobiographically.

Looking at the pictures of myself in my high school yearbook, I
seem asleep. My face has a flat, two-dimensional expression: not
pained, but not joyful either. A well-behaved teenager in a small
south Georgia town, I played in the band and made an occasional
attempt at playing football. Class president, class poet, I was the
kind of boy the mothers wanted their daughters to date. It was
assumed that I would go to Emory University, where my father,
who was a salesman, had earned a graduate degree.

Then my aunt Alice, my father's oldest sister, who was a school
administrator in Atlanta, asked an admissions recruiter from an
eastern college to send me a catalogue. Sitting in the swing on the
broad stone porch of our house on a crisp fall afternoon, I studied
the catalogue. It was the photographs of those old, ivy-covered
buildings that drew me in. There were thousands of books in the
library; many teachers for relatively few students. With a strange
excitement and a twinge of fear, I shut myself in my room for an
entire weekend with the application.

Fate, of course, involves more than the roll of a die. It is a living
thing, with reaching, branching tendrils, and it is rooted in history.
Though I didn't know it then, my aunt's sending me that catalogue
had a deeper significance.

Within families, even the simplest reaching out of one individual to another creates an encumbering complexity. My aunt's interest in me, which has been extremely important in my life, began
with her "parental" relationship with my father, who was the
youngest of five children in that family. As the oldest child, my aunt
Alice felt responsible for a number of the children, but she had a
special bond with my father.

I was born in 1938 into a matrix of charged and divided loyalties. When my father, who was a graduate student in biology, came

home from class in the afternoon, he had to make a decision: whether to enter the duplex apartment on the left, where his recently divorced sister (Alice) lived with their widowed mother, for whom, as the eldest daughter, she was the elected "caretaker"; or the apartment on the right, where my mother and I also waited for him. Often my grandmother would leave the door on the left open, and by the time my mother saw him, my father would have had a cup of coffee and talked about his day, and my mother would be quietly furious.

When my mother's father discovered how difficult this situation was for his eldest daughter (my father had married another "caretaker"), he bought my parents a house in the suburbs, though that hardly solved the problem between the various women who were in conflict over my father's loyalty.

With time and the growth of geographic distance between my parents' household and that of my aunt and grandmother (and my grandmother was really the controlling figure in this quiet struggle), I became an increasingly important link in the struggle. In order to introduce me to "culture," my aunt brought me to Atlanta from the smaller cities and towns where we lived; and though my mother officially approved of these trips, they always provoked in her a subtle and mysterious coolness toward me.

Nor did I understand the strange mixture of pleasure and dismay which my mother communicated several months later when a letter arrived from Wesleyan University in Connecticut informing me that I had been given a scholarship. It would be years before I understood that I had become a target for my mother's anger at my aunt and grandmother for their influence in first my father's life and then mine, or before I saw the other intricate teamings and schisms in our family to which I was subject. In the meantime, like my father, I had to decide which way to turn. I chose north.

The picture taken at the end of my freshman year of college looks more alert than the ones in the high school yearbook, but I am still sober, still looking away from the camera. Every morning for a year I woke up worrying, "Can I make it?" By the end of the year I was grasping with white-knuckled desperation at a tentative "Maybe."

I did not look up from my books until midway through my junior year. By then I was an English major, and doing well academically. "Time to meet a girl," I said to myself.

I had tried that before, of course, going on blind dates arranged by well-meaning friends who seemed to be using the misery-loves-company theory of mate selection; so of course these girls were also shy and reserved, and we had little to say to each other.

Finally Judy, dear Judy, my roommate Steve's girlfriend and later wife, said in a tone of mild exasperation, "Just what kind of girl do you want to date anyway, Gus?"

Drawing a sharp breath, I thought, "I'd better say this right." After a pause, I said, "Somebody bright, cheerful, interesting, and strong." Sometimes I wish I had left off the strong.

It was snowing that night, and having no expectations of this date either, I sent a fraternity brother to meet Margaret's train so that I could attend a lecture by Harold Stassen—announcing, I suppose, my career as a distancer. Eventually, an awkward introduction at Alumni House. I said hello, and this diminutive blonde with a bright, slightly playful smile and a confident manner said hello back. With a shock of pleased recognition, I said inwardly, "Aha." I had said hello, and someone who was clearly all those things I had said to Judy said hello back.

A rushed dinner at my fraternity: trying to look good but feeling embarrassed, trying to make contact across the noisy table. I liked her smile, sudden and warm, and the alert tilt of her head. I also sensed, with relief, her discomfort with the party-weekend scene. When the meal was over, she looked at me with a slight sense of panic as if to say, "Let's get out of here."

Nightfall, the crisp sound of our steps in new snow as we walked amid the nervous laughter of others like ourselves toward the evening's entertainment, a panel discussion. Remarkably, we found things to day: "This snow makes a nice sound," I ventured.

"Like eating cornflakes," Margaret answered.

"Or tearing paper," I replied. We were competitive, and we both liked analogies.

By the end of the panel discussion, we discovered that we agreed about people. "How dull can it get?" I asked.

"Pretty dull," Margaret agreed. "Except for James Gavin. He has nice eyes."

"And a sense of the tragic," I said.

Margaret liked to tease, something I found mildly disconcerting. "Sorry about not meeting the train today," I offered.

"It was a surprise, expecting a poet from Georgia and getting Mr. Brooks Brothers."

"How are poets from Georgia supposed to look?" I said warily.

"Pale and wan," she said with that smile again, "and a trifle threadbare."

"We travel in disguise when we're north of the Mason-Dixon line," I said, looking down at my Brooks Brothers jacket, bought so carefully on a trip to Atlanta with my father. "How should I stereotype you?"

"I suppose I'm still a St. Agnes girl."

"Is that a religious order?"

"It's more like a strong suggestion," she said, smiling. "Episcopalian schools are strong on ritual, but liberal underneath."

"I'm afraid Jeff Davis High wasn't very liberal," I said, "and the only ritual was on the football field. The band humiliated itself so the team would win."

"And did they win?" Margaret asked.

"With depressing regularity."

"Why do you say that?"

"Because I was in the band."

Testing, teasing, finding out things as we went. A girl from an eastern private school and a boy from a public high school in south Georgia—but that hardly seemed to matter.

The clusters of voices were softer now along the snowbound sidewalks. Margaret and I relaxed a little and moved closer to each other. As we stepped into the brightness of the hallway at Alumni House where she was to stay, I felt exposed and awkward, and touching her lightly on the shoulder, turned and fled.

In my solitary dormitory bed, I kept seeing her face, hearing her voice. Not even vaguely interested in sleep, I watched the moon move slowly across the limbs of a tree, like a single, bright finger. I was deeply, excitingly awake.

Brunch at the fraternity was frowsy and embarrassing. "I had a little trouble sleeping," I confessed, knowing that it was a risk.

"Me too," she said. "I didn't sleep very much at all." Then she added with smile, "It must have been that stimulating lecture."

"Yeah," I said, feeling awake again, and excited by what she had told me. Gathering my courage, I said, "Shall we cut the football game? Our presence would not help this miserable team."

"By all means. What should we do?" she said.

"How about a walk?" I felt about as poised as Holden Caulfield.

"Fine." She was also self-conscious.

Walking down a street of faculty homes near the campus, I took her hand. "Shall we try the graveyard? It's more interesting than the town."

"You frequent graveyards?" A quizzical look in my direction.

"Sure. It's a good place to read Emily Dickinson."

"You like Emily Dickinson too?" And we were off again, finding things to talk about.

"Which gravestone do you like best?" she asked.

"That one."

"Hey, me too."

One of us would notice something visually interesting—the way a broken branch lay on the sidewalk, the subtle colors of lichen on a stone, the intricate tracing of iron grillwork. "That's nice, isn't it?"

"Yes."

Then, in a bolder experiment, it was my turn: "Do you see what I see over there?"

Margaret said, "You mean the way the angle of that tilted gravestone parallels the angle of the roof? It makes a nice composition."

And that was truly remarkable. We could predict with uncanny accuracy what the other found visually interesting. We discovered that this world of light and shadow, of color and form, was very important to both of us; and wound up kissing, gently and shyly, but with an internal thrill that was clearly mutual.

The rest of the weekend is a blur. A Saturday-night dance we sort of attended, then left to kiss some more in the huddled dark. And the next day, ice skating with Steve and Judy; on borrowed skates, broken down and too big, I was a spectacle of awkwardness.

Margaret literally skated rings around me, taunting me with the toss of her braid, her gleeful smile. "Damn arrogant Yankees," I muttered at the three of them. "People weren't meant to do this." I felt unnerved by her teasing, and distressed that the weekend was ending.

Sunday evening, standing by the railroad tracks, talking softly, we were both sad but afraid to say it. The worn commuter train to South Hadley arrived, clanging and hissing, and I climbed the steps with Margaret, lifting her bag into the overhead rack. Then, as we sat there talking for the last delicious minute, the train pulled out, leaving the fraternity brother who had driven us to the station wondering what had happened. Embarrassed, laughing with delight, we rode through the countryside with the tired commuters to the next stop. Then I got off and called another friend, but it was too late. Whatever was going to happen had happened.

I have thought about it a thousand times, sorting each of those first impressions, trying to understand how we both knew, by the time the train left the station, that we were going to get married. The knowledge was to be severely tested in the years ahead, and sometimes the link between us held by the slenderest of threads; but these threads, as it turned out, were strong.

What is the nature of the link, the bond, the chemistry, the connection between two people? These hackneyed metaphors raise the issue of depth and commitment in marriage, and they are at the center of our inquiry. Of these physical symbols for relationship joining, the one I like best is chemistry. It connotes the linkage of atoms, the bonding of invisible structures to make a third thing, a new entity.

Are we drawn to someone who is like us, or different from us? If, as is likely, our mate possesses a complex combination of similarities and dissimilarities to us, is there some order in this mixture? As a general guide, it would be difficult to find a more cogent formula than one proposed by the nineteenth-century writer O. S. Fowler, who counseled:

Wherein, and as far as you are what you ought to be, marry one *like* yourself; but wherein and as far as you have any marked *excesses* or defects, marry those *unlike* yourself in these objectionable particulars.

We are all indeed in search of someone who will help us feel psychologically "complete"; and what better principle could we use than to marry someone in whom we see a similarity to our comfortable and valued aspects, and in whom we also see a possible complement to our faults?

But we would be mistaken to concentrate only on the qualities of the two individuals who marry. Each of us is profoundly and irrevocably the member of a family, and our choice of a partner establishes a new set of family ties. While we marry an individual, each of us is so deeply connected with the family we grew up in that both we and our mate are forever struggling with each other's loyalty to the family of origin. So we should consider the possibility that this loyalty is unconsciously taken into account in our decision, that we are drawn to the entire family of our mate. But let us begin with individuals.

SOMEONE LIKE ME

Only identical twins know the negative aspect of living with someone who is truly like themselves. The rest of us yearn for this kind of kinship with a partner who sees and experiences the world as we do. If there is a single principle in our selection of a mate, it is—in my view—that we marry someone who is a kind of psychological identical twin. Not, I hasten to add, a twin in obvious, surface characteristics, but in the deeper similarities of mind.

Shakespeare wrote, "Let me not to the marriage of true minds admit impediments." It is in this realm, the marriage of mental experience, that we find the deepest and surest link between people. We are attracted to each other physically, especially in the beginning; and I believe the physical characteristics of the partners play a much more symbolic role than is generally recognized. But physical attraction itself never sustains relationships. It is the commonalities in the way we experience the world that make us feel truly married; and some of these shared perceptions can only be built with time. But even the "kinship" we find initially in our mate is complicated, and comes from a number of sources.

The research literature is replete with evidence of "homogamy" in mate selection, or the attraction of people with similar back-grounds. Yes, we do tend to marry someone who is of our race, religious affiliation, social class, intelligence, age, and so on. These are the people we meet more frequently in everyday life, so of course we are more likely to marry them.

Let us look at demographics. Margaret and I were both serious students in highly competitive, single-sex New England schools. I suppose that was a start, though it had hardly been enough on other dates. But then I had gone to a public school in a small southern town, and she to an Episcopalian girls' school in a conservative Yankee suburb. Why was that disparity not an issue?

Far from being a problem, my background was partly respon-sible for Margaret's consenting to the date. "I was interested because you were a poet from Lumber City, Georgia, and had a funny name," she said later. As it didn't take me long to discover, Margaret's father, who was her favorite person on earth, had been raised in—a small town in Arkansas. Powerful, witty, smart, but still a bit rough-hewn, Paul was a successful businessman who never liked living in the northeast. Like my father, he took every opportunity to sneak away to fish and hunt. Though Margaret's mother had spent her early years in the state of Washington, her family's roots were in tidewater Virginia. Margaret had grown up in a displaced Southern family in which there had always been a kind of pensive discussion of moving south.

Some of our most important identifications are in the similarities of experience inside our respective family worlds. Not only were Margaret and I both from four-person Southern families, but also, though it took us some time to realize it, our families had both been somewhat isolated. As hard as they tried, Margaret's family never felt at home in their primly conservative suburb. "We were always doing the wrong thing," Margaret said. My liberal family also felt out of step with the conservative rural ethos in which I grew up. So of course Margaret and I found commonalty in our tendency to remain separate from the college weekend social scene.

As we got to know each other, we discovered that we had grown up in families that were superficially dissimilar but funda-mentally alike. Both our fathers, for example, were their mothers' favorites and had grown up as the family "princes." In different ways, our fathers also dominated the nuclear families they created; and our mothers permitted, if not encouraged, our fathers' domination of us all, in part through their willingness to be self-sacrificial.

Both families also contained some of the same themes of conflict. The descendants of Scots merchants and farmers, my mother's family was the inventive, practical, down-to-earth side. My father's side of the family was more intellectual, with a long tradition of education and achievement. Each "side" looked down on the other: the McLeans thought the Napiers were neurotic, the Napiers thought the McLeans were common. The same split occurred in Margaret's family, only it was Margaret's mother's family that was considered "educated and peculiar."

There is a good deal of evidence that similarities in values are critical in the attraction of mates, and of course value orientations are created within the family. The psychologist Bernard Murstein, the leading proponent of this emphasis on values in mate selection, has identified several different stages in courtship that are primarily concerned with couples' comparing their values. It did not take long for Margaret and me to learn that we weren't interested in going to church, or dressing up for the football game, or drinking heavily, or playing bridge; and that we were interested in a kind of gossipy analysis of people; in literature, music, and the whole world of visual imagery; and in the outdoors.

Since our shared values come out of our histories, they also allow us to connect with each other's family. My interest in poetry did not exactly help me with Margaret's businessman father (I shall never forget that memorable first dinner with her family when he asked me point-blank how a poet intended to support himself), but it provided me with an instant link with Margaret's mother, whose family loved literature.

I could describe other commonalities in our families, but the general point is made: *We are drawn to someone whose family world is in several important ways similar to our own.*

Eventually, Margaret and I realized that we also occupied similar role positions in our respective families. Even on that first weekend, both of us took a little time to study. From as early as each of us can remember, we have felt pressured to work hard, to be competent and successful, and to do things "right." We were our families' delegates. I don't remember what we said about our parents that first weekend, but I knew very soon that Margaret's father was the dominant influence in her life and that he was overinvolved with her. Margaret, much later, put it this way: "When we did go to church when I was a kid, my father would make a great to-do of polishing my shoes as I stood on the stairs. He would do it in a teasing, flirtatious way, and of course my mother would get furious with me. Knowing how jealous she was of his attention to me, I would spend the rest of the day trying to appease her." Oedipus, Oedipus. We were also both "marital" kids, which made it easy for us to find companionship with each other; but it also made sex an anxious area, especially in the beginning.

Let me hazard another generalization: *We are attracted to someone whose basic psychological "situation" in his or her family of origin is similar to our own.* That is, we identify with this person's "core problems," dynamics that were shaped in the early family.

This identification with the other's experience in the family "context" may lead people with similar positions in sibling order to marry each other (and there is some research evidence for this tendency); or the similarity may come out of their occupying similar family roles.

"But didn't many spouses have different roles in their childhood families?" the reader may ask. Vicki and Jack Gordon are a good case in point. Vicki was a parental oldest child, Jack an "infantilized" youngest. How could their dilemmas be similar?

Remember, it is the experience of the other which we identify with, not the exact situation that produced it. Through all her responsible caretaking, Vicki felt unseen and unnurtured—in short, emotionally neglected. Though Jack was sometimes hovered over by his infantilizing mother, he spent a great deal of time alone; and he was virtually ignored by his father. As we got to know him better, we learned that the central issue he carried over from childhood was emotional neglect. We also learned that Jack felt profoundly responsible for his mother's emotional welfare, something he was eventually able to articulate: "I think I had to be dependent on her because it helped her." This sense of responsibility for their mothers was another common link in their identification with each other.

However we arrived there, each of us sees in the other a vital and shared vulnerability, a common Achilles tendon. This perception of mutual vulnerability has great potential for development of empathy for each other; it also tempts us to see our own problems in our mate, and to blame him or her for our own feelings. As I listened to Margaret speak scornfully of Wesleyan's weekend revelers, I thought to myself, "She's a bit of a snob." Not realizing, of course, that I was as insecurely scornful as she.

I believe that we are likely to share not only some common situational dilemmas in childhood, but also some specific traumas. It may take us years to discover that certain particularly difficult events happened to each of us when we were children; and when we learn these facts, it may seem a little spooky that we could have somehow sensed these common early experiences. Though we dealt with the issue differently—I by being a "distancer," Margaret by being a conscientious "pursuer"—we later learned that we shared a sensitivity to abandonment or rejection. At first we were puzzled by our anxiety about this issue; soon it would cause us great difficulty. It would be many years before we fully understood its origins.

Our potential mate, then, is often a cleverly disguised emotional twin. This person offers us some purchase on life's terrible loneliness; he or she may have some chance of knowing what it is like to be us. This is someone who has:

- □ a similar tolerance for emotional closeness (or distance)
- □ approximately equal power, all things considered
- □ equal maturity
- □ equal courage
- □ equal commitment

Of course, I cannot expect the reader merely to take my word about these assertions. Evidence for these shared states accumulates with time, and with the playing out of the story.

SOMEONE DIFFERENT FROM ME

We are also excited by the sense that our mate is different from us. Sexuality itself is based on our biological incompleteness, and its exigencies create in us a profound and lifelong yearning for a ful-filling Other. There are many ways, however, in which we feel incomplete. We all have personal failings, and these compel us to link up with someone who will help us feel competent and whole.

Several weeks after we met, I drove to Mount Holyoke in a borrowed car; at the end of an afternoon of touring the countryside, Margaret noticed that we were nearly out of gas. With a sigh of embarrassment and relief, I pulled into a gas station. It was my first awareness of her attention to life's important details. I soon discov-ered that Margaret remembered when our engagements were sched-uled, thought about the sequences we had to go through to get to them, and noticed the other minutiae necessary to our negotiating the daily world. This rather dreamy poet soon came to depend heavily on her skills of attending carefully to the particulars of life, specifics of which I was often scornful—because, of course, my mother had looked after such things for me.

I also quickly learned that once we arrived at some unavoidable social function, Margaret was far more skilled than I in dealing with it. Though she had hated it at the time, the years of training at country clubs served her well. She remembered names and knew what to say. I also began to depend on this set of social skills. Every couple has its "social ambassador," or the partner who does more of the talking when they are together in a social setting.

So what did I contribute? While Margaret was acutely attuned to what was happening around her, she was often unobservant about her own internal experience. I was surprised to learn that she sometimes didn't know what she felt, and that she had little access to fantasy, or to the whole intuitive side of life. In this realm of private, interior experience, I shone. I noticed a pained expression on her face and asked about it; I shared my fantasies, my thoughts and feelings—sometimes more than she wanted to hear.

So we are also attracted by the asymmetries in our two sets of style and experience. If one of us is intuitive and impulsive, the other may be planful and cautious; if one of us is social and extro-verted, the other may be painfully shy. One of us may be assertive and parental, the other unassertive and childlike. One of us may be a lover of closeness, the other a connoisseur of separateness.

At least one major theorist, R. F. Winch, has advanced the

notion that "complementary needs" form the basis for mate selection. Of the "opposites attract" school, he feels that we seek someone whose needs are "matched" with ours: I may need to be a "caretaker," for example, and marry someone who needs caretaking; or I may have a high need for dominance, and marry someone who has a low need for dominance. Prominent in the sixties, Winch's ideas have not been strongly supported by others' research, but I believe there is merit to be found in them.

Whatever the "basic needs" of individuals, the history of marriage is indeed one of complementary adjustment and accommodation. Traditional marriage is rife with complementarity—though most of us would argue that a woman's "need" to be less dominant than her husband has been an artifact of enforced role playing rather than intrinsic need. Still, there are powerful forces that seem to compel us to seek out someone who is in certain respects different from us; and the same forces tempt us to "specialize" within marriage, each partner playing a particular role, or "representing" a certain attitude to life. I do not believe these tendencies are particularly healthy—often, they reveal our dependency on each other—but they do exist.

First, it is understandable that we would be hungry to link up with a person who has some quality that we covet. I want to learn from Margaret's affable sociability; she is intrigued by my access to the world of fantasy and intuition. Marrying someone is one way to gain access to a certain dimension of life.

Of course, rather than developing a certain skill in ourselves, we are likely to depend on our mate's ability to supply it. I don't have to learn to be more socially adept; I rely on Margaret to do that for me.

Second, regardless of our particular skills or abilities, once we are married, we are likely to take complementary (or asymmetrical) positions that allow us to become "specialists" within the relationship. These specialized roles fulfill a number of functions, from limiting competition to regulating impulsiveness; and we will examine the way they evolve over time.

I believe that while we are attracted to our mate's "differentness," and while we are strongly tempted to form contrasting patterns within marriage, our strongest identification with each other comes out of our similarities. Margaret was more skilled in social situations, but she turned out to be just as anxious about them as I was; and she felt better having me around to face them with her. We may have different styles or approaches for dealing with certain key areas of life—but they are areas about which we have very similar feelings.

Jack looked much more dependent and needy than Vicki, but, as we learned, there was within Vicki a hidden dependent self, deprived and unnurtured, which she gained access to in part through her relationship with Jack. If she couldn't take care of herself, at least she could take care of him.

The obvious and visible differences between us, then, may be "surface" differences: often, it is the hidden, unacknowledged part of ourselves which we recognize in our mate; and in linking up with this person, we attempt to make contact with this disavowed or undeveloped part of us.

Basic underlying similarities guide our selection of each other.

A FAMILIAR OTHER

What was it about her—that warm, brilliant smile, that alert tilt to her head, that lilting laugh? What was it in her very presence that made me feel dizzy, helpless, wonderful? How could someone so strange and new also seem familiar? "Have I met you somewhere before?" we ask. Though it is a complex illusion, it seems that we have.

Freud's notion was that we marry someone who reminds us of the parent of the opposite sex. While his views on this subject are not highly regarded by contemporary theorists, there is undoubtedly a component of truth in them. It was not until we had been married for several years that I noticed that Margaret's flashing smile was very much like my mother's. Every time Margaret smiled—mischievously, warmly, bravely—my heart melted; and of course my mother's smile had had the same effect on me as a kid. Her smile was one of the ways I felt loved by my mother. Then I began to notice other similarities between them—their delicately sculptured features, their large eyes, their short, slender frames (both were five foot two), their crisp, purposeful way of walking. Both were also extremely alert, bright, cheerful, strong, well-organized, helpful, anxiously overresponsible, controlling. At least in these respects, they were embarrassingly similar.

One cold early-spring day after we had known each other for several weeks, Margaret and I took a walk in the countryside near Wesleyan. Seeing a fire-lookout tower beside the road, I clambered up the steps—showing off, I suppose. At the top of the tower I felt the bite of the Connecticut wind, and sensed that fearful uncertainty which most of the time I tried not to think about. Solitary, exposed, I suddenly panicked about how I was going to deal with the world I saw below me, the world beyond college. At the foot of the tower, Margaret seemed small and insignificant; of no help to me. After staring for a while out into the anonymous countryside, I turned and hurried down the stairs. As I approached Margaret, I felt the immediate warmth of her smile, her voice, her very presence; and with a delicious sense of relief, felt safe. Taking her hand, I dismissed the thoughts of what I had seen on the tower.

A sense of safety is an important part of what our mate offers us; and his or her capacity to remind us of a parental figure is no small part of that special aura. Margaret's smile, and the other physical and behavioral cues that suggested my mother, were symbolic for me; they created the illusion that I was in the presence of a protective parent. The scared kid inside me leaned hungrily into this psychological shelter.

Our mate's ability to make us feel protected and safe may be the most powerful element in our attraction—stronger than our needs for sex or companionship. Since our mothers are the first and primary sources of our early security, it makes sense that Margaret would remind me of my mother. In fact, according to research by sociologist A. Aron, if we compare the personality characteristics of our spouse with the characteristics of both of our parents, our mate will be found to be similar in many respects to our mother. Apparently males and females marry people who remind them in important ways of their mothers.

I believe that this explanation, while plausible, is more true for men than for women. Many girls grow up with a strong involvement with both their mothers and their fathers (a tendency which we will explore further), and they often marry men who remind them of both figures. Indeed, as we thought about this issue much later, I seemed to be like both Margaret's parents. I look more like Margaret's father, but, particularly in my capacity for being reserved and sometimes distant, and in my ability to exploit Margaret's guilty conscience, I bear an uncomfortable resemblance to her mother.

If someone was not close to either parent as a child, he or she is—in my view—drawn to marry someone who is like the person—sibling, grandparent, foster parent—by whom he or she felt the most loved during childhood.

After years of trying to sort out our attraction to each other, and the marriages made by our clients, I have assembled a more complex idea of just who this person is who makes us feel so confused and dizzy when we first meet them. Yes, this is someone who reminds us of a certain vital, loved person in childhood who made us feel safe; but this talented individual may also remind us of *all* the key players in our childhood drama—mother, father, sister, brother, beloved aunt or grandmother. That is why we get so confused: we are confronted by a single person who can, and does, take all the important roles in our history. In Albert Pesso's terms, he or she is capable of creating all the important relationship "structures" from our childhood. And if this were not trouble enough, this sometimes maddeningly capable soul can also play *us*—particularly the part of us that we don't like or know very well—with great skill.

It is probably impossible to know whether our mate comes with a full-blown capacity to perform many of the important roles in our family of origin, or whether he or she learns these roles by being subtly reinforced for playing them. I did not think of myself as particularly parsimonious when Margaret and I married, but I have become so. I know when I remind Margaret to turn out the lights that I am courting danger; and that if I switch fields and after months of niggardliness about money suggest an extravagant purchase, I am inviting a storm of anger. But Margaret needed some way to deal with her anger at her mother about such behavior. So maybe I learned that one. But when I, as Margaret's father did, sit down and expect somebody to wait on me, I suspect my own natural proclivities, helped along as they were by my mother's willingness to do my bidding.

Our mate, then, has unusual powers. He or she can sometimes make us feel that we are literally enclosed by the family we grew up in. While this power may allow us to take comfort in our reassuringly familiar surroundings, some of the associations are of course negative. I am comforted by Margaret's tendency to direct me; I am also mightily annoyed by it.

The stage is set, then, for both of us to recapitulate our family dramas. We have married someone with the talent to help us stage the dramas; and particularly if each of us is to express the feelings we did not dare reveal in childhood, it is something we need to do. After Margaret and I married, and after about the third or fourth time Margaret suggested what I order at a restaurant, I exploded. Margaret was bewildered and hurt by my response, but I felt better.

This bewildering person also has the power to make us feel deeply frightened and vulnerable. Our greatest vulnerability comes in the implicit contract for caretaking. It is here that we risk searching for something we weren't given as children, and here that we risk recapitulating our historic injuries.

In most "unconscious contracts," as in ours, the nurturant, caretaking role is mostly on the shoulders of women (men tend to caretake by earning money, fixing flat tires, building furniture, and giving lots of practical advice, especially about money). So when Margaret was helpful to me, she was again repeating her role in childhood. Later she was to admit, "I guess I helped everybody in my family. When we went on a car trip, my parents couldn't agree on the route, and even as an eight-year-old I would take the map, figure it out, and tell them where to go. My mother would ask me what she should cook for dinner. My father would ask me what to do about Mother."

From the very beginning, the contract is often skewed, with women being givers. While most women are likely to fall into caretaking patterns in their marriages, women who as girls were in parental roles in their families of origin are the most vulnerable to this temptation. A variety of men are searching for such women. Men who as children were rejected or infantilized virtually require such a wife; but "delegates" like me who need someone to accommodate their needs and to facilitate the practical aspects of their lives are also in search of these generous women.

A DIFFERENT SENSE OF FAMILY

Fortunately, we are up to more than recapitulating history. I sensed commonality in Margaret's family, but also intriguing differences. At that first dinner, I was amazed at her family's aggressive teasing. "How can these people talk to each other in this way?" I asked myself. At first it seemed hostile; later I was attracted to the humor itself—the sense of hard edges, and of their challenging and pushing against each other. My soft, serious family could never talk so directly.

We often see such contrasts between a couple's two families of origin. Someone from an enmeshed family marries someone from a disengaged family. Someone from a disorganized family marries someone from a highly organized, planful family. Of course, such contrasts lead to difficulties, but the intent—to mix and blend two family worlds—remains valid.

In each family a story is playing itself out, and each family's story embodies both its hope and its despair. In our most skilled intuition in selecting a mate, we sense that there is something in the mixture of these family stories, and our respective involvement in them, that promises us both an opportunity to grow.

I was not conscious of it then, but a part of me knew that if I was going to be successful in my work, I needed a stronger model than my father's. I was drawn to someone who in addition to expecting me sometimes to behave like her mother, would also expect me to be like her father. Margaret simply assumed that I would be successful. Her expectation, and her father's example, would be useful to me—levers, pulleys to hoist myself into a role I had not seen at close range. If Margaret was to break out of her father's injunction that she not have a career, perhaps a man whose mother had to be the family stalwart, and who had a successful teaching career, could help.

In the mixture of these two families, then, as well as in the mixture of our own personalities and predilections, there is some purchase on change, and an imperative to change. If I was to hold my own with this very strong woman, and to compete successfully with the image of her powerful father, I had to be more successful than my own father.

Are there some general rules that we might apply to this intricate business of choosing a mate? Since each of us approaches marriage with our unique set of problems and needs, the variety of unconscious strategies in marital choice is dizzying. Perhaps these guidelines will help:

- ☐ Beneath the surface, our mate is very much like us, and comes from a fundamentally similar situation in life.

- ☐ There is also some kind of hierarchy in every marriage, and it is often based on an implicit contract in which one person plays "parent" to the other's "child." These behaviors are carried over from both partners' childhood roles in their families of origin. An oldest, overresponsible child may marry a youngest child who is accustomed to caretaking, for example. Or independent of sibling order, a parental child may marry a rejected child who didn't receive enough caretaking.

- ☐ These caretaking arrangements may be obviously mutual and shared; often, each person acts in a parental way toward the partner in at least some aspect of the marriage. But even if they seem highly unequal, there is always some form of reciprocity between the partners. Even when one partner seems to be "parent" in almost every respect and the other is in an exclusively "child" role, the parental partner is still meeting his or her dependency needs through caretaking the other partner.

- ☐ These "helping" contracts replicate in both partners the experience of living in their respective families of origin. These "hypnotic" associations inhibit many aspects of both partners' lives, particularly their freedom to deal openly with anger and to feel freely sexual.

- ☐ At some point in the marriage, these helping arrangements, which are the major impediment to an equal relationship, will fail. When this failure occurs, both partners will be required to face their childhood disappointments in their parents.

- ☐ Our partner will prove adept at making us face ourselves and our core problems from childhood. This person will expose our vulnerabilities, and call upon us to develop new strengths.

☐ The encounter with ourselves and our histories will sometimes become so excruciating that it will seem that unless things change, we will have to leave the relationship, or regress into some very frightening early-childhood experiences.

☐ If we survive these tests, this relationship has enormous potential for companionship, and for mutual support.

Finally, what makes us dizzy is the scope of the sheer depth of involvement which is created by the juxtaposition of our lives, and of the lives of our two families.

11

An Identity Crisis

IN EXPLORING THE DEVELOPMENT of marriage over time, we will encounter a number of predictable crises. The first crisis actually occurs before marriage; it is brought about by the approach of the ceremony itself. Though most people develop "a case of the jitters" before marriage, it can be a good deal worse than that. As our wedding day approaches, we may wake with a panic about our vague whisperings to ourselves in the night.

"What if it doesn't last?" the voice asks. We have friends who have divorced, or parents; we may have been through it ourselves. Even at some distance, we can see the devastation, the years of internal bleeding.

"What if it doesn't last?" Remembering all the silent couples in restaurants, remembering that frightening glaze in our parents' eyes, or their flat words with the edges turned down.

Questions that sound trite in the day are frightening at night: "What if she doesn't love me? Or I don't love her?" We yearn for certainty, and know there isn't any.

"What if he dominates me?"

"What if she smothers me?"

Some questions have no words; they appear only as vague waves of doubt.

Our fears are often the shadows of past injuries which we project onto marriage; our mate becomes the image of the hurtful parent, or, in the case of the previously married, the former spouse. But these anxieties and fears can also be an intuitive response to the marriage itself, and they may issue us with a warning that accurately predicts trouble ahead.

While a number of serious issues can be responsible for our anxiety, perhaps the most difficult worry is that we are not up to the challenges of marriage. Maybe we are not sufficiently autonomous; our identities may not be securely formed. The powerful forces between us thus threaten to swallow us up, and love seems to lead to the imminent loss of our precarious, embryonic sense of self.

The developmental psychologist Erik Erikson has said that a sense of identity must precede the development of intimacy. If we have reversed the sequence and become deeply involved before developing stable identities, we are likely to know that something is wrong; but few of us understand exactly what the problem is. We may only sense that we are not prepared to keep the promises we have made.

In spite of the midnight whisperings, most couples go ahead with the wedding. Unless they encounter a dedicated minister or rabbi who offers more than the usual "premarital counseling," most have little support for doing anything else. If they had the help they deserve at this critical moment, these anxious couples might not be so tempted to repress and deny their misgivings. Perhaps they could see that these anxieties have validity, but that they do not necessarily mean there is something fundamentally wrong with their choice of each other. With some help, they could look at the problems between them, and think about the preparation they need in order to be really ready for this long and taxing journey.

But most of us stand alone at this moment—hoping for the best.

My senior year in college was busy. Again I was the good "delegate"—class president, class poet—and I had an intellectual feast: writing tutorials with poet Richard Wilbur and with poet and novelist George Garrett; a course with Norman O. Brown, the psychoanalytic historian. Wesleyan was all I had expected it might be; it was especially a place where one had access to truly great teachers.

For the time being, I was well enough situated. I lived in an attic apartment in a professor's house, worked hard, and waited for the blue envelopes. They came at first from Paris, where Margaret worked on her French, toured museums, and wrote to me in a carefully composed hand about the streets, the people, the daily wonders.

After a month in Paris, she was off to the University of Geneva, where she was to study political science for the remainder of the year. I felt a twinge of anxiety when she arrived there, knowing what a cosmopolitan, and coeducational, environment she would be in. I sent her poems and long letters.

When you are twenty, a year apart seems forever. For about six months, we were both able to keep our images of each other firmly in place, and to keep intently focused on our long-distance courtship. Then, over the Christmas holidays, something in both of us shifted. I went back to Georgia, where my aunt, always making trouble, introduced me to a pretty, aspiring pianist. And Margaret went skiing at Zermatt, where she met a wealthy French medical student who immediately began pursuing her.

Back at Wesleyan, I wrote to the pianist, Ann, and also started dating Lin, a warm, bright girl from Smith. I was drawn to both girls; but in their presence, my heart stood strangely still. Having moved once, it refused to move again. I continued to write to Margaret, though I didn't mention the other girls.

Nor did she tell me about Antoine, and for that I suppose I can be grateful. If I had known about the world to which Margaret began to be introduced—the formal dinners, the art collection, the trips to Paris—I might have given up. In the spring I worried as her letters became less frequent and more cryptic; but then I was having difficulty writing too. After graduating from Wesleyan, I went back to Georgia. I visited my aunt often, and would walk over to Ann's parents' house and listen to her practice Chopin, Beethoven, Mozart, hour after hour.

As an aspiring poet, I thought that I might like to teach in a private secondary school, and in that interest, and to be near Margaret while she finished her degree at Holyoke, I had accepted a "teaching fellowship" at Phillips Academy at Andover, north of Boston. This fellowship was part of the Master of Arts in Teaching program at Harvard, where I was to spend a second year.

It was September, cool and beautiful in Boston, when I met Margaret for the first time in fifteen months. The person who walked toward me with that teasing, bright smile was a woman in a sleek blue dress, her hair done up in a bun. I felt disarmed by the change in her, but I also felt immediately the magnetism of presence: the lilt of her voice, the ease of her movements, the sensuous touch of her hand. All around me I could hear a familiar chord, the deep music of the world. And my heart moved again.

After the train ride to Andover, it did not take us long to find some countryside to walk in, nor did it take me long to begin to learn about Antoine.

Though I didn't know it then, by the time Margaret and I met that day in Boston, she had turned down his offer of marriage. I did know that he was rather desperately pursuing her, and that a week previously she had, in a tearful transatlantic call, broken off their relationship. Undaunted, Antoine was apparently attempting to transfer to Harvard Medical School. Yet here she was, smiling broadly, her arm in mine.

Years later, Margaret would say, "I don't think I ever seriously considered marrying him, though I did love him." And: "As dependent as I was in those days, it was too long a time to be away from you." And finally: "Antoine's mother died when he was ten, and I think she must have looked a lot like me. There was something too intense about his caring for me."

At the time, I felt deeply threatened, my complacency shattered. Margaret and I began seeing each other every weekend, and by the time the leaves turned in the country north of Boston, I had asked her to marry me. This time she said yes.

That fall, we were as intensely happy as two dreamy, poetic souls could be. I went to Holyoke, she came to Andover. Swept up in my relationship with Margaret, I began to ignore my job, and soon I heard negative remarks from my supervisor. I was absent too often; I got my papers back late; I wasn't attending to my dormitory duty. Having decided that I didn't like teaching in secondary school, I didn't care. I would teach in college.

As the bleak Massachusetts winter descended upon us, however, I began to grow strangely uneasy. I had applied to a couple of graduate schools of English, but I had difficulty imagining myself in one of them; I had even more trouble seeing Margaret and myself there together.

I would try to visualize us in an apartment in San Francisco or New Haven; Margaret would be teaching somewhere, and I would be studying hard. Most of the time I couldn't get the image clearly, and when I did, I felt a strange claustrophobia, a kind of suffocating feeling. I had begun to hear a new chord—dissonant, off-key. One day I was standing at a window at Andover, looking out into the winter day. I noticed a fly that had died between the screen and the window. "It couldn't get out," I thought to myself. It was then that I first realized that I felt trapped, and that I began to say to myself, "I'm not ready."

From the perspective of years, I can see us clearly: two naïve, idealistic young people, very much in love but very dependent on each other, and not at all prepared for the world of marriage. Able to study hard and to please our teachers, we were not ready to get jobs, rent apartments, buy cars. Nor were we able to be separate and distinct in relation to each other. We were two insecure kids standing stiflingly close to each other. That was what I feared—the lack of air, and my inability to define who or where I was in life.

At that time Margaret seemed confident, optimistic, self-possessed; but much of her confidence came from her somewhat dreamy idealization of marriage. In retrospect she can now say: "I placed all my hopes on our relationship. It offered me safety, and it permitted me to avoid thinking about myself and what I was going to do with my life. I was following the path I had been prepared for: to take care of a talented and ambitious man." Her inability to look at the challenges and the practical difficulties facing us left me to worry about them alone.

From the perspective of the present I can also see what was happening at that time in Georgia. My father was dying of heart disease; and unconsciously I sensed it. My relationship with him had been strained in recent years, and I needed somehow to reach him, to get with him. A second layer of anguish crept into the dissonance: it said, "Go home."

By the time I realized consciously how unprepared I was for the future Margaret and I had planned, it was late March and I had been accepted in the two graduate schools. Our wedding had been set for June, right after her graduation. During the spring I tried twice to talk to Margaret about the possibility of postponing our wedding, but she was obviously panicked by the idea. When I saw her alarm, there seemed nothing to do but go ahead. And so I did.

Spring came late to New England in 1961, and it was cold and disagreeable, as reluctant as my spirit. I continued to go to my classes, but my performance was worse than ever. Margaret and I still spent occasional weekends together, but increasingly she was in Albany, nudging along the machinery of the inevitable wedding. Our families seemed excited about it, and many people were coming. Everything seemed in order but me.

May arrived, in full flower, but still cool and overcast. I had trouble sleeping, and sometimes I didn't go to class, or showed up late. The headmaster called me in for a scolding, but his warning contained no invitation to talk about what was bothering me. I tried harder, but inside the abrasive chord became louder and louder, a shrill shriek that made it impossible to think. What to do? I felt totally, desperately alone. On a good night, I slept five hours; on a bad one, two.

In late May, three weeks before our wedding, I wrote to Steve, my old roommate. He and Judy had married, and he was now a graduate student. "When you come to be my best man, you will find a very unhappy groom. So please stand by me," I said.

As soon as he got my letter, Steve called me. "Listen," he said warmly, "you don't have to get married if you don't want to! And you really don't sound like you want to." His caring, confident voice was the first resonant note in a long time. Sitting alone in my room, I played the words over and over: "You don't have to get married if you don't want to." I had to do something, but what? The invitations had been sent long ago; the gifts were arriving.

Now, sleep eluded me altogether. After three completely sleepless nights, the dissonance in my head was simply unbearable. There seemed to be no choice at all, just the blackest despair. I sat down and started writing.

As I wrote, the words became a letter to Margaret—rambling, barely coherent, but with a persistent theme: "I can't do it; I'm not ready; I don't understand it, but I can't marry you. I feel totally overwhelmed by the demands of marriage. I hope you will be able to forgive me; maybe, at some time, we could try again." And I said that I loved her.

I packed some of my belongings and took the train to Boston, where I boarded a plane to Atlanta. Waiting for the plane, I felt that I was under water, where I heard random and distorted sounds. The only thing that kept chaos at bay was the idea of the plane. It was as though I was following a thin wire which led somewhere; maybe to air and light.

The plane made one stop, at Raleigh–Durham, North Carolina, and when it touched down, I decided to step outside. The sun was shining; the air warm, almost hot. "I'm home," I thought to myself, feeling a deep sense of relief. It suddenly occurred to me that I wanted to visit the University of North Carolina at nearby Chapel Hill. So I claimed my luggage, and took a cab to Chapel Hill's student-thronged main street.

For a while, I just wandered, bathing in the warmth of the sun, and in the deep familiarity of Southern voices. I still felt extremely confused, but now I worried less about the confusion. I found a cafeteria and had a sandwich; I wandered down the aisles of a bookstore and bought a book. For a long while, I sat on a stone wall and watched the students passing by. When the sun began to go down, I realized that I would need somewhere to sleep, but I didn't care where.

Though I was still extremely confused, and though every act required enormous thought and effort, I realized that I felt a strange kind of peace. I felt that for my whole life, I had belonged to someone—first to my parents and then to Margaret. Even when I boarded the plane in Boston, it seemed as though I was merely going home to the other people to whom I belonged. Now, for several hours, I had not belonged to anyone. In a primitive and disorderly way, I had betrayed them all. For the first time, it occurred to me that I owned myself.

Darkness was falling, and for nearly twelve hours, no one who cared about me had known where I was. I thought about my parents, and about Margaret. Looking around me, I felt a growing uneasiness.

As I dialed my parents' number, I could hear my heart beating in my ears. "Hello?" my mother's voice sounded uncertain, fearful. Suddenly I felt a wave of love for her.

"Hi, Mom," I said as cheerfully as I could manage. "This is Gus." She burst into tears.

"Where are you?" she was finally able to ask, and I told her.

"Will you call Margaret and tell her that I am all right?"

"Yes, I will," my mother said. "She will be so relieved."

Then I found a motel, and for the first time in months, fell asleep easily.

The next day, my parents met me at the airport. My mother was warmly accepting; my father looked disgruntled. Later he would mutter something about my throwing away my future.

That evening, I talked to Margaret. She too seemed warm and understanding, though her voice broke once. "You rest," she said. "When you're ready, I'll come down." Leaving her to disassemble a wedding, and to graduate from college, I turned to trying to find my way toward the next day, and the next.

My mother had gotten from a friend the name of a psychiatrist in private practice named Carl Whitaker. Carl was not a family therapist at that time; but during the early sixties, very few people were. Even then, the first meeting was with the entire family. Carl presided firmly, and from the outset I knew he was both smart and tough. Evidence of his caring would come later. He saw my mother's tendency to rescue me; saw my father's resistance to my being in therapy and labeled it openly. He had a name for what I had been through—"an identity crisis"—and for the intense panic itself, which he called a "fugue state." Toward the end of the interview, he recommended that I start individual therapy with him. "To accomplish anything substantial will take a year, minimum."

On the way home, my father said, "We need somebody like that for the entire family." He was right, but it was not to be.

By the time Margaret came to Atlanta a couple of weeks later, I had begun therapy and started looking for a job. In spite of what she was going through in New York, Margaret was the person I had always known: optimistic, warm, engaging. Though she didn't say it, she also looked relieved not to be getting married.

Margaret was immediately drawn to my father, and she and my mother got along well enough. The two of us sat in my parents' backyard, talking about alternatives. Carl had suggested that Margaret get her own therapist, and that we put our relationship on hold. Feeling my determination to work with Carl, Margaret said she would do it.

Having decided that, we smiled at each other, and I said, "Let's go camping." We borrowed a tent, loaded the family canoe on the car, and drove to an isolated lake in the Georgia mountains. There we found a small island on which we camped for several days: swimming naked in the moonlight, making love, talking, dreaming. After all the hours of loneliness and pain, it was truly wonderful.

Margaret had decided to spend the year in graduate school preparing herself to be a French teacher, and within a month she had been accepted both by Harvard's MAT program and Columbia's French department. Knowing that Antoine was now at Harvard, I held my breath. She chose Columbia.

When Margaret announced to her parents that she was moving to New York City and going into therapy, her mother threw herself on her bed and said that it was going to kill her. "Haven't you put me through enough already?" she cried. And when he discovered that Margaret intended to live in Greenwich Village with two other young women, her father had the same kind of reaction. "It isn't safe; I won't allow it."

By that time Margaret had already met Asya Kadis, an Adlerian therapist whose Park Avenue office was to become the center of her life for the next two years. Sixty-five, plump, with the accent of her native Russia, Asya sat amid her Chagall paintings, often sipping iced tea, and dispensed her unique blend of wisdom and care. Once Margaret had met her, none of her parents' hysteria had much effect.

At my aunt's suggestion, I applied for college teaching jobs this time, and, to my surprise, was offered an instructorship in English at a division of the University of Georgia in the small town of Carrollton, an hour's drive from Atlanta. As Margaret and her friends were moving into a basement apartment in Greenwich Village, I found a small guest house for rent on a farm near the college. While Margaret took the subway up to Columbia, I drove through the rolling countryside of west Georgia to my classes.

For most of that first year, both of us lived largely within the deepening confines of our separate but parallel therapies. Each of us had a therapist who met a deep need: Margaret had found a loving, accepting "mother"; I had found a strong, and as it turned out, caring "father." We had time, enough money to get by, and someone willing to listen very carefully to what we were feeling and thinking. Very quickly, we settled into the hard work of learning about ourselves.

How, within the brief confines of this chapter, can I begin to describe what happened to me during the course of therapy—the volumes of recorded dreams, the intimate conversations, the confrontations, the long silences while the expensive minutes went by, the flashes of insight that made my head spin, the moments of stark terror, the occasional boredom, the sheer sweat of trying to understand, trying to change myself. I can't, of course.

It was like going on a long and difficult journey to another country, a journey that required enormous amounts of effort and courage, and for which one received little recognition. While my classmates were getting doctorates and law degrees, I was writing down my dreams, sitting out the lonely nights in the vast expanse of sky over my little house, and talking about it all to Carl.

I liked teaching in college. Instead of lecturing, I broke my classes into small, family-sized groups, where I helped the students work on individual writing projects and encouraged honest conversation. Soon some of my students became friends, as did a couple of my colleagues, and my bachelor landlord.

When I wasn't teaching, I often roamed the countryside, taking photographs. I turned my kitchen into a darkroom. I also continued to write poems. All of these I sent to Margaret, who showed them to Asya; so that when she and I finally met, Asya and I already had a relationship.

I also went regularly to Atlanta, where I saw Carl, and visited my parents (my sister went to a nearby college, and she was often there too). After dinner I would sit out in the backyard with my father, talking quietly. He had stopped drinking, and, tentatively, we began to reach out to each other. Sometimes, when he was near Carrollton, he would drop by my house, though he would never call ahead, and often I wasn't there.

In some respects, these were ideal years. I look at photographs of that little white house on the banks of a farm pond, and I think of it as "my house." It was the place where I learned to live by myself relatively comfortably, the place where I got to know myself better, the place where I extended and deepened the feeling of owning myself that had begun in Chapel Hill.

I also think of those two years as a long and sometimes terrifying confrontation with being alone: finding that I had a dead battery and having to get my car going so that I would get to class; learning to get my papers graded on time; paying my bills; and sitting alone in that house, listening to the soft fluttering of the fire in the fireplace while the winter wind prowled around outside. Walking at night under the immense universe of the sky, feeling myself like the most insignificant and wavering candle. Lying still in my bed, wondering what I would dream about that night, and, as sleep came on, holding on to the image of Carl.

There were also moments of terror in my relationship with Margaret. As spring came to Georgia that first year of our separation, I was so engrossed in therapy that I began to resent Margaret's attempts to keep in close touch with me by phone. She seemed to want to talk at least weekly, and sometimes she would call twice a week. I began to resent the calls, partly because I could not afford to reciprocate. I paid my own bills out of my meager salary, while she got a healthy allowance from her family. "Look," I said, "let's alternate calling each other once a week." "Fine," Margaret said cheerfully; but she didn't keep the agreement. Soon she was calling twice a week again.

My mother had also begun to irritate me with the way she talked *at* me so incessantly when I visited in Atlanta. I know now that she was anxious about my father's health, but all I felt was that I wanted her off my back.

But it was Margaret who bore the brunt of my anger. After one of her calls, I called the phone company and had my phone disconnected. Before she could get my letter explaining why I had done it, she had called and gotten the brutally factual recorded message that, "at the customer's request . . ."

Somewhat to my relief, I did not hear from Margaret for a month. I wrote her an apology, but got no reply. Once I called her, but she was out.

Then one Friday night in early May, I had an uneventful dinner with my parents and sister. My father had become a real-estate salesman, and he had lost an important sale that day. He seemed tired and discouraged. My parents and I watched television together for a while, and then we all went to bed early.

I was awakened around midnight by my mother. She was taking my father to his doctor's office; he was having some chest pains. I told him I hoped it would be all right; he said he was sure it would be. Probably indigestion. I dozed off again. The phone woke me this time; it was my mother, telling me that he was dead of a coronary. At fifty-four, my father had collapsed in the car just as the doctor arrived. "Why," I was later to cry out, "didn't the doctor have them come to the emergency room?"

My mother, my sister, and I stood huddled together in the doctor's waiting room, all crying.

When I called Margaret to tell her, all her roommate would tell me was that she was in Boston. She didn't need to say more.

It was a long and lonely drive to Lumber City. After a funeral in the Methodist church that both he and I had attended as children, my father was buried in his family's plot in the cemetery by the river. The day was hot and steamy, with great cumulus clouds sailing over.

"Thank God for Carl," I thought, grieving for the father I had had, as well as for the one I hadn't, not knowing then that there was really no replacement for him.

And, I can say now, thank God for Asya, who said to Margaret, "Give this young man a little more time. He has lost his father." Margaret and I began to write again, politely and circumspectly. Meanwhile, I knew she was seeing Antoine, and possibly dating someone else in New York. Could I come to visit her in early September, just before my school began? She agreed that I could. I taught summer school that dry husk of a summer, feeling the vast emptiness of not having a father.

And so it happened again. Just seeing each other, just walking in the Village together, just talking over dinner. This time surrounded by her life, her friends; this time meeting Asya and falling in love with her too. I moved into Margaret's apartment with her two girlfriends, and for nearly a week, we lived together.

One evening, walking in Washington Square Park, I said to Margaret, "Could we talk about the future?"

"I think so," Margaret said.

"This time next year," I began, my heart beating fast, "let's be living together."

"I accept," Margaret said. "Your country or mine?"

"Mine," I said boldly.

For the rest of that year, Margaret came to Georgia when she could, and we had wonderful, intense weekends on the farm. I worked hard in therapy, knowing that it was the last year I would have in which to focus just on myself. On one of those weekend visits, Margaret and I walked over to my friend and landlord's house on the farm, and discovered that Claude's guest was the president of the college. I introduced Margaret, and she was her charming self. Two days later, after Margaret had gone back to New York, I called the president and asked if the college needed a French teacher. "If it's Margaret, we certainly do," he said.

In the fall, grieved over by her friends as if she were emigrating to deepest darkest Peru, Margaret moved to Carrollton, into an apartment near mine. In a small town in Georgia in 1963, our living together was out of the question. We had announced that we were being married at Christmas, at Margaret's parents' new retirement home in Florida; but, becoming more and more impatient with the awkwardness of our situation, we suddenly moved it up to Thanksgiving. We gave Margaret's mother three weeks' notice.

We were married in a chapel in Hobe Sound with only our families and a few friends present. I had not a flutter of anxiety; Margaret took the only tranquillizer she has ever taken. By Monday morning we were back in the classroom, to greet the rumors that Margaret was, as it is said in the South, expecting.

The first major task of adult life demands that we leave the protective world of the family and become an autonomous, independent person able to live on our own. Although I, like many young people, left my family physically, I did not master this developmental task. Instead, I transferred my dependency on my family to my alma mater; there I applied my habitual formula of trying hard to please, assuming that this effort would ensure that I would remain protected and taken care of.

For a time, this strategy worked. Within the insular world of college, I seemed to be adapting successfully to this stage of life. It was not until I had left the protection of this substitute family and faced the world of real career choices and the demands of marriage that I began to realize that something was wrong.

In my efforts to be such an ideal son, I had concentrated on what would please others; I knew little of what *I* felt, what *I* wanted in life, what *my* needs really were. When I faced the real demands of marriage, including the needs that Margaret also brought to our relationship, my inability to be a forceful and effective advocate for myself seemed to consign me to a lifetime of selflessness. All I could envision was being enveloped, swamped, surrounded by our largely unacknowledged dependence on each other. Whatever was genuinely mine would be lost.

According Erik Erikson, the critical struggles over identity take place during adolescence. During this period we begin to experiment with who we are, exploring new relationships, developing our own values, taking increasingly well-defined roles in the society around us. While many of these identity decisions are made and remade over a period of years, the commitment to an autonomous self begins in earnest during adolescence; and an important factor in our self-definition includes the capacity to defy at least some parental norms and expectations. While many adolescents link up with tightly bonded peer groups for support in this endeavor, it is not until the adolescent can make the terrifying leap of saying to the parental generation "I disagree with you!" that he or she begins to feel a genuine sense of self-ownership.

Erikson believes that the product of this sometimes stormy process of identity creation is the capacity for *fidelity* or loyalty. And certainly we see adolescents forming strong commitments to their peer groups and to their elected role models (coaches, teachers), a process of developing loyalty to those outside themselves which will later contribute to their forming lasting relationship bonds. But this stage of increasing selfhood is usually paralleled by the rejection of family stereotypes and of some family obligations.

My adolescence was much too placid and conformist. I did not seriously test my parents' rules, nor did I challenge their perceptions of me. I had some good friends and some good times during high school, but most of my energy went into pleasing others. It would be a good many years before I understood this "failure of nerve" during adolescence; and as Erikson would predict, it was related to earlier difficulties in my own life.

My struggles were also related to my hesitancy in identifying with my father. I loved my father deeply, but I hated what I saw happening to him. When I approached the demands of marriage and career and reached inside for a model, an example of what it was to be a man—I saw my father's struggles. With an ominous sense of foreboding, I knew I wasn't ready.

It was not until I had worked with Carl for nearly two years and felt deeply supported by him that I sensed the gradual diminishing of my panic about being overwhelmed by the force of Margaret's personality, by the dependence on me that she often concealed, and by the demands of marriage. By then I had begun to see the child that I had been: a boy whose father had been much too absent from his life, and who felt—especially during the war years—all too responsible for his mother and his sister. No wonder he felt burdened as a child; no wonder he later projected these feelings onto Margaret.

A great many young couples are strong and determined enough to ignore their misgivings about marriage. They plunge ahead, transferring their childhood dependency to each other. The marriage itself then becomes the background against which they struggle to create two separate identities.

Margaret and I were extraordinarily lucky. Not only did my failure of nerve gain us some precious time, and a measure of space in which to grow, but we happened upon two extremely capable therapists. These two compassionate people guided us through a confrontation with our own unconscious terrors and helped us accept some of the fundamental aloneness of life, an aloneness that we all hope marriage will alleviate but which it can only temper.

When we finally did marry, each of us had inner resources

which we had not had before, and which allowed us to keep a certain vital space between us. It was then that the romantic words of Kahlil Gibran which we had pored over during that first spring came back to us:

Sing and dance together and be joyous,
but let each one of you be alone,
Even as the strings of a lute are alone
though they quiver with the same music.

12

The Closeness Panic

THE FIRST YEARS OF marriage, like the first years of life, are full of enormous challenges; and they demand prodigious psychological growth. The greatest hurdle is learning to live closely and intimately with another person. Having spent the years of adolescence and early adulthood trying valiantly to become independent, we must suddenly manage to coordinate and to share every aspect of life with this omnipresent Other. One measure of the difficulty of this task is the fact that one fourth of all divorces occur during the first two years of marriage. These are years of hard and sometimes perilous work.

In some respects, the transformation in our lives wrought by the marriage ceremony seems magical. Overnight, we are free to rent an apartment together, and within it to do what we will. In a small town in Georgia in 1963, that seemed miracle enough for us. Margaret and I found a light, airy, second-story apartment on a tree-lined street near the campus and into it moved our two card tables and other surplus furniture from our families; and there we established a life. Hardly realizing that we were making decisions, Margaret started cooking our meals and taking care of our apartment, while I managed our new joint bank account, serviced our car, and took out the garbage. For a while, our cozily cooperative arrangement seemed easy.

At first, we all luxuriate in the newfound security conveyed by the institution of marriage itself. After years of anxiety about being alone, we finally *have* someone: here is a wonderful body to enjoy sexually (and we do a lot of that), to snuggle with hungrily in the night; and here is someone who is always ready to talk, always willing to help. It seems that a lifetime of loneliness is over.

And so we settle into enjoying the sheer presence of the other, soaking up the sex, the contact, the comfort, the deep mutuality of being together. What a great relief it is to feel so accepted, so "included" in this sudden expansion of life's possibilities.

It does not take us long to realize that all is not well. I am enjoying Margaret's cooking and caretaking so thoroughly that I fail to notice how hard she is working. She is in charge of so much that she fails to notice how much she directs me. Almost overnight, we realize that this wonderful person is running over us. I feel controlled; Margaret feels used. With a growing sense of horror, it dawns on us that we have married a selfish, pushy, willful person; and that we seem to be in a fight for our very lives.

Our first serious conflicts are about control. Do we see the movie she wants to see, or the one I want to see? Two weeks ago it didn't matter, as long as we were together; now it matters enormously. It feels as though we are losing most of the decisions, and that if we don't hold the line on this one, we are fated to be hopelessly and forever intimidated. And so we fight: about what foods to eat, what kind of toothpaste to buy, what to do Saturday night, whether to make love, how to make love, whether to take a walk, whether to buy a pet, what to name it, who is responsible for it.

During this stormy period, which began within a month of our marriage, Margaret and I found a convenient and slightly absurd metaphor for our anxieties about who was going to be dominant in our relationship: we started to play Chinese checkers.

Every evening, after preparing for the next day's classes, we sat down with our cups of tea and, with the solemnity of two chess champions, began to play. Fiercely determined, and bristling with defensiveness like samurai warriors, we poured our fearful hearts into these simple battles. If Margaret won a game, I'd have to win the next; and if one of us lost two games in a row, all was lost. Certain the two defeats meant being one down for the remainder of the marriage, we sometimes threw the marbles or the board across the room.

We also carried on a constant game of verbal one-upmanship; to be at a loss for words was even worse than losing at Chinese checkers. Before we knew it, this tension about control invaded our sexual relationship. If I approached Margaret, I wanted more than sex; I wanted sex on my terms. Angry about this pressure from me, Margaret became an artist at subtle resistance.

Before long, each of us seemed to be waging a campaign to change the other. Margaret was determined to get me to be more helpful around the apartment, and to sit down and talk with her more frequently; I was determined that we should have sex more often. As this coercive pressure increased, so did our mutual defenses. Soon there was a palpable impasse, with each of us saying, "I will not give in until you do." We were firmly dug in, convinced that capitulating would invite still more pressure, which would require still more capitulation, until we would finally be reduced to a helpless, completely vulnerable state. At least that is how I felt; and I later learned that Margaret felt the same way.

The psychological environment of early marriage is highly symbolic. Everything we say and do feels charged, dreamlike, almost larger than life. This volatile atmosphere is caused by a number of forces, not the least of which is the symbolism of the institution of marriage. When a representative of the society says, "I now pronounce you husband and wife," all the associations of being a couple, and by extension a family, come into play. Suddenly we are not Gus and Margaret, but Husband and Wife, and our preconceptions about these roles well up in us. It is as if we find ourselves back inside the family we grew up in, playing parts that were written by our parents. We feel trapped and burdened by these roles; and we are inevitably worried about repeating our parents' histories.

But the major panic of this period is that we will be forced back into *childhood vulnerability;* that if we are not vigilant, we will fall into perpetual, helpless servitude to this demanding, controlling person we are married to. Our tendency to perceive our mate as having "parental" power comes in part out of the fact that he or she does resemble our parents to some degree, but it is also caused by the "amateur psychotherapy" that is taking place between us.

Deeply worried about facing the "real world" of adulthood, and relieved at discovering our access to each other, we have allowed our long-repressed dependency needs to surface. We ask each other for reassurance, and we give it to each other freely; we may also give advice, and even offer "interpretations" of each other's problems. This exposure of our dependency makes us feel vulnerable to being controlled. Each of us has brought to the other our "child" self, saying in effect, "Please meet my needs." When the other to whom we have turned begins to exert power, we feel especially threatened. We hardly notice the needs that we are bringing to this person, but we do notice our partner's controlling behavior. When we cry out, "You are controlling me!" we are ignoring the fact that we are more controlled by our own dependency than by our partner's behavior.

How could I be threatened when Margaret suggested what I order in a restaurant if I were not in some measure seeking such advice? Today, I would laugh if she tried to do that; in the first year of our marriage I didn't laugh—I bristled angrily.

To this atmosphere of anxious helpfulness, which creates a kind of psychological "time warp," threatening to cast us back inside the family we have been trying to leave, we add the volatile ingredient of sexuality. However sexually liberated we may seem to have been before marriage, the marriage ceremony grants us a deeply welcome permission to be freely sexual. And most of us take ample advantage of this freedom: in the first year of marriage we may make love almost every night, and on the weekends we may have sex several times. We try new positions; we do things we have never done before. This intense sexual interest is of course fueled in part by our dependency needs; we are also seeking the cuddling and the deep body contact that accompany sex.

While we know rationally that our mutual helpfulness is merely that—the attempt of peers to reassure each other—and while we know that our sexuality is appropriate and healthy, the combination of intense helpfulness and intense sexuality is confusing, especially on an unconscious level. The unconscious mind may become alarmed by this combination, and though few of us would allow ourselves to verbalize such fears, our unconscious interpretation of our behavior may be "I have married a parent, with whom I am having sex." Such a statement may sound humorous to the rational mind, but in the shadowy region of our subliminal fears, it is not amusing. We know that we are suddenly very close to someone, and that something in the closeness is threatening.

The control battles that begin to dominate our relationship serve two functions: they force us to be less dependent on each other; and they erect protective barriers against the pervasive threat of unbridled sexuality. If we are fighting over which movie to see, we are less likely to be anxious about the sex we might have when we get home. So our fights are partly an expression of anxiety about too much closeness, and they offer us an unpleasant but perhaps necessary protection from each other.

The major problem in early marriage is the psychological process of transference, a phenomenon first identified by Freud in which we "transfer" feelings about one person to a second individual, whom we perceive as if he or she were the first. As we have seen previously, the most charged and difficult instance of transference occurs when we transfer feelings about our parents to someone in our everyday life—friend, mate, employer. Because of the symbolism of marriage, and because of the "pseudotherapy" that takes place in early marriage, our partner is particularly likely to become the target of our repressed and denied feelings about our parents. Sensing that our partner is *like* our parent(s), we become alarmed that our partner *is* a parent.

The prevalence of transference feelings in early marriage results in both partners' experiencing symbolic "intrusions" into the marriage. These bewildering episodes seem to come out of nowhere, and they create a sense of constant vulnerability in both partners. One couple, April and Blair, described such an incident.

April said, "We had been shopping for groceries together, and when we started to bring the bags into the house, Blair was carrying a particularly heavy sack. When he got in the door, he just stood there holding it, and he said in this whiny voice, 'Where do you want me to put this?' I know it was a logical question, because the kitchen is my territory, but suddenly I just saw red. I said to myself, 'How stupid can you get? Why don't you just put it on the counter?' But my reaction was far too strong. I guess it was the helplessness in his voice. It made me so mad that I wanted to hurt him; I literally had the fantasy of throwing a huge can of tomatoes at him."

"All I did was ask a simple question," Blair complained, "and I got this furious outburst. It didn't make sense. It still doesn't."

Of course Margaret and I began to ask April about the intensity of her reaction. Was there anyone in her family who acted in that dependent way? Anyone who would seem helpless and confused and would wait for direction?

"Now that you mention it, my father would act like that a lot. Even when I was a kid, I realized that he wasn't very strong, and that he waited for my mother to direct him. He would get this whiny voice . . ." then she paused, realizing the parallel. "I see what you mean. I guess that's why I reacted so angrily to Blair. I really didn't respect that little-boy quality in my father."

These "intrusions" from out of the past occur in part because we have married someone who reminds us of our parents; but they also occur because we simply have so much accumulated feeling about our parents that any fleeting reminder of them in our spouse's behavior acts like a lightning rod in attracting these pent-up feelings.

Another source of panic in early marriage comes out of our suddenly being much closer to our partner emotionally than we are accustomed to being with anyone. While we enjoy being close to our partner, this closeness can also be confusing when it comes to sorting out our own feelings from those of our mate. Suddenly, we aren't sure who is who.

One reason we lose perspective is that we both project our own feelings and motives onto our partner. It is natural to see ourselves in someone we have chosen in part because of his or her similarity to us. But it is particularly tempting in this panicky early period when a couple has not established separate psychological "territories" within the marriage. There is great anxiety between the newly married about the loss of identity, and mutual projection merely heightens this stress.

The dominant theme of the second crisis in marriage is a *closeness panic,* in which the mechanisms of transference and projection create a great deal of mischief, leading each partner to feel invaded and threatened by the presence of the other.

As if all of this were not trouble enough, we must also contend during this period with a massive reorganization of our loyalties to our families of origin. Few of us are prepared for the problems we encounter on this front.

After we had been married for several months, Margaret and I visited my mother in Atlanta for a weekend. On the surface, Margaret and my mother's relationship was cordial and friendly. In fact, several times I had felt jealous of the developing closeness between them. I knew that my mother had her own needs for female companionship, and that there was a genuine warmth between the two women; but it did not occur to me that my mother was also cultivating this relationship to maintain her access to me.

That Saturday morning, Margaret had left to run an errand, and for the first time since we married, I found myself alone with my mother. While we sat drinking coffee, my mother chatted casually about a variety of things, but the content seemed superficial. Then she shifted direction, and said very warmly, "Gus, I like Margaret so much. She is so warm and friendly, and I have enjoyed getting to know her." I thanked her for her response, and felt good about what seemed to be her approval of my choice of a partner. Then my mother added offhandedly, "It's a shame she isn't prettier." With no time for me to reply, she quickly changed the subject, and I discounted the remark as petty jealousy. I knew that Margaret was a beautiful woman.

It was at least three months later when Margaret said, "Gus, you never tell me that I am pretty anymore." Before we married, I spent hours photographing Margaret; and I was always fascinated by her face and her body. It now occurred to me that Margaret was right, and that recently I had felt disappointed in her appearance. A number of times, I had found myself thinking, "It's a shame Margaret isn't prettier." I reassured Margaret that I still found her attractive, but part of me remained unconvinced. The nagging thought returned.

Several weeks after the conversation between Margaret and me, I recalled my mother's offhand remark. With a sudden flash of anger, I realized that this casual comment had worked its way into my unconscious mind. As soon as I remembered my mother's comment, my doubts about Margaret's appearance began to dissipate.

This was not the last of my mother's covert, and probably unconscious, attempts to undermine our relationship. A couple of years later, when Margaret had some minor health problems, my mother became convinced that Margaret was dying; and she repeatedly suggested that she make out her will. Then, as we began to make decisions as a couple that would take us first to North Carolina and later to Wisconsin, my mother lost few opportunities to remind me that Southerners often had difficulty with the winters "up north." This persistent campaign to get me to stay in the South indeed made it difficult for me to avoid feeling guilty about living away from my southern roots.

Margaret had some of the same difficulties with her father. Before we married, her father apparently took her aside and, in the same offhand kind of way, warned her that I was an impractical dreamer, and that she would have to be careful to keep me from making unwise financial decisions. "You will have to make those decisions," he counseled.

Soon after we married, Margaret's mother gave Margaret the passbook for a savings account she had begun contributing to when Margaret was a baby. Since we were struggling financially, this was a welcome gift, and we began to talk about how to use the money. Those were the go-go years of the 1960s bull market, and everyone we knew was making money in the stock market. "Why don't we invest some of it in stocks?" I suggested. "Maybe half of it." Margaret said nothing, but it was clear that she felt threatened by the idea.

When I persisted, Margaret became cool and aloof. She didn't want to do that, and she could not say why. I pressed harder; she resisted. I felt that my suggestion was sensible; and I had done a good bit of reading about the stock market. "We can buy top-quality stocks," I argued. "I'm afraid we will lose it all," she countered.

Within days, we were in a major fight. Even though I didn't know about the conversation between Margaret and her father, I sensed her mistrust of my judgment, and I knew the issue was her loyalty to her family's financial conservatism. I was determined that she was going to side with me; she was just as determined to remain loyal to her father's warning. One day, as we were leaving in our car to run some errands, we started arguing about the investment decision. I was driving, and while we waited for the traffic to clear at the intersection where our street crossed a busy highway, I felt a mounting fury at Margaret's quiet resistance to my suggestions. Suddenly, with no awareness of what I was doing, I started to make a left turn onto the highway. "Gus!" Margaret screamed. I looked up, just in time to see a massive truck bearing down on us. Slamming on the brake, I narrowly avoided a collision that would have put Margaret's side of the car directly in the path of the truck. Margaret burst into tears; I began trembling uncontrollably.

This incident was so disturbing that it changed the course of our fighting. Margaret eventually revealed the conversation with her father, and she talked about feeling torn between her loyalty to him and her loyalty to me. I began to see her dilemma, and I backed away from my demands. In turn, Margaret expressed her willingness to invest some of the money in the stock market. Together, we chose a broker, and we chose the stocks together as well. Fortunately for our marriage, we doubled our money.

When a young couple marries, their relationship threatens to disrupt both partners' ties to their parents. When those parents have relied heavily on their relationships with their children, and particularly when there is a "marital" coalition between a particular parent and an adult child, the parent feels unconsciously betrayed by the marriage of the child. These overinvolved parents often attempt to undermine the marriage; and though they are usually not conscious of this effort, it can have a devastating effect on the young marriage.

Parents can oppose their adult children's marriages in a number of different ways. In the most blatant instance, they may openly campaign against the marriage; as we shall see, they may even offer their child money to break the engagement. Such open disapproval is in some ways easier to oppose than more covert methods, because it usually angers the young adult and mobilizes his or her defenses. When open disapproval does not block the marriage, the parents usually change their tactics; they may become superficially accepting of the relationship, only to engage in more subtly undermining tactics.

Indirect attacks on the young marriage can be surprisingly effective. My mother's comments about Margaret were not so subtle, but they were brief and "casual," and, like most hypnotic suggestions, easy to dismiss. We should remember that our parents have been our primary security in life, and that they learned to influence us when we were tiny, helpless infants. Even when we are adults, our parents have a powerful capacity to speak to our unconscious mind. However it is conveyed, the message "I do not approve of your marriage" usually registers in a very destructive way in the young adult. The most common result of parental disapproval of a marriage is for the "bound" adult child to retreat emotionally from his or her partner. When such a loyalty triangle is created, the adult child "solves" the dilemma by becoming emotionally distant from the parents and from the partner. That is essentially what both Margaret and I did when our respective "Oedipal" parents attempted to undermine our confidence in our partner: we pulled back emotionally from each other. It was only when we realized the divisive effect of our parents' attitudes that we were able to begin to fight such interference.

Often, parental invasion is disguised as helpfulness. Here are Joyce and Thomas, speaking about Joyce's father's presence in their lives:

Joyce said, "I think it began when my father noticed that we hadn't cleaned out the gutters on our new house. He made some joking remark to Thomas that he wasn't taking care of the house, and Thomas joked back with him that he was too busy to do it, but that if Daddy wanted he could help him."

"I didn't mean it seriously; I just wanted to shut him up," Thomas said. "The first thing I knew, he was over here with his ladder, cleaning the damn things out. So I let him do it, though it made me a little uneasy. Now he thinks it is his duty; I guess he thinks he is taking care of his baby."

"Well, I didn't help things," said Joyce. "When I asked Thomas several times to put up some shutters for me and he didn't do it, I asked my father; and of course he jumped at the chance. The problem was, when he was there hanging the shutters, he began to make snide remarks about the sorry man I had married. He said it in a joking way, of course, and if I tried to ask him not to talk like that he made it sound as though I was making something out of nothing. Well, the point is, his 'helping' us out started over a couple of little things, but he used it to get inside our house. Now he comes over whenever he wants to and seems to think he owns a right to comment on the way we do things."

As Joyce recounted her father's invasiveness, it was clear that her father enjoyed pointing out that Thomas was an inattentive and not thoroughly competent man, and that his ability to make such remarks had a destructive impact on their marriage. Joyce went on, "Now that I think of it, our sexual problems began around the time my father started coming over to 'help' us. Once he even made some snide remarks about our sex life, something like, 'I suppose you two are still at the stage when you do it every night.' I was so flabbergasted that I didn't know what to say. Then he said, 'Enjoy it while it lasts,' which I understood to mean that he and my mother didn't have sex anymore." After a thoughtful pause, she said, "That was the time when our sexual problems began, it really was."

It would be enough for a young couple to deal with the symbolic intrusions of past family experience into their new marriage, and with the natural blurring of boundaries which is caused by the sudden and intense involvement with each other; but many couples must also deal with the concurrent interference of one or both families of origin. The real wonder is that only a fourth of divorces occur during this period of panic and turbulence.

Most young couples have a moment of truth. There is a critical incident, and often it is a frightening fight, one that changes the course of the marriage. For Margaret and me it was when I almost drove in front of a speeding truck. Sometimes one partner will walk out and spend the night in a motel; sometimes someone gets hit. However the realization arrives, it becomes clear that the escalating and destructive blaming must stop; that some peace must be found with each other.

A truce is called. There is an effort at equilibration: we try to balance the injustices, to deescalate the fighting. The problems have not been solved; they are merely shelved. For the time being, one solution to the fighting is learning to play the serious roles of adulthood.

If we are able to back away from our struggles over control, and if we can work out a more comfortable balance of closeness and distance, we often enter a period of relative calm and satisfaction. In fact, this stage of being "just a couple" can become one of the most enjoyable times in marriage. If both of us are working, we probably do have enough money to live comfortably; and, unencumbered by large mortgages or the responsibilities of children, we may explore the world together, pleasuring ourselves and each other in a way that may be much more difficult to manage later on.

We sleep late on Saturday morning, and after breakfast in bed, we make love. Then we get up and run a few errands together, perhaps looking dreamily at new cars, or at the furniture we wish we could buy. In the evenings we meet other unencumbered couples for dinner or movies. We take long walks in the park, discover favorite television shows, read the same books.

We may also travel together, taking weekends or longer periods to explore new geography. We go camping or canoeing; we dream of going to Europe. In fact, we do a lot of dreaming: our whole lives lie before us, and anything seems possible.

We may have learned how to support each other without the troublesome "parenting" which we attempted earlier. Like two nation-states that have agreed not to use certain ultimate weapons, we have learned—through painful experience—that certain forms of psychological attack are so destructive that we had better not engage in them. Threatening divorce, hitting, walking out on a disagreement, attacking each other's family of origin, casting aspersions on the other's sexual performance, impugning the other's basic motives ("You're a manipulator!"), and certain other kinds of blaming interpretations ("You're just like your mother")—these tactics produce so much alarm and anger that we gradually use them less and less. Perhaps we have to put each other through a kind of trial by fire in order to find out that we can be worthy foes; but once we learn that we can in fact hurt each other profoundly, and that we both have this power, we are inclined to back away from the use of this kind of power.

We may also learn how to "trade," or negotiate. It begins with someone offering to "give in," or to help in some way; it ends with the discovery of the miracle of reciprocity. Margaret may say, "If I wash the dishes tonight, will you do them tomorrow?" These simple beginnings may eventually lead to more complex negotiations, such as, "I will demand less sexually; will you be willing to initiate sex more often?"—though it often takes quite a while to get beyond the simplest negotiations.

As we learn to be less blaming, we may also learn how to lose face, to admit fault, to apologize: "I'm sorry I got so angry." When we are afraid of being overwhelmed by the other, admitting fault feels positively dangerous; but as we get more secure, it gets easier, particularly as we learn that it can achieve positive results.

Once the turbulence of early marriage begins to decrease, this period is particularly satisfying for men, because we have our wives' more or less undivided attention. We feel comforted and benignly reassured by this togetherness, and the fact that both we and our wives work also gives us some needed separateness. Women too are more contented during this period, when their work often provides them with satisfaction and income, and when the only obvious inequities in the marriage may stem from women's larger responsibilities for meals and for care of the household. We may fight about these chores; but if a man is willing to participate at all in such duties, whatever imbalance there is in the couple's workload may seem endurable to his wife. Even during this first stage of marriage most women feel that their partnerships are inequitable; but this era is relatively satisfying, in part because men and women are more equal during this time than perhaps at any other.

After the initial struggle over learning to live together, the average couple enters a period of fairly high satisfaction with marriage. At least that is what couples report. There is a great deal of anxiety about coping with the adult world, and many problems, which have been temporarily shelved, lie in wait; but for the time being, things are not so bad.

For some couples, there is no truce, no equilibration. Instead, their conflicts escalate. The differences between couples who reach an accommodation with each other, versus the couples who proceed to even more serious conflict, are of degree rather than kind; but they are related to the seriousness of the issues both partners have brought to the marriage from their families of origin. Especially for couples whose basic marital ties are weak, this period may present them with more stresses than they can cope with.

*   *   *

Twenty-seven, and married for a year, Felix and Holly worked for the same large high-tech company—he in engineering, she in personnel. Often the envy of their colleagues, this bright, attractive, ambitious couple seemed determined to solve their problems. Conscientious and therapy-wise, both had been in previous relationships that had failed; and as they began therapy around the time of their first anniversary, they were convinced they could work out their difficulties.

They were already well entrenched in very separate positions. Felix complained, "You hound me all the time about doing things with you. All I want is a little time with my friends to play golf, and some time to watch sports on television, I feel I deserve that."

Holly said, "Our apartment feels like a fraternity house—you are always having your friends over or doing things with them. You never spend any time with me. And when you are home, you have your face in the television."

Holly felt persistently rejected by Felix, and she seemed to be, in Felix's words, either "whining for attention, or blowing up like a volcano." He responded to her demands by withdrawing, which of course created more hurt and anger in Holly. And the angrier she became, the more hounded Felix felt. While they seemed to be in a pursuit–distance struggle, there was a deeper issue: their commitment to the marriage itself.

Instead of developing a steadily deepening commitment to Holly, Felix seemed more like the separating adolescent who proclaimed, "My friends and I come first." At a time when couples are usually settling into an intense togetherness, Felix seemed to be in a rebellious and defiant search for more autonomy. When Holly talked about wanting to be close, wanting commitment, Felix revealed a brooding reserve and got a panicky, evasive look in his eyes.

They had met at work, soon after Felix had been rejected by another woman. Depressed by this loss, he was attracted to Holly's energy, cheerfulness, good looks, and independence. She was also a sympathetic listener and seemed to understand his feelings. Soon he felt better, and their courtship bloomed. They discovered they had many similar interests, and within six months after they began dating, they were engaged.

Their first conflict occurred during a visit to Holly's mother and maternal grandparents, soon after their engagement was announced. Holly's mother, who was from a wealthy Charleston family, had married a man her parents considered beneath her. Holly's father never managed to be successful enough for his in-laws, and he had been divorced by Holly's mother when Holly was in her early teens. The bitter divorce had been traumatic for Holly, who had been close to her weak but charming father.

Holly felt abandoned by both her parents around the time of the divorce. Her father had withdrawn from both Holly and her younger brother; and Holly's mother went into a long depression, leaving Holly feeling responsible for her mother and her brother. "When she recovered," Holly said, "she was often angry, and very controlling with me."

Holly was understandably anxious about bringing Felix to meet her still distant mother and her controlling, proper grandparents. Felix had bristled at her request that he "be on good behavior," complaining that it was "just like the shit I grew up with—be nice, don't make waves."

Felix's father had been a high school principal who insisted that his four children, of whom Felix was the oldest, must not embarrass him. Once, during high school, Felix and some other boys had been suspended by Felix's father for minor misbehavior, but that was the only such incident. "I was into a good bit of mischief," Felix admitted, "but that was the only time I got caught."

Later we would learn that the social veneer in Felix's family covered a miserable marriage between the parents, and that it had exploded in a most public way when Felix was an adolescent. His father had an affair with his secretary, and when it was exposed, he was transferred to an administrative post in the county office. Felix had learned about the affair before his mother did, and, like many oldest children, he felt caught up in his parents' problems, and somehow responsible for them. After a bitter and embarrassingly public divorce, Felix's father married his secretary.

At the memorable dinner given by Holly's maternal grandparents, Felix had not behaved himself. He wore a plaid shirt with a plaid jacket to dinner, where he also told several off-color jokes. He didn't open doors for the women or help seat them at the table;

and he was almost openly hostile to Holly's mother. Alarmed at the prospect of history's repeating itself, the grandparents took Holly aside and—somewhat unbelievably—offered her financial support "if the marriage doesn't work out." Their dutiful grandchild politely declined, but privately she was also worried. When Holly's mother joined in the opposition to Felix, Holly was furious; and she and Holly had several heated arguments about the impending marriage. "Just put it off for a while," her mother pleaded.

Angered by the pressure, Holly fought back. "Your parents tried to dictate who you married, and you're not going to do that to me!" This interchange was the beginning of open tension between Holly and her mother. "When I look back," Holly recollects, "I realize that I found someone who would fight with my controlling mother, and I was probably more attracted to Felix because my mother didn't accept him. Of course, I was just substituting one controlling person for another."

Back in Atlanta, the engagement dinner given by Felix's father and his second wife didn't go much better. Dressed in jeans, Felix came late and got very drunk, embarrassing his own family. "Are you sure you want to get married?" Holly asked him tearfully the next day.

"Of course I do," he replied, "You'll never find anybody who will love you the way I do." Skeptical, but a little worried about her advanced age of twenty-six and feeling that she was in love with Felix, Holly decided to risk it. In a voice so faint that she barely heard it herself, she said, "I'll give it two years." They both felt ambivalent about the marriage, but, caught in the trappings of officialdom which began to surround them, neither seemed able to call it off.

"Our wedding was very nice," Holly said. "It amazed me that we got them all there. At first my father talked as if he might not come, and Felix's mother said she wouldn't come if Felix's father's second wife was there. But they both backed down." After a pause she added, "It was a beautiful ceremony in this ancient church in Charleston. All our friends were there, and we even got our parents together in a few of the pictures."

I know that Margaret and I had the same thoughts then, glancing at each other briefly, seriously, tenderly, out of our own earned knowledge.

At the beginning of therapy Felix and Holly seemed to work productively: defining issues, exploring the roots of some of their problems in their families of origin, working on better communication. Each made some behavioral accommodation to the other: Holly curbed her demands for closeness, and tried to contain her temper; Felix made some efforts to be at home more, and to share more of his feelings with Holly. For a while, their fighting decreased, and we felt hopeful about their marriage.

But the struggle over Felix's commitment to the relationship continued. He would do something that signaled his distancing from Holly—watching television all weekend, or staying out very late with his friends, or just being silent during dinner; and Holly would first get angry, and then retreat into wounded depression. Either reaction seemed to drive Felix to retreat farther. While Holly felt rejected by him, he looked frightened of her anger and emotional needs.

In an effort to work on the roots of this pursuit–distance pattern, we brought in both families of origin. Holly's parents were willing to cooperate, but they would not meet in the same room. They came on separate days, and both interviews were rough for Holly. An attractive, cheerful woman, divorced now for the second time, Holly's mother seemed to want to help. She talked about Holly's father in a somewhat condescending manner, but she acknowledged the interference of her parents in their marriage. Yes, they had never accepted her husband; but then he had let them all down in a number of ways. Yes, she had felt that Holly was on her father's side, and she had at one time felt jealous and angry about their coalition. But that was over now, wasn't it? Though she was trying to be helpful, she was clearly unwilling to deal with Holly's feelings. She had a bright, cheerful kind of evasiveness which we could not seem to penetrate. After the interview, Margaret remarked: "She is still obviously angry at Holly's father, and though she would deny it, at Holly."

She did not look once at Felix during the entire interview, nor did she in any way acknowledge his presence. This cool denial of

Felix seemed so obvious that both Margaret and I worried about it. "Felix is getting the same kind of cold shoulder that Holly's father got from his in-laws," I said to Margaret. "Of course, he isn't exactly waging a campaign to gain acceptance."

Holly's father seemed distant and removed. He did not want to come to the interview, and he was barely willing to talk about the divorce from Holly's mother. What he did say placed the blame on his ex-wife, and on his interfering in-laws. A quiet man, he had clearly been deeply hurt by the divorce, and he still seemed distant from both Holly and her brother.

There were remnants of deep fondness between Holly and her father, but they were unspoken; and Holly tended to treat him as if he were fragile. He did seem almost entirely focused on his second marriage and his job.

After the interview, Holly was angry, hurt, and worried about him. "How can I be angry at him for letting me down, or for being so dishonest, when he doesn't look like he can take it?"

We cautioned Holly that she had many reasons to feel hurt and disappointed by both her parents; and that she was probably unloading many of those feelings on Felix. On an intellectual level she seemed to agree; but her anger remained focused on Felix. "He is the one who is letting me down now," she countered defensively. Nor did it seem logical to her that her mother's refusal to accept Felix could be unconsciously influencing her own attitudes toward him.

The interviews with Felix's parents were in many respects similar; again, they would only come separately. Felix's mother had not remarried, but she appeared self-confident and relatively content with her life. After the divorce she had started selling real estate, and she was now the head of her own agency. Attractive, poised, articulate, she was determined not to be seen as her ex-husband's victim.

Felix was surprised by his mother's confidence, and by her warmth toward him. He had worried about his mother's depression following the divorce, and his sense of responsibility for her had been a burden. While Felix was close to his mother as a young child, during his teenage years, a time that coincided with the dissolution of his parents' marriage, he and his mother had become alienated. Felix had seen his mother as cool and critical, and he had learned to live a very separate life from her—from both of his parents, in fact.

The interview with Felix's mother led to a warmer relationship between mother and son. Felix was relieved to see his mother doing well, and this perception allowed him to feel less guilty about not helping her more.

Felix's father was a handsome, distinguished-looking man. Felix and his father had had a fairly warm relationship over the years; and during the period before the divorce, Felix had been his depressed father's chief confidant. Having known about the affair before his mother did, Felix felt implicated in the divorce. Felix's relationship with his father had clearly been parental; the child was father to the man.

But it was now the father who was concerned about his son. He expressed support for Felix's marriage, and he clearly liked Holly. He urged his son not to give up the way he had, but to work hard to preserve the relationship. It was a well-meaning plea; but when Felix made a tentative effort to discuss what had happened between his parents that led to their divorce, Felix's father dodged. This explosive end to their family had never been discussed; and it seemed destined to remain mysterious.

"I love my father," Felix said after the interview, "but it's hard to trust him. I wish he would come clean with what happened. I know my mother was pretty critical and controlling, and that my father felt dominated; and I know his own father was an alcoholic; but I can't get out more than that."

From as early as he could remember, Felix had felt concerned about one parent or the other—before the divorce it was his father; after the divorce he worried about his mother. He also seemed to have gotten little support from them. When he was a teenager, all his support had come from his peers; and most of these relationships he had kept secret from his controlling, moralistic parents. It was this sense of burden which he seemed to see in Holly; her needs, her anger, all seemed to make him feel both guilty and responsible.

We kept reminding Felix how bound he felt by his family, and how likely it was that he was transferring this sense of burden to Holly. We urged him to confront Holly when she was too demanding; we tried to help him learn to ask her for support. Felix made an effort to look at his own issues, and he tried to learn to fight with

Holly, to say to her, "My needs matter too." But much of him remained separate, aloof, at a distance from Holly and from the therapy.

Again and again, the cycle repeated itself: Felix would distance, and Holly would react. Unable to get either partner to have much insight into his or her own part in the marriage, Margaret and I began to feel discouraged. Felix and Holly seemed pitted against each other with implacable determination. Then we began to notice the strange, evasive darting in Felix's eyes. He looked anxious, and extremely uncomfortable. When we asked what was wrong, he evaded our question. "It's work," he complained. "I'm under a lot of pressure with this new computer system."

Felix did seem to be under a great deal of stress at work. He had been teamed with another salesman, Jim Bowen, in an attempt to market a new computer system to a very large potential customer. There were numerous trips out of town, and many late hours at the office. During this period, we did not see the couple for several weeks; when we did meet again, Margaret and I felt out of touch with them.

At the first session after the interruption in the meetings, Holly looked extremely upset. After several minutes of casting about for something to say, she launched in, looking both frightened and angry. "Apparently this has been the talk of the office for weeks," she said, her eyes blazing, "but somebody finally had the consideration to tell me."

"Tell you what?" Felix said, looking extremely apprehensive.

"That you were sleeping with Jim Bowen's secretary." Silence. Felix looked wooden and pale. "Is it true?"

For a moment, Felix's eyes darted here and there in the room, as if seeking escape. Then he looked directly at Holly and said, "Yes."

What followed seemed almost preordained, as if both had rehearsed it. At first Holly was so stunned that she could neither speak nor move. Then tears began coursing down her face, and she said, "How could you, Felix?" Perhaps it was the fact that he said nothing that enraged Holly, and she suddenly stood up, weeping, not knowing what to do or where to turn. Sure that she was coming at him, Felix bolted from the room, leaving the office door open as he fled down the stairs. "I'm not taking this anymore," he shouted over his shoulder, making it sound as if the whole bitter scene was Holly's doing.

"I hate you!" Holly screamed at him. Then he was gone, the sound of his car scattering gravel in the parking lot outside. For a while, Holly paced back and forth in our office; then she finally sat down and started to cry. Margaret and I sat on either side of her and held her while she cried deep, wrenching, inconsolable sobs.

Felix lost no time in moving out of their house and into an apartment with the secretary, who had immediately quit her job. He refused to come to more sessions, saying that he would not tolerate being yelled at anymore. Holly was alternately enraged and extremely depressed; and while we attempted to give her support, we also tried to get Felix to agree to meet with her. I argued with him: there had to be some agreement, some resolution, and they needed to do it face to face. "I will meet with her only if she agrees not to yell at me," Felix said firmly.

With our assurance that Holly had agreed not to yell, we had a last meeting with the two of them. It was a scene we had witnessed before, and would again, but one we always dreaded—two people, sometimes with their children, trying to give up on a marriage. It is like witnessing a death.

"I just can't go on," Felix said. "I can't take the demands, and especially I can't take the anger. I won't take it, either." His face was haunted, tragic, tears streaming down his cheeks.

"I can change all that," Holly promised desperately. "I know I can."

"I'm sorry," Felix said firmly. "It's over, Holly."

They were both crying then. In the space between their anguished faces, an almost palpable, visible thing was being rent, torn apart. Perhaps it was an invisible sleeve of caring, of connection; Felix had removed himself from it, and Holly, still inside, was falling. Margaret and I sat with them, trying to give them what we could; but we felt almost as helpless as they did. Our words probably sounded hollow: reassurances that they were both worthwhile people, encouragement to talk out their feelings, to try to make decisions together.

It wasn't over, of course. Felix refused to meet jointly anymore, so we worked individually with both of them. The legal proceedings were beginning. Felix kept a tough stance with Holly, but in separate sessions he wept about the collapse of the marriage. "None of it makes any sense," he said. Had he not heard anything we had said about his need to escape the entrapment in his family of origin, and about how Holly's needs and demands had replicated that dilemma for him? In such a storm of emotion, the voice of reason is faint.

In spite of the fact that several months prior to his affair Holly had been threatening to divorce him, she was devastated. Felix's abandonment of her, which she had partly provoked, was like a primal wound that seemed to call up all the rejections of her past, and out of this injury poured a great turmoil of grief and anger. As they tried to divide their property, there were several almost physical confrontations between Holly and Felix. And in our sessions with her, she raged helplessly at him for his deceptions, his lies, his "gutless evasions."

Eventually the couple reached a legal settlement that involved the sale of their house and the equal division of their assets. As they sorted out their belongings and began to have less contact, they began to relate to each other relatively politely. It soon became clear that Felix's relationship with his lover was going to continue, and that they had numerous issues to work on in their own relationship. Margaret and I continued to see Holly supportively, and we referred Felix and his lover to another therapist. It was just as well; though we cared about Felix, and understood his side of the marriage fairly well, it was difficult not to be angry at him over the way he chose to end his marriage.

But Margaret and I realized that we had contributed to this stormy ending. In our liking for both people, and in our persistent optimism about the possibility of their working out their problems, we had lost contact with Felix. We had not seen clearly enough, or helped him verbalize, his lack of commitment to the marriage. Since we did not "read" his position accurately, Felix began to mistrust us; and as he had done in his family of origin, he began to lead a double life—not only hiding his feelings from Holly, but from us too.

Nor had we confronted Holly sufficiently about her own "scripting" of her rejection at Felix's hands. We had pointed out the unconscious effects of her family's lack of support for her marriage, but maybe we hadn't done it forcefully enough. Certainly we could have been tougher on her about the way she dealt with her feelings of rejection: lashing out when she was hurt, rather than talking about the hurt itself. And maybe we could have gotten her to engage more with us, and to demand less of Felix.

Maybe. But we had to remember the ambivalence both felt about the marriage from the very beginning. Holly herself had said, "I'll give it two years." And two years was how long it lasted.

There are undoubtedly as many ways of getting divorced as there are of getting married. There are "underdetermined" divorces in which the partners just drift apart with no apparent conflict or crisis; and there are deeply regretted divorces of committed partners, in which the protagonists surrender only after years of work in therapy. Most divorces, however, are surprisingly like Holly and Felix's: painful firestorms of misunderstanding which take place amid a superabundance of feeling and a scarcity of insight.

Psychotherapy is obviously not a universal panacea for troubled marriages, but it is unfortunate that only a small fraction of divorcing couples see a therapist. Most fight it out alone, feeling devastated and deeply wounded by the experience, and injuring their children—probably permanently—as they proceed.

The dynamics of divorce are complex, and no single cause of divorce is to be found. Most divorcing couples have certain common characteristics, however.

I believe that most couples get divorced as the result of a multi-generational process; that is, the origins of the couple's difficulties are firmly rooted in the problems of the prior generation. Often, there is a covert, unacknowledged split between both sets of parents of the divorcing couple; and the present schism is a kind of "acting out" of what has been hidden in the parental generation.

In Felix and Holly's case, their parents had already been divorced, and it is possible to see this young couple's divorce as an unconscious attempt to "understand"—through acting it out—what happened between their parents. In fact, there were certain similarities between both sets of parents: neither had talked honestly about the divorce to their children, and both Felix and Holly had grown up feeling mystified and traumatized by their parents' divorces. There were also similarities in the dynamics in both parental marriages; both were wife-dominated partnerships, and it was Felix who was unconsciously elected to "defy" his "demanding" partner. And of course there was the close parallel between the father's affair and the son's. Though we did not witness these conversations, after Felix's divorce, he and his father finally had some honest talks about the father's affair.

But the major factor in divorce is the dependency that the partners create in the marriage, and the unexpressed rage that both bring with them out of their childhood. As the partners disappoint each other, this pent-up, repressed fury surfaces; and the couple is overwhelmed by the force of the emotion. Like Margaret and me in our first attempt at marriage, neither partner has enough self-possession, enough independence, enough securely separate identity to withstand the feelings that emerge between them. Like a dry forest with no firebreaks, the relationship is consumed in a conflagration of feeling that threatens to force both partners back into positions of extreme childhood vulnerability. So divorce appears as the only obvious alternative to the traumatic loss of the sense of self. For so many couples, the scripted reenactment of the dilemmas of childhood is more than they can bear; getting out becomes the only alternative to going crazy.

When I see a couple like Felix and Holly, so passionately engaged in perceiving each other as images of threat and harm, I sometimes imagine that I am watching a nightmare version of a psychomotor "structure." It is as if each person has chosen a marriage partner who has agreed to role-play the negative aspects of his or her parents. As each partner acts out for the other the intricacies of that negative role, helped along by the process of role induction, the long-denied feelings that properly belong to the parents begin to be expressed. Felix feels threatened by the trap of Holly's demands, and by her anger; Holly feels abandoned and unsupported by Felix's withdrawal, just as she did when her parents failed her during her adolescence—when her mother retreated into years of depression following the divorce, and when her father also withdrew from her emotionally.

These "cooperative" role plays take place simultaneously. Holly's pressure on him reinforces Felix's conviction that she cannot be trusted; his retreat convinces Holly that he cannot be trusted. The defenses that each person employs when confronted by the other exacerbate the tension. Before long, both are engaged in what systems theorists call a "runaway," an out-of-control reactivity which escalates to the point where the relationship breaks down.

Into this atmosphere of threat and mounting anger one partner is likely to introduce another role player: someone to play the role of the ideal parent, or the ideal mate; someone who will be different from this "negative" person. If the couple is lucky, they may choose a professional to represent that image of the ideal; and even though no therapist can fulfill such a role in real life, perhaps he or she can take advantage of the symbolism to gain a slight purchase of influence within this supercharged system.

The affair is, of course, just such an "election" of the ideal image. In the midst of adversity, this is someone who will not be critical or rejecting, someone who really understands us, someone with whom we can feel freely and intensely sexual. If we can recall that distant time, this dream partner is someone who offers the promise that our present "negative" partner once held out to us.

Of course the affair will cool, and this person too will prove as human, and as carefully chosen to confront us with ourselves, as the one we are leaving. But in the meantime, the lover presents an alluring dream; and it is one with which psychotherapy is ill-equipped to compete.

Though Felix rejected Holly in a most brutal and painful way, such affairs often have a more complex underlying structure than meets the eye. The "transgressing" partner often feels one down in the marriage, and has been unable to confront his or her mate. This betrayal expresses the rejection and hurt which this person has felt—not only in the marriage, of course, but also in childhood at the hands of his or her parents.

The "wronged" party is also usually guilty of a subtle and indirect infidelity to the marriage. In Holly's case, her loyalty to her family of origin was probably considerably stronger than her loyalty to Felix; and her commitment to the marriage probably no deeper than his. So affairs are usually thoroughly two-sided; and the "transgressing" party is usually the person who first felt betrayed in the marriage. In Felix's case it was Holly's shift from an independent stance to a more dependent mode that left him feeling wronged and mistrustful.

The sad fact, however, is that the real injuries done these two individuals began in childhood; and the rage that pours out between them does not properly belong to either of them.

Today, Felix and his lover are married, and they seem to be doing well together. Holly is still single, and she is satisfied with her present life. She has a new and more demanding job with a different company; a new apartment; and several men in her life. But she is in no hurry. "I've learned a lot about myself, and about what I want out of marriage," she says. "This time I'm going to be ready."

Holly has grown impressively in the two years since the divorce; and though our meetings have become less frequent, Margaret and I both still meet with her. After growing up with divorced parents, it seems to be helpful to her to see us sitting together, working together, caring about her together.

Occasionally Holly speaks nostalgically about her marriage to Felix. "It's a shame it didn't work out," she says sadly. "We had a lot in common, and a lot going for us."

13

Giving Birth

WITH A MIXTURE OF excitement and relief, we turn from the intensity of early marriage to the high seriousness of learning to play our parts in the larger world. As we enter an era in which productivity will be our primary focus, we face major decisions and commitments: there are houses and cars to be bought, careers to be launched, and perhaps children to be conceived and raised. While the decision to have a child is only one of many which we confront during this time, it is by far the most important; and it is one of the few in life that is irrevocable.

Before we take this momentous step, we should have worked out the rudiments of living together. Having learned to balance two sets of individual needs, we should have negotiated some basic intuitive "agreements" that allow us to function as a unit. We need to be able to communicate easily, to make decisions together, and to offer each other support and encouragement. We should also be able to deal openly and directly with conflict.

We will also need to be able to lean on each other. For years we will be called on for an intense outlay of emotional energy; and we will turn to each other for comfort, for solace, and for the mutual pleasure that allows us to feel rejuvenated. If this pleasurable and supportive "we-ness" is not available, everything that follows becomes much more difficult; and the products of our efforts—our household, our children, our careers—may come to substitute for what is missing between us, and thus eventually be divisive rather than uniting.

Of course, few of us manage life in its proper sequence. Some couples begin marriage by getting pregnant, which puts them at a horrendous disadvantage in creating the kind of supportive relationship which they deserve as a context for parenthood. Most of us get married too early, forming an overly dependent "we" before we have accomplished the job of becoming autonomous individuals. Then, while we are still struggling to build a relationship, we discover in our midst this explosively demanding creature, a child. But I am jumping ahead.

For Margaret and me, the decisions came quickly; and we made them without much thought. After all, we had grown up in the placidly traditional fifties, when so much seemed predetermined.

Not long after I went into therapy with Carl, I realized that I was much more interested in my students' lives than in the content of their papers, and that I was spending most of my time with them talking about their personal problems. Deeply fascinated by the unconscious mind, and by the process of psychotherapy, I decided to become a therapist.

When Margaret and I married, we lost little time in setting goals, and in moving toward them. Margaret hurried to finish her master's thesis in French so that she could support us by teaching; and I began accumulating the necessary course work that would get me into graduate school in psychology. We spent the second year of our marriage in Atlanta, where Margaret taught college French and I took undergraduate psychology courses; then we moved to the University of North Carolina at Chapel Hill, where I had been admitted to a doctoral program in clinical psychology. By that time Margaret had become interested in working with troubled children; and while I dived into the doctoral course work, she enrolled in nearby Duke University in a joint psychology–education degree in working with emotionally disturbed children.

For a while, we worked side by side on our studies. Then, as our second anniversary approached, we not only felt increasingly confident about our academic work, but we began to feel the pressure of our advancing years. Margaret was twenty-six; I was twenty-seven. Tentatively at first, but with growing boldness, we began to talk about having a child. We realized that with my fellowship and a loan from Margaret's family, we could manage financially. In the last weeks of 1965, after calculating the time that it would take Margaret to finish her master's degree, we decided to have a baby.

We did not admit it to each other at the time, but internally, we had taken stock of our marriage. Both of us had apparently decided that we were going to make it.

No one approaches such a decision without ambivalence, and we had the requisite share. On balance, having a baby seemed to me like a wonderful *idea* that came out of my feeling for Margaret. For her, there was much more—a deep magnetism, a creative impulse that beckoned almost irresistibly. In Margaret's decision to have a child there was a quality of acquiescence to an undeniable hunger. In me, there was interest in being a father, and love for Margaret.

When a couple decides to have a child, making love begins to seem purposive, almost like work; but since sex now contains an element of danger—which is how we have learned to perceive the possibility of pregnancy—it is a risky, exciting task. Of course, nothing happens for a while, and some couples become so tense about conceiving that pregnancy is delayed by this stress. There may be months of false alarms and disappointments.

When a woman misses her period—which happened to Margaret very quickly—we look at each other in disbelief. Could this be true? Our world seems strangely unaltered.

Up to now, both of us have been canoeing down approximately the same experiential river. As soon as it becomes apparent that a woman is pregnant, however, we notice the thin sliver of an island before us. Soon, we have been pulled onto opposite sides of this at first insignificant strip of land. I continued life as before; nothing strange or different was happening to me—except the changes in Margaret. I was puzzled by her somnolence, her fatigue, her nausea. I also noticed that she seemed preoccupied: often she was dreamy and self-absorbed. While she recovered her interest in sex by the middle months of the pregnancy, during the first trimester she didn't feel like making love. By the third trimester Margaret not only felt ungainly and uncomfortable, but, like most other women, she also began to worry (her doctor's reassurances to the contrary) that intercourse would precipitate an early delivery.

Like most husbands, I felt vaguely jealous of Margaret's emotional self-absorption, and I felt positively betrayed by her lack of interest in sex. So many of the emotional needs of men are focused on the sexual relationship that this interruption causes significant difficulty for most of us. We may have an intellectual understanding of women's issues during pregnancy, but inwardly we feel abandoned, and angry about the abandonment; and we are usually unable to talk about any of it.

A significant number of men have affairs during this period, and the affair represents an unconscious retaliation for what the husband perceives as rejection. Jealousy over their wives' absorption in pregnancy is only one of many instances of this kind of possessiveness and insecurity in men, but it can be a powerful phenomenon that is puzzling to both partners.

As a woman begins to face the fact that she is alone with the physical aspects of pregnancy, she too feels betrayed. "It's not fair that men don't have to do this," Margaret complained, and of course she was right. Her anger, however, barely masked her panic about the mystery of delivery, the possibility of complications, the worry about the baby's health and safety. While the technology of modern obstetrics provides some reassurances, there are still many risks to the woman and the child, and she knew it. It was Margaret, of course, who had the fears about deformed babies.

In the last months of pregnancy, the current picks up and the psychological island between the couple widens. We can still see each other, but it is apparent that we are now traveling on two increasingly divergent courses. In a moment of panic Margaret wanted to turn back; and then she knew that she could not. Unlike anything she had ever known, this current was swift and powerful; Margaret did not feel in control of her body. With our shared fantasy of symbiotic oneness ruptured by the body's imperatives, we came face up against our essential biological aloneness. I wanted to help her; I knew that I could not.

These fears and anxieties are of course the shadow side of pregnancy. After the initial nausea decreased, Margaret was remarkably healthy during her pregnancy; and generally she felt confident and good. Almost instinctively, we began to do "nesting" projects together. When spring came to Chapel Hill, we grew a garden of flowers by the terrace of our small house; and I built a wall of carefully chosen stones, and a desk for Margaret. We wandered the aisles of bookstores, saw every movie that came to town, and when we weren't studying, spent time with friends. As the pregnancy progressed, we savored the remaining time together. It was only as the actual delivery approached and we began assembling furniture for the baby's room that we became consciously anxious.

In the last weeks before delivery, time seemed to stop. Sensing the passage of an era, we walked as if in a dream through the waning days of being a couple. In the little time we still had alone together, we took a weekend trip to the mountains, a trip that we both still remember with startling clarity. A few days later, we dropped in on friends and asked them to go to a movie with us. Looking at us with knowing smiles, they said, "We'd like to go, but we'd have to get a sitter for our children." Then the wife looked at Margaret, and added, "You'll have to start thinking like this soon, too."

"Oh," we replied, embarrassed at having forgotten such a contingency.

During the mid-sixties, when Sarah was born, the medical profession seemed to conspire actively to separate us. Margaret's visits to the obstetrician were always alone, and as the delivery date approached, I felt more and more excluded. Margaret also got little support from her obstetrician; she had to pry even the simplest information from this distant physician.

Two weeks before her due date, Margaret went into labor. Sarah's room was carefully prepared, but we were not.

I sat beside her bed, anxious and eager, while a sleepy resident followed Margaret's rapid progress through labor. We talked animatedly; I read aloud to her. Four hours after her first contraction, the resident suddenly gave Margaret an injection. "What are you doing?" Margaret protested. Before either of us knew what was happening, she was wheeled away to the delivery room.

Sarah's birth was fast and uneventful, and soon I was allowed to see Margaret. As she looked up at me from the pillow, Margaret said groggily but with ecstasy shining through her face, "That was wonderful! I want to do it again!"

Then I saw Sarah, a tiny and lusty crier, through the glass of the nursery. It was several hours before we were assembled in Margaret's room as a tremulous, tender little family. It was a magical moment, taking awed and worshipful possession of our child, the first gathering of this deep interlacing of lives which becomes a family. Until now we had been a social construct, a marriage of minds; our relationship was now literally embodied in a new life.

While many couples still have such "traditional" deliveries, the alternatives of natural childbirth offer today's couples a marvelous advantage. Supportive "classes" bring the spouses together with other couples, and they provide an atmosphere and a structure through which husbands find a role—in helping their wives relax and in providing them with emotional support. The comfort that this experience gives couples is deeply reassuring; and the encouragement for husbands and fathers to identify with the process of childbirth can change for life their involvement with their children.

For women, the experience of giving birth is usually far more exciting than if they are sedated, and the pain is in many cases managed by the techniques they are taught. And the babies they deliver are more alert.

By the time Julia was born, this revolution had occurred, and we benefited greatly from it. During Julia's delivery I stood by Margaret's head, held her hand, and was actively engaged with her during the birth. I saw Julia's head emerge, then her shoulders, then her whole gleaming and life-convulsed body. Before she was given to Margaret to hold, the nurse took her over to a "warming" lamp, and I stood by her, putting my outstretched finger in her tiny hand.

During these powerfully charged moments surrounding the birth of a child, a man can develop a level of empathy for his wife's struggle that almost transcends their biological separateness; and he can fall in love with his child. An early involvement in the childbirth process cannot erase the centuries of conditioning that have separated men from infants and young children, but it can help tremendously. I know that the level of "connectedness" which I feel with Julia is related to those first magical moments with her. I wish I could have had them in this way with my other children, and I would give this advice to prospective fathers: participate as fully as you can in your wife's pregnancy and delivery, and make as much physical and emotional contact with your newborn child as possible. Men have a right as well as an obligation here, and if necessary we should be prepared to fight with the medical profession for it. These are critical moments in life, and we should be physically and emotionally present!

In spite of the advances in obstetrical care, far too many couples are separated by the experience of childbirth. A perfectly ordinary and normal birth is a watershed event, and it can be a time when misunderstanding begins, and when the life streams of the partners diverge. This is particularly likely to happen if the husband, unconsciously angry about the demands of the pregnancy, is absent or seriously inattentive around the time of the delivery. A woman feels profoundly abandoned in such instances, and may have great difficulty trusting her husband again.

This is another moment when couples need far more support than they usually get. They need help learning to work as a couple throughout the delivery; and men especially need help in bonding with their infants, and in staying connected with them.

As we bring our first child home from the hospital, we are as terrified as we are ever likely to be. Here is this terribly fragile, helpless little person who is totally dependent on us for survival. No one but us to keep her alive—to feed her, to bathe her, to cradle and protect her life. And what does she need? Why is she crying now? Why won't she ever sleep? Oh, why won't she ever sleep? She is a strange little creature, swept by mysterious storms of anguish, which, try as we may, we sometimes cannot seem to calm. And she needs so much attention, and is so evidently, so totally vulnerable and defenseless that we are in her thrall, slaves to her need.

I say "we," but the same swift and deeply cut river that catapulted a woman into delivery is now likely to continue its course, pushing onto her the major burden of child care. He may offer to get up in the night too, but, especially if she is nursing, the tie between mother and child is very powerful and may subvert their intention to share this load.

The mountainous weight of tradition also rises between them, forcing these fragile streams farther apart. As a couple approaches the birth of a child, each moves into the time-honored role of Mother and Father. In adopting these roles, each encounters the overweening presence of the same-sex parent. Cast back on his father's historical model, he quite unconsciously begins to repeat it. The same happens to her: whatever her mother did now looms before her like destiny. Unless both partners make a conscious, determined effort to change these patterns, they will unwittingly repeat the actions of their parents.

Confronted by this tiny, needy being, a woman has in her "memory bank" the experience of being nurtured by her own mother, in whose role she now finds herself. So even if she has not cared for a child before, a woman has had the experience—being nurtured by a woman—that she is now being called on to produce for her child. While a man may have many memories of active contact with his father, rarely does he have "father memories" from this period of his own development. In all likelihood, his father did not care for him during his infancy; and when he reaches inside for "information" about how to parent an infant, he comes up with a blank, unrecorded tape. Instead, he finds the male model which tells him to get busy and earn a living, a prospect that is demanding enough, but less anxiety-provoking than the emptiness of not knowing how to respond to an infant. So he defers, in effect giving the child to his wife—who does not feel that she has any option but to assume its care. The sheer momentum of precedent usually carries the day.

A man's emotional retreat from the needs of his infant is certainly overdetermined. Not only is it traditional, but this withdrawal probably contains his fear of the dependent, helpless part of himself, which he dare not encounter at such close range. He is also afraid of his wife's powerful pull on him for support; it feels like a familiar trap. The childhood dynamics that make men phobic in the face of a woman's emotional needs (I will get to those soon) are at full alert at this moment. Alarmed by the whole scene, he finds it easy to distance into that increasingly safe haven, work.

In the not too distant past, women with new babies were supported emotionally by other women in their families, especially their mothers. But today's urban family is likely to find itself far from the extended family, and the independence-conscious mother may be reluctant to invite her mother to help. So unless she has an unusually secure support network of women friends, the young mother often finds herself terribly alone with the care of her infant. While a woman may love much about her baptism in the sweet flesh of her child's infancy, a fatigued, isolated, beleaguered mother also feels deeply angry about the inequity of her situation. Some of this anger may be directed at her child, and she may develop fantasies that something terrible is going to happen to it. She is inevitably very angry at her husband, though she may be afraid to allow herself to be conscious of just how angry she is.

Today, women with infants often have the added inequity of responsibility for a full-time job in addition to the major responsibility for their children. With inadequate day care, insensitive employers, and unsupportive husbands, they confront seemingly insoluble dilemmas.

But even if the couple is able to share the care of their child, they must face the enormous task of learning to give emotionally to this new generation. After enjoying the reciprocity of marriage, we must make peace with the fact that, at least in the beginning, we give far more to children than we get back from them. Eventually, we will find many satisfactions in parenting, but young children require that we sacrifice many of our own needs.

There is ample research evidence that all couples experience the birth of a child as a full-fledged crisis. The sleeplessness, the fatigue, the immensity of the responsibility, the sheer weight of the child's needs, the tension between the couple about how they will meet these needs—all these complex pressures leave the couple's emotional resources strained to the breaking point. The third crisis in marriage, then, is caused by the birth of a child; and each child produces a new crisis. The first child is difficult because we are so inexperienced; the second is difficult because we must also meet the needs of the first; by the time we have a third we are more experienced, but we are also more fatigued.

The decisions that couples must make today regarding the care of their children are also clouded by controversy. Where once there was only one "right" solution to the needs of children—women stayed with them and raised them—there are now complexity and doubt. The majority of women with children work outside the home, and the percentage of women who choose this option—or have it forced on them—will inevitably increase. As a society, we must address the needs of children much more conscientiously, yet without calling for a return to the family of the past.

Only recently have women had enough societal "permission" and support to begin to articulate the real source of their anger about their situation, which is at their husbands, and at a social system that casts them in the exclusive and undervalued role of primary care giver to children. Most women want to have children, and they want to be deeply involved with them; they simply want more emotional support in raising them—especially from their husbands. It is time for men to assume a much more influential position in providing that care. We have a duty here, but we also have, as I will try to show, an opportunity.

As they move toward dual careers and dual involvement in parenting, some couples today are succeeding in changing these old patterns, though women are being much more successful in breaking into the job world than men are in caring for their children, especially young children. While estimates of the amount of time fathers spend caring for their children vary, most observers believe that fathers today do about one third as much child care as their wives; and they tend to do the pleasantest kind of care, such as taking a child to the park. Since, when both parents work (and 50 percent of women with children under the age of three were employed in 1985), they rely heavily on paid care, the actual amount of time these fathers spend with their children may still be meager. A recent study (by Teresa Jump and Linda Haas) of "committed" dual-career couples in which the women had meaningful, well-paid jobs, found that of the child care provided by the couple, 38 percent was done by the fathers. These men tended to be highly educated, and were generally supportive of their wives' careers. They were largely satisfied with their experience with their children, which usually consisted of direct interaction with them rather than cooking for or cleaning up after them.

These dual-career couples found their lifestyles to be demanding and difficult, especially if the husband's career was a challenging one, and almost all complained of the lack of adequate day care, and of a dearth of support for their attempts to parent their children together. The husbands in particular found little encouragement for what they were attempting to do. And even in these exceptional circumstances, the women still felt unfairly burdened by their greater responsibility for their children's needs.

Though an increasing number of businesses are providing day care for their employees' children, the general atmosphere in the workplace is still decidedly insensitive to the needs of parents to care for their children. This is of course even more true when a man seeks flexible scheduling or time off for child care. Dual-career couples also find little support elsewhere in society for the stresses they face.

One obstacle in the path of shared parenting, however, lies in the ambivalence some women feel about relinquishing their "emotional territory." A woman may be fatigued and angry about the burdens of motherhood, and she may consciously want to share these demands. But part of her feels anxious and guilty about giving up what history has defined as hers. Will her identity as a woman be compromised if she shares the care of her children with her husband? Is she prepared to deal with the competitive world outside the family?

Many women in such circumstances ask their husbands for help with child care, but they ask in an anxious, irritable way that makes their husbands feel resistant to their demands. "You don't do enough with Johnny" is a complaint, but it is not really a clear request for change; and it keeps the locus of control with the woman. The implication is, "You don't do enough with Johnny *for me.*"

In the face of such a message, her husband can be a compliant little boy and try to "help more," meanwhile feeling silently resentful about being in his wife's "employment"; or, in order to defend his autonomy, he can balk, and feel like a bad father.

Successful negotiation in this area is difficult to accomplish, and I will later suggest strategies for both partners who want to make new agreements in their relationship. A woman must be very clear about really wanting to share parenting, and she must make forceful, direct requests, not just for "help," but for shared *responsibility.* And a man must be diligent in insisting on shared control as well as shared duties. Just as men must give up economic control when their wives share the responsibility for the family's financial well-being, women must give up exclusive parental control when their husbands assume more responsibility for child care. The best format for making these changes is a firm and clear contract that specifies definite duties for both partners.

For men, a major difficulty in making such changes comes from the literal model of our fathers. Even the man who badly wants to be a more responsive parent faces a difficult battle with his history. Whenever we attempt to break with our same-sex parent's model, we not only feel guilty, as though we were doing something wrong, but we also introduce an element of strained, effortful work into an area of life where we hope to be spontaneous and intuitive. The man who tries to learn to care for an infant when his father was not involved with him at that age must construct a careful image of himself in a new role, and he must consciously "coach" himself through a set of deliberate, planned acts. It is as though he is inventing a new role, and "parenting" himself as he tries to fill it. He may read books about child care, go to lectures, and talk to other men who are trying to make the same changes. This kind of planned change takes a great deal of mental energy, and it often leaves him feeling drained and irritable.

The conscientious father will almost certainly fear being called "feminine" by other men. The fact is that all men begin life being cared for by their mothers, and their earliest and most profound identification is with Mother. Boys are taught quite early to be ashamed of this historic connection with "mothering," and to become distanced from this part of our lives. All too soon, we pull away from that "childish" link with Mother as we put on the difficult armor of masculinity. In order to deal successfully with children's needs, we men must be willing to do battle with these early terrors of being found out to be "feminine." And most men need help from other men in feeling more comfortable with the feminine side of themselves. Only when a man feels a strong, supportive link with other men—who he will discover have similar anxieties—will he feel safe from his fears of engulfment in the feminine side of life.

If a man succeeds—by dint of will or determination—in

expanding the role his father occupied, he may be able to do things for his children that his father never did for him: spending time with them and being much more supportive than his own father. The danger in this kind of "willed" change is that it may leave him feeling empty inside, and angry at his children because they are beneficiaries of a kind of fathering that he never received. He may find himself lashing out at the very children he is trying to help.

None of us can make major changes in our behavior without a great deal of will and determination. When we are attempting to break the patterns set by our parents, however, I believe it is a mistake to underestimate the power of our loyalty to those parents. Our chances of making lasting changes are greatly enhanced if we have clear and open permission from our parents to break with their models. For example, if a woman who is attempting to enter the career world can talk with her mother about her feelings of guilt, and about the mixed messages that she gets from her mother about her career, she may be able to get consent and encouragement for what she is attempting. This parental sanction can be tremendously freeing; and the lack of it can be a powerful barrier to change.

A man may be able to get from his father the same kind of permission: in his case, to be a more nurturing and involved father. The encounter between the father and his adult son may bring up the son's resentments and the father's regrets, and it may culminate in an apology from the father. This older father may be able to say, "I want you to be free to be the kind of father I couldn't be." So binding is our loyalty to these loved, imperfect people who are our parents that only when we receive such sanction do we realize how much we have been hampered by its absence.

As we try to give our children an important emotional experience that we have not had, we need to make an effort to have that experience for ourselves. In this instance, a man should not assume that he can "invent" male nurturance out of an emotional vacuum. If he merely tries to act out a nurturing role, sooner or later he will find himself feeling resentful. He needs to experience, especially in relation to other men, what he is trying to provide for his children. If he is to be a truly nurturing man, he badly needs to have felt nurtured by men.

As we work later in this book on the practicalities of change, I will discuss strategies for dealing with these problems. Even if our parents are reluctant to talk about these topics, or are totally unavailable to help us, there are many things we can do. Men, for example, can benefit greatly from women's experience in forming support groups; and I will discuss one such group of which I am a member. In the absence of the "ideal father," men can share the effort to create for themselves new images and new examples of masculinity.

It is extremely important that men become more intimately involved with the early lives of their children. Not only do our wives need support, but our children need our deep involvement in their lives. If this period of primitive needs and primitive caretaking passes without us, it is lost to us forever. We can be involved in other ways, but never again on this profoundly intimate level. The deepest connection between parent and child occurs during those very first days and months and years; and if we men are excluded from this experience, we lose a great deal of life's richness.

By the time we are in our forties, many of us realize what we have missed with our children. We see the continuing bond between our wives and our children, and we also see the limitations of the career world. Whether or not we achieve them, wealth and fame look ephemeral by middle age. We tire of competitiveness and stress; we begin to crave intimacy and emotional involvement. But the relationships that seem most important—those within the family—may seem closed to us. When we approach our kids, they dodge our attempts; and though they may not say the words, we hear them anyway: "Where were you when I needed you?"

It is never too late to try to change a pattern, but I would advise the young father to start now, at the birth of the first child. Get as involved as you can, and stay involved.

The consequences of the father's involvement with his children extend far beyond his own pleasure. In examining the pattern of traditional father absence, we will find that it has had a profound impact on us all; and as we see the impact of these trends, the need for fathers' involvement will become even clearer.

At the time that Sarah was born, Margaret and I were both firmly under the spell of the traditional family model. When I was a young child and my father came home from work, my mother had me ready for bed; he would then play with me for a while, and he and my mother would have dinner. My mother looked after me and my sister almost entirely, and it was not until I was well into grade school that she began her teaching career. Margaret had also been raised in a traditional family. Her mother gave up teaching when she married, and though she had an active volunteer career, most of her energy went into their home.

Because I was a student, I had a fair amount of time at home during Sarah's first year. I helped with her care, mostly by being Margaret's "assistant," and by "keeping her" to give Margaret an occasional break. I loved playing with Sarah, and I was fascinated by her development. I followed her everywhere with my camera. But I was still on the sidelines of the real responsibility for her life. It was Margaret who felt frightened that she wasn't getting enough to eat, or that she might be getting sick. It was I who woke up in the night terrified that I would not be able to support this family financially. So, regardless of our respective duties, the burdens we each assumed were far too separate, and too solitary. In our own way, we both felt alone.

When Sarah was about six weeks old, her colicky crying began to subside, and she started sleeping through most of the night. When this happened, we both felt grateful in our very bones. The sun came out; it seemed that we would survive.

Margaret had begun to feel more confident in her ability to take care of Sarah, who was steadily gaining weight and looked plump and happy. I was still worried about supporting a family, but as life with a child became more routine, we settled into a new kind of peacefulness. Gone were spontaneous outings to see friends, but they were replaced by a kind of "nested" enjoyment of each other, and of this tiny being around whom our world now turned. Not only did we have a new weight to carry, but our marriage had a new center and a new heart.

Once the initial panic about parenthood begins to subside, we parents discover that in our midst another miracle is occurring: slowly, but with a secretly guided surety, our child is growing and changing. Her eyes begin to focus on and follow our faces, and then she gurgles and smiles in response to our smiles. Soon there is a wonderfully liquid exchange of babbling and cooing and touching between us, as if we are pouring love from our lives into hers, and she is pouring it back purer and more joyfully than it came to her; she is, after all, closer to the sources of life.

At first she seems to swim in a primal sea of feeling; while storms of distress sometimes sweep this world of hers, it is all one vague and dreamy blur. Gradually she seems to become aware that her world contains shapes and "entities." Her safety, her food, her rescue from the panic of the seemingly endless pain of a diaper rash come from this presence with the soothing voice who enters the room and takes her up in her arms and mysteriously makes her feel better. There is a definite "thing" out there which is this all-important mother. There is also another thing who lifts her up into the air and swings her around and makes her laugh. He is not there as much, but he also has the power to make her feel good. At first she does not sense herself as separate from these figures, especially the soft-voiced one who appears so regularly. Since this one responds so readily to her needs, she thinks of her as part of herself. In time she will learn that she and the mother are separate, but for a long time she doesn't want to know that.

She also learns about other objects: her foot, her fingers, the red ball, the shiny spoon. Everything that seems to be outside of herself, including her foot, she wants to put into her mouth. For a while it seems that she wants quite indiscriminately to eat the whole world, including her mother. Soon she will learn that her foot is part of herself and therefore different from the spoon or the cup. In thousands of personal "experiments," she learns that there is an inside and an outside of her; that she is also an entity in the world.

In rapid succession, the miracles unfold: she crawls (backward first), pulls up on things, standing there swaying like a drunken sailor, then takes a few staggering, hand-held steps. Soon she will stand alone, and one day she will launch bravely into the abyss of space: one step and a fall, two steps and a fall. She is on her way. Before we know it the naming of the world will begin.

The family with a young child is being swept by change. Whatever stability the couple has established in their relationship is profoundly disrupted by his little engine of growth. Not only does she demand that we acquire entirely new skills, and a new capacity to give of ourselves, but she awakens in us the deepest memories of our own childhoods. Her birth jerks us backward in time to our own beginnings, and as she moves forward she takes us with her through our own histories. Parenting is a profoundly reciprocal process: we, the shapers of our children's lives, are also being shaped. As we struggle to be parents, we are forced to encounter ourselves; and if we are willing to look at what is happening between us and our children, we may learn how we came to be who we are.

14

The Childhood Years

HOW DID IT HAPPEN that the bucolic college town where I stepped off the plane that warm spring day in 1961 became the place where Margaret and I began our careers, and where we started our family? A generous fellowship offer made the University of North Carolina a logical choice for graduate school; and the three years we spent in Chapel Hill turned out to be intently focused, hardworking, good years. By the end of that time we had Sarah, Margaret had finished a second master's degree, and I had completed most of the work for a doctorate.

As I began to look for an internship, which is usually spent in a medical setting, I knew that I wanted to learn to work with families. During one of my early clinical placements in graduate school, I tried doing individual therapy with delinquent adolescents. When that proved frustrating, I brought in the adolescents' families, but I felt totally bewildered by the complexity that I encountered. A young professor, Doug Schoeninger, encouraged my interest in family therapy; and the two of us went to one of the first national family therapy conferences. It was held in Philadelphia, and there on the podium with the other pioneers in this emerging field was Carl Whitaker.

Already nationally known as an innovative therapist and

teacher, Carl had made a major career change. Though he had long been interested in families, a move to university teaching accelerated that focus; and he was now one of the leaders in the fledgling field of family therapy. Though Carl and I had corresponded occasionally, I was delighted to meet him on a different footing; and I lost little time in applying for the internship in the University of Wisconsin's psychiatry department, where Carl was a professor. When I was accepted, Margaret and I assumed without much discussion that we would move there.

With my father's canoe on the car, and pulling a rented trailer, we started out for Wisconsin. By then Margaret was seven months pregnant with Mark. As we drove through Chicago at rush hour, Sarah woke up, bewildered by the tumult of traffic, and started crying. Looking at each other frantically, we plunged on, hoping this was not an omen of things to come.

Without realizing it, Margaret and I had committed ourselves to a year in which we had to deal with a new city, where we knew no one but Carl; a new job for me, which involved full-time clinical work, including my being on call many weekends and evenings; the completion of my dissertation, which eventually stretched to 400 pages; and a new baby. During that frantic year I was gone almost all the time, leaving Margaret terribly alone with Mark, who was a demanding and energetic baby, and two-year-old Sarah. "I don't think I would have survived that year if it hadn't been for the other women in our neighborhood who also had babies," Margaret said. "And every time I think about what I went through, I get angry."

It was not the only year of such stress. Fascinated by family therapy, I was also obsessed with the notion that I had to succeed at my work. The specter of my father's problems drove me to work too hard and too long. I merely substituted workaholism for his alcoholism; and it did not help that my mentor, Whitaker, had the same penchant for overworking.

Margaret confronted me repeatedly about my daily, weekly abandonments of our family. It was during the first year in Madison that she fought with me to take an hour on Saturday mornings so we could walk together. She pleaded with me to make more time with the children. Later, when I began my private practice, she struggled to get me not to have five o'clock appointments; and to do fewer workshops. "When you are fifty and your children are gone, who in that workshop will remember what you said?" she argued. Though I tried to hear Margaret's arguments, my panic about not succeeding made me resist. I made some compromises in my schedule, but it took years for me to change my priorities.

THE PRESCHOOL YEARS

Within a few years, however, our lives in Madison became more settled, and more satisfying. I learned that I could earn a living; and I began to set a few limits on my tendency to overwork. Margaret and I both became more confident about our abilities as parents. We made friends with other couples; we bought a house.

The era in which we have preschool children has its difficulties, and we often feel fatigued from the energy drain of having new careers and young children. But it is also a protected and insular time, when we are drawn into the deep intimacy of living with children. After the initial shock of learning that we must discipline our kids—a fact that the rebellious two-year-old teaches us—we often settle into comfortable domesticity. Later, when we are struggling with the problems of adolescence, we will recall with nostalgia that halcyon time when we stood firmly between our children and the larger world; when we could set a bedtime and enforce it.

As we acquire a more secure sense of being a family, there is much to enjoy. We begin to develop our own rituals, particularly around birthdays and holidays. We discover favorite foods, special places to go, familywide games, pet names for each other. As they emerge from infancy, our children become interesting, engaging *people*, and we begin to delight in their personhood. We take them to the zoo, and to museums; we find a beautiful lake north of Madison which we reach by taking a ferry across the Wisconsin River, and where we have magical picnics. Whatever the burdens of parenthood, our love affair is now enlarged to include our children.

Captivated by their innocence and spontaneity, we begin to use our children's intimate language. Sarah calls jelly "gaggie," and so do we, at least in private to her. Mark calls Sarah, "Dara," and so do we. Almost from birth, Julia becomes "Jubie." Later Julia calls me her "double big brother," and the family smiles. She and Margaret have a nose-rubbing game which is accompanied by Julia's saying, "Pickle, pickle." We read to these children in tender tones, loving the snuggled warmth of their bodies, delighting in their baths and hairwashings and in their little clothes; enjoying the feel of their hands in ours on our long, naming-the-world walks. At these charmed moments there is within the family a kind of love-feast.

Children are so openly caring and (if they are emotionally safe to do so) so frankly angry, and so obviously grief-stricken, that they reawaken in us intimations of an emotional life which we have forgotten, or learned to hide. In doing so, they are vulnerable to that underlayer of denied emotionality from out of our childhoods, and to the subterranean currents in our marriage. All is not well in our household; and as our children grow, they are powerfully shaped by forces that none of us sees very clearly at the time. Some of these forces are the monolithic social norms which we unwittingly teach them; some are the more particular tensions and taboos which have been passed down from our two families of origin and are now the special province of this new family.

A FAMILY TRAUMA

Like their parents, children are vulnerable to the accidental violence of an unstable world. I was thirty when I got my doctorate, and just as I was beginning to take on the stresses of being an "official" therapist, my mother died suddenly of a heart attack. This terrible blow plunged me into deep and bewildering grief. Margaret struggled to be supportive; I did my best to cope with this loss, and to confront being orphaned.

One day in early April, only a few weeks after my mother's death, Margaret came home from running an errand, dismissed the children's sitter, and sat down to feed them lunch. As she supervised Mark's messy food play, she noticed on his neck two small closely spaced puncture marks. Alarmed, she called our children's pediatrician, who saw Mark immediately. He too didn't know what to make of these wounds, but he called a physician friend who was a dedicated naturalist and whom he thought might be able to recognize the animal that made them.

When this doctor saw Mark a couple of hours later, he said cautiously, "I believe that this is a bat bite." Then he added, "Mark has to start the rabies shots immediately."

With the thirteen-year-old sitter's help, we then reconstructed what had happened. She had left Mark near our house and gone down toward the lake, where Sarah had wandered; when she returned with Sarah, she saw a bat lying on the ground. Mark stood nearby, with a plastic baseball bat in his hand. Not knowing what had happened, she took both children inside. In his two-year-old speech Mark finally told us that a bird flew around his head.

Mark had to have fourteen shots in the abdomen. Margaret took him to the doctor's office every morning for two weeks, and as she helped the nurse hold him down, he screamed and fought every one. I tried to support both Margaret and Mark; we showered Mark with attention and tried to explain. He, of course, did not understand what was happening.

After the shots were over, and during the incubation period for the disease, we learned that the vaccination was sometimes not effective for bites on the head and neck. There simply might not be time for the immune response to block the virus's progress from the wound to the brain. During that very anxious period, Mark suddenly came down with a very high fever.

The pediatrician, who thought Mark might have a systemic blood infection, hospitalized him. As a precaution, he put him in an isolation room and started injections of penicillin every four hours. For two days, Mark fought and screamed with every shot. Frantic with worry, Margaret and I sat beside him, holding his hand, trying to comfort him.

During the second day of those shots, Mark began to retreat emotionally. He looked disoriented, and of course we began to assume that he might have rabies. At the very worst moment of our fears, a woman physician came into Mark's room and said to us in reassuring tones that neither of us shall ever forget, "Mark does not have rabies." Hours later his fever broke, and the lab work came back. He had strep throat and a double ear infection.

Rejoicing, but deeply shaken, Margaret and I were both exhausted. We resumed our usual lives, and Mark seemed to recover. Within a week, he was almost his usual self, though not quite as cheerful. Margaret and I did not have such resilience. Still grieving over my mother's death, I tried to get support from Margaret; she did not have it to give. We began to fight over insignificant things; our relationship was electric with tension.

It made me uneasy to do it, but Margaret and I turned to Carl, and to his wife, Muriel, for help. Carl and Muriel had begun to work together as co-therapists, and they saw us as a family for about nine months. I got support in dealing with my grief about my mother, and we later worked on my difficulty in supporting Margaret, and on her tendency to be self-denying. Muriel, who was both confrontive and very warm, helped me see the need for a deeper involvement with my kids. Able to hear from her what I resisted hearing from Margaret, I made a decision to try to change this "absent father" pattern. A few years later, when Julia was born and Mark felt displaced by her birth, I was able to be available to him in a way that would not have been possible before. Seeing him struggle so painfully and valiantly during the rabies shots had captured my heart, and it essentially made me his father.

The kind of devastating simultaneity which the world arranged for us in Mark's second year is common enough in family life. A man loses his job around the same time that his wife loses her mother; and months later they have a third child. When they come in clusters, these "ordinary" stresses can overwhelm the resources of families, throwing them into acute crisis. The marital crisis comes later, after the immediate stresses have passed. Post-traumatic stress occurs in soldiers following wartime; it also happens in families.

Sometimes a family's crisis coincides with a particular child's developmental stage, so that not only is the child particularly vulnerable to psychological injury, but the child's "stage" exacerbates the family problems. The period when a child is around age two is such a time.

From the child's perspective, this is a vulnerable time because he is beginning to separate psychologically from the early and intense ties to mother. Part of this separation process involves the child's belligerent and defiant rejection of parental control. Children who are separated from their parents during this time, even for relatively brief periods, unconsciously assume that their anger has caused them to be rejected, and they may have lasting psychological difficulties as a result of this separation.

Because the parents of a two-year-old are having to deal with a confusing belligerence in their child for the first time, they may also be threatened by this developmental stage. Their own childhood struggles regarding control and rebellion may come to the forefront and spill over into their parenting. A certain amount of rebelliousness in children is healthy and normal (it returns in kids at age four, and again at six, and of course it occurs with greater intensity during adolescence); but parents who have been abused themselves, or who are experiencing acute stress, may not be able to handle these angry outbursts in their children; and child abuse may begin around such developmental changes.

Most of us suffered some kind of trauma during the years before we reached school age; and few of us remember these events. These early blows are recorded in the unconscious mind of the child who experiences them, and they affect his or her adult functioning. Often we learn about these early psychological injuries as we try to understand why certain situations cause us difficulty. It is instructive, of course, to talk to our parents about what was happening in the family around the time of our birth, and during our early childhood. These stresses affected our earliest experience of life, and we need to understand them.

THE INVISIBLE CRISIS

Another developmental struggle is so common, and so much a part of the fabric of the family, that we tend to think of it as inevitable. Subtle, pervasive forces shape the way male and female children are experienced by their parents, and these forces have profound effects on the problems which these children later bring to marriage. As usual, I found it easier to see these difficulties in others' families than in my own.

At the small, informal mountain resort where we have gone for many years, our kids' favorite spot is the community pool. One summer morning several years ago we arrived there early, laden with books and snacks, to find the area nearly empty. A mother and her four- or five-year-old daughter were in the shallow water, while the girl's older brother, perhaps eight, was practicing diving. The morning was warm, and steamy with moisture from a recent rain. While our children began to swim, Margaret and I took reclining chairs and, with the sun streaming down through the morning mists, enjoyed the scene.

After looking at my own children for a while, my attention was drawn to the mother and daughter. The mother was trying—not very purposefully—to teach her daughter to swim. She was playing with her daughter in the warm, sunlit water, guiding her gently and lovingly, now on her back, now on her stomach, bobbing her easily and safely in and out of the water, never letting her head go under; and, as she did so, talking to the girl in a liquid, caring voice that had in it bright moments of laughter, and teasing, and long, caressing syllables of encouragement. Lost in this play, the two of them were oblivious of us, and also of the boy on the diving board. "Hey, Mom," he called out eagerly, "watch this!"

Her reverie with her daughter interrupted, she raised her head for a moment and then said warmly, "That's nice, son, very good." Then she drifted back into her water trance with her daughter and was again absorbed in their play. The girl struggled to get away from her mother, walking on tiptoe toward the side, giggling gleefully, while the mother pursued her, caught her, swept her up into her arms. Again the boy called out, and once more she smiled toward him warmly and offered him encouragement. This cycle continued for nearly a half hour; and I could not take my eyes off it, especially this delicious, seal-like body play between mother and daughter.

Eventually I realized that this could well have been a scene in the year before my father returned from the army, when my sister was four and I was eight—except that our family swam on a bone-white sandbar in the dark, tea-colored water of Little River.

The next day Margaret and I were again reading by the pool when a water polo ball came whizzing by our heads and clanged into the chairs behind us. Soon the ball made a high arc over us back into the pool. When the same thing happened again, I looked behind me to discover this same mother. This time the girl was sitting near her mother reading, and the boy was making contact with the mother by throwing the ball to her from the pool.

The boy beckoned to his mother to join him, and after one more interchange with the ball she did so. As soon as she entered the water, the boy began to tease her aggressively. He jumped on her back in an effort to dunk her, but she was too large for him. Then he splashed her playfully, and she responded in kind. "This is a very good mother," I thought to myself. Soon they were swimming together, and after a couple of side-by-side laps, they went to the diving area, where she watched him proudly run through his dives.

This scene caught my attention in part because I had recently read *The Reproduction of Mothering* by Nancy Chodorow, a psycho-analytically oriented sociologist; and these patterns of behavior were consistent with some of her ideas.

With a number of other feminist writers, Chodorow points out that although both boys and girls are mothered during childhood, it is largely women who inherit the role of "mothering," or caring for children in a nurturing way. Chodorow asks: why aren't men more likely to perform this vital function? What interferes with our learning to care for children?

After a thorough review of the psychoanalytic and child development literature, Chodorow believes that the answer to this most important question lies at least partially in the way boy and girl children are perceived by their mothers. According to Chodorow, this perceptual difference occurs so early and is so consistent that it shapes the expectations of both sexes. Her argument also has a direct bearing on some important issues that men and women bring to the marriage relationship.

As in our scene by the pool, Chodorow points out the absence of male influence during the period of early childhood. I thought nothing of the fact that the father of the children in the pool was absent; he was undoubtedly back in Charlotte or Atlanta, at work. With fathers often absent from the child-rearing process, children are extremely dependent on the mother's support, and she has enormous power in their lives. Because she holds such power, mother becomes a highly ambivalent figure to her children and is both loved and feared.

According to Chodorow, a mother begins quite early in her

life to perceive her girl and boy children differently. She looks at her girl child and sees someone like herself; she looks at her boy child and sees someone separate from, and different from, herself. These perceptual differences influence how these children learn to see themselves, and how they grow into adulthood.

The mother identifies with her girl child, projecting her own feelings and experiences onto that child. If she feels lonely, for example, she is likely to comfort her daughter with special emphasis. This intense identification sets up a special bond between mother and daughter, and it often leads to a blurring of the emotional boundaries between the two. That is what I was seeing between this mother and daughter, a kind of liquid immersion in each other's lives. This can be a wonderful experience in many respects, and something we males have a right to envy; but this closeness also makes it difficult for girls to separate from their mothers.

Boys, on the other hand, are from an early age seen by mother as different from her. They are parented and loved as "separate entities." This difference in the way mother sees them may make it easier for boys to develop emotional separateness, but it may force them to confront being separate too soon; and it may make them vulnerable to becoming symbolic for mother of various "others" in her life, especially her father and her husband. One result of a mother's perception of her son is her tendency to sexualize her relationship with him. That is what I was seeing between this boy and his mother. He was being aggressively flirtatious with her—trying to dunk her, splashing her with water; and one can assume that he learned at least some of this behavior from her.

This boy also attracted his mother's attention through his achievements on the diving board; and in the years to come he will find in this realm—achievement—his most reliable way of not only keeping his mother's attention, but gaining his father's as well. Many men can clearly recall this early impression: I get noticed through what I do to make them proud.

While these perceptual differences begin early in the child's life, their effects first become apparent in children around the time of the Oedipal period, that still controversial staging of the "family romance" defined by Freud. While some child-development experts question the importance of this stage, we clinicians find plenty of evidence for its impact within the family.

This Oedipal stage, which both boys and girls experience, and which occurs when children are aged between four and six, signals the *fourth* crisis in the evolving family. Not only are important and stressful shifts taking place in family coalitions, but the family is facing the entry of its first child into school. From this point onward, our child will be seen, measured, evaluated; and we parents are anxious about the feedback we will receive. How will our child, and thus we the parents, be judged by others? For mothers who have been deeply immersed in the child's life, there is the pain of separation to be dealt with, since this is the first of many rehearsals for the child's eventual graduation from the family. This period is the most stressful with the first child, but these tensions recur as each child approaches school age.

The gamelike and flirtatious "family romance" that begins to develop between a child and the opposite-sex parent during this time is also a rehearsal of sorts. All children "practice" heterosexual relationships with their parents which they will later transfer to peers. But Chodorow maintains that by the time this stage arrives, the experiences of boys and girls have already been strongly affected by their different perception by mother.

THE GIRL'S DILEMMA   As she reaches the Oedipal stage, the girl's relationship with her mother is already so intense that her emerging "romantic" ties with her father are often not strong enough to compete with the depth of her relationship with her mother. Instead, the young girl adds the flirtation with father to the deeper, more significant bond with mother. So the girl's Oedipal relationship with father is an "add-on" to the tie with mother, which remains firmly in place. The young girl thus develops a "triangular" orientation (being loyal to both father and mother) which may help her learn to handle complex relationship ties later in life. In my view, these divided loyalties may also lead eventually to her marrying someone who resembles both parents.

Father, of course, enjoys the link with his daughter, and there is some research evidence that he attempts to teach his daughter the games of flirtation. But according to Chodorow, the tie between father and daughter is strengthened in part because it provides the daughter with an alternative to the sometimes frightening bond with mother. For the girl, father becomes a way of separating from the too powerful, potentially engulfing mother; he provides his daughter with the first "alternative" to mother. The young girl takes some of her positive feelings about mother and attaches them to father, allowing her negative feelings about mother to surface for the first time.

Though there is now conflict between mother and daughter (and what mother has not experienced a period of noisy conflict with her six-year-old daughter?), it is usually not motivated by intense rivalry over the father. This mother-daughter battle is largely the result of the daughter's need to separate from her mother. As they compare themselves with their mothers, girls of this age find themselves feeling inadequate and insecure. They become preoccupied with their appearance and may argue with mother about what to wear to school, and about other "territorial" issues as well. The theme beneath these conflicts is the young girl's need to identify with her mother, and her conflicting need to develop independence from her. The daughter's struggle for emotional autonomy from her mother is, according to Chodorow, the major issue of her lifetime.

It is my opinion that the competitive rivalry between mother and daughter is not as intense as that between father and son because the mother has usually not been absent to the extent that the father has. Since mother has been more visible and present in her parenting role, her daughter has not been so tempted by the omnipotent fantasy of replacing her. Since father is more likely to be absent, boys have ample opportunity to imagine themselves as taking over his role.

For girls, the primal scene between mother and daughter which I witnessed at the pool remains a dominant metaphor; this kind of enclosed, boundaryless experience is so seductive, and so intense, that the challenge of the girl's life is to be able to leave it. A major difficulty for the young girl is that in order to complete her identification with a mature role model, she doesn't have to *leave* her mother (in the way that a boy has to separate from mother in order to form an identification with his father). The girl's model is right there, ready to help her learn to be a woman—or to overhelp her, as the danger lies. There are simply too few incentives for girls to learn separation from their mothers.

The appropriately involved father can be very helpful to his daughter in her effort to "individuate" from mother. He can be an alternative source of support, he can teach his daughter that the world outside the family is less frightening than it might seem, and he can even actively intervene if the mother overparents the daughter. But many fathers fail to help in this way. Some fathers are neglectful, while others are overinvolved with their daughters. The underfunctioning father, who leans on his daughter for support, is certainly of little assistance; and the father who sexualizes his relationship with his daughter adds a major stress to her life, often driving her back toward her mother.

THE BOY'S DILEMMA The boy's side of this skewed parenting arrangement also carries distinct liabilities; and because more has been written about the childhood difficulties of girls, I will spend more time on the boy's experience.

Because his mother sees him as different from her, a boy may not receive as much nurturance as his sister; instead, he may be treated all too separately and distinctly. I am reminded here of a picture taken by my father as my mother was bathing me when I was about six months old. My father took hundreds of photographs of me as a child, but this one always puzzled me. In the photograph, I am lying on my back in a small tub, and my mother stands over me, smiling. Her smile always intrigued me: it is almost a smirk. Not until I read Chodorow's book did I realize that my mother was embarrassed by having her photograph taken as she was bathing a naked male baby. It was my penis that was the problem.

Only as a symbolic Other can the infant boy be seen in this way. By "sexualizing" her relationship with her male baby, the mother not only creates a sexual connotation in the relationship, but she also sets the child apart from her. These very issues resurface in marriage, as this boy's eventual wife complains about being treated as a sexual object.

But other forces in the male's life lead to his feeling separate, distinct, and solitary. During the Oedipal years, the young boy's "crush" on his mother results in his poignant announcement that he is going to marry his mother when he grows up. While mother smiles and explains the tragic facts of her prior commitments, this is an unsettling development for the family. Mother may in fact be uneasy about her son's romantic ideas about her, and pull away; father may be jealous and become punitive; alarmed himself, the boy may decide that this situation is dangerous, and, as Freud described, renounce his ties to mother. Rather than competing with father, he decides to become like him.

When a girl begins to identify with her mother, and to try to become like her, the mother is close at hand. The girl doesn't have to travel very far to study and learn from the mother; as Chodorow and others point out, mother and daughter remain perilously close.

Her brother, on the other hand, must separate from mother in order to establish his identity as a male. Thus he must renounce his ties to the person from whom he gets the most support. Boys are tragically torn between their need for support from mother and their need to be identified as males. All the forces of society dictate that the boy must put aside such childish needs and become independent and strong.

The boy's "retreat from femaleness" is bolstered by his watchful peers, who tease any boy who seems feminine. The most fearful weapon boys wield in this cruel hazing is to call each other gay, an epithet that creates a profound anxiety in boys about their connection with their mothers and about the "feminine" side of themselves. They learn to keep their own counsel, and to conceal their emotions, especially their vulnerability.

The father to whom we turn for help in learning the art of being male is often an inept parent. While he may be an effective role model for learning to be competitive—and we observe him very carefully—he is not likely to see how much emotional support his children need, nor is he good at providing support. Since he is likely to be afraid of his own vulnerability, he may be punitive in relation to his son's. How many times have I raged inside as I watched a father at a park try to "teach" his son some activity in a harsh, demanding manner. It is as if the father looks at his son and sees the awkward, unconfident boy inside himself; and of course he communicates these self-punitive attitudes toward his son.

Even if our fathers are more benignly helpful, and even if they spend time with us teaching us what they know, rarely do they tell us what they feel. They stand apart emotionally: strong perhaps, maybe caring in a nonverbal, implicit way; but their internal world remains mysterious, unseen. "What are they really like?" we ask ourselves. "What do they feel about us, about the world, about themselves?"

Though the process begins in boyhood, many of us males spend our lives trying to "reach" our fathers. We need to contact them emotionally, to understand what their experience is like, and, above all, to gain their approval. Since our fathers have been so elusive, we may resort to all manner of indirect strategies to attract their attention, from getting into desperate trouble to trying desperately to achieve. But perhaps the most reliable way of "contacting" this mysterious figure is to model our life on his. "Maybe," we say to ourselves, "if I do what he does, I will not only learn what he feels, but I will get him to approve of me." Father is the cipher whom we try to understand through reliving his enigmatic pattern.

With regard to his mother, the young boy has a painful dilemma. Because he is threatened by his mother's potentially engulfing "femaleness," because he is threatened by the triangle with his father, and because he needs to develop his own identity as a male, he must retreat emotionally from his mother. When he does this, he does not get much support from his father. So there he stands: looking strong, perhaps; but too insular, too separate. Having renounced his needs for mothering, and with little consistent help from father, his only predictable source of support seems to be his peers.

Sensing her son's decision to pull away, a mother struggles to find a way of relating to her mistrustful charge. One thing her son will accept from his mother is her time-worn habit of doing things for people. And so a little sadly, the boy's mother falls into pursuing her son with favors and requests. She picks up after him, fixes special meals for him, takes care of his clothes; and when he, like his father, doesn't take out the garbage or do the other things she asks him to, she prods him, reminds him, nags him. Thus mother and son establish between them the final link in what may become the son's lifelong addiction to a woman's fond, frustrated helpfulness.

The boy's tie with his mother isn't satisfying for either of them, but it seems to be the only one they can manage; and it becomes as important to him as it is familiar to her.

When, as a man, this boy succeeds in finding a woman who will—however subtly—pursue him and be his caretaker, he will in all likelihood conceal his neediness through his habitual distancing; but if his wife attempts to move away from him into her own world, he will be terribly reluctant to let her separate from him. Perhaps more than any other force in men, our needs to complete our "unfinished mothering" are responsible for our attempting to keep our wives dependent on us and close by. Then we can try to extract from them the same kind of fond, frustrated caretaking that we got from our mothers. Soon, our wives will give up on getting support from us, and they will turn to rearing children in order to attempt a deeper satisfaction of their needs.

Though most boys are not conscious of these feelings during childhood, they are often terribly jealous of the intense attention their sisters get from their mothers, and often from their fathers as well. The boy on the diving board kept calling to his mother to notice him, and these calls had a frantic, urgent quality. He of course saw the delicious play between mother and sister, and part of him wanted to be the recipient of this loving, intimate contact. But since these wishes were in conflict with his emerging sense of masculinity, he probably did not allow himself to be conscious of his jealousy. If his father was also involved with this sister, the boy would have double cause for jealousy.

I believe that boys are often fiercely jealous of their sisters, and this is especially likely in a boy who has a cuddly, charming younger sister. My sister Jane and I are good friends now; but when Jane was three and I was seven, I "playfully" pushed her out of a rubber life raft, and she nearly drowned. Whatever the sibling order, boys have a difficult time competing with the mother-daughter bond, and this often unconscious jealousy may surface in later life. Though I have never *felt* very jealous of my sister, I have been extremely jealous of Margaret at times; and since she had a jealous mother, these issues have collided painfully in our marriage.

This connection may not be apparent at this point, but the boy's early jealousy of his sister's bond with mother may also be the underlying issue in the young father's deep jealousy of the mother-child bond. The feelings are simply transferred from the childhood relationship.

As the Oedipal boy pulls back from involvement with his mother, she often continues to approach him—but now with a confusing irritability. One of the reasons the boy feels it is unsafe to be close to his mother is that she sometimes treats him as a highly charged, symbolic "object." Remember, mother tends to see her son as "Other"; and if she is unhappy with her husband, any child whom she identifies as being in coalition with her husband—but simply because he is male, especially her son—is likely to become the target for her anger. Perhaps *because* he is separating, and "leaving her" like his father, her son unconsciously becomes the lightning rod, the conduit, the vulnerable target.

Margaret and I first saw Ed and Roberta Dunn immediately after Ed confessed to Roberta that for two years he had been having an affair with a co-worker. The revelation ignited a firestorm of anger in their marriage, and for a while the couple teetered near divorce. Roberta was a slight, rather angular but pretty woman, and her face literally shone with rage: her body was taut with it, her voice poured it out with geyser force. For her, the worst part of the betrayal was Ed's deception. "You lied to me!" she screamed. "You plotted to hide what you were doing, and you deliberately carried this out behind my back!"

Ed was deeply contrite and apologetic at first, but, as the couple continued to confront the issue of the affair, he gradually began to expose his discontent with the marriage. He had some genuine complaints, one of which centered on his frustrations with their sexual relationship; and he had finally found in a lover someone who responded to his needs.

Margaret and I worked hard to help the couple see the problems in their marriage, and they attempted to change these patterns. Within a fairly short period, Ed had broken off the affair and the couple settled into the hard work of therapy. We brought five-year-old Tommy and eight-year-old Beth into the therapy after the initial storm had subsided a bit; and though they didn't know the sexual details of the affair, they of course turned out to be caught up in their parents' relationship struggles.

Several months after the kids entered therapy, Tommy began to act like a perfectly normal five-year-old: he began to lie. If a vase got broken, it was the cat that did it. If he forgot to pick up his pajamas, it was because his door got locked and he couldn't get in. Most kids go through such a phase, which is designed to test their new discovery that they can conceal their thoughts and actions from their parents.

Most parents take this kind of lying lightly: "Now, Tommy, did the cat really break the vase, or do you think you might have done it and been afraid to tell Mommy?" This was not Roberta's tack. She began to get really furious; and Ed's attempts to intervene only made matters worse.

During one session our discussion centered on the allegation that Tommy had taken some of Beth's allowance money from her dresser and hidden it in his room (we later discovered that he was jealous of his sister's ties to their mother, and that his stealing was an indirect attempt to communicate his jealousy). When Beth found her money, Tommy of course denied taking it. "I don't know how it got there," he said innocently.

Suddenly, Roberta began to yell at Tommy, who was sitting on the floor in the middle of the room, playing with Lego blocks: "Dammit, Tommy, you do know how it got there, because you took it, and you're lying!" Her face was red, and she sat rigid and erect in her chair. Obviously frightened by his mother's anger, Tommy did not look up; he simply went on playing with the plastic blocks.

Incensed by Tommy's lack of response, Roberta stood up. I thought that she intended to take the Lego from his hands, and to make him talk to her. As she stood, Tommy looked up at her, his face full of terror. Though she was a slight woman, Roberta towered over this diminutive boy; and he clearly thought she was about to hit him.

"Roberta!" Margaret said sharply, and the mother stopped abruptly. Then in a softer voice, Margaret continued: "I think he's frightened of you; that's why he's having trouble talking to you and telling you the truth." Then she explained once more how normal it was for a kid this age to tell lies. Disarmed by Margaret's words, Roberta sat down—though she still looked angry, and Tommy still looked frightened.

Having watched this scene intently, I spoke to Roberta. "Do you see the parallel between Tommy's lying and Ed's behavior several months ago?"

Roberta seemed startled by the connection: "I hadn't seen that. Maybe I'm still angry at Ed." After a pause she concluded, "Maybe I am." She was, of course, and there was much more work to do in helping her deal with her anger.

The image of this slight, angry woman literally towering over her son has remained with me as an illustration of the boy's vulnerability in the face of an angry or otherwise unhappy mother. While Roberta's vulnerability was obvious from our perspective, she was an extraordinarily powerful and threatening force from her son's point of view.

As a result of her tendency to see her son as a symbolic "object," the mother is likely to "come at him" with a variety of confusing pressures. In addition to the rejecting, blaming posture which Roberta took with Tommy, a mother might also bind her son to her:

☐ If her son resembles her idealized father, for example, she may look up to her son in an ingratiating way, and the son may become grandiose and omnipotent. She could also see the son as the nurturant father whom she never had; such sons are at risk for becoming therapists.

☐ She may of course see her son as a sexual figure, or as a companion.

☐ Since she feels abandoned by her husband, she may infantilize her son as a way of keeping at least one male close to her.

Boy or girl, the child with an unhappy mother is at risk. For a good many years, we clinicians have pointed out in great detail how mothers injure their children, but we have often failed to see the destructive effect of the father's absence from the child-raising process. It has fallen to feminist writers like Nancy Chodorow and Dorothy Dinnerstein to point out the pathology of the arrangement in which only mothers raise children. Yes, the lonely, unsupported mother may bind her girls to her; she may set her boy children apart, and she may use them as scapegoats in a variety of ways. As we have seen, if a girl is in coalition with her father, an angry mother may use her as a scapegoat. But father's emotional absence from the difficult job of rearing children has an extremely powerful effect on these dynamics.

STRATEGIES FOR FATHERS

Rather than blaming mothers, or accepting as inevitable the patterns which I have described, we need to change them. We need to insert into this problematic scenario a caring, active, involved man: some-one who knows how to give his wife emotional support, and who knows how to parent children. While we men don't yet know how to do our part of that new job, we need to set about learning how. And no time is any more appropriate than during these childhood years when there is so much to be done.

Maybe we didn't feel comfortable with babies; maybe we were preoccupied with our own careers during our children's infancy. But the childhood years are an ideal era for us to become important players in the interior life of the family.

First, we need time with our children, and there is no substitute for our finding it. One way to develop a more intimate connection with our children is to be alone with them. If we are on the spot with their care, we will learn to provide it. When Julia was a newborn and Mark was struggling with feeling displaced, I took him camping, and later backpacking. These experiences away from the family can help us develop a more intimate connection with a child, but our contact needs to be more regular than such occasional outings.

We need to contract for regular periods when we are solely responsible for our kids; and we should commit to as much time as we can manage. Maybe we can't do more than a couple of evenings a week and one weekend day; but perhaps, if we are determined, we can find ways of being in our children's lives every day. Maybe we can fix breakfast and do the car pool in the morning; or our schedule may make it easier for us to take the late-afternoon shift and the dinner hour.

In addition to being "on duty" for certain times, we may also contract for responsibility for particular activities or concerns. A father may take on the job of helping a child learn proficiency in a certain sport, for example, or for tutoring his child in math, or for following a certain child's problems at school. With younger children he might agree to supervise bedtime, including reading to children who need help "settling in." (The process of contracting is treated in more detail in Chapter 16.)

Whatever the structure of our contact with our children, we should try to avoid being dutiful and resentful about "having" to do it. The best way to avoid this "set" is to let ourselves enjoy interacting with our kids. Margaret once said to me, "I realized that as long as I had to do car pools, I might as well enjoy them. So I started having fun with the kids as I drove. I would sing with them, or try in some way to get into a more active interaction with them."

Giving ourselves permission to enjoy interacting more spontaneously with our kids is especially hard for men, since we may be embarrassed about being "childish," or concerned about how to interact in an open, personal way with a child. Recently I found myself alone with Julia in our family room. Margaret was at a meeting, and Julia and I were eating dinner together. The television set was on, and Julia kept glancing at it. I had picked up a newspaper and was reading the headlines. Suddenly I realized what a nonexperience this was, and I put down the newspaper and asked Julia if she would turn off the television. Then I looked directly at her, and struggled to find something we could talk about. Within a couple of minutes, she was busily telling me about her day at school, and we went from there to talking about her favorite history class.

If we are to have something to talk to our kids about, we need to know what is happening in their lives. When we first moved to Atlanta, and before I plunged into my usual overwork, I volunteered in each child's classroom for a while. Not only did I get to know their teachers, but I met their friends and classmates; and I still draw on those experiences. Every time I see Sarah's friend Jody, who is graduating from college this year, I am reminded of her as an eighth grader, telling a vivid dream to the class in which I lead a discussion about dream interpretation.

As we try to connect with our children, we men need to remember that we have much to teach them; and that if we aren't too heavy-handed about it, our skills and knowledge can be a valuable way of bridging the space between us and them. My interest in the outdoors and in photography has helped me find meaningful and enjoyable links with my children. The man who is knowledgeable about automobiles, or computers, or who is good at sports has much to impart to his kids.

If our kids are to learn from us, we need to be patient, to take them where they are, and to lead them only to the next step; and we need to listen carefully to what they find interesting, and to what they find difficult or anxiety-provoking. Doing something with a child is far better than giving that child a lecture or demonstration.

Though our wives can be a great help to us, we would also be advised to consult our own independent child-care expert. Becoming knowledgeable about child development can be very helpful in anticipating the stages in our kids' lives, and there are a number of excellent books on this subject. Knowing that temper outbursts are typical for an eleven-year-old girl, for example, can help us be calm when they occur.

In our effort to be more involved fathers, we should be prepared for resistance on several fronts.

Our wives may plead for us to take a more active role in parenting; but when we begin to do it, they may get anxious about losing their importance in the children's lives, and they may subtly undercut our effort. As I have become a more consistent parent, Margaret and I have realized that we are sometimes competing for importance in our kids' eyes.

Many men will have to struggle hard with their employers to find the time to do what they need and want to do with their children. As in every aspect of this role alteration, there is no substitute for determination. This fight, for the time and energy to do a good job of parenting, is worth having!

But the major fight will be with ourselves. As we try to change, we will discover within us a fierce struggle between our loyalty to that battle-scarred victim of his own childhood, our father, and the father we want to be. We must meet our childhood father at close range: get to know him, learn to forgive him, and somehow, go beyond him.

We men will need to help each other with this project. If we remain alone, the inertia of the past will prevail. Until the time when the intrinsic rewards and delights of parenting become as obvious to us as they have been to women for many centuries, we should find similarly minded men and ask for support in seeking these difficult, vitally important new directions.

15

Coming Apart:
The Adolescent Years

LIKE THE PASSING OF spring storms, the crises of the Oedipal years dissolve into that placid and seemingly uneventful summer which Freud termed "latency." Because the child's sexual feelings and aggression are somewhat hidden from view, and because there are no dramatic developmental shifts during these years, researchers once assumed that there was little of note to study. Glad for any respite in our children's unremitting growth, we parents are also easily lulled into a fixed and somewhat complacent view of them during this time. For a while, our kids seem to stay kids, and they become almost predictable.

Our sense of family deepens and becomes more stable. The relationship alignments that occurred during the Oedipal years seem to reverse: boys identify with other boys and with their fathers; girls remain deeply involved with their mothers, and they form intense and sometimes rivalrous friendships with each other. At school our children study basic skills, and though we may have to relearn how to add fractions, we can usually help them with their homework.

They also begin to grasp the rudiments of what it means to be men and women. Boys study their fathers closely, and involved fathers may coach their sons' athletic teams, take them camping, and teach them to fish. In this "sexist" stage, in which children are imitating the behavior of their same-sex parent, girls also learn their mothers' skills; and long before they reach adolescence, they and their friends rehearse in secret the rituals and romance of being grown-up.

During latency, children and parents tend to trust each other. Parents know what is happening in their kids' social lives because their kids tell them; and parents still have a good deal of control over their children's behavior.

Beneath the surface , more is going on than meets the eye. Our kids may feel slighted and hurt by us, but often they don't admit what they feel. They also have more sexual interest than they reveal. Boys begin to masturbate regularly, and girls may masturbate as well. But sexuality runs in two separate streams in both boys and girls, with each afraid to approach the other. Sexual feeling increases gradually, with girls far ahead of boys in sexual development. Recently our thirteen-year-old Julia complained, "Boys are so naïve!"

We parents believe that this benign summer of childhood will last forever. Father and son will fish endlessly down a placid river; mother and daughter will talk eternally about anything and everything. Before we know it, hurricane season is upon us, and the clouds are gathering.

THE STORMS OF ADOLESCENCE

It starts with a clap of thunder, which just might be the slam of a door. Augmented by a recent infusion of hormonal energy, our child's secret growth has proclaimed itself, bursting our cozy dreams. A suggestion that a few months ago would have brought compliance now elicits fury. "I don't want to pick up my room!" twelve-year-old Sarah yells, slamming the door. "It's *my* room." We know that adolescence has begun; and, as always, we are not ready. The difficulties of our having adolescent children, coupled with the stresses of their having middle-aged parents, precipitate the *fifth* crisis.

While adolescence seems to begin quickly, this extremely complex stage actually occurs quite gradually, beginning at about age eleven for girls and a year later for boys. It takes our skinny, vulnerable kid who is afraid to go to parties and is struggling to learn basic algebra, and six or so years later gives us someone who not only looks like an adult and may tower over us physically, but who also can do calculus, drive a car with better technical proficiency than we, and may be engaged in a passionate sexual relationship. In the interim, these profound changes do violence to every relationship in the family.

We are surprised to find that not only is our emergent teenager unpredictably angry and moody, but he or she is sometimes boldly sexy—with us! This outbreak of sexual energy in our midst is confusing and upsetting.

A twelve-year-old girl may be flirtatious and seductive with her father; and he may get very anxious when she suddenly starts kissing him on the lips. He is likely to withdraw, making her wonder what she is doing wrong. But he need not worry: within months she will be acutely conscious of her sexual feelings, and frightened of them herself. She will then pull away from Father into a whispered conspiracy with Mother in which they purchase bras and discuss the mysteries of menstruation. She remains extremely interested in her father, but may be very shy about admitting it.

Though it occurs a little later, the same sequence happens in boys. Their romantic feelings for their mother are rekindled, but they are somewhat concealed; and adolescent boys quickly turn to their peers for support in sexual exploration. They generally have little help from their fathers in making this transition. Adolescent males are usually obsessed with sexuality, and may engage in compulsive masturbation. When they finally get up their nerve to approach girls, they are driven by "goal-directed" sexual fantasies; because girls have more romanticized fantasies, they are confused and upset by this object-focused approach.

If the species-wide prohibition against incest is to be obeyed, the adolescent has no choice but to turn away from the family toward his or her peers. This biologically driven flight is as healthy as birth, but in the family in which there is a troubled marriage, or a lonely parent, it can create emotional chaos. The inevitable separation of parent and child is disturbing for everyone: parents feel betrayed by their kids' increasing separateness; and though adolescents complain bitterly that their parents are restricting them and treating them like children, this dilemma is much easier for them to deal with and carp about than their very real fears of leaving home.

There is usually some breakdown in trust between parents and their teenagers. Our adolescents feel that we don't understand their need for autonomy; and we become suspicious about what they are doing in their fiercely defended privacy. Soon they begin to plot with each other with conspiratorial glee to evade our rules, and often they succeed. The fifteen-year-old girl who would not have thought of such a thing last year now schemes with her best friend to tell both sets of parents that they are spending the night at the other's house; they then go to an unsupervised party where the parents are out of town. They experiment with alcohol, pot, and sometimes cocaine; and by the time they graduate from high school, the majority of them will be sexually active.

Though it can easily escalate to extremes, this painful adversarial atmosphere, where we parents become "the enemy," is almost universal. Frightened of eventually leaving home, our kids are also fearful of the power of their dependence on us. Seeing us as adversaries not only helps propel them into the arms of their co-revolutionaries, but the rules we are forced to enforce give them a way of learning to deal with the structures of society. Unfortunately, we are the ones they get to practice on as they struggle with having to live within a social structure. We are the lucky ones who must try to puncture their outrageous omnipotence, which makes them believe that they are invincible and immortal. Since we seem to be making them grow up, we are easily seduced into "carrying" for them the anxiety about the world which they are afraid to feel. In order to avoid worrying about themselves, adolescents are extremely skilled at getting us to worry about them.

Only about 20 percent of adolescents have stormy and openly troubled relationships with their families; but if one adds depressed and quietly alienated kids to this category, the majority of teenagers will be found to be seriously distressed at some time during adolescence. Some of this unhappiness is created by the dramatic hormonal changes in our children's bodies; some is due to their anxiety about facing the world outside the family; but much of it is caused by us.

We fail our children in a variety of ways. Often, they have been unhappy with us for years, but we see only evidence of our failures when our kids enter adolescence. Sometimes it is our excessive reaction to their growth that precipitates a crisis. Often our teenagers have been trapped in the bound, delegated, rejected, and rule-breaking roles which I have described.

Even if our adolescents don't have really stormy rebellions, this period of life is difficult for every family. The statistical curve of marital satisfaction, which took a tumble at the birth of the first child and has continued downward since, takes another plunge as our children enter adolescence. Most of us who survive our children's leaving home will—after a sometimes stormy "period of adjustment"—experience a sharp, euphoric rise in marital satisfaction as the last child exits the house. But a significant and increasing number of marriages founder during these turbulent years. Although the average length of the marriage that ends in divorce is between seven and ten years, the peak divorce years are in early marriage, and as the children are leaving home.

It is not surprising that many marriages collapse as adolescents attempt to separate from home. Fathers who turned to their daughters for tenderness they didn't find in their marriages are betrayed for pimply-faced boys with cracking voices; and mothers whose daughters gave them companionship and whose sons gave them adoration feel similarly deserted. Finally, these couples must face what is between them, and what is not.

But before we get to face each other, we must survive being the parents of adolescents, a task that demands that we be almost impossibly calm, adult, and flexible. Bombarded by other stresses, grieving about the loss of our child's childhood, and confronted by an angry and demanding almost-adult, we falter. Should we hold firm on a rule, or make an exception? Should we intervene, or let our child learn from experience? Should we confront forcefully, or offer our sympathy? It is difficult to imagine making such decisions in the face of our child's threats and alarms without a supportive peer who can be our "consultant."

By the time we reach this stage, every marriage is burdened with its own history. Whether or not she had a career, a woman who sacrificed her own interests for twenty years, and who was caretaker to her husband as well as her children—this woman is furious about the costs of her self-denial. A man who has carried the preponderance of the financial burden of the family for the same period, and whose only emotional support has come from his increasingly irritable wife—this man is deeply fatigued by the stress and isolation of his life. Both feel alone with their own burdens; and both are angry about the thousands of failed attempts to change each other. They are especially tired of trying so hard to please *everyone*.

Those of us with adolescents also find our sexual relationship increasingly compromised. With incredible intuitive skill, our kids seem to be waging a campaign against our sex life. Why does Julia need to talk to her mother in our bedroom about some problem at eleven o'clock at night? How is it that on Saturday afternoon when we find ourselves alone in the house and decide to risk making love, Mark decides instead of going to the movies to bring three of his friends home to listen to rock music?

The ubiquitous and acutely conscious presence of our adolescents is a major problem, especially since much of their consciousness seems to be focused on sexuality—ours and theirs. They expect us to ignore them if they are kissing their dates in the family room; but let us so much as wink at one another, and they whistle loudly.

In fact, our children have been inhibiting our sexual relationship for a good many years; and since the days when we could put our kids to bed at eight-thirty and expect them to stay there for the night, this problem has only gotten worse. Unfortunately, their watchful awareness of our sexuality can easily remind us of the critical, judgmental eye of our parents. As we "protect" our children from exposure to our sexual relationship, this self-inhibition puts our kids in the role of "censor," and thus we transfer to them our guilty self-consciousness about sexuality itself.

THE BURDENS OF THE WORLD

But there are many other intrusions and hardships in this era, not the least of which is the failure of our aging parents. At a time when our demanding, narcissistic adolescents are abandoning us, our parents are also becoming needy and burdensome. They have serious health problems; they are coping with retirement; they are not getting along; they are coming to visit for long periods; they want to come to live nearby, or with us! One parent may die suddenly, leaving the other in a terrible state of crisis.

The death of a parent during this tumultuous period creates a profound crisis in our weary, middle-aged lives. Though we say to ourselves that we are adult and should be able to cope with a parent's death, the eternal child within us feels bereft and orphaned. Our parenting, our work performance, our marriage—all are deeply affected by our grief. Most of us get little support during this crisis; nor is there respite from the demands of our daily world. Our surviving parent is confronted with life's most stressful crisis—the loss of a spouse—and needs our help. If, in an effort to gain security, this parent comes to live near us, family-of-origin coalitions from childhood are powerfully reactivated.

When Harold's father died suddenly, he and his wife Betty tried to convince his mother to stay in her home community in New Jersey, but she insisted on moving to a retirement home in Atlanta. Missing not only her husband but her lifelong friends, she became extremely dependent on Harold, and her increasingly intrusive involvement in the couple's lives created major strains in their marriage. They knew they were in for difficult times when in the first week she was in Atlanta Harold's mother tried to rearrange their living-room furniture.

Even if their health is reasonably good, older parents are moving inexorably toward that moment when the adult child becomes an almost literal parent to the parent. Often older parents want from their children a level of support which they have never given their children; and they may remain controlling and directive at the same time that they extort emotional caretaking. How ironic and unfair for the daughter who felt unloved as a child to find herself as an adult having to care for the mother whose attention she always wanted. Somehow, she must relinquish her lifelong fantasy of being nurtured by her emotionally limited parent and find support elsewhere. Often she must mobilize her siblings to share the burden she carries.

Without noticing it, we have become the generation on which the entire world depends. If there is trouble at the office, we are called to help. If there is a church committee formed to raise money, we find ourselves on it. We are called on to get a cousin into college or into a drug-treatment program; one of us has to cook the thousandth Thanksgiving dinner (guess who?) at which we listen to our parents carp at each other and see them look askance at our teenagers.

Of course we must pay for this impossibly expensive undertaking: for orthodontic work, for soccer camp and music lessons, for vacations, for the outrageous clothes our kids wear, for the tapes and CDs that assault our sensibilities, for the cars that threaten our kids' lives and which break down daily, for the leaking roof, and for the perfectly serviceable sidewalk in front of our house which the city decides to replace. Saving frantically for college tuition, we worry about the retirement which we are sure we will not live to enjoy. Bone tired, we complain constantly to each other. Finally, Margaret and I had to ban the use of the word "exhausted" from our vocabulary.

This can be a particularly discouraging era for men. While women whose children have left home can often look forward to having more energy to devote to their own interests or careers, many men face an indefinite future of working at jobs of which they have long since tired but which they cannot leave. Trapped "in harness," and feeling increasingly unappreciated by their families, many men become acutely depressed at the prospect of such joyless perseverance. Having sacrificed the riches of personal relationships—particularly with their children—they don't know how to break out of the traps that their role has set for them.

Some men become so depressed during this period that they give up emotionally, and like my father, die. Some plunge on, waiting for retirement. The most courageous men begin to face their emotional lives, and make a deeply held decision to live more fully. They may learn to relax and enjoy life more; they usually reach out to their children and try to repair the damage created by their years of absence.

BROTHER AND SISTER

As they approach adulthood, it becomes obvious that our boy and girl adolescents have responded differently to the pressures surrounding them. While the new freedoms offered women are narrowing some of these male-female differences (Julia plays soccer with a physical aggressiveness which her mother was never allowed to express, and Sarah is more assertive than either of her parents), there are still strong contrasts between brother and sister. These differences shape the way boys and girls approach marriage, and the expectations they each bring to it.

The challenge for many girls is to develop more autonomous, separate lives. As Chodorow points out, the major battles occur in leaving mother. Because mothers have projected their own feelings and needs onto their daughters, and because they depend on the companionship their daughters provide, the adolescent girl's needs for independence create a real struggle between her and her mother.

Mothers and daughters usually select a central metaphor around which they structure their battles. Because the link between them can be so intimate, the metaphor often involves the daughter's right to control her own body. This battle may begin at age six, when the daughter fights with mother over what she will wear to school and what she will eat for breakfast. While other "body-related" issues arise during adolescence (such as the girl's sexual behavior), these earlier themes may persist. Struggles over food, for example, may escalate during adolescence and can result in extreme cases in the daughter's becoming anorexic.

Often, mothers insist on "helping" their daughters with decisions which the daughters are perfectly capable of making. When the daughter senses that her mother is overriding her own initiative, she rebels. Because their relationship boundaries have been blurred, and the daughter has not been given permission to take a stand and fight with her mother openly, she fights indirectly. Rather than saying, "Mother, you are treating me like a child and I won't stand for it," the daughter fights back within the metaphor. "You don't eat enough," the mother chides her daughter. "You're right," the daughter says, and eats less. "You should wear your hair longer," Margaret counseled Sarah. So Sarah cut it short.

These mother-daughter battles can become terribly intense. Mother knows intuitively that she is approaching her daughter in a way that invites rebellion; daughter knows that the indirect way in which she fights with Mother invites the mother's continuing intrusiveness. The daughter's dilemma is that she must define herself as separate, but she is also unconsciously aware of her mother's need to keep her dependent. The daughter's "rebellious dependence" is a way to find a compromise between her needs and her mother's. Though some mothers and daughters may scream at each other, both participate in maintaining their conflictual, but highly involved drama.

When daughters sense that their mothers lack support from their husbands, or that they don't have meaningful careers, they are powerfully tempted to sacrifice their fledgling independence. The biblical parable of the Prodigal Son should be rewritten to include the Prodigal Daughter. The daughter may "fail" at school and return home to her depressed, isolated mother. Or in the space of a year a young woman may get pregnant, married, and divorced, bringing home to mother an infant who becomes the lonely mother's cuddly "therapist."

While daughters' unconscious loyalty to their mothers is a powerful obstacle to their independence, young women also fail to get support from society itself in becoming autonomous. At school, the adolescent girl is already feeling the effects of the different ways boys and girls are treated.

Within the family, adolescent girls need their mothers to stop overhelping them, to set firm limits that require independent behavior; and they need their mothers to find other sources of support—from their husbands, and from their own interests.

Underlying the anger between mothers and daughters there is often sadness about the impending separation, especially in the latter stages of this long process. Margaret and I recently saw a family in which the mother and her twenty-one-year-old daughter were fighting over the daughter's wedding plans. The daughter felt criticized and controlled by her mother's "helpful suggestions," and the mother felt hurt and rejected by the daughter's attempts to be autonomous. After an hour of bickering, both finally admitted their sadness about the transition in their lives which the wedding would bring, and wound up crying together.

A supportive, appropriately involved father can play a vital role in helping his daughter separate from her mother. The supportive father can also help his daughter develop greater confidence in dealing with the competitive world. He can teach her that traditionally male activities need not be so intimidating. She *can* learn about automobile engines, computers, and the stock market; and she can be successful at sports. Many women with successful careers got an early start through the encouragement of their fathers. Working closely with their fathers can also give girls a sense that men can be reliable sources of emotional support.

There is substantial research evidence that girls with good relationships with their fathers have more successful heterosexual relationships, do better schoolwork, and have more successful careers than do girls whose fathers have been physically or psychologically unavailable. We fathers do have a key role in the lives of our daughters!

Unfortunately, many fathers don't see themselves as being important to their daughters. Assuming that girls are their mothers' responsibility, they essentially ignore them. Some of these neglectful fathers may have had close ties with their daughters earlier in childhood, but the onset of the daughters' puberty made them anxious. Vaguely aware of sexual feelings for their daughters, they withdrew emotionally out of embarrassment. How many times have I heard adult women say, "My father and I were close until I became a teenager, and after that he was very reserved with me. I never figured out what I did wrong, and I felt very hurt."

Other fathers who are stimulated by their daughters' sexual development react by being inappropriately sexual with them. Even if this father doesn't make an overt pass at his daughter, his suggestive remarks and too close hugs make her feel terribly uncomfortable. In his presence she becomes guarded and defensive, and she feels unable to gain support from him; instead, her father is an additional stress in her life. This tragic and all too common situation pushes the daughter back into an even more intense relationship with her mother, and often into self-sacrificial sexual encounters with males.

The "marital" girl, whose overcloseness to her father makes her mother feel extremely jealous, may have little difficulty getting her mother's permission to leave home; but the girl's attractiveness may so threaten her aging mother that the stage is set for bruising confrontations between mother and daughter. With an angry mother and an exploitative father, this girl may feel terribly alone with the terrors of facing the world outside the family.

The adolescent boy's struggle to leave home is often very different from his sister's. Few boys have such an intensely involved relationship with either parent, though there are exceptions to this rule. We tend to grow up surrounded by much more psychological space than our sisters; and our fears tend to be of intimacy, rather than of aloneness.

By the time boys reach adolescence, they have become more aware of the roles which await them. Boys who were shy and academically unconfident in the earlier years are suddenly dominating discussions and making better grades. They know college or some other competitive challenge lies ahead; and society has been preparing them for competitive situations.

Some of this preparation takes place in that giant social metaphor, the world of sport. It is here that we get pushed and kicked and yelled at; and if we complain, told to shut up and run three laps. Most of this conditioning is done by men, though it is often encouraged by both parents. My mother reinforced my attempts to play high school football; and though at a hundred and sixty pounds I sustained a number of injuries, she helped me through them and tolerated my return to the field.

Like columnist Russell Baker's mother, whom he describes in *Growing Up* as "having decided to make something of me," my mother seemed to have a similar intent. Not only did she make it clear that I was not to date girls with shady reputations and that I was to make good grades, but she seemed determined that I not be a sissy. During the junior high years she sent me to Boy Scout camps, and in high school she helped me find a number of summer jobs that felt like boot camp—digging ditches, loading watermelons on my uncle's farm, unloading lumber from boxcars, pushing wheelbarrows laden with cement. There was no mistaking the message: get out there and face the world.

Not only do adolescent males get such messages consistently, but we begin to see the advantages for us in obeying them. There are awards to be won, and there is the omnipresent, sacred admiration of girls to be sought.

At home, however, we do not fare as well. Often, we get very little help from our fathers in learning to be adult. The lucky boy has a father who helps him rebuild an old car, or who hires him as his assistant carpenter; but these lessons do not include dealing with the emotional world of men. Those doors remain closed, mysterious; what do our fathers feel, we wonder to ourselves? Nor do they ask us about our inner world.

In many families, the adolescent son has been drawn into a too adult coalition with his mother; brimming with teenage arrogance, which is fed by his relationship with his mother, he collides with father. Determined to remain powerful, father comes down hard, and the ensuing confrontations can be brutal. I periodically revisit one scene between my father and me when I was about sixteen. I had built a hi-fi amplifier kit and assembled a set of speakers, and when my father tried to give me too much advice about where to put them in the living room, I bristled. "I know more about this than you do," I said angrily; and the fight was on. We wound up screaming at each other, and not speaking for some time afterward.

Often, boys whose parents are divorced grow up at a considerable psychological (and sometimes physical) distance from their fathers, and their attempts to get adequate fathering are terribly discouraging. Even if they are physically present, however, many fathers abandon their teenage sons psychologically, especially if the fathers are depressed or alcoholic. My father's alcoholism became obvious during my latter high school years, and I certainly experienced it as an abandonment.

Teenage boys also tend to feel unsupported by their mothers, who may direct at their sons a very confusing mixture of feelings. While a mother may have "parentified" her son and leaned on him heavily at times, when he becomes an adolescent she may not only sexualize her relationship with him, but find herself furiously angry at him. It feels bewildering to have Mother overinvolved with him one moment, and furious the next.

Sixteen-year-old Norm Hale had been seriously depressed. Meeting with me in a separate session, he described a recent conflict with his mother: "I had come in from school and was watching TV. My mom came in the door with some groceries, and when I didn't get up to help her, she said something sarcastic. Then, when she came over to talk to me, all she said was, 'Have you done your homework? Why are you watching television?' She said it in that angry, bitter sort of tone that she uses with me a lot. I suppose I said something smart back to her and went on watching TV, but I felt lousy. I know I should have helped her, but all she ever says to me is, 'Have you done your homework?' or, 'Did you take out the garbage?' I don't know why she is so angry with me all the time."

"What happened then?" I asked.

"After dinner, I was in the family room. I was lying on the floor reading my history, and Mom was walking in and out of the room doing something. She asked me to get up and get something for her—I think it was a book. The strange thing was that this book was closer to her than it was to me, and she was standing up! It was like she was by God going to get something out of me. Her voice had that shrill sound that I can't stand. It affects me like somebody scraping their fingernails on a blackboard."

"Let me guess," I said. "You said something smart."

"Yeah. And the first thing I knew, Mom was screaming at me at the top of her voice that I was lazy and arrogant and never did anything for her." He hesitated as he recalled the moment. "I guess I just lost it. I stood up and started yelling too, and I made a mistake—I shoved her up against the wall. That scared her, but it stopped her yelling. It seemed like I was going to die if she didn't stop that. But it scared me too, and I turned and walked into the living room. I could hear her crying a little in there, and after a while she went upstairs."

"Was your father upstairs?"

"Uh huh, and a few minutes later he came down, angry as hell. He is usually so quiet and withdrawn at home, or busy with his work, but this time he was different. He started yelling at me that I couldn't treat my mom like that, and that he would clobber me if I did it again. I said to myself, 'I'd like to see you try it,' but I didn't say it. Strange, but it was almost a relief when he got mad at me, like I'd been wanting him to. Sometimes I think he is a wimp with all of us. After a while my dad cooled off, and later he and Mom talked to me together about my bad temper. I wound up feeling more depressed than ever, like I had caused the whole thing."

He hadn't, of course. We lost no time in convening the family again, where for the first time some of the background issues came to light. Norm's mother, Emma, who was the oldest of three children, was a strong, directive woman, and certainly the dominant figure in her marriage. For many years she had subordinated her own needs to those of the family, and she had been a caretaker for her very successful but often depressed husband. She had gotten little support from anyone in her family—except Norm's older sister Esther, who had recently left for college.

As we began work on their wife-overfunctioning marriage, Emma was able to say how worried she often felt about her husband, and how little support she got from him. It was her anger about that inequity that was directed at her "unsupportive" son, whose depression—which reminded her of her husband's—made her feel even angrier.

The mother-son fight was unconsciously scripted to bring father in as a more active and forceful presence in the family; though of course that needed to happen in a much calmer and more predictable way. The parents began to address their marital issues; and as Emma saw how painfully rejected Norm felt by her constant criticism, she was much more caring with him, and his depression began to lift.

Teenage boys are much more vulnerable than they seem. They often feel unsupported by their fathers, who may be harsh and strict with them; or absent or emotionally unavailable. In the early adolescent years, these boys feel threatened by their mothers' involvement with them; but as their inevitable teenage irritability surfaces, they frequently become the target for their mothers' anger at their husbands. Feeling blamed by both parents, they withdraw, turning to peers for support.

CASTING THE DIE

As a young woman approaches marriage, she expects in this relationship the same level of intimacy that she experienced with her mother, her sisters, her women friends. Like her husband-to-be, she may also have significant deficits in fathering. Unconsciously, she hopes to find in her husband some of what she did not get from her father—be it playfulness, nurturance, strength, sensitivity, attentiveness.

Her future husband has grown up fearing the power of his mother's emotionality. Because of his struggles with his mother, he may be afraid of a woman's dependency, her sexuality, her anger, her rejection.

When, as soon as they are married, his eager, intimacy-seeking wife approaches him, he is likely to retreat. "Be close to me!" his wife implores.

"I'm frightened of your needs!" he might say if he recognizes his panic.

This male retreat is even more likely if he has not had adequate fathering. He senses his wife's need for something from him *which he has not gotten from his own father*. Once more, father's emotional absence looms over them both. "Be helpful to me!" his wife cries out. "I don't know how to do that for a woman," he might say if he knew what his anxiety was really about. "My father didn't do it for me, or for my mother."

After a lot of frustration in attempting to get her needs met in her marriage, the young woman is likely to do exactly what her mother did: she begins to believe that her only chance of real closeness lies in giving to a child. So she has a baby, and in turning to this child for support and intimacy, begins the cycle again. It is the woman's turning to motherhood as a solution to her dilemmas that Chodorow credits for "the reproduction of mothering."

REWRITING THE SCRIPT

During our exploration of the long progress of the family's development, from the courtship days to the trials of adolescence, we have seen how easy it is for fathers to become separated from the family's inner circle. This displacement begins at the birth of the first child, when father often feels unable to compete with his wife's intense involvement with the newborn. Unless both parents make a determined effort to overcome their social conditioning, the consequences of father's failure to become deeply bonded to his children, and to be intimately involved in their lives, become more and more pronounced with time. By the time children reach adolescence, father's emotional distance from the family can become a critical issue. With the possible exception of the birth of children, at no time in the family life cycle are fathers more needed than during this era.

The hidden agenda in the families of adolescents is often father's lack of involvement with parenting. While mothers may be able to parent young children alone, adolescents are another matter. Many adolescents are unconsciously motivated to make emotional contact with their fathers before they leave home, and to pull father into a more active parental role in the family. This motive is especially strong in boys, who often cry out for more structure, more involvement, and more help from their fathers. Most adolescents' unconscious strategy for getting fathers involved is to create a crisis of such proportion that there is simply no other alternative than his being a more active parent. Finally, his wife says to him, "You've got to help me with this," and this time, the stakes are a child's life.

There are so many ways that we men can help during this period, but none is more critical than our being able to team equally and intimately with our mate around issues involving discipline. Our problems in this arena are often related to our power in the family. If we have been dominant overfunctioners, we must learn to be softer, kinder, more understanding with our wives and our kids; if we have been one-down underfunctioners, we must learn to take a stand with our kids as well as with our wives. Adolescents sense the drifting separateness of their parents, sense the conflicts in the marriage, and they usually create a series of challenges that force us to confront each other and to begin to deal with our marriage issues. Norm's father needed to be more assertive in almost every aspect of his life, and his son was unconsciously trying to "teach" him how to make these changes.

These angry young revolutionaries seem to confront every aspect of the family: they attack the family's denial, its deadness, its rigid injustices; they lay siege to its endless repetitiveness; they make war on the trapped, joyless, hopeless regions of the family's interior; and while they have genuine concern about the parents and siblings they are trying to leave behind, they also act out of self-interest. They need to test their parents' marital "togetherness," for they know intuitively that only if their parents are satisfied and thriving can they become the secure "base camp" which these young voyagers need in their ever widening journeys into the lonely beyond.

One of the major ways we fail our teenagers is by not addressing our subterranean marital wars, thereby "triangulating" our child in the midst of our disagreements. A dominant father ignores his wife's desire to talk out an issue with a teenager and imposes harsh discipline; and rather than disagreeing openly with him, his intimidated wife subtly signals the child that it is permissible to get around father's rules. When each parent uses the adolescent as a pawn in a cold war, the teenager inevitably loses. Sensing that they are needed to play this role, these triangulated teens often stay close by; they know unconsciously that if they weren't there, and causing trouble, that the parents' marriage might founder.

But we men can be helpful in many other ways than in dealing with structure and discipline. We can teach our kids what we know about the larger world; we can stand by them and support them as they do their own battle with getting established in that world; and we are often much better than our wives at being calm, reassuring "consultants" to the leaving-home process. One of the contributions we can make is in sensing when *not* to help the fledgling adult.

Even as our kids leave home physically, fathers will still have opportunities to parent. Many kids with unfinished agendas with their fathers will return home for an extended period, or live nearby, in order to work out these issues. There are also many instances in the lives of young adults who are established away from home when they need some help, but not too much. Fathers are often the best prepared to supply this kind of parenting.

In spite of all this talk of crisis and struggle, the years in which our kids are adolescents can be, and often are, enjoyable. The wonderful discovery of this era is that our children have become informed, intellectually curious, excited young adults. Amid the instability of this era we can develop a sense of deep companionship with our teenagers.

Finding that the family can be a team, and a source of mutual enjoyment, is also heady and invigorating. Though they will not occur nightly, evenings when everyone is hanging around together, telling stories, reminiscing, teasing—these are even more delightful for the willing and witty participation of our almost adult, worldly-wise visiting nomads.

16

Strategies of Change

WE DON'T PLAN THE patterns into which our marriage falls, nor are we usually conscious of how predictable we are: the feint and parry of practiced argument, the ritual touch with which we initiate lovemaking, the heavy familiarity as we move through the responsibilities of our days. As long as our relationship works, we don't think much about it. The doubts arise because of a vague disturbance, a deep misgiving in the very sinews, the muscular understructure of our marriage. Some element in love's body grinds against itself repeatedly; something in this chosen, worked-at, cherished assemblage which is our life together—hurts, feels wrong. We know intuitively that this pain is part of why we chose each other, that it comes out of our need to face our own truth. But it is never because growth looks like fun that we decide that something must change. We change because we must.

Not until we deliberately try to vary our "automatic" responses to each other do we realize how powerful are the psychological forces that impel us to behave in certain ways. A woman, for example, who tries to alter her tendency to be helpful and self-denying will soon discover—particularly if her partner is skilled at eliciting this kind of behavior from her—that she faces a formidable challenge. Because we tend to encourage certain habitual responses in each other, couples need to work together in order to change these patterns. Many of us will also need help from a therapist; but there are steps we can take on our own.

Somebody has to take a very firm stand to get things started. When Margaret found herself floundering and depressed when we moved to Atlanta, she made a forceful, confrontive, and impassioned plea for change. She told me exactly what she was unhappy about, and what she wanted from me. There were a number of such confrontations, and they awakened me to her dilemmas in a way that nothing else could have.

The studies of marital satisfaction leave little doubt that traditional marriage was advantageous for men; and because many women today still have their usual responsibilities in addition to full-time work, their unhappiness may be even greater than their mothers'. In the past, women have been more likely than their husbands to go into therapy individually, and to initiate marital therapy. Though there is some evidence that more men are initiating therapy, this trend may be due to greater anxiety in men that their self-sufficient, working wives might leave them. Three fourths of divorces are in fact filed by women, though it would be a mistake to assume that this statistic is an accurate measure of the proportion of marital unhappiness.

In my view, the hardest work in changing habitual patterns in marriage must be done by men; and I take up these issues in the next two chapters. But many of us must be jolted, confronted, or in some way awakened to the need to do our part of that work. And this is a job that still falls predominantly to women.

STRATEGIES FOR WOMEN

When Margaret and I begin work with a couple in which the wife's complaints clearly underlie their coming to see us, our first move—after hearing both partners' views of the problems—is to ask the wife to take a look at her role in the couple's difficulties. Any woman who wants change in her marriage would be wise to follow the same train of thought: what is my role in our problems? This question leads to a larger one: what is my role in our marriage?

Understanding the dynamics of one's marriage can provide a valuable clue in knowing how to proceed. A woman who wants more intimacy and closeness with her husband, for example, should assume that she is inadvertently doing things that make it difficult to achieve what she wants. Often she is engaged in a high-pressure campaign to "reach" her husband, and the quality of urgency in her needs is part of what is driving him away. The woman who finds herself in this "pursuing" position should take a hard look at why emotional closeness is so important to her. While it is certainly legitimate to want an intimate marriage, if we bring to the marriage an intense yearning which comes out of our unmet childhood needs, our partner is likely to feel anxious about this emotional pressure, and to recoil. We men have plenty of work to do on our side of the impasse, but it is difficult for us to become aware of our problems as long as we are spending so much effort fending off our wives.

If the woman pursuer can take control of her own anxiety and *stop pursuing*, turning instead to activities and interests where she can be assured of getting support, her husband will inevitably become anxious about this change; and he may be much more interested in establishing contact with her. *This kind of change should not be undertaken manipulatively or secretly.* It is best to be open about what you are trying to do: "I am tired of being the one who tries to get us together, and I am going to make an effort to avoid pursuing you." Women friends and work are the best place to turn for support. Turning to one's children involves them in a marital issue; and the threat of an affair introduces complexities that may make the situation worse. If your husband begins to initiate intimacy, respond positively; but don't escalate your requests.

It is just as critical for the woman who wants change in the balance of power and vulnerability in her marriage to understand her role in maintaining this pattern. The overfunctioning wife who is strong, organized, helpful, and giving inevitably feels depleted and drained; and she wants more support and help from her husband. But she needs to remember that she will unconsciously resist changing the very role that burdens her.

Overfunctioning wives tend to stay in their mobilized, empowered "modes" as they approach their husbands, and they often present themselves as critical, directive, controlling. For the underfunctioning husband who had a dominating mother and/or a weak father, his wife looks *formidable*. It is very tempting for such a man to take an accommodating, wife-pleasing stance: "Yes, dear, I'll do it," he says; anything to get his wife to be quiet. Then, in secret, he fights back passively—forgetting to pick up the laundry, or letting the burned-out light bulbs in the upstairs hall that only he can reach go unchanged.

The woman who finds herself in this burdened position needs to be able to acknowledge the needy, unnurtured part of herself, *and to reveal this part of herself to others,* but especially her husband. Instead of helping, she needs to learn to ask for support, and to be vulnerable. For someone who doesn't trust that she will get support, this "asking" can feel like an immense undertaking. While she is tempted to complain angrily to her mate, "You never change the light bulbs," she needs to be able to say, "I'm very tired, and I get so discouraged that I can't do it all. I really need your help with our house." And she needs to stop doing more than her share of the household work.

Most overfunctioning women find that they need help in breaking their addiction to helpfulness, and to being in control in their relationships. The wives of male alcoholics are almost all in this category, and the organization Al-Anon is devoted to helping such women learn to nurture and care for themselves, and to give up this lifestyle of helpfulness and self-denial.

In addition to being willing to surrender a certain amount of control, the overfunctioning wife must also be willing to hurt the person she normally protects. It took us a long time to get one wife to say to her husband, "I'm not attracted to you sexually because you are overweight; and I don't respect you when you always bring your work problems to me. I wish you would be stronger, and more assertive." When she began to share her own needs, and to assume that her husband was adult enough to deal with her feelings, the pattern began to change.

The underfunctioning wife who feels one down in her marriage must of course take the opposite tack. She needs to learn assertiveness, and to be able to exert power. Often, she must confront her husband about the conditions in her marriage which make her unhappy. Many women find this kind of confrontation extremely anxious, especially if they had mothers who were unassertive, or who were extremely critical and demanding, and thus seemed like unpleasant "models." It is of course very difficult for women who are economically dependent on their husbands to risk being confrontive. Women who do not have paid jobs can still exert equal power in their marriages, though it is an uphill battle.

It is tempting for the woman who feels one down to remain silent, and to use indirect ways of gaining power: making her husband feel guilty, refusing sex, flirting with his boss, overspending, turning to the kids for support, and the thousand other ways women have learned to exercise influence in a world dominated by men. The vast literature of the women's movement, and the support groups that have helped so many women, are a vital adjunct in tackling these issues; but it is also important to examine critically the family-of-origin issues that play into women's one-down status. Women who were youngest children, for example, are often at a disadvantage in dealing with power issues; as are women who had critical, unsupportive parents; as are women who had early loss experiences—the list is long.

Many women fear confrontation because they anticipate that it might lead to divorce; and they are understandably alarmed at the prospect of being alone. When we men discover this fear in our wives, we are tempted to use it to intimidate. The fear of aloneness begins early for many women, and it is partially grounded in the tendency of mothers to overprotect their daughters. Learning to brave the prospect of aloneness, confronting the fear itself, is an important part of women's claiming their power in marriage.

In order to be able to live in a relationship successfully, we must be willing to lose it; otherwise, we are slaves to our need for the other. In addition to having less training braving the terrors of aloneness, women have fewer attractive opportunities in the work world; and, especially if they are older, they face the discouraging demographics of remarriage. These forces make confrontation with their husbands all the more anxious.

Women who badly want their marriages to change but are anxious about confronting their husbands should remember that the level of dependency in a marriage is usually equal. We men are skilled at hiding our dependency, but it is a powerful force in our lives. In fact, most of us turn only to our wives for "therapy." Women who feel one down in their marriages should try to see the vulnerable aspect of their husbands; seeing it may allow them to realize that they have more power than they claim. Claiming this power involves relinquishing the image of the man as the protective "father," but this is a necessary and inevitable loss.

In describing the end of his first marriage, one remarried husband said: "I never gave my life a second thought—everything seemed fine. I was successful at work, and I thought I had a good marriage. Then in the same year I lost my business and my wife left me for another man. That was ten years ago, and I have been depressed ever since." I already know enough about this man to see what must have made his first wife unhappy: his reserve, his rigid domination of the family, his deep mistrust of women. I will probably never meet his first wife, but he obviously cared enough about her to spend ten years being depressed about the failure of his marriage. Had she seen past his tough, taciturn surface to the lonely, frightened person I see (and of course he bears responsibility for not revealing that part of himself), she might have confronted him, fought with him, demanded that they get into therapy. Perhaps he, and they, could have changed.

This man is working hard in his second marriage, and his wife recently described how intimidated she felt by his strident, authoritarian statements: "I feel that you are sometimes hovering way above me." Then she demonstrated, raising her arms in a threatening gesture. "It makes me feel small inside, like I'm a child and you are an adult. And it doesn't feel good." After a reflective pause, he replied, "I'm sorry I have that effect on you. I don't mean to. I'll try to change that."

Some women who are unhappy with their marriages turn for support to individual therapists, who in the past have often been male. This can be a kind of emotional affair, an idealized relationship which can encourage women to stay in frustrating, unfulfilling marriages. For the woman who wants change in her marriage and who cannot get her husband to work with her on this project, I would suggest that she hire a therapist as a *consultant*. Her request should be: "Help me work out a strategy for getting us [husband

and probably children too] into therapy; and also help me look at my resistance to changing myself."

DEFINING THE ISSUES

One of the toughest challenges for couples is defeating the notion that one person has "the problem." Just as families tend to use one of their kids as a scapegoat, most marriages maintain the fiction that one partner is more responsible for the couple's difficulties. In one family in which the wife was extremely depressed when they began therapy, the husband had subtly aligned himself with their four children, and the consensus in the family was that mother was "impossible." The husband's mother turned out to be the real target of his anger, but his wife had an extremely difficult time extricating herself from her role as the family's problem person.

Many boys grew up feeling the impact of their mothers' anger at their fathers, and, like most kids, they assumed their mothers' unhappiness was their fault. When they become adults and their wives approach them with their own anger and frustration, these men, prepared to feel blamed, retreat readily from what feels to them like an ambush. Fear of being found out to be "the real problem" is responsible for the reluctance of many men to enter therapy.

It is difficult to do, but every couple beginning the process of change should make a firm commitment to thinking about their difficulties as "systems problems." In the overfunctioning–underfunctioning pattern, for example, we should not say, "She dominates him," because we label the wife as the cause of their conflicts. Instead, we should assume that each of us plays a role for which our childhood family trained us, and that the dynamics of our roles determine the outcome.

In the initial stages of working on our problems, an objective, intellectual approach may help us avoid blaming and name-calling. We should acknowledge that we created these patterns together, that we have done so because they are familiar, and because we have needed to work on the conflicts we brought with us from childhood. We need to see the origins of *our own position* in the

343

marriage; and we need to make a mutual commitment to changing these repetitive interactions.

FINDING A WAY OF WORKING

It is when we try to talk to each other about how we feel that something goes wrong, often badly wrong; and most of us become so engrossed in these conflicts that we don't understand how they occur. Nothing is more vital than learning a productive way of verbalizing the anger, the pain, the often intense frustration of living in close quarters with this usually loved, sometimes hated Other.

In marriage, rarely is the absence of communication the problem. In fact, in close relationships, it is impossible to avoid communicating our feelings. I know very quickly when Margaret is angry or upset, though my only cue may be a slight inflection of voice, or an unusual silence. The problem is that the *origin* of our feelings may be hidden, even from the person who has the feelings (Margaret may still be angry at her dead father, for example, and I may trigger those feelings). Just as the true source of feelings can be hidden, the person who senses or hears about these feelings can also misinterpret them. Perhaps Margaret is angry with the client she saw in the last hour, and, sensing her coolness, I think she is angry with me.

The other problem in marriage is the sheer intensity of our feelings, which are sometimes so powerful that one or both of us believes that our relationship cannot stand this intensity. Even though our attempt to block, repress, or otherwise avoid communicating our upset (particularly anger) is doomed to fail, we still try it. This denied anger pervades our relationship, poisoning every aspect of our lives: our ability to cooperate, our trust in each other, our sexuality. Learning how to deal with anger is perhaps the major problem in marriage.

THE UBIQUITOUS "YOU"   Blaming is the scourge of marriage. We all do it, and it is always damaging and unproductive. While the diagnostic cue is the overuse of the word "you"—"You always forget our anniversary," "You are just like your mother," "You never clean up your messes"—much more is at stake than the overuse of a certain pronoun.

Since we have transferred our dependency on our parents to our mate, our blaming is really a product of this dependency. If I say to Margaret in an anxious, angry tone, "You never pay attention to our finances," I confess by my tone of voice that I am anxious about money, and I imply that she is failing me in some way. What I am really saying is that she is responsible for my anxiety; if she were only a better money manager, I would not feel this way. *So the essence of blaming is the denial of responsibility for the self.* Perhaps I could say, "When you don't notice what we're spending I get very anxious, and I feel alone with the responsibility for our finances."

We learned to blame from our parents, who dealt with some of their anxiety about life by attacking us. How many times have I seen an anxious, harried mother literally savage a two-year-old in a grocery store? I recently heard one such mother say to her toddler in a chilling voice, "I'm going to kill you if you do that again!" This habitual, daily abuse happened in different degrees to all of us; and when our anxious, stressed partner blames us, he or she triggers our own sensitivity to this kind of attack. So we retaliate, or defend, or retreat.

As we begin work with a couple, Margaret and I explain the three-part division of the personality popularized by Eric Berne, in which we have a "parental self," which is an internalized version of our parents' attitudes toward us; and an "adult self," which represents our rational, problem-solving capacity; and a "child self," that vital, perennially troublesome part of us that needs love and encouragement, and can so easily become hurt and discouraged. Margaret and I sometimes suggest that each partner get a photograph of themselves as a child—one that expresses the way they often felt. These photos can help each partner visualize the way he or she feels about and deals with this "child" aspect of themselves, and with that part of the partner.

An initial hurdle is helping couples see that we are all tempted to bring this "child self" to our partner for help. Margaret and I take an immediate stand on this issue, announcing firmly that our partner cannot be a substitute parent; and that we should not bring such expectations to marriage. We suggest that they neither request "parenting," nor give it.

Here is Janice, a young office worker, addressing her husband: "I get depressed sometimes because of my situation at work, and I just wish you would notice when I'm feeling that way and ask me about it. Offer me a little support. You seem to think I'm made of steel."

Tom replies, "If you would ever listen to my advice, maybe I would be more interested. You let your supervisor run all over you. If you'd either stand up to her, or ask for a transfer, maybe you would feel less depressed."

This brief interchange illustrates a common failing, and one that we begin work on immediately. For the partner in Janice's position, we counsel: *don't ask your mate for parenting*. As children, we had a right to expect our parents to see what we needed, to seek us out when we felt depressed, and to take care of us. While we need to be able to get support in marriage, we should not expect our spouse to anticipate our needs. We need to mobilize the "parental" and "adult" aspects of the self, and those parts of us need to be in charge of getting our needs met. If Janice's "internal parent" sees her depressed "child" and feels empathy for her, she can then mobilize the "adult" aspect to problem-solve for this unhappy part of herself. Janice may decide to go jogging, or she may decide to ask Tom for support. If she asks him for support, she should know what she wants, and be explicit: "Would you just sit down with me and let me complain for a while?" She is asking for support, but she is still in charge of getting her own needs met.

Since we didn't have ideal parents, our "internal parent" is usually ill equipped to meet our own needs. We tend to respond to our feelings in the way our parents treated us; and whatever our initial hopes that marriage will be "therapeutic," we eventually project our parents' mode of relating to us onto our spouse. As we begin work on more effective "self-parenting," we are forced to face the deficits in our experience. We must learn to distinguish between the needs we can legitimately expect our partner to meet, and those needs which he or she cannot meet. *Our unmet needs for parenting should be addressed with a therapist.*

A very important part of the early stage of marital change, then, is to limit one's expectations of marriage. Expect companionship, caring, support, sex, shared work; but don't expect your mate to be responsible for your life in the way that a parent would. Don't ask for help with your sense of self-worth, and don't ask your partner to solve any of life's fundamental agonies: being alone, being bored, being frightened about dying, having to work.

Janice's husband, Tom, is making another fundamental error: he is assuming an older-generational, parental position. We may attempt to seduce our partner into being parental, but few of us like it when he or she succumbs. Most of us have had enough advice, direction, analysis, and criticism for a lifetime. But because many of us had parental positions in our family of origin (and thus learned these "skills"), and because both we and our partner usually had inadequate parenting, there is a powerful temptation to repeat these patterns in our marriage. As we have seen, some marriages are organized with one dominant "parent," but in many relationships both partners are parental with each other.

First, we need to be aware when we are making parental statements:

"You should do that today." (direction)

"I think it would be a mistake not to take that offer." (advice)

"You're nagging me the way your mother nagged your father." (analysis)

"Give me that pen." (command)

Then we should make a two-sided commitment to avoid such one-upmanship. The partner with a propensity to be parental should resolve to abstain from such statements; but since he or she will inevitably lapse into old habits, the other should be prepared to challenge this stance. As we will see, there is a way to confront one's partner without provoking a major crisis.

Trying to learn to approach one another as peers can be a discouraging endeavor. We are so tempted to slip into ingratiating, pleading, dependent positions; or to take righteous, superior stances with each other. It is lonely to claim responsibility for ourselves, and to see the other as someone like us—a companion, a fellow traveler. But if we can make this transition, we can achieve deeper intimacy than if we pretend that the other can be parent to us.

DEALING WITH ANGER

The real test of our ability to communicate effectively comes when both partners are upset and angry. There are no easy solutions to such situations, but there are some effective—if difficult to follow—rules for dealing with anger that can make the process much more constructive.

Don't put off talking about something that makes you angry.

If we accumulate anger over time, it can build to frightening proportions. In recent years, Margaret and I have learned to have on the average a couple of brief "collisions" a day. These tend to occur over misunderstandings, or they arise out of the tensions and situations of the day. We still have larger, longer, more significant fights, but they tend to be more focused, and more centered on the issues at hand, than they once were.

Most of us grew up in families that had difficulty expressing anger constructively. Although we didn't learn this from our parents, we can "normalize" anger (it can become as easy and natural to express as humor), and express it as it arises.

Develop a list of "weapons" that are off limits.

Some of these are obvious; others will become evident and can be dropped as you become more efficient fighters. Some of the worst offenders:

- ☐ Threatening divorce when you don't really mean it (on an unconscious level, it terrifies your opponent).
- ☐ Leaving the scene of the fight. This dramatic move is often symbolic of an underlying threat to leave the relationship, and it has almost the same effect as threatening divorce.
- ☐ Attacking your mate's character, motives, or worthiness as a person. The intent behind our anger is of vital importance. Fight to be heard, and to reach the other; but not to assassinate. At times we all want to wound our partner; but this impulse almost always occurs when a childhood injury has been activated by the conflict.
- ☐ Attacking your mate's family of origin (such attack makes your mate feel guilty, and inevitably provokes a defense of the family of origin).

☐ Shifting the focus. When we are losing an argument, it is tempting to bring up the past, or to shift to a variety of other topics: "You've always done that, and you do this and this and this too!" Try to stick to the present issue.

☐ Bringing others in. "Your brother agrees with me about you" is an attempt to marshal support from others. The worst example of this kind of fighting is when parents literally drag a child into an argument: "Don't you agree with me that your father is irresponsible?" This is a terribly destructive thing to do to a child, and it also invites retaliation. Before you know it, both partners can line up their own cadres of support. Learn to do your own fighting!

☐ Feigning defeat. It is terribly difficult to fight with someone whom your anger seems to devastate. Some of us are skilled at using our own vulnerability in order to disarm our opponent. "I feel so guilty and depressed when I realize that I have slipped and had a drink again"; what this says to the angry mate is "Don't be angry at me, because I'm already so angry at myself." Regressing into tears, depression, or conspicuous self-reproach can be an unconscious way of disarming our mate. People who use this method of avoiding conflict are often genuinely afraid of anger, but they also have difficulty taking responsibility for themselves.

☐ Being defensive. "You're wrong about that; I didn't mean to do it. Besides, you did the same thing yesterday." As natural as it feels, defensiveness gets us nowhere. Our mate, angry or upset about something, feels unheard, unnoticed, and may try harder to get the point across. And especially if his or her approach to us is blaming and critical, we may become even more defensive.

Learn the arts of self-disclosure, and of empathic listening.

We all need to learn a method of expressing strong feelings, and especially anger, to our partner; and we need to learn to hear and to take in such feelings about ourselves. Like many growthful endeavors, the method I suggest will feel artificial at first—largely because we were not taught it by our parents. There are several prerequisites in the use of this approach:

First, we need an empathic attitude toward our own feelings. We simply must be able to respond in a caring manner to our own emotional states and dilemmas. Second, we need to be able to step outside our experience, and to observe ourselves: "Am I off base in what I am asking?" "What am I really upset about?" "What am I really feeling?" The capacity for self-observation allows us to modify our own responses. Third, we must be responsible for knowing what our feelings are, for communicating them, and for asking for appropriate responses from our partner.

Most of us need help from outsiders in learning such a method. Margaret and I took the Minnesota Couples Communication Course, which is offered in most major cities; and we found it extremely valuable. Our own approach to communication issues has been heavily influenced by the Minnesota group. But there are many other such structured workshops on communication.

All conflicts take place in a context, a situation; and the context includes everything surrounding or influencing the present moment. For example, when Margaret and I come home from work in the evening, we face a situation which is often difficult. We are both tired and hungry, and we have ourselves and a teenager to feed. My agreed-upon job is to clear the dining table of extraneous items, such as the bills I was paying the night before; to set the table, pour the drinks, and to help Margaret with the meal if she asks for it. After dinner I cajole and coerce Julia into helping me with the cleanup.

When I come home, my inevitable tendency is to collapse into a chair, and, tired of attending carefully to every word said to me, space out. Conditioned by years of being on duty, Margaret charges into cooking like a runner on the last lap of a race; she likes to collapse after dinner. So it was inevitable that Margaret would find herself nagging me about getting the table set; and that I would find myself getting angry. "Would you set the table?" she would complain irritably. "Would you leave me alone? I'll do it in a minute," I would reply irritably.

Margaret and I certainly broke every communication rule in dealing with such issues; sometimes when we were exhausted we found ourselves yelling at the top of our voices over this ridiculous situation. But we have gradually improved our abilities to deal with such conflicts, and these are some of the rules that have helped us:

1. Describe the context you are in. Margaret might say, "When I'm tired like this and you don't set the table the way you've agreed to . . ." Already, I have two important pieces of information about the context: she's tired, and she is responding to my failure to set the table. She hasn't said that I am a bastard and that I never do anything for her. She has just described the *stimulus* which seems to be provoking her anger: in this case, my failure to set the table.

This part of the process of communication may seem unimportant, but it is not. Margaret may be tempted to get to the heart of the matter and focus on me, but she is deliberately resisting attack. She is also being somewhat objective: her feelings seem to come from this situation. She is implicitly allowing me to explain my point of view.

2. Describe your feelings. This is perhaps the most crucial step; it is certainly difficult to do. "When I'm tired like this and you don't set the table the way you've agreed to, I feel let down, disappointed, discouraged. I feel alone with all this work. I'm also starting to feel angry." In order to be able to disclose feelings, we have to know what they are. Rather than just jumping at me for my negligent behavior, Margaret pauses, asks herself what she is feeling, and tries to describe those feelings to me.

Face to face with our partner—and especially when we are angry—it is very difficult to stop, to search around, and to describe what is going on internally. It is even more difficult to do this in a nonblaming, nonjudgmental way; that is, to leave the interpretation of our partner's behavior, and especially his or her motives, undefined. Maybe this day I had a traumatic session with a client the last hour; or I'm worried about one of our kids. Margaret really doesn't know why I'm behaving like this—though she may have made a pretty good guess.

One can describe any set of feelings: "I feel so absolutely enraged that I don't know what to do!" Or: "I feel hurt, lonely, ignored." In general, our vulnerability is the hardest to reveal; and often, feelings of rejection or hurt underlie our anger. If we are able to describe our vulnerable side, our partner is usually able to hear us much more successfully than if we talk only about our anger or frustration. In marriage, nothing is more vital than the honest, open, disclosure of the self. Over and over I say to clients: *describe your feelings*.

3. Make a request. It does little good to complain if we have no idea what we want. After telling me about the situation she is in, and the feelings it engenders, Margaret needs to ask that I do something differently: "I wish that when you come home, you would set the table without my having to ask you, and that you would do it before you sit down. In fact, I wish you wouldn't sit down at all. I always need help with dinner, and I'm as tired as you are." Sometimes requests need to be made after the emotional exchange has occurred and anger has subsided, but they must be addressed. They represent a way to prevent a recurrence, and they open the way to negotiation.

4. Take part of the responsibility. Even if you are acutely upset and believe that you have a right to be angry at your partner, listen carefully to that self-appraising part of yourself that introduces an element of doubt. Maybe you are overreacting; maybe you are part of the problem. So Margaret might say, "I know when I'm tired I get critical, and I'm sorry if I jumped on you; but I still feel upset that this happens so often." This admission communicates to the partner bearing the brunt of the anger that he or she is not the entire cause of the distress; and it makes it easier to hear a complaint.

5. Respond to your partner's self-disclosure. When Margaret has taken the risk of exposing her feelings, I must respond by acknowledging them. I may be tempted to say that I was about to set the table when she made me not want to, or I may want to sullenly start slapping the forks on the table; but I should do something else.

First, I should look at her. She's tired, angry, frustrated. Perhaps I can see the situation she is in; at least I signal her that I am ready to listen.

Second, I should let her know that I have heard her; and that even if I don't agree with her, I take her feelings seriously.

My acknowledgment is more convincing if my voice conveys empathy, and if I repeat some of her own words: "I understand how you would feel disappointed and let down, and I don't blame you for feeling angry."

Third, it sounds rather trite to say, but if you are convinced you have made a mistake, admit it: "I'm sorry; I'll try to change this."

Admitting one's faults can have an almost magical effect in an argument.

6. Ask for something in return. Few issues are one-sided. In this everyday example, Margaret tends to remind me about a chore before giving me time to do it in my own way. So I make a counterrequest: "I will work on my side of this, but I wish you would stop reminding me. I will get the table set before dinner is ready, but I don't want to be prodded. I want to sit down for a few minutes and read the mail."

Most of the time, we cannot move so quickly to an apology; nor are the issues so clear-cut. Margaret may be angry with me about something much more personal, and I may be just as angry with her about another issue. In this instance, we both need to be heard and our feelings acknowledged; and we may have to sort through a great deal of distortion and misunderstanding to get there. Even when we are dealing with simple issues, of course, the process is never as tidy and logical as this example.

Several months ago Margaret and I had a fight about some trivial issue, and after yelling at each other briefly, we realized that the fight was going nowhere. Finally Margaret said, "Well, I feel hurt and disappointed." I said, "And I feel unjustly criticized." Margaret then said, "I'm sorry you feel that way." I said, "I'm sorry you feel that way." Suddenly, the fight was over, and the inconsequential subject matter relegated to obscurity. The resolution was not at all sophisticated, but it had the basic elements: self-disclosure, and acknowledgment of the other's feelings. We were stressed and tired, and not really interested in the fight; we just needed a way to extricate ourselves honorably.

7. Keep your sense of humor. There is an absurd quality in many of our arguments, and if you feel tempted to smile at the ridiculousness of your own arguments, give into the impulse. You may both wind up laughing, but so much the better.

Communication is much more problematic when one or both of us brings symbolic issues to the argument, or when both are under a great deal of stress. If Margaret screamed at me and broke into tears as she was complaining about my not setting the table, I would know immediately that something else underlay her distress, and I would try to find out what was happening. Seeing "through" our partner's distress to an underlying issue is a parental activity, but for short periods it can be helpful. If I guessed that she had just talked to her mother's doctor about her mother's cancer, I would be much less likely to retaliate; and rather than becoming embroiled in a defense, I might be able to offer her support.

CONTRACTING FOR CHANGE

In this age of psychological sophistication, some of us become skilled at saying the right thing. We offer insight and empathy, and we apologize for our mistakes; but then we turn around and act in exactly the same way. Apologies and empathy are rarely enough. If it is to be convincing, attitudinal change must produce behavioral change. We want action!

Unfortunately, most couples fall into rigid patterns in which each pressures the other for certain changes, and then resists his or her mate's similar pressures. "Won't you ever pay attention to the children?" she chides. "Won't you ever pay attention to my relatives?" he nags. Breaking such patterns is difficult, but change is more likely to occur if both partners agree to "work on" the issues together.

Almost any pattern from the trivial to the most serious can be addressed through a bilateral contract for change. But if our plan to change a pattern is to be successful, several elements are required.

1. We must really want change. As noxious as they sometimes seem, our conflicts have served a purpose in our lives. If we are to change our behavior, we must be willing to find healthier replacements for the subtle rewards we have derived from them. Largely because it reminds me of something my mother did, Margaret's prodding and pressuring me to do my household jobs may be both vaguely comforting as well as irritating; and for that reason I may resist giving it up. In order to make lasting changes, I may need to learn new ways of making emotional contact with Margaret—other than seducing her into being a nag. In the same vein, if Margaret feels guilty about giving up some of her traditional territory, she may pressure me in a way that will make me feel rebellious; and

thus unconsciously encourage me to resist making the very changes she is asking for.

Lasting change addresses not only the symptoms of our distress, but the underlying needs of both partners.

2. It must be a bilateral agreement. If I am attempting to please Margaret and accommodate to her needs, and if she is not doing the same for me, our relationship could easily fall into a parent-child game in which I am the compliant, and resentful, child.

Two-sided agreements to change force us to look at the bilaterality of our relationship. Women tend to have their lists of "Desired Changes in Husband" close at hand; while men may have to search around a bit for their "Re-design of Wife" blueprints. But we both have such hopes, and we need to expose them, and to negotiate for change.

Since women are more likely to be able to verbalize their discontents, it is especially important that men learn to do the same. One way to ensure this parity is to have balanced "equations": if a man agrees to try to initiate certain changes, he should make parallel requests of his wife. Many men have difficulty speaking assertively about their emotional needs; but unless they learn to do so, they will, out of their hidden resentment, subvert their own intentions to change.

3. Our goals need to be clearly and behaviorally defined. We may not need to write down the specific behaviors each promises to change, but they should be so clear that we are able to.

4. Both partners need time and space in which to make changes—without being reminded or prodded. If we have agreed to change, we should be taken at our word, and not "supervised." Assume that there will be lapses and false starts; and that each of us will test the other's ability to stop reminding and pressuring. I will forget to set the table, and tempt Margaret to nag me about it.

5. Log your own progress. Each person should keep a diary of his or her own behavior in relation to an agreed-upon change. I record my own attempts to initiate conversation, for example, or my progress in getting the table set on time. Monitoring one's own activity takes over the partner's tendency to be that supervising, monitoring agent.

6. Plan a formal review of both partners' changes. Allow time for

changes to occur, but assume that there will be a day of reckoning in which we will sit down and look at our efforts. This "session" should be scheduled at a time when we are likely to be rested and relatively rational.

7. *Regardless of what your partner does, change your own behavior.* Assume that I am so addicted to Margaret's prodding me that I can't seem to give it up. Is she helplessly consigned to being a nag? Of course not. She could go right ahead fixing dinner, and let it sit there getting cold while I, embarrassed, scramble to set the table. This is a simple example, but the principle is vitally important. Contrary to the way it often feels, our behavior is not determined by our partner's behavior. As family therapist Murray Bowen has often counseled, discovering our own freedom to act autonomously is the most important single aspect of breaking out of habitual relationship patterns.

The realization that we can act independently allows us to claim our adult power in a relationship in which we often feel childlike and dependent. This shift in our consciousness represents a kind of infidelity to our established system of games and countergames; but it is a very healthy "betrayal." Jack Gordon's realization that he didn't always have to follow Vicki's directives is a good example: "Then one day last week I realized that I could just say, 'No, Vicki, I can't do that, at least not right now.' It was a small thing, but in a way it felt very big."

We can learn to recognize when we are being induced into playing a role in our partner's "script." We may be at a critical point in an argument, for example, and realize that at this point we usually become defensive, or start yelling, or make some deeply familiar response. Learning that we can make a choice to behave differently, that we can make a truly independent response—this is the beginning of the realization that we have adult freedom in marriage. Our partner will be alarmed when we start making such autonomous moves, but one person's exercise of autonomy legitimizes the other's claiming the same right.

Support is different from "parenting." It is essentially the loving and empathic attentiveness of a peer. In giving support, we do not take resonsibility for the other, though we do care about the other. Often support is communicated through small personal favors, through sensitive acknowledgment of the other's feelings, and through physical touch. We lend our presence, our good will, our caring to the other; and we expect it to be returned in kind.

Women have often learned to be supportive of others. They helped their siblings grow up; and they watched their mothers model this giving response, which women have learned from centuries of caring for children. Because of their histories, women tend to be able to be more supportive of their husbands than their husbands are of them; but they have difficulty asking for and accepting support for themselves. In balancing the marital equation so that both persons feel supported, women often need to be able to ask more directly and forcefully for support; and they may need to learn how to accept it when it is given.

We men have a different set of problems. We probably didn't see our fathers modeling this nurturing, giving response. We also may feel threatened by the idea of giving emotionally to a woman, since we felt threatened by the power of our mothers' emotional needs, needs for which we felt vaguely responsible. Since we "renounced" our needs for mother during the Oedipal period, many of us males also grew up feeling somewhat undernurtured.

Thus we tend to feel threatened by our wives' emotional needs, at the same time that we need their support. We often "sneak" indirect support from our wives: we get them to nag us the way our mothers did; we complain about being overworked; we steal nurturing through sex.

Many of us men also need to learn to ask for emotional support directly, and we need to face the fact that our wives cannot be our only sources of such support. Many of us need deeper levels of male friendship. Some of us need the support of a therapist.

Men also need to learn how to feel loved and cherished for their ability to give emotional support. This was one of the most difficult shifts for me to make: learning that I could get love, attention, good feelings—by giving emotionally to Margaret. It is an absolutely vital shift for men to be able to make, and I will return to it shortly.

Whenever one partner is attempting to be more emotionally responsive to the other—and it is often men who are engaged in this endeavor—that person needs appreciation, encouragement, positive attention for making such changes. One of the best and most satisfying rewards is direct, honest verbal appreciation: "It really feels great when you do these things for me. It makes me feel loved, and I really appreciate you for it."

When I have made an effort to be responsive and attentive to Margaret, that kind of warm, genuine appreciation for my efforts has felt wonderful; and it has been essential in my learning that there were benefits for me in being a more giving partner.

There are dangers in expressing appreciation, of course. If said condescendingly, such comments make us feel like children. Appreciation needs to come from the heart, which never condescends.

17

Men's Work

WHEN WE MOVED TO Atlanta and Margaret began to confront me about my role in our family, I felt defensive, confused, and a little frightened. Was I about to lose my marriage? I didn't think so, but it was clear that our basically traditional relationship was not working. Deeply uneasy about how to make the changes in my own behavior that were obviously in order, I tended to blame myself. It would be some time before I saw Margaret's contributions to maintaining our habitual patterns.

Yes, I was narcissistic, and I counted on Margaret to sacrifice her needs for mine. I did think mainly about myself.

Yes, I was a distancer. Even after nearly fifteen years of marriage, I still found it easy to occupy myself with various projects when I knew that she wanted me to sit down and talk with her over a cup of coffee.

I also realized that I tended to dominate our relationship, though not in a traditional, heavy-handed way. I had *important* things to do; I had many stresses; I needed support. Too nice much of the time, I also had a blazing temper when I finally got angry. A subtly demanding "delegate," I seemed to be able to play the role of Margaret's ambitious and sometimes very angry father, and also the role of her self-sacrificial, but self-centered, mother.

I seemed to assume that Margaret was unremittingly strong; and that whatever happened, she would handle it.

As I thought about myself, I realized with a wince of recognition that I was very much like my father. I had his omnipotence; his neediness; his fierce, sometimes petulant temper; his addictive personality—though mine was to work; his preoccupation with tomorrow; his tendency to neglect those closest to him. In the beginning of that realization I thought mainly of his faults; later I would recall the things I loved about him: his gentleness, his sensitivity, his brilliance, his diverse interests, his easy friendliness. What I had to face was my powerful, but ambivalent, identification with him. Though I was more successful occupationally, in many respects, I had repeated his life.

Attempting to understand myself and my role, I discovered that I had not allowed myself to think much about maleness, or about the forces in men's lives that shape us. Though it seemed puzzling to me at first, I realized that I had actually lived my conscious life in reaction to women. I had apparently struck a bargain with my mother: in return for my being the family's delegate, she would without complaint take care of everything else. When Margaret refused to carry out my mother's part in my script, I felt confused and betrayed. Though it was defensive at first, my instinctive reaction was to reach out to men for support. With something of a shock, I realized that although I had "friends" in Atlanta, I had no close friends. The two men I had developed deeper friendships with, both also students of Whitaker, were in Wisconsin.

For several years, as Margaret and I struggled to get established in Atlanta, and as we also struggled with our own issues, I was conscious of the lack of male friendship in my life. Then, about five years ago, an important shift occurred. Our practice group had recently bought the old house in which we work, and we were busy renovating it. During the several Sunday afternoons we spent scraping and painting, our partner Gail brought her husband Billy to help. Bearded, scrappy, and an incessant talker, Billy is a widely respected ophthalmologist; but something in his offhand remarks made me wonder if he too was a little thrown by the recent changes in his wife. After their four children had left home, Gail had gotten a social-work degree, and she was tremendously excited about being a family therapist. Billy looked a little bewildered by her sudden plunge into her career.

As we worked, Billy and I started talking about men. Though he didn't say it directly, Billy also seemed unhappy about the lack of male support in his life: "I've been operating at this hospital for twenty years, and I don't think I've ever heard a really personal conversation between two male doctors. One guy who had a locker near mine in the surgical dressing room got divorced and I never knew it. We talked twice or so a week, and he never said a thing to me. What kind of life is that?" Billy had made some attempts to develop deeper and more personal friendships: "I invite some of my friends out to our cabin in Colorado to go skiing every year; and even though we have a great time, we rarely talk about anything very personal. We don't even talk about medicine!"

Gail's immersion in the world of psychotherapy had had an effect on Billy; he seemed to be envious of her more intimate work, and of her female friendships. He was also distressed about her recent preoccupation with her clients. Sensing our parallel dilemmas, I finally said to Billy, "Why don't we do something about this lack in our relationships with other men? Let's start a group of men who want to talk more honestly to each other." Billy said he would like to do that.

Each of us came up with three names, and we agreed to call our own candidates. When a couple of weeks passed and neither of us had followed through, Billy finally admitted, "I'm afraid these guys will turn me down." "Me too," I said. So we set ourselves a deadline. As it turned out, everyone we called was eager to join.

There were eight of us: two psychologists, two physicians, a dentist, an architect, a minister, and a commodities broker. The first meeting was at Billy's home, and it was an anxious, uncertain experience. Why were we meeting? "To learn to talk more personally about anything that bothers us, or that interests us," Billy and I suggested. We defined the group as a kind of organized attempt at developing deeper friendships, but not as psychotherapy. The one thing we all seemed interested in talking about was our careers; and so on that theme, which was to be raised again and again, we began a process that four years later is still an active and important part in our lives.

At my suggestion, we also talked about our family histories; and we had not gone very far into those stories when it became obvious that we had all been somewhat mystified by, and often hurt by, our fathers. Initially, these enigmatic figures pervaded our talk. One occupationally successful member was openly scornful of his father, whom he had always seen as weak. "Whatever I got, I got it from my mother," he said. Another described being physically abused by his father, with whom he had never been reconciled. A couple of people had quietly companionable but largely uncommunicative relationships with their fathers, and one of these had helped his father run a family business. One person had been the quiet scholarly son to a tough-minded athletic father whose approval he had never earned. One man saw his well-known father devote his life to a job that seemed to make him unhappy: "As a consequence, I think I have done too much playing in life." Though we had a variety of feelings about our fathers, none of us felt that we really *knew* them.

I felt relieved to be with men who were willing to talk about their relationships with their fathers; and as it turned out, about other aspects of their lives as well—their work, their kids, their marriages.

As we settled into the uncertain work of finding a way of relating to each other, we found common purpose: to deepen our sense of what it was to be men, and to make that experience less lonely and isolated. We all had reasonably satisfying careers; we were all in stable marriages; and we were all interested in being better partners and better parents. We also wanted to have more fun in life. Only one person—whose father had a joyless career—wanted to learn to work harder.

We met every other week for an entire evening in each other's homes; and we had no set agenda. Sometimes we joked and talked trivially; but after a while we settled into serious and increasingly intimate talk. For the first time in my adult life, I felt around me the possibility of peer male support; and I welcomed it.

While this group got down to what felt in the beginning like work, but which later became increasingly enjoyable, the question with which I was struggling at the time continued to haunt me: why do we have such difficulty breaking with our fathers' models? Even if we react like my "playful" friend and devote our lives to the opposite lifestyle, we are still dominated by our fathers' examples. As I thought about this and other questions about men, I began to discover in my clients a new source of information about myself and my own male heritage.

THE LOST OBJECT

John Walker became our client by an inadvertent but for him appropriate route: he married one of our long-term clients. I had begun work with Melanie Lindstrom several years previously, as her first marriage was collapsing; and after a disastrous attempt to work with her abusive family of origin, Margaret and I started seeing her individually. A beautiful woman and an extraordinarily talented sculptor, Melanie had been deeply wounded by her chaotic family; and she was subject to bouts of intense depression.

John is the kind of man who would never have come to therapy for himself, but several months after he and Melanie married, he did come to "help Melanie." In fact, he was the son of a very unstable mother whose rescuer he had been, a stance he transferred to Melanie. A seemingly tough young lawyer in a firm of which his dead father had been a partner, John was impatient with therapy, and impatient with me. "What action can we take today?" he would say irritably. I would suggest with a smile that we could work on helping him be less helpful to Melanie.

At first John would only watch us work with Melanie, and sometimes he offered advice that interfered with what we were trying to do. After we had several tense fights with him about his being an amateur therapist, he became less contentious and just observed. Then, slowly but gradually, Melanie began to bring him into the therapy. "Why do you put up with your work?" she would ask quietly. "The phony parties, the constant pressure, the adversarial crap? I know you don't agree with it all, or you wouldn't have married me." Then she helped us see that part of him that had attracted her: he too was an artist, and he painted beautiful watercolors. He volunteered for the Legal Aid Society. He read widely in psychology and philosophy. And all of this he hid from his colleagues.

With Melanie's subtle encouragement, the gentler, more contemplative side of John emerged; and with it, we became aware of
a quiet battle within him. A part of him was fiercely competitive,
and very ambitious; another part wanted a different kind of life. It
was the second part that had attracted him to Melanie. "Why don't
you leave that place?" she kept asking him. "I don't know," he
admitted.

Then he began to talk about his father. "He was very successful,
very strong and rational in a household that wasn't always that
way"—referring to his mother, whom he always seemed to have
felt responsible for. "My mother was—how can I say it?—not
stable." Though his father sounded like a traditionally well-de-
fended, somewhat driven man, he was stable; and John had idealized him.

John's father died suddenly of a heart attack when John was
barely twenty. "The pressure killed him," John said in a rare tone of
sadness.

"I'm worried it will do the same to you," Melanie said lovingly.

"I know," John admitted, "but I can't seem to stop what I'm
doing."

This battle within John became more pronounced with time,
and it became a source of conflict in their marriage. "I can't stand
the parties," Melanie would complain. "I'm not going to them."
John went alone; jogged to deal with the stress; and when he had
time, painted.

One day John came to a session looking extremely sad. When
we asked what had happened, he said, "I don't know what is going
on. I was elected to the management group in the firm. When they
announced it, there was a lot of applause; and later, some of my
father's old friends came up and said they knew he would be proud
of me. When I got home and told Melanie about it, I started crying,
and I couldn't stop. I have some idea what's going on, but I certainly
feel confused."

"Something to do with your father, I would guess," I said.

"You're probably right," he admitted. "He was the head of the
management group when he died. It's like I made it to where he
was."

"When he died, did you grieve about him openly?" I asked.

"I don't think so. There was my mother to look after."

"My thought is," I said, "that you have been trying to reach him by being like him. Trying to find out what his life was like, what he was like. And, I suppose, trying to earn his approval as well." After a pause, I added: "And you've done it. Reached him, as it were. And now you can grieve."

John looked at me warmly, tears streaming down his tanned, lawyerly face. After composing himself for a moment, he said with a smile, "I know what that's called. Identification with the lost object. Freud."

"That's exactly right," I said.

For the next year, John would find himself thinking about his father, and suddenly he would be crying. He stayed on the management group and did well in his job. But as he grieved about his father, who had been dead for ten years, he began to lose interest in the large, high-stakes firm that had cost his father his life. And with rather wide eyes, he began looking around for what he wanted to do with the remainder of his own life.

While Freud referred to the tendency for someone like John who has lost a parental "object" (or person) early in life to become *like* that person in an effort to replace or to know them, I began to see a larger significance in John's experience. It occurred to me that we men have such difficulty breaking with our fathers' examples in part because our fathers are all to some degree "lost objects." That is, we don't know them; we yearn for them to be a more intimate presence in our lives; and in order to understand what their lives felt like, we repeat some aspect of their histories.

Only after John had "joined" his father symbolically—and one could also do this by failing in the same way that one's father did—was he able to turn him loose, grieve over his death; and not only be released from him, but from the way his father had lived his life.

Many men of course live very different lives from their fathers; indeed, some of us seem determined to be almost the polar opposites. Even then, however, we are dominated by our fathers' examples; we simply attempt to live the life they did not live. Sometimes this effort makes us identify with a single, hidden aspect of our fathers. My friend in the men's group who saw his father as so purposeful and joyless, and who has been just as purposefully "playful," is of course "acting out" his father's unexpressed side.

Margaret and I are currently working with a family in which the son is struggling with painful feelings of inferiority in relationship to his powerful, driven, "successful" father. What this creative, emotionally open and expressive young man has a hard time seeing is that—partly in response to his mother's needs for companionship, but partly in response to the buried emotionality in his father—he is the kind of person his father needs to learn to become more like; and that he has a lot to teach his father. As this impressive young man reaches out to his father through a history of rejection and neglect, often crying as he does so, he forces his father to confront the long-denied, tenderly emotional "boy" within himself.

Whatever our "agenda" with our fathers, we seem to be searching for them, hoping to complete our relationship with them. This search occurs in women as well, though it is not as central to their being able to form identities as women; it is, however, important for girls to have a warm and caring relationship with a male figure from childhood if they are to have healthy and successful marriages.

As I began to see fathers as "lost objects" in the lives of their sons, I discovered that a great many of our male clients fit this pattern. Even if these men's lives were superficially different from their fathers', their feelings about life, and their essential emotional dilemmas, were very similar to their fathers'. There are obviously better ways of knowing our fathers than repeating their patterns. If a man's father is alive, he can make a concerted effort to get to know his father more intimately; and many older fathers are willing to reveal more about themselves than they once were. Even if a man's father is dead, however, it is still possible to get to know him.

SEARCHING FOR MY FATHER

Perhaps because I had a forum, and incipient support from other men, I began to try to learn more about my father. I went through old photographs, reread my old letters from him; finally, I allowed myself to see the obvious: my beloved aunt, my father's oldest sister, lived several blocks from me, and she knew a great deal about him.

I saw Atu, a nickname coined by one of her younger siblings who couldn't manage Alice, regularly; and so on my weekly visits to the retirement community where she lived, I began to ask questions.

Now in her late eighties, Atu is a tall, gracious, distinguished woman whose presence conveys warmth and friendliness, and also commands respect. She was an admired teacher and school administrator, and her former students often pay the kind of call on her that I did: basking in her warm company, seeking her wisdom. Sitting amid the paintings and books that recalled my childhood, we talked about the latest course she was taking at Emory University, about her other "pleasure reading," and, with increasing regularity, about my father.

Sensing what I needed to know, she proceeded cautiously, but willingly. "What was my father's relationship with his father like?" I eventually asked.

"I don't think it was very good. Father was often harsh with him, and cool. They were just not close. Of course," she added, "Father believed in discipline. Both he and Mother did, and there were whippings from them regularly. I suppose today you might call them beatings."

"But he was especially harsh with my father?" I asked.

"Yes, I think so. I believe that Father was jealous of him; and in a way I can understand it; Gus was very special in Mother's eyes." I urged her to go on. "You know about Rene?" I knew that he was one of my father's siblings who had died when he was an infant. "It was such a sad thing. He was a charming, wonderful baby, and one day when he was about a year old he got very sick; he was dead in a week. It was terribly hard for us all, but because he was a doctor, Father felt helpless at not being able to save him. And Mother was devastated, really devastated. She was very depressed for months. Then, when she became pregnant with your father, she seemed to improve." So my father had been born just after the death of their youngest child.

"I remember clearly the night your father was born. I was about eight years old, and Leroy and Jean [her younger brother and sister] and I stayed up all night, listening for sounds in Mother's and Father's room. Of course Father delivered all the children. Once we heard crying, and then we drifted off to sleep; when we woke up

Gus was here, and we all went in." She paused, describing the house, the sunlit rooms, the hushed gathering around the new baby. "Later, when I was older, Mother told me that when Gus was born, the room was flooded with rosy light. She said that she knew then that he was a special, blessed child, sent to her from God to replace Rene."

Silence, while I took in what I had sensed: that my father had struggled all his life with his mother's obsession with him; that he had repeatedly tried to break away from her, probably unsuccessfully. "So that was what made my grandfather jealous—her fixation on my father?"

"I think so," she said softly. "She always favored Gus, and the rest of us were jealous too. I know we picked on him." She looked sad, regretting what she now understood.

A flicker of memory prompted my next question: "Didn't Grandmother also lose a parent early in life?"

"Both of them, really. It's a painful story." I encouraged her to go on. "Your grandmother was the youngest of thirteen children. They were planters, and before the war they were very well off financially; but who can take care of that many children? Then, when Mother was three, her mother died. For a while she lived with her father, but when she was nine he got into a fight with a man who was trying to take the family's land, and he was killed. It was the Reconstruction Era in the South, and that happened often then. Mother went to live with an older brother and his wife; but she was finally taken in by another couple who were dear friends of the family. They were really her adoptive parents, I suppose."

"So when Rene died," I suggested, "it would have reawakened the losses from her early years."

"I'm sure it did," Atu said pensively. "I hadn't thought of that."

"And when my father was born, he became her savior, as it were. The one who comforted her in her grief." How old this story is, women seeking comfort in caretaking their children. I thought about my grandparents: first my grandmother, who by the time I knew her had broken her hip and was being cared for by Atu. Even in her weakened condition, she seemed vaguely problematic for me as a child. She was fragile, imperious, demanding, and everyone circled obediently around her; and she could make me feel guilty about any number of things, from the way I sat in a chair to my table manners.

And then my grandfather, whom I knew only through his stern, serious photographs; and from the stories about him. A beloved physician, he had traveled to see his patients over a fifty-square-mile territory. In spite of his harshness at home, Atu spoke admiringly, almost reverently of him. My father had never spoken of him at all. "Tell me about your father's family," I asked.

"He was the fourth of eight children; and all of the boys in that family were successful. They were lawyers and doctors and college professors." That was a theme we had talked about before, but it was not what interested me.

"Who was he closest to, which parent?" I asked.

"I don't think either parent; or I never heard him speak of them in those terms. I think he was closest to his sister Alice, whom I'm named for." I remembered her clearly, a staunch, proper, unmarried Victorian who had taught mathematics in a Georgia college for fifty years.

On a guess, I asked; "Was there a younger brother whom he might have felt jealous of when he was a child?"

"Perhaps it could have been Jack, the baby of the family. I believe he might have felt jealous of him." Then it all made sense: my father's mother fixated on him, and his father, who had grown up lost in the middle of eight children, was jealous of him, as he had been jealous of his younger brother.

When I heard these stories, and others that came as we talked, my anger at my father began to give way. I could feel it slipping into forgiveness—and into a kind of melancholy empathy for him. It was hard to be angry at any of them, those harshly disciplined, well-meaning people who struggled with life as it was then, when parents and children died suddenly and too early, and when there was little permission for anyone to cry out, much less ask for help. Atu talked on, and I took notes; but the essential shift had occurred; I had forgiven my father.

I systematically revisited several painful scenes. In one of them we were having a picnic on a sandbar on the river, and he kept coming at me with hard, biting criticism; then he would turn to my sister and speak tenderly to her. I could now see him in my role, and his father coming at him in that way. So he did to me what his father had done to him.

I also began to recall things, mostly experiences, that my father had given me. The beagle he had brought me on one of his army leaves, the time he had smuggled me into the belly of a B-29 bomber at the base where he was stationed, the feel of his standing beside me as he taught me how to hold his army pistol, the fishing trips that came later when he was out of the army, the time we sweated together cutting the brush out of the garden when he moved our family back to the house he had grown up in. The times he had tried to get me to work in his garden with him. I could feel his presence, sometimes strong and loving; only occasionally abandoning and harsh.

And I remembered several stories he had told me. Most of them were oblique comments said as we were cutting wood together for the fireplace, or fishing together. One was about the loneliness of being financially responsible for a family: "It feels very anxious to know your whole family depends on what you earn." Several were confessional: "I'd had a number of serious relationships with women by the time I was your age." But one was about courage: "When I was about twenty years old and fresh out of college, I was pretty frail and thin, and the doctor told me that I would never live to be thirty. It made me mad, and I said to myself, 'I'll show him.' So I started swimming three miles a day, up and down Little River, and I did that for the year I was teaching school there. And that was the last time I heard that kind of talk from a doctor."

Although a combination of forces which I had probably never encountered had finally defeated him, I realized that at least as a young man, he had been fiercely determined; and that discovery helped me identify with him in a new and more hopeful way.

SEARCHING FOR A PLACE TO STAND

Learning that I could forgive my father for some of his failures—his angry outbursts, his criticism, his frequent neglect of our relationship, his drinking—did not actually remove my anger. It merely placed it in a larger context in which I could feel empathy for his life situation. But I still felt angry about some of the things that had happened between us.

During that period, I was a member of Al Pesso's training groups. Pesso's approach—which the reader will recall from the angry confrontation that the young psychologist had with a role-play "father," described in Chapter 2—is ideally suited to someone attempting to come to grips with strong feelings about a person who is dead or otherwise unavailable. Even though Al was in Atlanta only twice a year, I realized that his visits offered me an opportunity to work "symbolically" on my relationship with my father.

The remarkable thing about Pesso's approach is that it allows one to do things in a symbolic environment which would never be possible in "real life." We tend to accept what happened to us at the hands of our parents as law, as emotional "givens." The power of psychomotor structures lies in their capacity to reorganize our perceptions of what is possible for us. "I could never express such anger to my parents," we say to ourselves, giving up on our feelings. "I could never have a parent love me in that way," we say with a sigh.

Our lives have an implicit order. Within this form we carry out dialogues with important figures, and we live out our part in a complex story which involves many others. We become psychologically "stuck" in this history when there is a blatant injustice, or an incomplete sequence: "My father and I loved each other, and although he told me he loved me, I never told him that I loved him." Since he died before I could tell him that I loved him, I am a prisoner of unexpressed emotion within this relationship. The same could be true of anger: "My father got furiously angry at me, but I could never get angry back." So I am a prisoner of this unexpressed emotion, which is my side of the angry "dialogue."

We also become caught in our historical families by our sense of injustice: I deserved to be loved by my parents (a universal human longing), but I wasn't. Therefore, I am imprisoned by what should have happened between us, but didn't. I can't leave my family psychologically until I feel loved by them.

We would all prefer to work out these dialogues in person, to "balance" them by expressing our side of the relationship; and we would like to have been treated justly by our families. But it is not always possible. After having failed us in childhood, our parents refuse to talk with us, they become frail, they die. Sometimes we have to finish the dialogue within our own heads, to "make it right" symbolically—so that we can go on with our lives; and so that we can find what we need from others. Psychomotor work allows us to do such things safely, and within our own control. It is not as satisfying as honest talk with real parents, or as useful as a healthy childhood. But if we need it, it can be extremely helpful.

I did several "structures" with Al, but I remember the first one most clearly. It took place in the same bare, carpeted room which I have already described, sunlit and circled by other students. Sitting in the center of the circle before this smiling, jeans-and-sneaker-clad figure as he set his electronic timer, I felt extremely anxious. What would I say that I wanted to work on? I wasn't sure, though I sensed that it had to do with my father.

Suddenly I was talking: "I want to work on my father. His problems, my problems with him."

"Can you tell me something about those problems?" Al asked warmly, watching me carefully as I talked about my family history.

As I described some of my anger at my father, I said, "I think what bothered me most was the sense of his weakness"—and my voice broke—"and the realization that he often wasn't there." Then I added, "But I have difficulty even feeling my anger toward him."

Al pointed out that my voice had broken when I used the word "weakness," and then he waited to see what my reaction would be. Sensing the accuracy of his probe, I felt tears welling up inside me; then just as rapidly, they receded. "You close down on your feelings very quickly," he observed. I knew that it was true; insight into myself I had. What I didn't have was the freedom to feel strongly and spontaneously.

Silence, while Al thought, the group watching intently. Outside in the hall I could hear the quiet hiss of the coffee maker. "Let me make a suggestion," he said. "Why don't you choose someone to role-play an ideal father, someone who would be strong."

At the mention of this possibility, I felt a roil of excitement, fear, anxiety. "Okay," I said tentatively, looking around the room. Finally I settled on a tall, strong-looking man whom I liked. "Would you role-play an ideal father?" I asked.

"I will role-play an ideal father," he said in the ritual convention of Pesso's work, rising and walking out into the center of the room. I immediately stood up.

"That's interesting," Pesso said, noting my getting up to meet this new figure. After another moment of silence, he said, "What do you feel like doing?"

"I don't know," I said tentatively. "I don't trust him, somehow."

"Of course not," Pesso said. "Why would you?" Then he added, "Let me make a suggestion. Why don't you try pushing on him, to get an idea of his strength." Then he instructed the role player to take a stand, one leg braced behind him to resist my efforts, and he showed me how to place my hands on the front of his shoulders. I recalled one of the drills in high school football in which one player braced himself while the other tried to push him backward.

As I sensed this man's solidity before me—he was slightly larger than I was, and carefully positioned—I felt a rush of energy. With a broad smile, I pushed hard, and he struggled to maintain his balance. "That's where your energy is," Al said with interest. "You liked that."

I was about to push again, harder this time, when Al interrupted me. "Wait. You might repeat your history here." He was apparently worried that I might overpower the role player, and experience him as unreliable. Turning to the group, he quickly enlisted four other men to brace the ideal father. "Now try," Al said with a smile.

This time when I pushed, the ideal father didn't budge. He was a solid wall of masculinity. I pushed harder, straining to keep my feet from slipping. "Take your socks off so you can get a good grip on the floor," Al advised.

Eager to try again, I quickly stripped off my socks and braced myself before the role-play father. Feeling another sudden burst of energy, I put my hands against his shoulders and pushed with all my might. This time my feet held firm, but so did the ideal father. The sense that this man was truly immovable released in me a primitive mixture of rage and delight. "You look like you still think you can defeat him," Al said. "Try it again," he urged.

Aware of my father's vulnerability, and his punitiveness, I had learned to monitor and conceal much of my own power. My contact with a "strong" figure allowed me to feel that my force could be contained, bounded by someone outside myself; and thus I was able to feel and to express my feelings, particularly my anger, more directly.

With almost certain conviction that I could topple not only this figure but the four men who backed him up, I put my shoulder aggressively into the ideal father's stomach, lowered my stance to gain more power, and pushed with all my might. Although the ideal father staggered slightly behind my push, and exhaled with surprise, the men supporting him held firm. I tried again, this time letting out a long, agonized groan as I strained repeatedly against this immovable group. Somewhere in this long groan, which was a mixture of agony and relief, something in me gave way, gave up. Perhaps it was my lonely omnipotence, my conviction gained during my father's long absence in the war years that I was responsible for the entire world and must somehow manage to be all-powerful. Perhaps it was the sense that I could overpower my father. With this giving way came a great relief.

Suddenly all my impulse to challenge the ideal father was gone, and like a defeated boxer, I sagged toward the floor. Seeing the shift in my bearing, Al guided me. "You look like you want to rest." Breathing hard, exhausted from all the physical effort, I sat down on my knees in front of the ideal father. It was a moment of vulnerability: defeated by the exercise, I felt lonely, conspicuous before the group.

My head must have tilted toward one side, because Al then commented, "You look like you want to lie down." Accepting his sure interpretation of my body's language, I lay down on the floor, curling up protectively. Now I felt even more alone, and of course Al saw that too. "Would you like some support from the ideal father?" he asked gently.

"Yes, I guess so," I said.

"Why don't you kneel beside him," Al instructed the ideal father. "What if he put his hand on your shoulder?"

"Fine," I said, feeling better as the man followed Al's instructions. "What is going on? What are you feeling?" Al asked.

"I'm remembering a time when I was a kid," I said dreamily. Perhaps it was the solitariness of lying curled up on the floor, but I suddenly had a memory from the war years. My mother, my sister and I had gone to spend the summer with my father, who was stationed at a base in New Jersey, and we had just taken up residence in an apartment near the base. On one of our first days there, my father took me—I must have been four or five years old—with him to the army base. I suppose my mother had instructed him that I would need a nap in the afternoon; so after a morning of seeing the wonders of guns and barracks and marching men, I found myself on a wood and canvas cot in an enormous, sunlit tent, instructed to take my nap. My father was an officer, so I suppose he was allowed to take a nap too. His cot was on the other side of this great, sun-buzzed space, and before long he was sleeping soundly.

Delighted to be with my father again after nearly a year's absence, and stimulated by all that I had seen in the morning, I was too excited to sleep; so I lay there feeling a mixture of pleasure at having a father again, and frustration and loneliness at the immense distance at which his cot and his sleeping seemed to place him. I had the clearest, most agonizing impulse to go over and snuggle up with him on the cot, to nuzzle into his great male armyness, to soak up the fathering I had missed. But I knew it was forbidden; that he would only be angry if I did it. And so I lay on the cot waiting forever for his nap to be over, listening to the sound of a fly trapped in the tent like the hot, airless sunlight itself.

As I recounted the outline of this memory to Al, he said warmly, "Maybe we could recreate the scene as you would have liked it to have been." Suddenly I felt anxious, exposed, and my posture must have tightened visibly, because Al said, "That make you anxious?"

"Yes," I said flatly.

"Your father wouldn't have approved," he suggested.

"Good old homosexual anxiety," I said, acknowledging my awareness of this common issue for so many men.

Al said, "We could go several ways with this. We could work on your father's anxiety about closeness to his son, or we could stick with the ideal father. Do you have any sense of which way you want to go?"

I could still feel the reassuring presence of the ideal father beside me, and I communicated this awareness to Al. "Let's have him say what you would have wanted to hear from an ideal father, then," Al suggested. When I nodded approval, he added, "What would that be?"

"He would say that he would not be anxious or disapproving if his son who hadn't seen him in a year wanted to curl up and snuggle with him."

Al instructed the ideal father, who said, "If I had been your father, I wouldn't be anxious or disapproving if I hadn't seen you for a year and you wanted to curl up and snuggle with me." As the ideal father said the words, I could feel myself relax a little. I remembered the warm containment of the tent again, the sound of my father's breathing. "Anything else?" Al asked.

I said, "He could say that it would be all right if I curled up and snuggled with him."

The ideal father said: "It would be all right if you curled up and snuggled with me."

"Do you want to try this?" Al asked matter-of-factly.

"I guess so," I said, still keeping my eyes closed, hanging on to the memory of my father.

With some coaching from Al, who took his cues from me, the role player lay down beside me on the floor, facing in the same direction that I was, and draped his arm over my side. For a moment I felt anxious again, but then I recalled the ideal father's reassuring words, and relaxed into the fantasy that this was a father who was not worried or ashamed about his son's healthy need to be comforted physically. Aware of the group's also relaxed, beneficent presence, and of Al's easy comfort with this scene, I drifted into a reverie of contentment, feeling the heavy, protective arm of the ideal father over me. I have no idea how long I had been lying there, half-asleep, relaxing into the floor and into the fantasy, when I heard the tiny beep-beep of Al's electronic timer.

"Take a little longer," Al said, and for another minute or two I held on to the scene, clasping in my memory the reassuring comfort of this kind of father. When I finally opened my eyes and blinked as I looked around the room, I was greeted by the caring, respectful faces of the other participants. The ideal father resigned from his role with a smile and said his own name, and I rose and again took my familiar seat by the wall.

I did a number of other structures with Al in the next couple of years: one very angry one in which I vented much of my frustration with my father; one in which my ideal father became playful and humorous; and one tearful one in which I said goodbye to the aspects of my father that I loved. But the first structure I have always carried as a special talisman, and over the next few years it became a metaphor around which I built my struggle to be that kind of man: one who stands firm and strong, and who can bend to nurture. To this group of images I attached all the principles of this kind of maleness, this kind of being; a model toward which I tried, often with difficulty, to live.

SEARCHING FOR MY CHILDREN

While Margaret's confrontations with me at the time of our Atlanta move helped catalyze my efforts at being a more attentive husband and father, those arguments between us, and my efforts to change, had been going on for a long time. But I don't believe that I really addressed my role inside our family until my role outside our family—my work—had begun to be successful. However much I would like it to have been different, at the time when I was needed most, it seemed imperative that my work take precedence.

Margaret dates Julia's birth as marking the real change in my attitude toward my children. "You seemed a little afraid of infants," she said to me recently, "but I never doubted your love for our children. You played with them, read to them a lot, took them to the zoo and the fire station. What I had difficulty with you about was the level of your active responsibility for them. I had problems getting you to worry about them the way I did, and getting you to be more assertive in intervening in their lives—going to school conferences, for example. Keeping up with when their medical checkups were due. Remembering that it was time to start thinking about their summer plans."

Not only was I involved in Julia's birth, which helped me feel deeply connected with her; but when she was born I felt a great deal of responsibility for Mark. Having had a captivating younger sister, I saw his jealousy of Julia very clearly, and I realized that I could help him. He and I began going camping together, and we did other "male" things which helped him feel a little less displaced. Those activities broadened with time to include backpacking, canoeing, and eventually kayaking. When we moved to Atlanta and Mark began playing soccer, I became an ardent fan; I went to every game. Sometimes I would get extremely angry with Mark, but my involvement with him was clear. At times I have been too attentive to Mark; and afraid of neglecting him the way I felt neglected by my father, I risk instead being indulgent.

I found it more awkward to parent my girl children, especially Sarah, who always seemed so strong and competent, and with whom I sometimes fought. Sarah dealt with both Mark's and Julia's births by becoming Margaret's "co-parent," a role that put us in conflict as I became a more active parent. Sensitive, intense, and extremely verbal, Sarah has always reminded me of a combination of my mother and my sister; an association that has both helped and hindered our relationship. As she got older, Sarah and I discovered that we had a great many interests in common. We both like to write, both enjoy photography, and, as it turned out, we are both psychologists. We have worked on being less competitive, and over the years our relationship has eased into a friendly and companionate one.

Perhaps because of her sunny disposition and her sense of basic security, parenting Julia has never seemed conflictual. We have had a friendly, fond relationship, and one that I have tended to take for granted, as if she would be our child forever. I worry that in an effort not to make Mark jealous, I have subtly neglected Julia. I have trouble setting limits with her, and following what she is doing in a close and attentive way. Thankfully, we also have several interests in common—writing, soccer, the theater—and several more years together. This time I will get it right; this time . . .

Over the years, I have learned to worry about my children, to parent them more actively, to be in their lives in a more direct and supportive way. But in actuality it has never been easy. Margaret's confrontations and entreaties have helped; but most of the effort has come out of my own determination. And perhaps I got that from my father.

It has been useful to have the men's group to turn to, and to feel supported by the efforts of other men who were working at being better parents. I have seen some group members with older children struggling to help these adult children deal with the problems that came out of their early histories, and these early warnings have enabled me to anticipate some issues in my own family. This is also one of the benefits of being a therapist: learning from the mistakes of others—not that I don't still make plenty of my own.

Today when I see young fathers in the airports and grocery stores—those vast arenas in which I do my nonclinical research—I envy the easy way in which they hold and care for their children; and wish I had begun earlier on being a more deeply involved father. But then I see those preoccupied, harried, staunch carriers of briefcases, those men whose children are never with them and who look oblivious to their needs, and I feel a little better. I am at home most evenings; I go to the school conferences now; and even if I'm not at every soccer game, at least I know the score.

This part of being a man, changing the way we parent, happens only when we want it to. It changes because we are determined for it to change; and the motive for changing often comes out of wanting to be the kind of parent we didn't have. Our parents wanted the same thing, and though we will fail as they failed, the effort, the will, the intent to parent effectively and lovingly eventually makes a difference. For all his difficulties, my father's determination comes back to me: I hear it in the slow, steady slip-splash of his arms rising and falling as he swam past the white sandbars, under the low-hanging willows, beside the cypress swamps; and the sound echoes through my life.

18

Couple's Work

As I began work on this chapter, I felt strangely uneasy. "How," I asked myself, "does one write the conclusion to a continuing story?" Of course I knew I had to face where Margaret and I had been, and where we seemed to be headed.

My anxiety about ending the book made me irritable for several days, and I found myself provoking petty fights with Margaret. One night after one of these conflicts, I took our dog for her usual walk, and found myself having a half-conscious internal dialogue with a decidedly superstitious voice in my head.

"What if I reveal that the two of us have worked out some critical struggles in our relationship?" I proposed.

The voice answered: "I'm not sure I'd recommend that. You wrote *The Family Crucible* as you were leaving your ties with Whitaker. Maybe you'll do the same thing with Margaret. Maybe you'll keep acting like this, for example."

"And what would happen?" I asked the voice.

"Maybe she'll leave you." There it was again, that old fear, like a hole in my tooth that I couldn't keep my tongue out of. "Then think how ridiculous you will look."

"All the evidence is to the contrary," I replied. "I am the distancer, and the one who left her the first time we tried to get married."

The voice wouldn't give up. "But you know that is a defense, that in your heart of hearts you are afraid she will leave you. So always you leave her first." Then the voice added: "Do you really think she will stay with you for the rest of your life? Think about what your mother did," recalling an early incident of which I had recently become aware.

I had to admit that I was skeptical. "Maybe you're right," I admitted.

Then I heard another voice, a woman's, friendly and firm. "As a child you didn't have many choices. But as an adult you do. You can't control what Margaret does, but you can certainly influence it. And you don't have to stage your childhood issues in your relationship with her." It was Jackie Damgaard, an Atlanta psychologist whose clients we had been for the past two years. Sometimes that is all it takes, a friendly voice in the night, someone to interrupt all that anxious doubting.

"So I'll risk writing about it," I said to myself, "and I'll be as honest as I can." Like the uncertainties of fate, the doubting voice was still there, but it was quieter now.

The changes in my relationships with our children which I have described were helped along because for a couple of evenings a week over a period of several years, Margaret left me with them. In spite of my effort to support her interests, Margaret's increasing involvement with Paideia School felt to me like a kind of abandonment. I tried to ignore these feelings; I finally coped with them.

In October 1982, after her responsibilities on the Paideia board of trustees had been growing for several years, Margaret got a distressing call from her parents, who were at their home in New York. Her father was very ill, and was on the way to the hospital when he called. "He sounded terrible," Margaret told me later. "He said, 'I guess this is it for me, baby,' in the saddest voice, and I almost broke down on the phone."

It would be Margaret's last real communication with this captivating, powerful man. In the weeks that followed, her father struggled to survive a devastatingly virulent pneumonia. And through the extreme medical intervention of Paul's physician, who had also been his friend, Paul's body did survive; but the person he had been did not. For the next cruel and agonizing year, Margaret's father edged day by day toward death. In and out of the hospital, sometimes he would recognize us, and sometimes he would not.

Flying back and forth from Atlanta to Albany, Margaret did what she could to help her mother with Paul's care. There were special nurses, but most of the burden fell on Margaret's mother; and since her sister Elizabeth lived in Arizona, on Margaret. Again, I looked after our children when Margaret was out of town.

As his condition worsened, Paul began to be more disoriented, and he sometimes had terrible anxiety attacks. Throughout the long ordeal of that year, Margaret's mother was loyal, dutiful, and stoic. She had always felt overshadowed by Paul's charismatic presence; and now, as she faced the horrors of his decline, Clora felt abandoned by Paul, frightened by the intensity of his needs, and resentful of her burdens. She badly needed someone to listen to her frustrations and anger, and she turned to Margaret.

In June 1983, Margaret assumed the chairmanship of the Paideia board; and it soon became apparent that she would have to oversee a multimillion-dollar fund-raising effort for a new gym and theater. A month later her father died, incoherent and in agony. I had made some of the trips with Margaret, and I wish I had made more, especially at the end. After the last visit to Paul's bedside, Margaret's face seemed vacant, staring into the tragedy of her father's dissolution; and then came the call that he had died. I held her, and we both cried about the loss of the cheerful, vibrant, witty man he had been.

And then nothing happened. It was as if there was a great long silence. Paul had not wanted a service, and Clora didn't approve of them either; so there wasn't one. Composed, exhausted, Clora pulled herself together; and the rest of us stood there, wondering how to mourn this man we had loved. "It was almost as if he had never existed," Margaret said of her mother's refusal to grieve.

Years of living with her mother's jealousy of her relationship with her father blocked Margaret's ability to feel her grief openly. I could see Margaret edge toward her tears, and then back away. Turning to her own life where there was plenty to do, she mourned silently and alone. "You need to cry," I said. "I can't seem to," she said.

Now it was Margaret who escaped into the many hours of work which the Paideia board required. She was at the limits of her capacity, and for some reason I wasn't able to help her. I tried, of course, but she often didn't ask for much help; and I was frequently preoccupied with myself and my own projects. Outside our home, both of us were taking on too much work, shouldering too many burdens. As Paideia's demands increased, Margaret simply asked more of herself: meeting with parents, visiting classrooms, working with the headmaster and with another board member to meet the two-million-dollar fund-raising goal. All this was in addition to her practice, and the still strenuous demands of our kids and our complex household.

At home, I was able to let down and rest, partly because Margaret continued in her usual role—shepherding, directing, looking after us all. For a while, this frenetic pace may have helped her avoid her grief, but her rage at the unfairness of her situation began to intrude into our relationship. She was demandingly critical of me, and of the kids; and yet, with a kind of fierce determination, she didn't seem willing to change the way she lived.

Gradually recovering from the ordeal of Paul's care, Margaret's mother began to face being alone. She wanted to travel, to do some of the things she had been denied in the latter years of her marriage; and she wanted company. Always eager to please her mother, Margaret invited her for long visits, and Clora went with us on several family vacations.

Though she was so active, and often seemed cheerful enough, I knew that Margaret felt alone and depressed. She not only had difficulty talking about her feelings, but her overworking left little energy for the two of us. Though she felt deserted by her father, and unsupported by me, I also felt abandoned by her. For the first time in our marriage, I began to have serious fantasies of having an affair. "Somewhere," I said to myself, "there must be a woman who will offer me something, who will be supportive, understanding." Knowing it would be a mistake to act on these fantasies, I began to look for a therapist for the two of us.

Finding a really skilled therapist is a chancy, difficult business; and it is especially hard for therapists themselves, who may be good at helping others but often resist being patients. I had met Jackie

Damgaard when she asked me to consult on several of her cases. After these brief consultations, I found myself talking openly to her, and a couple of times I felt vaguely uneasy in her presence. Though I didn't know at the time what my discomfort was about, I sensed that this woman had a lot to give me. Working without a co-therapist, she was tough, smart, and very warm. It was that unusual combination of qualities that drew me to her, and that led me to suggest to Margaret that we see her.

Skeptical, Margaret agreed to see Jackie largely because she was concerned about the way our stresses were affecting Sarah and Mark; and for most of the first year of our work with Jackie, we saw her as a family. During that time Jackie and I had the first skirmishes in her long battle to get me to be a patient. I tended to align myself subtly with Jackie, and to offer my family insight into our problems.

With a disconcerting mixture of warmth and firmness, Jackie challenged me. "Gus, your family needs to hear about your feelings; they don't need your professional self. They need to know *you*." When my helpful insights were blocked, I floundered, slipping into self-blame. "I know I let them all down. I often fail my family, particularly Margaret."

"Can you see how that kind of self-attack affects them?" Jackie said, challenging me further. "It makes them feel guilty about asking things from you." Margaret had been worried that she would be labeled the family's problem, and seeing Jackie confront me about being a patient helped her accept the therapy.

As our marital issues came more to the foreground, we began meeting with Jackie as a couple; and she intensified her assault on my "expert" status. I gave her plenty to work with. I came late to sessions; I paid our bill late; I insisted on challenging Jackie's interpretations. "Gus, it's fairly subtle, but you have an arrogant, almost omnipotent quality, as though you don't trust anybody to help you. And you seem determined to stay in a one-up position with me."

I had to admit that it was true. My mother had deferred to me; Margaret had tried extremely hard to please me; I wasn't sure I trusted a woman therapist to be strong enough for me to lean on her. With that annoying combination of warmth and toughness, Jackie kept coming at me. "Gus, I want to hear your feelings, not your ideas. You are not the therapist here. I am. And I want you to stop interpreting Margaret." Then she added, "I know what this is like, because I have been guilty of exactly the same thing. The cost of this kind of 'parenting' in your intimate relationships is not only putting your partner at a distance, but also means that you are not getting any real support yourself."

Jackie's challenge of my helpful, expert role made me furious; it also left me feeling confused and strangely tearful. Feeling her strength, and the caring that lay within it, I began to feel supported by her as well. Eventually I would be grateful to her for taking me on.

In a much gentler way, Jackie also reached out to Margaret, attempting to offer her support, and also challenging her self-sacrificial, overextended commitments to others. "I worry for your health, Margaret," she said repeatedly. Hearing the terrible bind Margaret felt in with her difficult-to-please mother, she encouraged her to limit what she did for her, and to be on guard against her often indirect criticism.

Jackie also helped us see the structure of our relationship more clearly, and she issued clear and emphatic directives to help us change. We already knew that when power issues were clear and out in the open, Margaret and I were equally matched. I was a parental, oldest kid in a family in which males had special status; and I was also a delegate. An atypical youngest child, Margaret was the family mediator; and in addition to being her family's delegate, she was parental with both her parents. She had also learned a lot from her father about controlling people. When we squared off, each of us brought a lot of power and authority to an argument; so much that we tended to be afraid of head-to-head confrontations. "You have a good deal of accumulated anger at each other," Jackie said matter-of-factly. "We need to find a way for you to deal with it constructively."

But in dealing with each other's vulnerability and needs for support, we tended to miss each other. I complained that while Margaret often tried to please me by doing special things for me, I didn't feel that I got much emotional support. "What I see, Gus," Jackie countered, "is your using what the transactional therapists call 'racket feelings,' or feelings expressed to gain attention manipulatively. You complain in a martyred kind of way about your stresses and needs, with the implication that Margaret is supposed to make things right for you."

That stung, but it felt right. I remembered my mother clucking anxiously over my temperamental father. Jackie wouldn't let up. "Furthermore," she said, "when Margaret tries to talk to you about her needs, you tend to bring the conversation back to you. Or you get defensive. Or you blame yourself in a way that implies that she is being unfair to you." And as Margaret and I negotiated with each other, Jackie began to interrupt me when I started to maneuver Margaret's attention back to my needs.

She also began to be a little more confrontive with Margaret. "You have such trouble letting yourself be vulnerable," she chided her. "And you rarely let anyone support you. Like me, for example." Pointing out how often she had tried to give Margaret support, and how often she had been rebuffed, and reminding Margaret that when she asked me to do something for her she often turned around and did that very thing herself, Jackie made a forceful plea to Margaret to allow herself to ask for and to accept more emotional support from others, but especially from me.

I was forbidden to talk to Margaret about my stresses, and encouraged to bring those issues to Jackie. Margaret was instructed to make regular requests of me. Jackie also helped me begin to listen more carefully to Margaret's feelings and needs, and to respond to her requests for "special favors." With Jackie coaching me, I began to initiate social events—like buying tickets to a concert series that I knew Margaret would enjoy. Systematically, with the assumption that we would need to practice making these changes, Jackie coached us on reorganizing our relationship so that Margaret's needs got much more attention from me.

"Look at her," Jackie would counsel. "Try to acknowledge her feelings first. Then find out what she needs from you—specifics. You aren't responsible for her life, just for being a supportive partner." They were things I had said to men a thousand times, but they were difficult to comply with. I much preferred to assume that she was strong, and to let her worry about me.

As she pushed me to be more responsive to Margaret, Jackie offered me support. Like so many men's, most of my security needs had been met in my marriage. As Jackie extended herself toward me, I found myself fighting her away. What was wrong? Why couldn't I let myself trust her? "It feels like an early-childhood issue," Jackie said. "Does anything in your history come to mind? Any reason you wouldn't trust your mother?"

"Couldn't I just assume that you are untrustworthy?" I kidded.

"Sorry, too easy," she replied.

"What occurs to me is that a woman might leave me," I said, "or reject me. But I don't understand why I would make that assumption."

"Let's see if we can find out," Jackie suggested. "Why don't you schedule a session with me, and we'll work on it."

I said, "I have an idea. Let me first do some research."

My mother's best friend and younger sister Dorothy lives with her husband Reid in central Georgia on the edge of the enormous ranch where they raised their two sons. A perceptive, gregariously friendly, eminently practical person, Dorothy was another important person in my childhood, and at critical points she took care of both me and my sister. Dorothy is so like my mother that seeing her is always an ambivalent experience: I feel glad to be with her, but sadly reminded of my mother. I knew that she would be the person to ask the question that needed answering.

Rather than wait the several weeks it would take me to get to see Dorothy, I called her. I must have been abrupt, but I didn't waste time getting to the point: "Dorothy, was there a time in my early childhood when I was separated from my mother?"

"Don't you remember—no, of course you wouldn't. You were too young." Then she sighed. "Yes, and I took care of you."

"Can you tell me about it?" I said.

"Let's see. You would have been about eighteen months old. You were talking, but not very well. Your family was living in Atlanta then, and I was still living in Lumber City. It was late in the summer, and your parents wanted to go on a vacation to Florida; so they left you with me at your grandmother's house in Lumber City. Your mother always felt guilty that they didn't tell you they were going."

"What?" I said incredulously.

"They were afraid you would cry and make a scene, so they

sneaked off while you were taking a nap. When you woke up you were terribly upset."

"How long were they gone?"

"Two weeks, I believe. It seemed like a long time to me, because you stayed upset. You had trouble sleeping, and you didn't eat well either."

I thought to myself, "If it felt like a long time to you, what was it like to an eighteen-month-old with no sense of time? For a kid that age, two weeks might as well be forever." One of the problems, of course, was that while my aunt and grandmother were familiar and secure figures for my mother, I had seen them infrequently. They were not strangers to me, but they probably seemed like it.

Dorothy continued: "When your parents came back, you said the saddest thing to your mother. You said that the walls of the house fell down." She seemed apologetic, as if she should have done something she didn't do. "Didn't your mother ever talk about it? I know she felt guilty about leaving you."

I remembered that my mother had made vague references to the time when I was a child and she and my father had taken a vacation. But I had not known how old I was, nor any of the circumstances. Dorothy and I talked for a while longer, and I thanked her for sharing this information. Then I sat by the phone for a while, thinking about what that experience would have been like for me. An eighteen-month-old child is beginning to be rebellious and testy, and he would think unconsciously, "My badness made my parents leave me." So he would try very hard to please so as not to get left again. I also realized that he would find it difficult to trust his mother.

Suddenly I recalled the abrupt and traumatic way I had broken off our "first marriage." I could see Margaret at her dormitory at Holyoke, bewildered and frightened by my sudden disappearance. "That's why I did it that way. It was an unconscious revenge for what my mother did to me."

I began thinking about all the traumatic things men do to women, and I wondered how many of them are unconscious reprisals for the inadvertent traumas that boys suffer at the hands of their mothers. Then it occurred to me, "Why am I blaming women? My father left me too. No, in fact he didn't, not in the same way, because he wasn't there to begin with to the degree that she was." Here I was again at that central problem, the psychological absence of fathers, realizing once more that mothers are often angry about being abandoned by their own husbands to raise their children alone, and behind that anger there is the anger at their fathers for not parenting them. I wondered if there could be any end to this chain of betrayals visited across the generations—except through a new commitment by men to their children.

I rose and went in search of Margaret. I thought I should tell her what I had learned.

Understanding that early experience helped me trust Jackie a little more, and it allowed Margaret and me a way to talk about my precipitous flight from Andover. I was so preoccupied with my troubles during that period that I seldom thought about their effect on Margaret; in fact, she had been haunted by what she perceived as my rejection of her. "I guess on some level I am still frightened that you will leave me," she said. "After all, you have done it once already."

"This is ridiculous," I said with a smile. "You are the one who is going to leave me."

"But you actually did it," Margaret countered.

Thinking about her involvement with Antoine, I started to object, "But you—"

"Listen, you two," Jackie interrupted. "This *is* ridiculous. But let me say, Margaret, that I do take your anxiety about being abandoned seriously, though I don't understand it as well as I do Gus's."

In fact, we were making progress. With Jackie's coaching, I was learning to be more aware of Margaret's needs. Sometimes I would catch myself looking at her as she was doing something at home, and I would deliberately think to myself, "What has her day been like? What is she feeling now?" Gradually, I was moving away from my own egocentrism toward greater awareness of the context of Margaret's life—her situational dilemmas, her interests; and of my place in this context. I had never doubted Margaret's importance in *my* life; but it was strange to realize that I had a powerful influence on the way she experienced life. Had I discounted my own impact on her, my significance to her? Apparently. Then I realized that it was part of the process of transference. If I derived security from her, this made her a symbolic "mother." So of course my own importance to her would seem less—to me. The part of me that had felt responsible for my mother's needs would also feel anxious about her needs: they would seem overwhelming. Better to see her as strong and to lean on her than feel that kind of responsibility.

One of the reasons that Margaret had resisted being in therapy was that she didn't want "hired" support from someone else; she wanted it from me. And Jackie seemed to see Margaret's point. Not only did she confront me repeatedly about my significance to Margaret, but she helped me feel empowered in relation to Margaret's life. "You can make a profound difference to her," she said. As I set about trying, I of course found that there were many skills I didn't have, but I felt encouraged by the results of my efforts.

Jackie helped here too, because she repeatedly encouraged Margaret to thank me for being attentive, supportive, thoughtful. "When he succeeds, give him praise, love, attention," she counseled. "He needs to learn on a deeper level that he can feel secure and valued through giving emotionally to you. Like most men, he only knows how to feel connected through being 'parented,' and many times he tries to create that connection in a negative way, such as getting you to nag him."

I discovered that what Jackie and Margaret were asking me to do wasn't as difficult as I had thought it might be, partly because I had had a younger sister whom I had learned to support emotionally through some of our childhood family struggles. I did know how to be supportive of a woman—if I could see her as needing me in some way.

"It's no wonder I have been jealous of your attentiveness to Janie," Margaret said. "Why can't I have more of what you give her?"

"Wait a minute," Jackie interrupted. "Don't forget—he is actually doing more of that."

"I know," Margaret said. "I just get angry when I think of how often I have occupied his mother's role over the years."

"Margaret." Jackie was persistent. "I think what he said is accurate. It will be easier for him if you reveal your vulnerability, if you ask for what you want and need. And that really isn't easy for you. You do insist on staying alone with so much."

"Okay, Jackie," Margaret conceded. "I'm trying too."

During that period, I was grateful that Jackie respected my need for male support. She encouraged my participation in Pesso's groups, and my membership in the men's group. Though I had some anxiety that she was attempting to bring me under "female control," her support of these other involvements allayed that worry. I also felt reassured that she seemed remarkably able to see both men's and women's dilemmas.

In the spring of 1985, as part of our efforts to work less hard and to enjoy ourselves more, we had planned a family trip to Tortola, in the British Virgin Islands; and we invited Margaret's mother to go with us. One evening, toward the end of the trip, we were walking with Clora up an unlit, rocky path toward her cottage when she slipped and fell. It was not a serious fall, and we thought nothing would come of it. The next day Clora was in intense pain and could barely get out of bed; she seemed to have injured her back. She was still in some pain when she returned to Atlanta with us, and an x ray indicated a collapsed vertebra—"Probably the result of osteoporosis," the doctor said.

Then, a month later while she was exercising in her swimming pool in Florida, Clora broke her collarbone. "I just made a sudden movement," she explained to us over the phone, confused and frightened. It took a week of exhaustive tests for her doctors to arrive at a diagnosis: multiple myeloma, a blood cancer that, among its other assaults on the body, affects the bones. The doctor who made the diagnosis told Clora and Margaret—who had of course flown to Florida—that Clora might, with chemotherapy, live up to three years. "I don't think she heard him," Margaret later said to me. "She's still blaming it all on that fall on Tortola."

At a time when Jackie was inviting her to let down, to accept more support, to work less hard, Margaret's life would not let her take the advice. The fund drive at Paideia was in full swing, and there was a constant flurry of meetings and phone calls. In Florida, Margaret's mother was battling for her life. There was another broken bone, and an internal hemorrhage that was the result of the chemotherapy. With every one of her mother's crises, Margaret was on another plane.

During one of Margaret's trips to Florida that first summer of her mother's illness, I walked by Julia's room and saw the photograph of Margaret as a girl—she must have been about four—that Julia keeps on her desk, perhaps because it looks so much like Julia at the same age. In the hundreds of times I had looked at that photo, I always saw a flirtatious, scrappy, strong little girl ready to take on the world. Now as I looked at it I realized I saw someone different— a rather lonely and beleaguered girl with much too much on her shoulders. I had a poignant image of her parents fighting about which route to take on a car trip, and of Margaret trying to read the map, trying to take charge. Something had shifted in me: this time I saw Margaret's vulnerability.

When Margaret discovered that her mother was dying, she felt what one feels at the prospect of a mother's death: frightened, profoundly sad, abandoned. But she also felt a ray of hope. Maybe her mother could survive; but if she didn't, maybe they could come to a more intimate understanding of each other's lives. "I'm going to do all that I can for her, and I'm going to try to get her to talk honestly to me."

After several months of crises, Clora's condition stabilized; and though there was never any hope of recovery, for nearly a year she was able to live a somewhat normal life. During that year Margaret did everything she could to see that she was comfortable and had as much pleasure as possible. She worked closely with Clora's nurse, and visited her often, usually bringing one of our children with her. In spite of all her other responsibilities, Margaret's attention to her mother never wavered.

She also struggled for more intimacy with her mother. There were so many unanswered questions: what had her mother's childhood in British Columbia been like? Did she remember her father, who died suddenly when Clora was six? What were the dynamics of the family that remained, one headed by a literary mother (Margaret's grandmother), who moved them to Spokane, Washington, where she taught English to support Clora and her two brothers. How had Clora met Paul? What made her suddenly decide to break off her engagement to another man to marry him? All these vital questions—which only she could answer—Clora dodged. She changed the subject, refused to speak. She would talk about her bridge scores (she won regularly until the week she died), about politics, about the treatments that were getting her well, she thought; but she would not reveal her feelings.

There were a number of pleasant, easy hours when their talk ranged across many superficial topics; and in one of these conversations Margaret's mother happened to mention a time when she and Paul had been on vacation in Bermuda. "When was that?" Margaret asked. "I didn't know you and Daddy had been to Bermuda together."

"You wouldn't remember it," her mother replied. "You were a baby."

"How old was I?" Margaret asked, intrigued as she remembered my recent discovery about my parents' vacation. "And how long were you gone?"

"Oh, you were about eighteen months old," she said. "I think we were gone for three weeks."

"Who stayed with me?"

"The housekeeper we had then. I think it was Belinda." Later Margaret would say to me, "I couldn't quite believe what I was hearing. My head started spinning, particularly when I realized that she had no idea that such an absence would have been traumatic for me at that age. At least your mother felt guilty." This discovery made both of us feel relieved; no wonder we both had anxieties about abandonment. When Margaret gave up on getting her mother to talk about her feelings and tried to reveal her own feelings, hoping for a sympathetic response, she often felt punished. Once, talking to her mother on the phone, Margaret confided that a friend had hurt her in some way and said offhandedly, "Maybe she's competitive with me; I don't know why she said what she did."

Clora replied coolly, "Margaret, you are the most competitive person I have ever known." I can still see Margaret standing by the phone, looking as if her mother had struck her.

This hurtful remark came out of a long history in their relationship. How could Clora not feel jealous of the weekends when Paul took Margaret fishing with him in Canada? How could she not envy the conspicuously flirtatious attention that Paul had given Margaret since she was five or six years old? Mother and daughter loved each other, but even after Paul's death, this triangle still held them distant from one another.

"I don't know where to go with her," Margaret complained to Jackie. "She can't seem to talk about herself, and she can't seem to hear my feelings either." Margaret paused, attempting to formulate her complicated feelings for her mother. "I do love her, and I admire her courage, her determination to live; but I wish we could reach each other."

Could it be only a year ago that we were caught up in the swirl of parties and celebrations surrounding Mark's graduation from Paideia? Has it been just one year since Clora insisted on attending that happy event, her only excursion away from home since her cancer was diagnosed? There she stood, in an elegant new dress, talking cheerfully with the other parents and grandparents at the reception, a proud, brave, fiercely determined fighter who would not be denied this event. There she is still in a photo, laughing at a student skit in which her grandson played a part.

The trip took an enormous effort for Clora, and following it, she declined rapidly.

I stuck close to Margaret that summer, and I saw her, in those last painful months when Clora sank day by day into darkness, struggle valiantly for some more intimate response from her mother. "If she could only talk about her fears, if she could acknowledge her impending death, if we could just comfort each other," Margaret said to me. But it did not happen.

Margaret and two women nurses, both of whom had come to love Clora, formed an intimate and caring team. Day by day they tried to ease Clora's pain, to make her comfortable, to help her die. Seeing Clora's sudden decline, I remembered the times as a kid when I saw woodcutters fell a tree. After it was cut it would hang there for a while in its magnificence, then it would list a little, and finally it would come crashing with incredible violence into the ground. These women saw Clora's impending fall: lovingly, carefully, meal by meal and bath by bath, they eased her body down as it inevitably crashed into itself. "When I die," I thought to myself, "I should be lucky to be surrounded by such women."

It was mid-August, hot and humid in Atlanta. Mark was packed for college, and tense and excited about the three weeks of soccer practice that lay ahead of him before school started. I drove with him to Earlham College in Indiana, and on the way there we talked about his career interests, about cars, about our homespun philosophies of life, about his grandmother. All too soon we arrived at the college, and Mark was swept into the furies of a new life. As I walked away from the practice field where he and the other players were beginning to be tested, I saw him looking small and vulnerable under an immense cloud-filled sky. That night, on my way back to Atlanta, I wondered what my father had felt after driving me to Wesleyan; wondered if he felt abandoned by my emerging adulthood in the way that I felt by Mark's.

Mark won the starting goalkeeper's spot in the team's first game, which was played a week before the opening of school. Midway through the game, while Mark was on the ground with the ball in his arms, a frustrated player from the other team collided with him, smashing his tibia. When I arrived in Richmond that evening, one of the players told me he heard the break from the sidelines.

Mark was devastated, and in more pain than I had ever witnessed before. Even in a massive leg cast, the slightest movement made him want to scream. The campus was empty except for the dorm counselors and the sports teams, and the soccer team was about to leave on a road trip. In too much pain to travel, Mark didn't want to leave. "I'm afraid if I go home, Dad, I won't come back."

So I moved into his room, and for the next ten days took care of him: brought him his meals, helped him dress, changed the tapes on his hi-fi, brought him books to read, and stood by him while he ever so painfully hobbled on crutches to the shower. Gradually, the pain began to ease, and though he winced with every step, Mark began to get around on crutches. When his roommate returned from the soccer trip, I moved to a hotel for a few days; then, anxious about leaving Mark, and admiring his courage, I went home.

Clora died three weeks later, and as the family convened in Florida, Mark hobbled off the plane on his crutches. In the beautiful living room that she loved, we had a brief memorial service for Clora. I wrote and read a eulogy; and Elizabeth's husband, Keith, who is an astronomer and an excellent musician, played several of Bach's Goldberg Variations.

And so we returned to our lives. We worried about the stock-market crash, saw our clients, tried to make sense of Clora's estate. I picked up this long-abandoned manuscript, and, trying to keep in touch with Margaret, started writing again.

I was worried about the outcome of the struggle that I knew Margaret was facing. She had formulated its terms herself. "There were times when my mother looked at me angrily, as if she were saying to herself, 'She is going to live, and I am going to die.' I wished beyond everything else that she could have said to me, 'I want you to live and enjoy your life.' I know that consciously she wanted that, but the other jealous, abandoned part of her keeps haunting me."

Since she did not get that wish, I knew, and Jackie certainly knew, that Margaret would have to decide to claim her own right to life, and to a good life. "I'm worried about you," Jackie kept saying to Margaret following her mother's death. "I want us to do some intensive work on your unconscious scripting to deny your feelings and sacrifice your own needs. Unconsciously, you probably feel very guilty about your mother's death; and I'm concerned that you might sacrifice yourself."

As she had before, Margaret resisted Jackie's efforts. "I don't know why, but I just can't make myself work 'intensely' with Jackie. I did that once with Asya; I'm too old for that kind of work."

I also knew that it would be very easy for me to abandon Margaret following her mother's death: easy to get preoccupied with my own work, easy to drift away into my own needs. So I watched myself as well as Margaret; and I tried to stay close by.

In December, after I had started writing again and Margaret's desk was piled high with the paperwork related to her mother's estate, we made a shocking discovery. Margaret had a lump in her breast. While we both struggled against our panic, there was an inconclusive mammogram, then a referral to a surgeon. During the seemingly infinite time that it took the surgeon to see her—it was a couple of weeks—Margaret got very depressed. "I just know it will be bad news," she said to me. "That seems to be all that we get anymore." I tried to be comforting, but I felt frightened.

One night during those two weeks, I came home a little late, and after dinner I remembered that we had some rented videotapes that were overdue. "I think I'll return these," I said, picking them up and starting toward the door.

"Sure, go ahead," Margaret said, with the slightest tone of irony in her voice. Turning toward the sofa in the family room where she sat, I saw that she looked extremely sad.

"On second thought," I said, "I don't think I will," and I sat down beside her.

"Look, I'm all right," she said angrily. "You go ahead. You wouldn't want to pay extra for those tapes." She was trying to be earnest, but not succeeding. It was a sore point; mine and her mother's stinginess. Anything to save a dollar.

"I'm staying," I said. "I can return these later."

My determination to stay seemed to provoke more anger: "Listen, you will be angry at me later if you don't return those, so go and do it. I *want* to be by myself."

"I don't care," I said firmly. "I'm not leaving." Seeing right past the anger to her conviction that I too would abandon her, I put my arm around her shoulder. "I want to hold you."

"Go away!" she yelled at me.

"No," I said again. For several minutes I just sat there, and gradually, she let me move closer. After a while she relaxed in my arms, and leaned against my shoulder. I looked down and saw the glimmer of tears on her face. For nearly an hour we sat there together, my arms around her, while she cried silently.

The next week she had the biopsy, which gave us blessedly good news. "The first piece of good news," Margaret said, "which I can remember in a long while."

Jackie shared our relief, but it was not enough for her. "I'm still worried, Margaret, about your scripting—about your mother's messages to you, and about the way you don't take care of yourself. I think we should do this work. If we don't, the next time you have a health problem, the news might not be good."

Finally, weeks later, Margaret agreed to work further with Jackie. With that decision, I felt deeply relieved—not absolved of responsibility, not certain of the outcome for either of us—but grateful for what the decision seemed to represent: Margaret's decision to live, and to live fully.

*   *   *

Sometimes, changes in a marriage occur suddenly and dramatically. One partner has an affair that forces the couple to confront their problems, or one spouse gets fed up with pursuing and turns to some other activity; sometimes a one-down spouse declares open rebellion against a history of marital tyranny. At these moments there is what we term an "existential shift," or a change in the way the marriage is experienced by both partners.

An existential shift can also occur more slowly, as it did in our marriage. The changes between us took place over several years, and we both worked hard to make them happen. I struggled to be less focused on myself; and not only to be more aware of Margaret's feelings, but to be strong, giving, and supportive in relation to her. Rather than waiting until I was furious with her, I also attempted to be more calmly assertive, and to take that stance more frequently.

Margaret, on the other hand, worked to be less self-sacrificial and focused on others. She tried very hard to identify her needs, and to allow herself to ask for and to accept more support from others, but especially from me. Of the two of us, I think Margaret's job was harder, because as a kid she was so unaccustomed to being supported that she had a very hard time believing that it was possible for her to get emotional support on a deep level. There were also so many people in her life who took advantage of her competent, take-charge approach to life.

Jackie helped us a great deal. Her challenge of my "poor me" racket and of my omnipotent delegate's mission was critical, as was her tough confrontation of my narcissism. But her support also helped me need less from Margaret, and it allowed me to have more to give her. But I believe the pivotal moments came in Margaret's willingness to accept emotional support; to break with her mother's long-suffering denial of her feelings and needs. Jackie's challenge of Margaret's script of self-denial was essential; but so was the accumulation of stress which exhausted Margaret's defenses, and which made her risk being vulnerable to a husband who was, finally, there for her.

Since I have described the most stressful times in our lives, it may seem to the reader that Margaret and I have had a turbulent marriage, and that it took us twenty-five years to achieve some modest gains. Some may wonder how we were able to help our clients through these stormy times. In fact, our relationship has usually been satisfying and intimate. The first year of marriage was conflictual and difficult, and so was the fourteenth year, when we moved to Atlanta. The last three or four years have been the most trying, but during that time Margaret lost two parents and we graduated two children; and we each had major career demands. Even during these highly stressful two years surrounding Margaret's mother's death, we have had many good moments; and we have managed to be competent parents and successful therapists.

We have always been able to talk to each other, and to say almost anything that was on our minds. Sometimes we didn't say it smoothly, but we didn't keep secrets, and we didn't stay silent for days at a time. Our capacity to talk about anything and everything has been a sustaining element in our marriage.

There has rarely been a time when we didn't look forward to being in each other's presence. After only a few hours' absence, I look forward to seeing Margaret enter a room. I anticipate with pleasure her quick, staccato walk, and her bright smile. I want to know what she has been doing, what has happened in the interim. Even when we have been working side by side for several hours, we find that we have lots to say to each other—reactions to what we have seen and heard, feelings about the people we have been working with.

We sometimes worry that we are together too much, and are too dependent on each other. In recent years, however, Margaret's separate practice has grown, and I have done more supervision and writing. But the core of our professional lives is our co-therapy. We enjoy it; we are good at what we do; and we intend to continue working together. Sharing a career has given us a set of common experiences that seems to far outweigh the disadvantages of too much togetherness.

It has helped us immeasurably to have shared values, and to have remarkably similar ways of seeing the world. We are still surprised and pleased when we like the same painting, have the same opinions about people, enjoy the same books.

Our sexual relationship has been a sustaining aspect of our marriage. Though fatigue and stress sometimes take their toll, we have always drawn solace and comfort from sex; and today we find it more deeply exciting than ever. Feeling less guilty and being more relaxed about sexuality has progressively opened this area of our lives to more and more enjoyment.

Our capacity to fight openly and productively has also enriched our relationship. Since the earliest days of our marriage, we have been committed to dealing with anger honestly and forthrightly; and that commitment has never wavered. It has always been anxious for us to confront each other, but again and again, we have done it. Sometimes I wonder where courage comes from, how I get up the nerve to tell Margaret that something she is doing makes me angry; but I have no doubt that it is necessary.

Over the years, our fights have gotten quieter and more efficient. We spend less time being defensive and attacking, and more on saying what we feel, and on what we would like to be different. We haven't mastered the art of dealing with conflict, but we are still learning. Being able to describe our own anxiety, hurt, and vulnerability seems to help a great deal.

It has been reassuring to rediscover again and again that neither of us seems to be able to run over the other. I felt challenged by Margaret the first time I met her, felt myself having to bring up some internal force to meet her wit, her teasing, her strength of character. She has also felt challenged by me. "You intrigued me partly because you fought with me; you called me on my tendency to manipulate." Finally, we do seem to be equally powerful, a match for each other; and each of us seems to have kept in fighting trim.

Trust is a complicated issue in marriage, but on a very deep level we have trusted each other. Trust is never complete, never guaranteed. I know that there are men in Margaret's life to whom she is attracted, just as there are women in mine. Though we don't act on these attractions, it seems important that they are there. Some element of danger, some possibility of leaving each other seems vital to our staying emotionally alive. It is, after all, still a competitive world.

But in the darkest moments, we have not abandoned each other. Some thread, some interior commitment, has held. Our bond could break, of course; but the fact that it hasn't, that we have not definitively betrayed each other, gives us enormous reassurance. Perhaps we will finally defy our scripts.

For now, our family seems to have recovered from the stresses of Clora's death. Sarah is a rising senior at Agnes Scott College in Atlanta, a psychology major and the editor of the campus paper. Mark has made a beachhead in college life at Earlham, and is doing well academically. His leg has healed, and he is looking forward to another run at the goalie's job. Julia, about to be a high school freshman, is an excellent writer and a good soccer player, and she would like to be an actress.

Margaret's wounds are beginning to heal. She is smiling again, reconnecting with friends; and retired from the Paideia board, looking forward to not acquiring any new responsibilities. We are both beginning to allow ourselves to get excited about a forthcoming trip to Europe; and we will rejoice together the completion of this manuscript.

We know, of course, that there are challenges ahead. There is a sixth crisis in marriage when the last child leaves home; and it is not unlike the first year of marriage, when issues of closeness and power must be negotiated. In this instance, they must be renegotiated. For the moment, we are grateful to have Julia still in our midst, but we feel that we will be all right when she leaves us. We have several projects planned, and we enjoy doing so many things together.

There are, of course, dark clouds on the distant horizon, and there will be other crises as we face the failure of our bodies and our own inevitable deaths. We hope that we have some time before then, and we are determined to enjoy the time that we have: we want to work less hard, to play more. And when those clouds loom before us, we hope to march into them together.

Bibliography

Aron, A. 1974. Relationships with opposite-sex parents and mate choice. *Human Relations* 27:17–24.

Bach, G. R., and P. Wyden. 1969. *The intimate enemy*. New York: William Morrow.

Bank, S. P., and M. D. Kahn. 1982. *The sibling bond*. New York: Basic Books.

Boszormenyi-Nagy, I. 1965. A theory of relationships: Experience and transaction. In *Intensive family therapy: Theoretical and practical aspects*, ed. I. Boszormenyi-Nagy and J. L. Framo, 33–86. New York: Harper & Row.

Boszormenyi-Nagy, I., and G. M. Spark. 1973. *Invisible loyalties*. New York: Harper & Row.

Bowen, M. 1978. *Family therapy in clinical practice*. New York: Jason Aronson.

Bronstein, P., and C. P. Cowan, eds. 1987. *Fatherhood today*. New York: John Wiley & Sons.

Burgess, E. W., and P. Wallin. 1953. *Engagement and marriage*. Philadelphia: Lippincott.

Carter, E. A., and M. McGoldrick. 1988. *The changing family life cycle*. 2d ed. New York: Gardner Press.

Chodorow, N. 1978. *The reproduction of mothering*. Berkeley: University of California Press.

Cromwell, R. E., and D. H. Olson, eds. 1975. *Power in families.* New York: John Wiley & Sons.

Dinnerstein, D. 1976. *The mermaid and the minotaur: Sexual arrangments and human malaise.* New York: Harper & Row.

Erikson, E. H. 1968. *Identity, youth and crisis.* New York: W. W. Norton.

Faber, A., and E. Mazlish. 1987. *Siblings without rivalry.* New York: W. W. Norton.

Fogarty, T. F. 1979. The distancer and the pursuer. *The Family* 7:11–16.

Fowler, O. S. 1859. *Matrimony.* Boston: O. S. Fowler.

Fraiberg, S. H. 1959. *The magic years.* New York: Charles Scribner's Sons.

Gardner, H. 1978. *Development psychology: An introduction.* Boston: Little, Brown.

Gibran, K. 1923. *The prophet.* New York: Alfred A. Knopf.

Gray-Little, B., and N. Burks. 1983. Power and satisfaction in marriage. *Psychological Bulletin* 933:513–38.

Guerin, P. J., L. F. Fay, S. L. Burden, and J. G. Kautto. 1987. *The evaluation and treatment of marital conflict.* New York: Basic Books.

Hoffman, L. 1981. *Foundations of family therapy.* New York: Basic Books.

Hoopes, M. M., and J. M. Harper. 1987. *Birth order roles and sibling patterns in individual and family therapy.* Rockville, Md: Aspen Publishers.

Jump, T. L., and L. Haas. 1987. Fathers in transition. In *Changing men,* ed. M. S. Kimmel, 98–114. Newburg Park, Calif.: Sage Publications.

Kramer, J. R. 1985. *Family interfaces: Transgenerational patterns.* New York: Brunner/Mazel.

Lamb, M. E., ed. 1981. *The role of the father in child development.* 2d ed. New York: John Wiley & Sons.

Lederer, W. J., and D. D. Jackson. 1968. *The mirages of marriage.* New York: W. W. Norton.

Leman, K. 1985. *The birth order book.* New York: Dell.

Levinson, D. J. 1978. *The seasons of a man's life.* New York: Alfred A. Knopf.

Miller, S. 1983. *Men and friendship.* Boston: Houghton Mifflin.

Miller, S., E. W. Nunnally, and D. B. Wackman. 1988. *Connecting with self and other.* Littleton, Colo.: Interpersonal Communication Programs.

Murstein, B. I. 1976. *Who will marry whom?* New York: Springer.

Napier, A. Y. 1971. The marriage of families: Cross-generational complementarity. *Family Process* 9:373–95.

———. 1978. The rejection-intrusion pattern: A central family dynamic. *Journal of Marriage and Family Counseling* (January):5–12.

Napier, A. Y., and C. A. Whitaker. 1978. *The family crucible.* New York: Harper & Row.

Osherson, S. 1986. *Finding our fathers*. New York: Free Press.

Paul, N. L., and B. B. Paul. 1975. *A marital puzzle*. New York: W. W. Norton.

Pesso, A. 1969. *Movement in psychotherapy*. New York: New York University Press.

————. 1971. *Experience in action*. New York: New York University Press.

Pogrebin, L. C. 1983. *Family politics*. New York: McGraw-Hill.

Rose, P. 1983. *Parallel lives: Five Victorian marriages*. New York: Alfred A. Knopf.

Sager, C. J. 1976. *Marriage contracts and couple therapy*. New York: Brunner/Mazel.

Scarf, M. 1987. *Intimate partners: Patterns in love and marriage*. New York: Random House.

Sheehy, G. 1976. *Passages: Predictable crises of adult life*. New York: Dutton.

Stierlin, H. 1981. *Separating parents and adolescents*. New York: Jason Aronson.

Toman, W. 1969. *Family constellation*. New York: Springer.

Walster, E., G. W. Walster, and E. Berscheid. 1978. *Equity: Theory and research*. Boston: Allyn & Bacon.

Winch, R. F. 1958. *Mate selection: A study of complementary needs*. New York: Harper & Row.

About the Author

Augustus Y. Napier was born in Decatur, Georgia, in 1938 and graduated from Wesleyan University (Conn.) with high distinction in English. After deciding to become a therapist through a personal therapy experience, he earned a Ph.D. in clinical psychology at the University of North Carolina. During an internship in the Department of Psychiatry at the University of Wisconsin–Madison, he began to work with Dr. Carl A. Whitaker as a student co-therapist, an experience that formed the basis for the book *The Family Crucible*. Dr. Napier later served on the faculties of the Department of Psychiatry and the Child and Family Studies Program at the University of Wisconsin. He now directs The Family Workshop, a family-therapy training institute in Atlanta, Georgia, where he works frequently with his wife, Margaret, who is also a family therapist. A frequent consultant, he is the author of numerous papers. The Napiers have three children: Sarah, 21; Mark, 19; and Julia, 14.